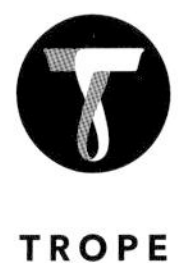

TROPE

ABOVE & ACROSS

SAN FRANCISCO

EDITED BY

SAM LANDERS

MICHELLE FITZGERALD

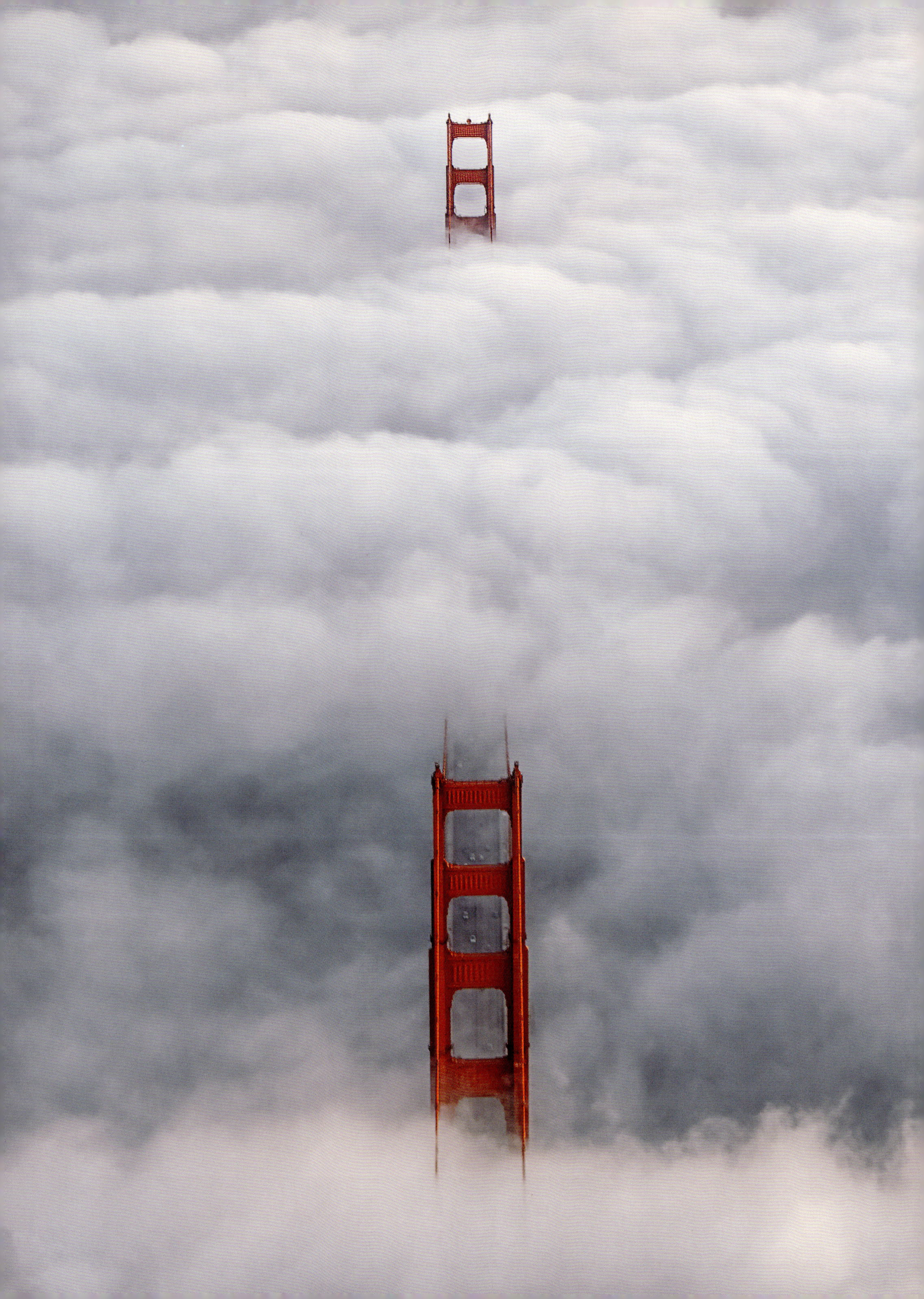

PHOTOGRAPHS BY

COCU LIU

DIANE BENTLEY RAYMOND

HOWARD KINGSNORTH

JACK LANDAU

JAY HUANG

JEFFERY XIN

JOHN MONTOYA

KRIS KUGANATHAN

LICHAO LIU

FOREWORD BY

STACY WILLIAMS

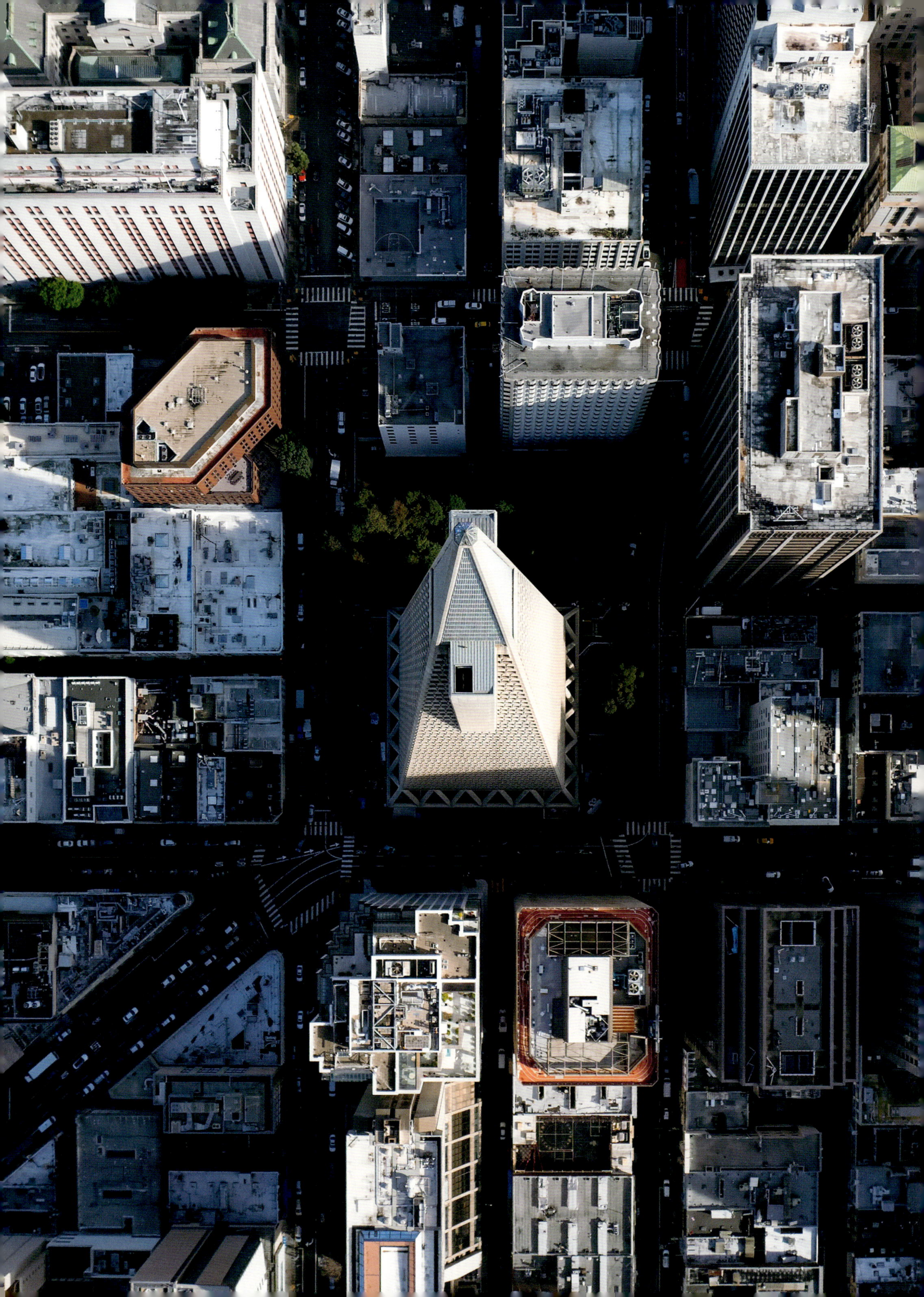

"Leaving San Francisco is like saying goodbye to an old sweetheart. You want to linger as long as possible."
—Walter Cronkite

Above & Across San Francisco is a curated collection of aerial photographs of San Francisco from nine independent photographers.

Fondly nicknamed the "City by the Bay," San Francisco is known for its iconic bridges, hilly terrain, vibrant and diverse neighborhoods, and picturesque views. The images featured in *Above & Across San Francisco* represent a contemporary view of the city. Photographed in all weather conditions and times of day, from the persistent fog blanketing the Golden Gate Bridge to the sunshine of the Presidio to the evening lights of downtown, each image captures a snapshot of the city's multifaceted character.

San Francisco is a vibrant and eclectic city recognized globally as a cultural center and a hub for innovation. The photographs in this collection, taken from helicopters and observation decks, atop buildings and hills, and with the use of drones, capture the essence of San Francisco as seen by both locals and visitors alike. From the Ferry Terminal to the Transamerica Pyramid to Coit Tower, San Francisco's skyline is instantly recognizable, creating a vision of a city that is both iconic and fluid.

Let *Above & Across San Francisco* transport you to the city and experience the breathtaking beauty of San Francisco — from above & across.

Sam Landers & Michelle Fitzgerald
Editors

"San Franciscans know we live in the most beautiful city in the world, a jewel on the edge of the Golden Gate."
—Gavin Newsom, Governor of California and Former Mayor of San Francisco

San Francisco is a vibrant, contradictory city where breathtaking views meet practical challenges, and old-world charm exists alongside innovative design. Nestled between the Pacific Ocean and the San Francisco Bay, this unique cityscape is shaped by dramatic geography and often shrouded in the iconic fog known locally as "Karl." This fog acts as a lens and veil, casting a shifting light that transforms the skyline, rendering familiar structures like the Transamerica Pyramid and Coit Tower mysterious and elusive.

The city's interplay of light and shadow creates an atmosphere like no other. On a foggy morning, these structures emerge as if from another world, softened and blurred. On a clear afternoon, the city shines, revealing vibrant details. This ephemeral quality enhances the architectural experience, allowing each building to reveal different facets throughout the day and seasons.

The architectural landscape here is a study in contrasts, marked by a history of resilience and reinvention. Stately Victorian homes in Pacific Heights stand alongside the sleek, modern towers of SoMa, and the Painted Ladies of Alamo Square overlook a skyline forever changing. Each neighborhood, from the colorful murals of the Mission to the intricate alleys of Chinatown, is a microcosm of San Francisco's cultural fabric, capturing the spirit of the communities that shape them.

San Francisco's hills and valleys have forced architects to adapt creatively. The city's topography has necessitated innovation from terraced homes and multi-level streets to the iconic cable cars that still run today. Landmarks like the Golden Gate Bridge and the Bay Bridge go beyond utility; they symbolize San Francisco's connection to the larger Bay Area and embody the architectural ingenuity that defines the city. Designed with seismic resilience in mind, buildings here are a testament to endurance, standing firm amid shifting ground.

Living in San Francisco is a balancing act between marveling at its beauty and navigating its peculiarities. Amidst the stunning architecture and breathtaking views, there's an undeniable challenge: the scarcity of affordable housing. Yet, this, too, is part of the city's character, sparking a continuous dialogue on how to make this iconic place accessible to all who wish to call it home. For those of us captivated by its charm, we embrace the city's quirks — its fog, its hills, and its enduring spirit — finding ourselves looking past its challenges to the promise beyond the mist.

Above & Across San Francisco offers a unique view of this ever-evolving city, capturing its beauty and complexity through stunning aerial perspectives from nine talented photographers. These images showcase the intricate layers and interwoven landscapes that make San Francisco a city like no other. Whether you're a longtime resident or a first-time visitor, this book provides an opportunity to rediscover a city that embraces change and invites you to fall in love with San Francisco. I hope you do.

Stacy Williams
Executive Director,
American Institute of Architects,
San Francisco

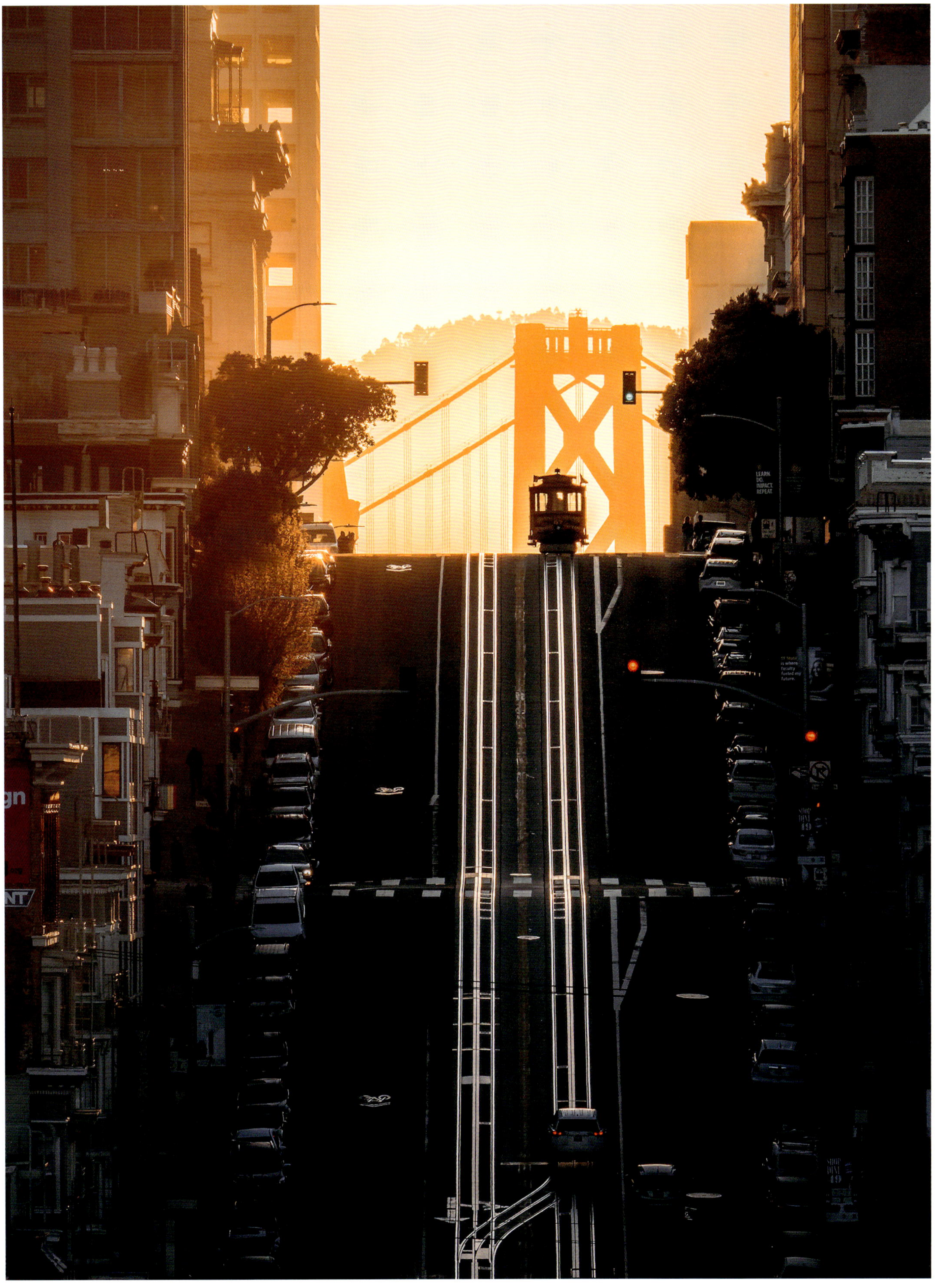

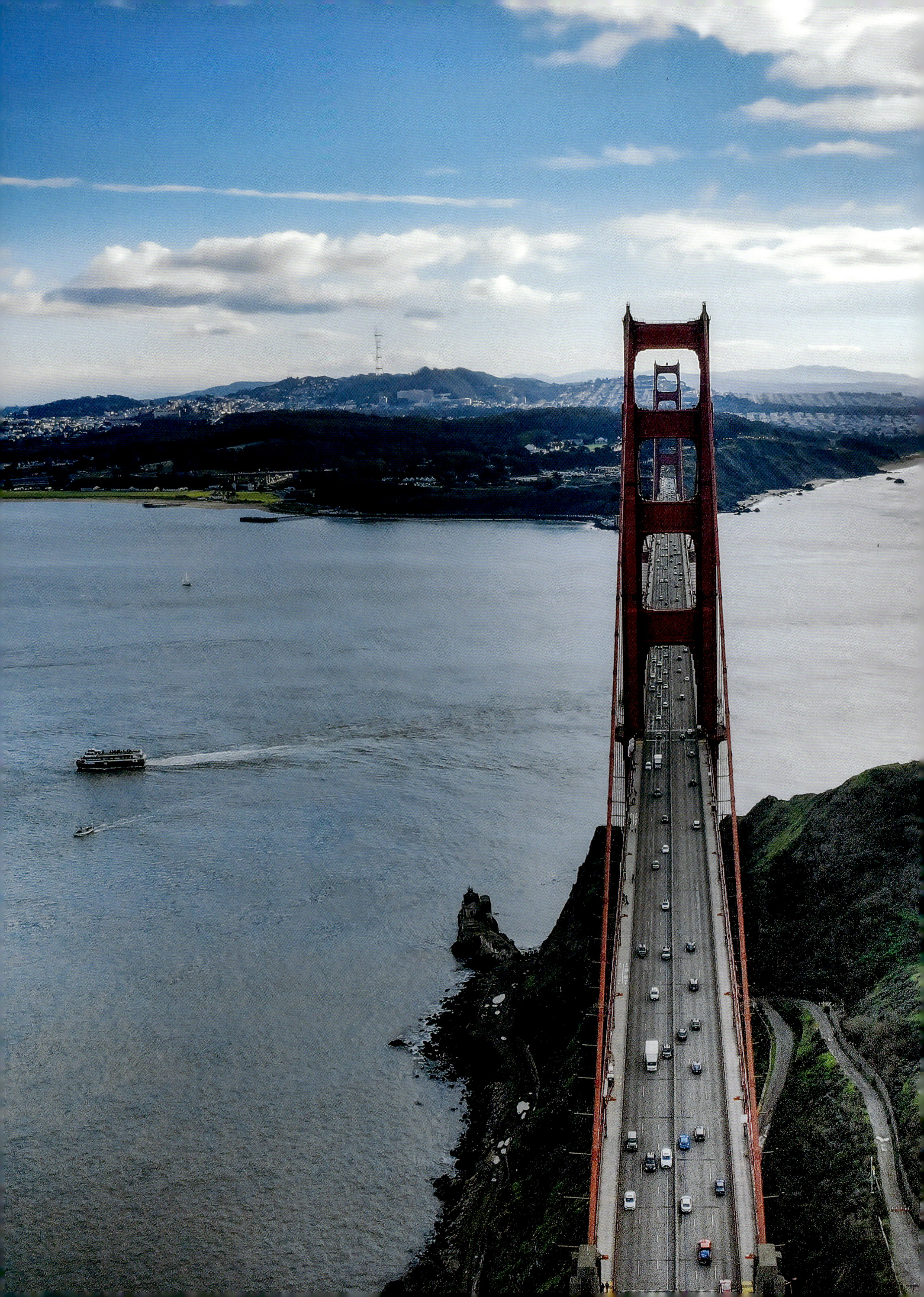

City by the Bay ♦ San Francisco is situated on a peninsula, bordered by the Pacific Ocean to the west and the San Francisco Bay to the east, and is often referred to as the "City by the Bay." The city has approximately 28 miles of coastline with landscapes ranging from rugged cliffs to sandy beaches like Ocean Beach and Baker Beach, to iconic waterfront areas such as Crissy Field and Fisherman's Wharf, offering breathtaking views of the city's bridges and natural beauty. ♦ The San Francisco Bay, one of the largest and most important estuaries in the United States, not only supports a vast array of wildlife, but is also a major hub of recreational activity, including fishing, sailing, kayaking, and windsurfing. Historically, the Bay was essential to the city's growth. During the California Gold Rush of the late 1840s and 1850s, the port of San Francisco welcomed thousands who came to the city seeking fortunes. ♦ To the west, San Francisco faces the vast expanse of the Pacific Ocean. This location makes the city a major port city and a gateway for international trade, particularly with Asia. The Pacific also makes San Francisco appealing as a tourist destination. A walk around San Francisco isn't complete without a stop at a landmark like Lands End or Cliff House to catch a view of the city's stunning coastal scenery, beaches, and sunsets.

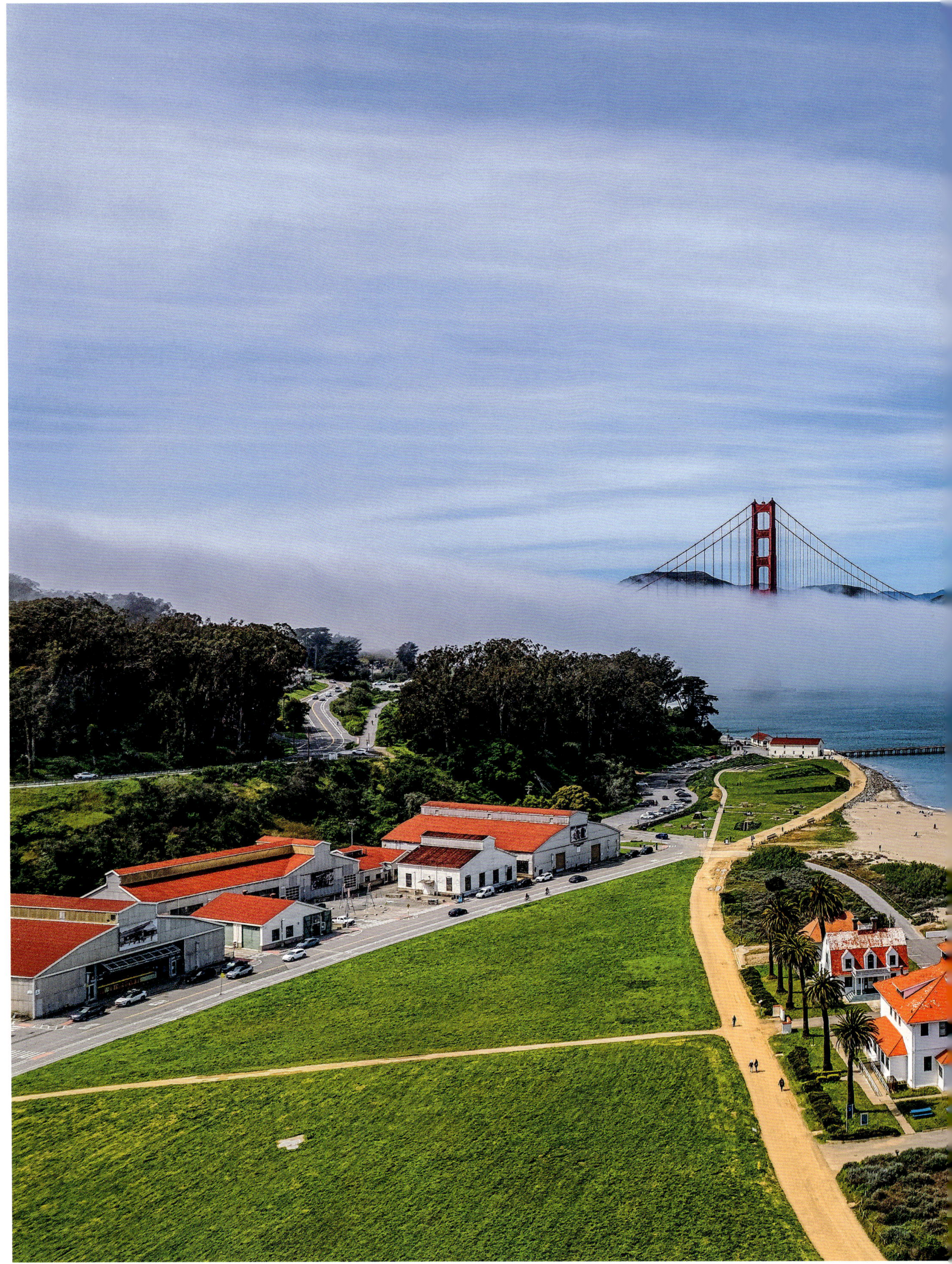

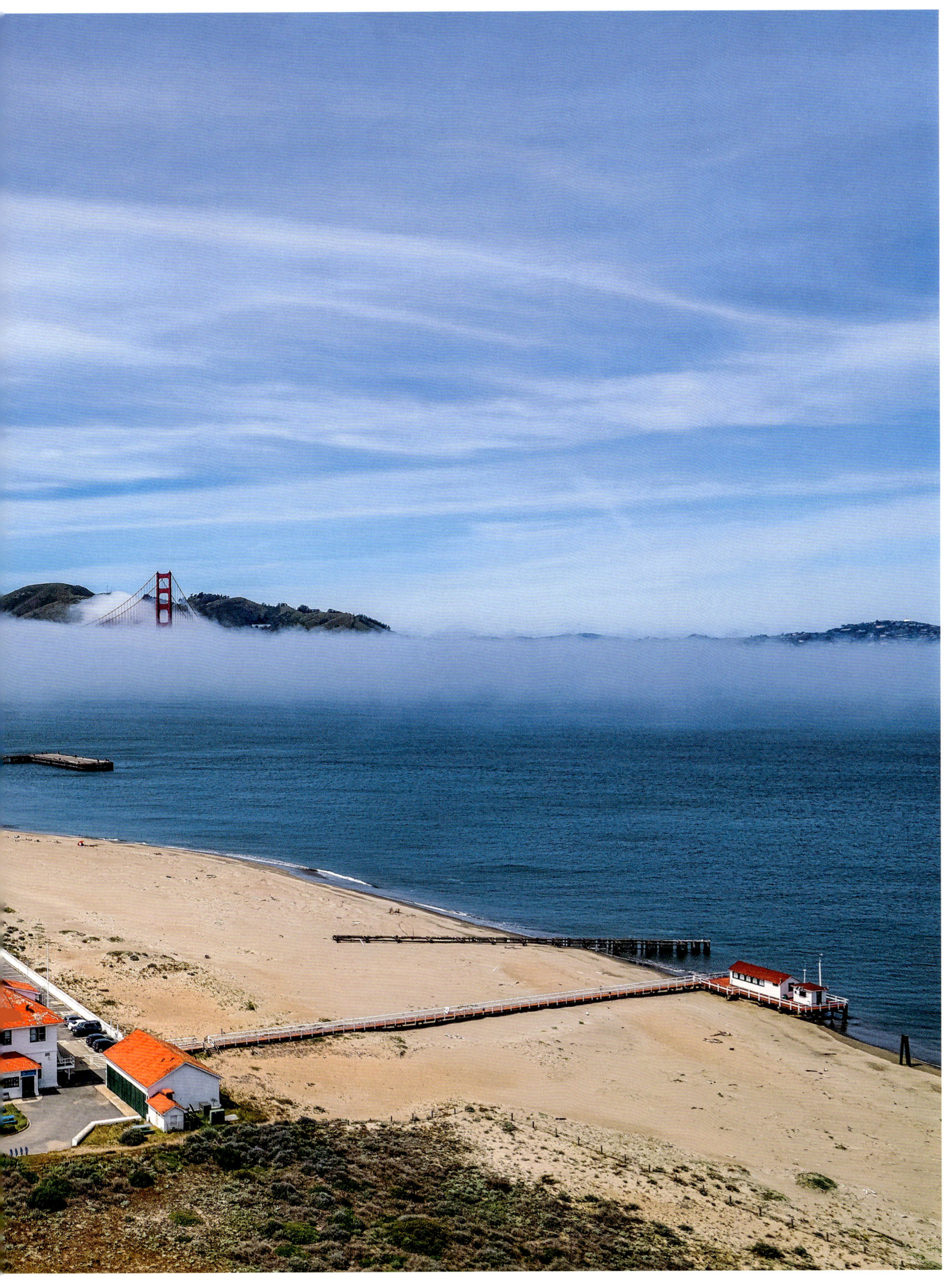

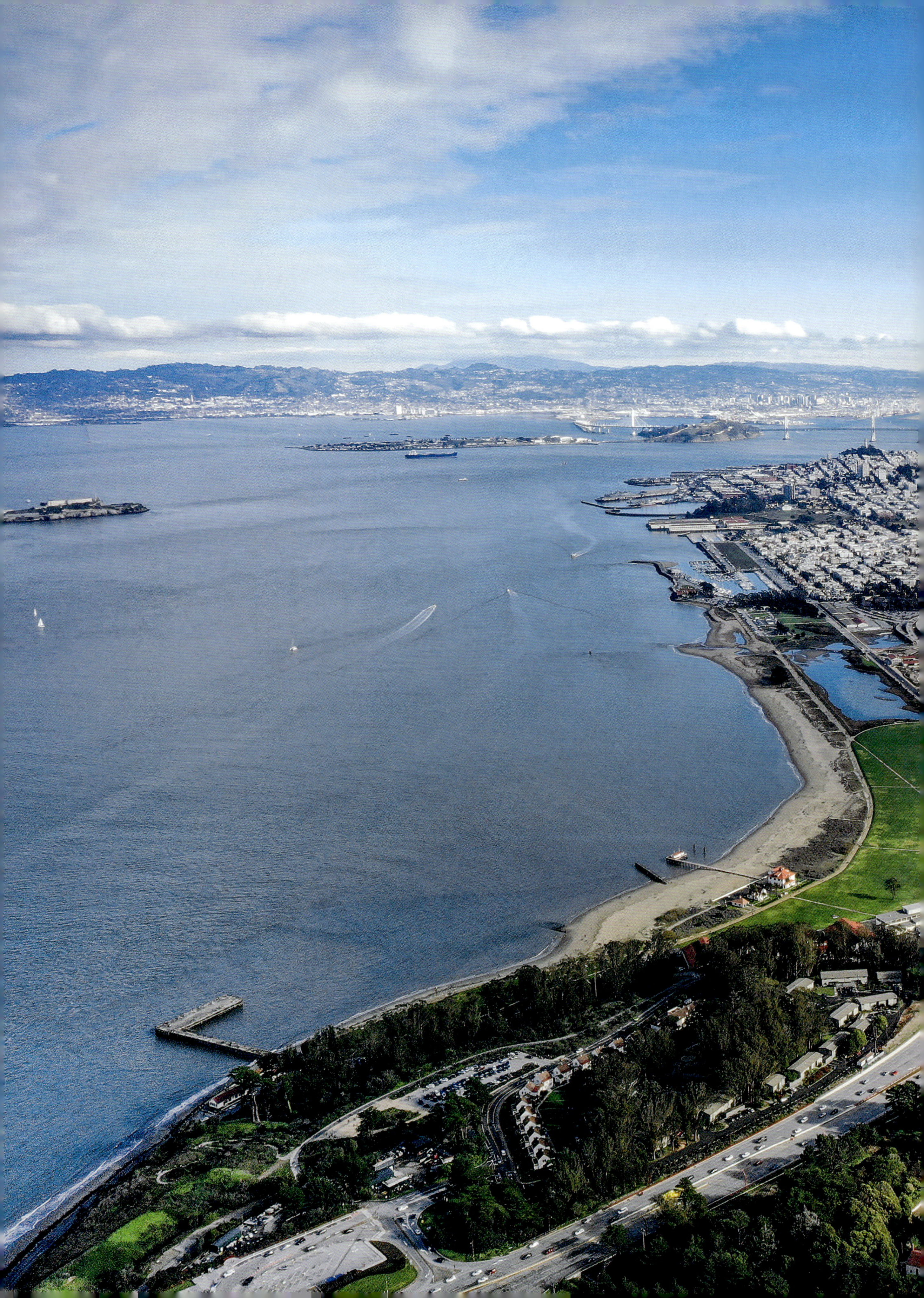

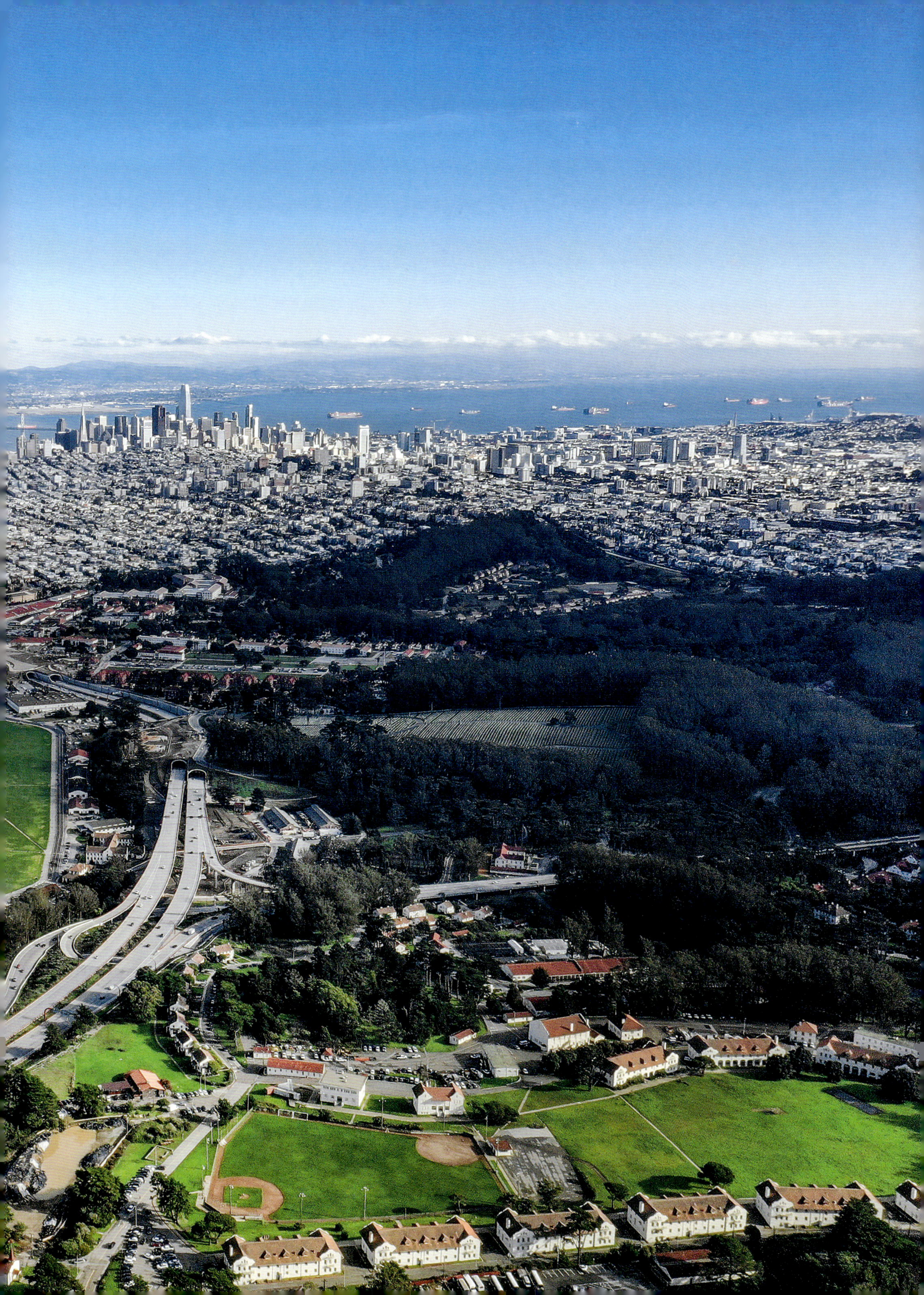

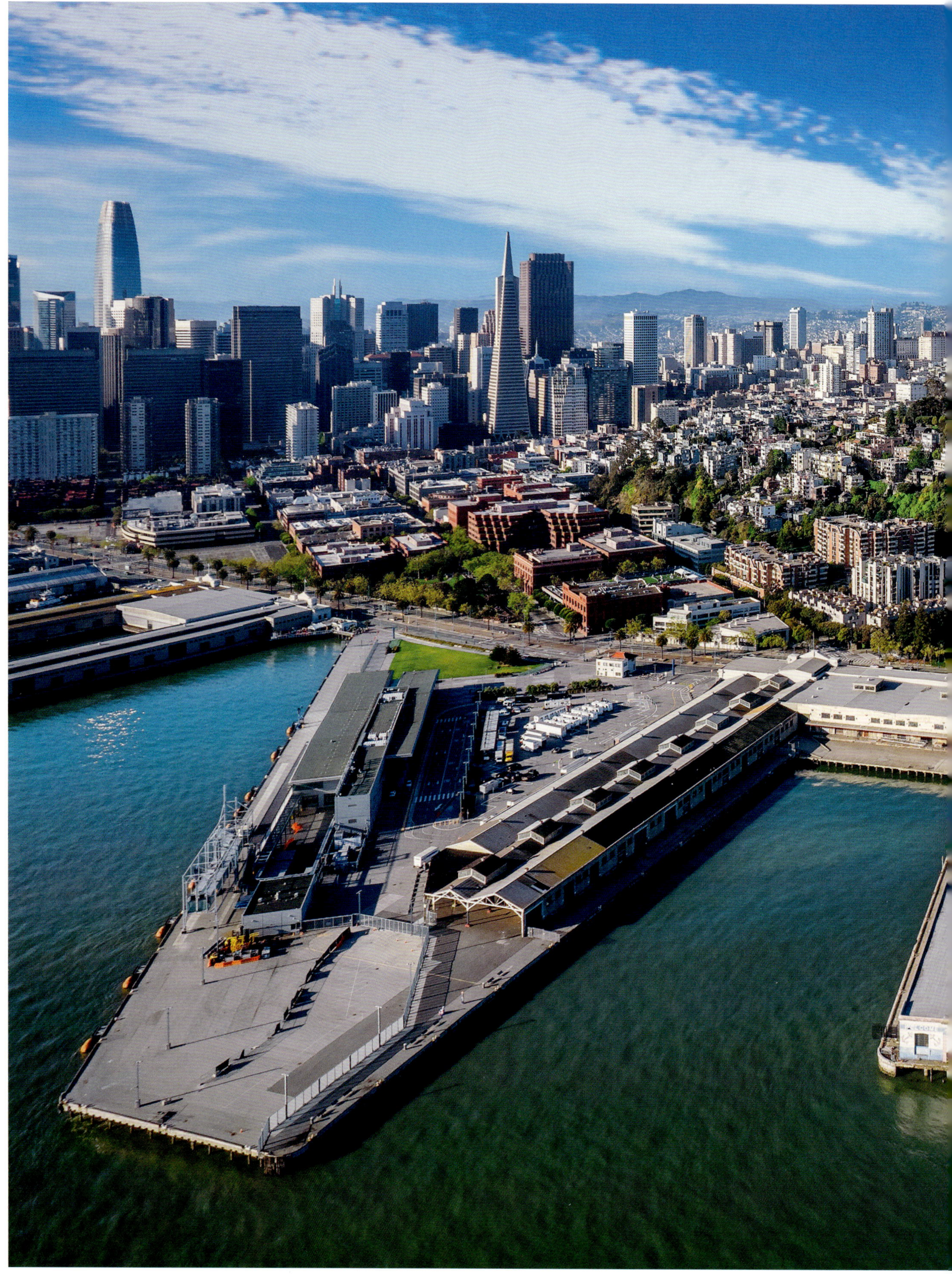

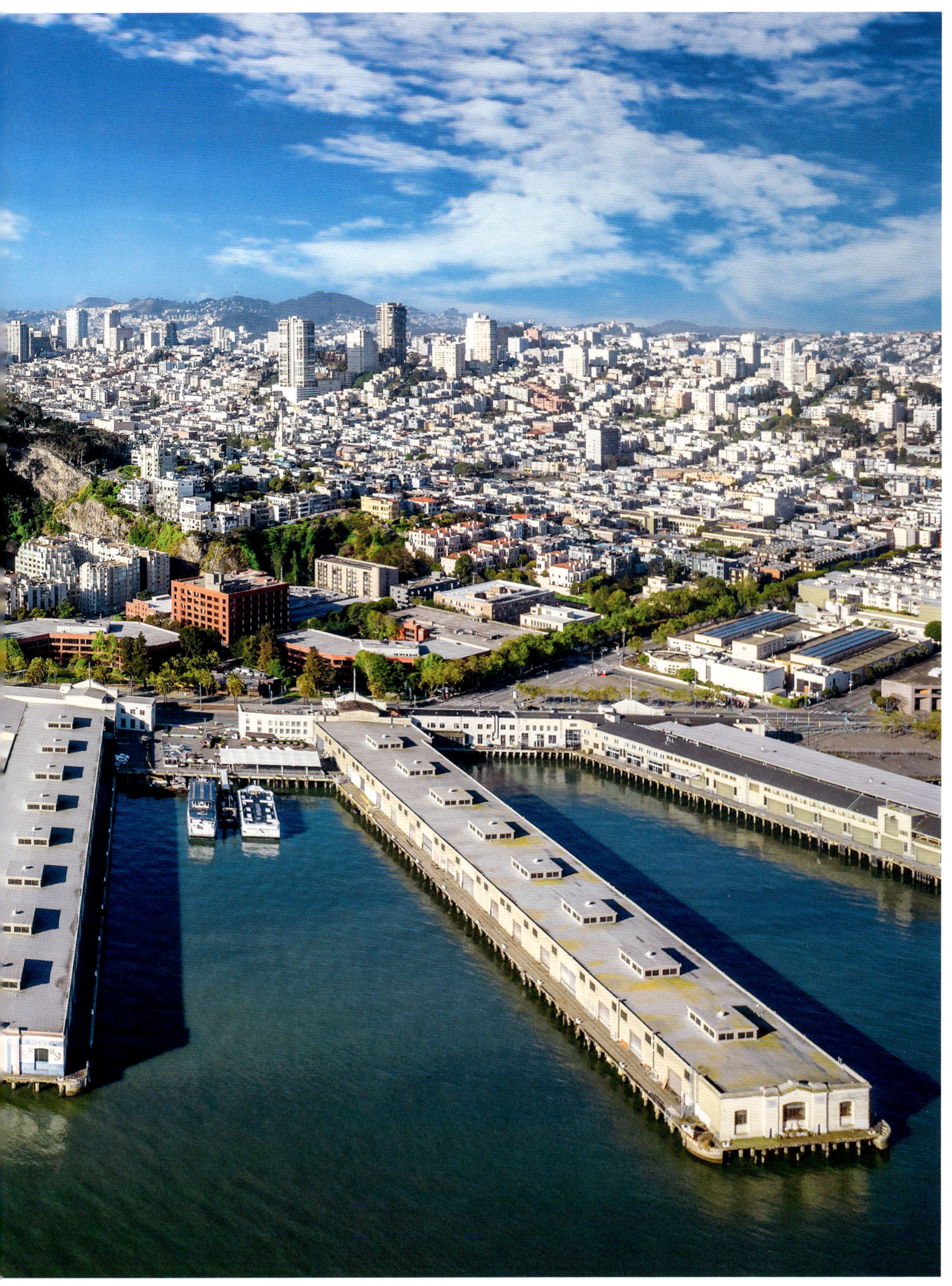

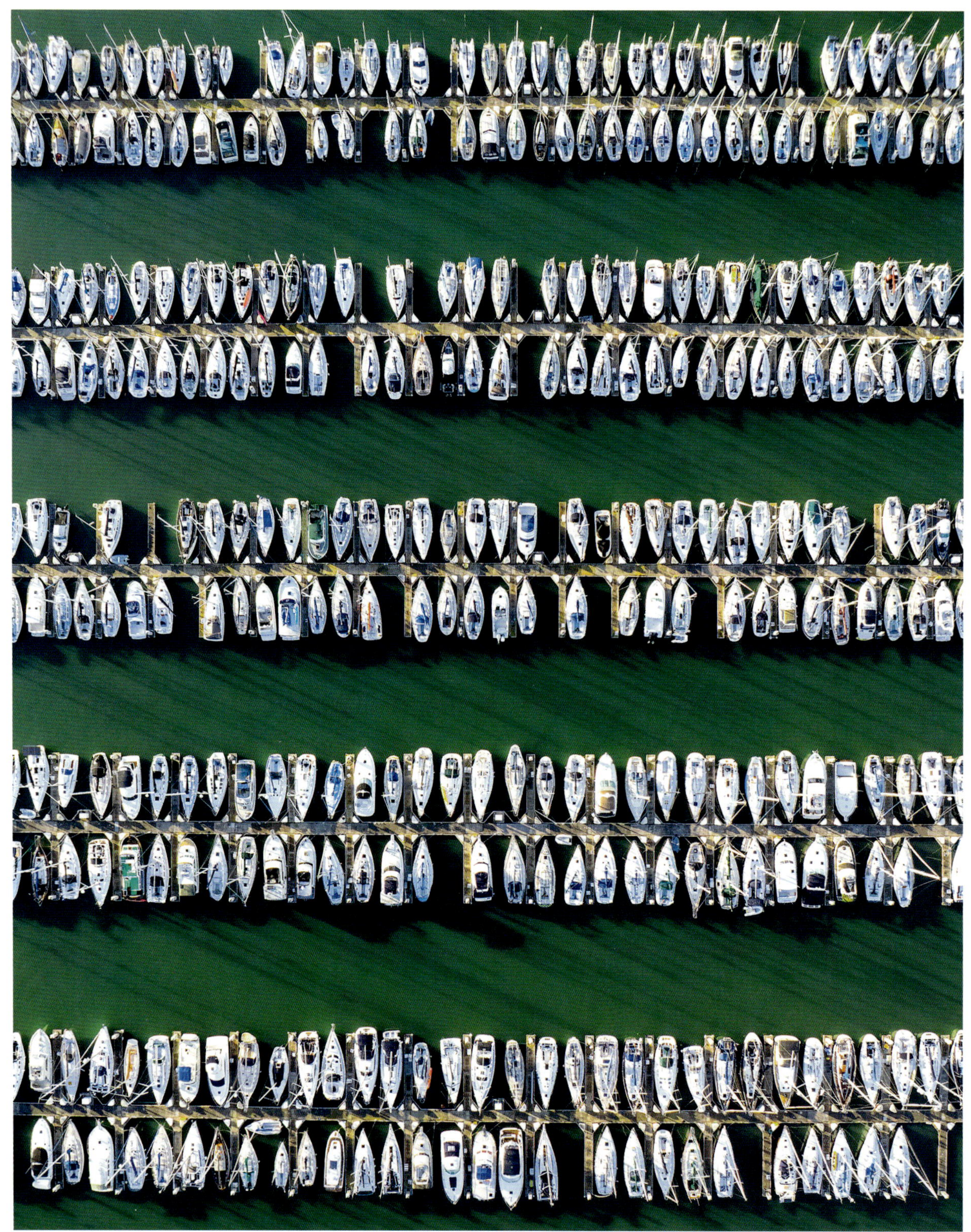

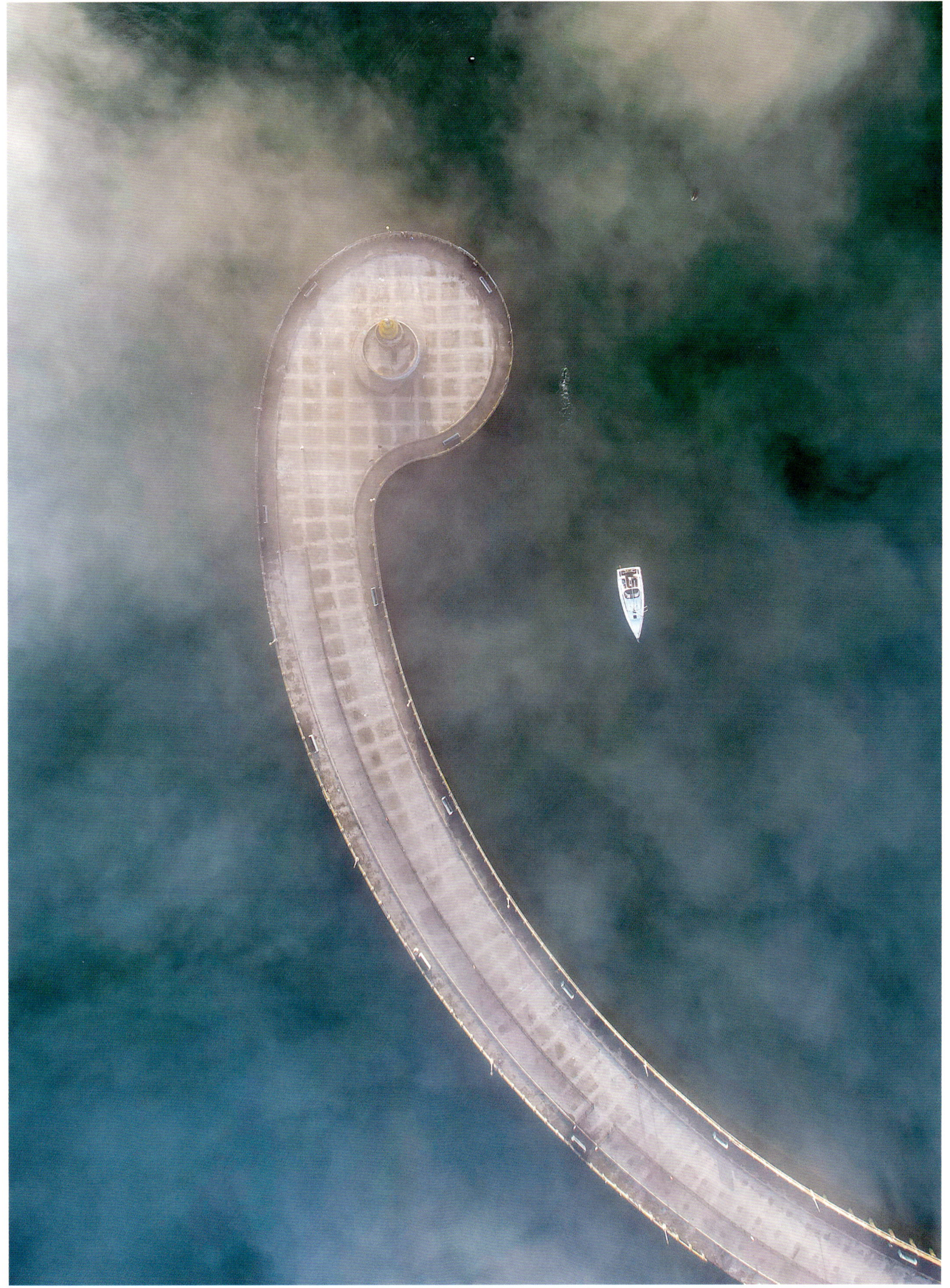

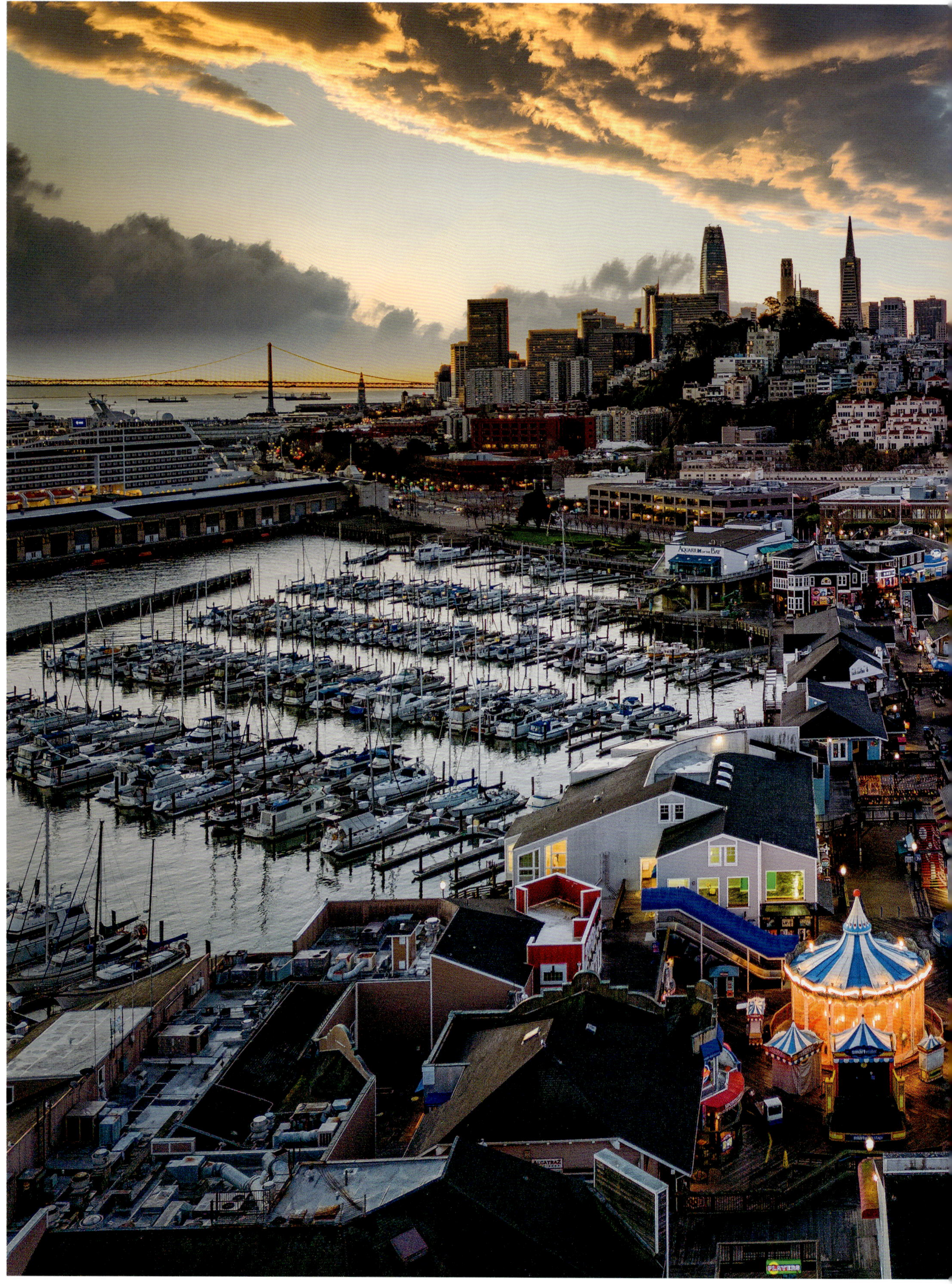

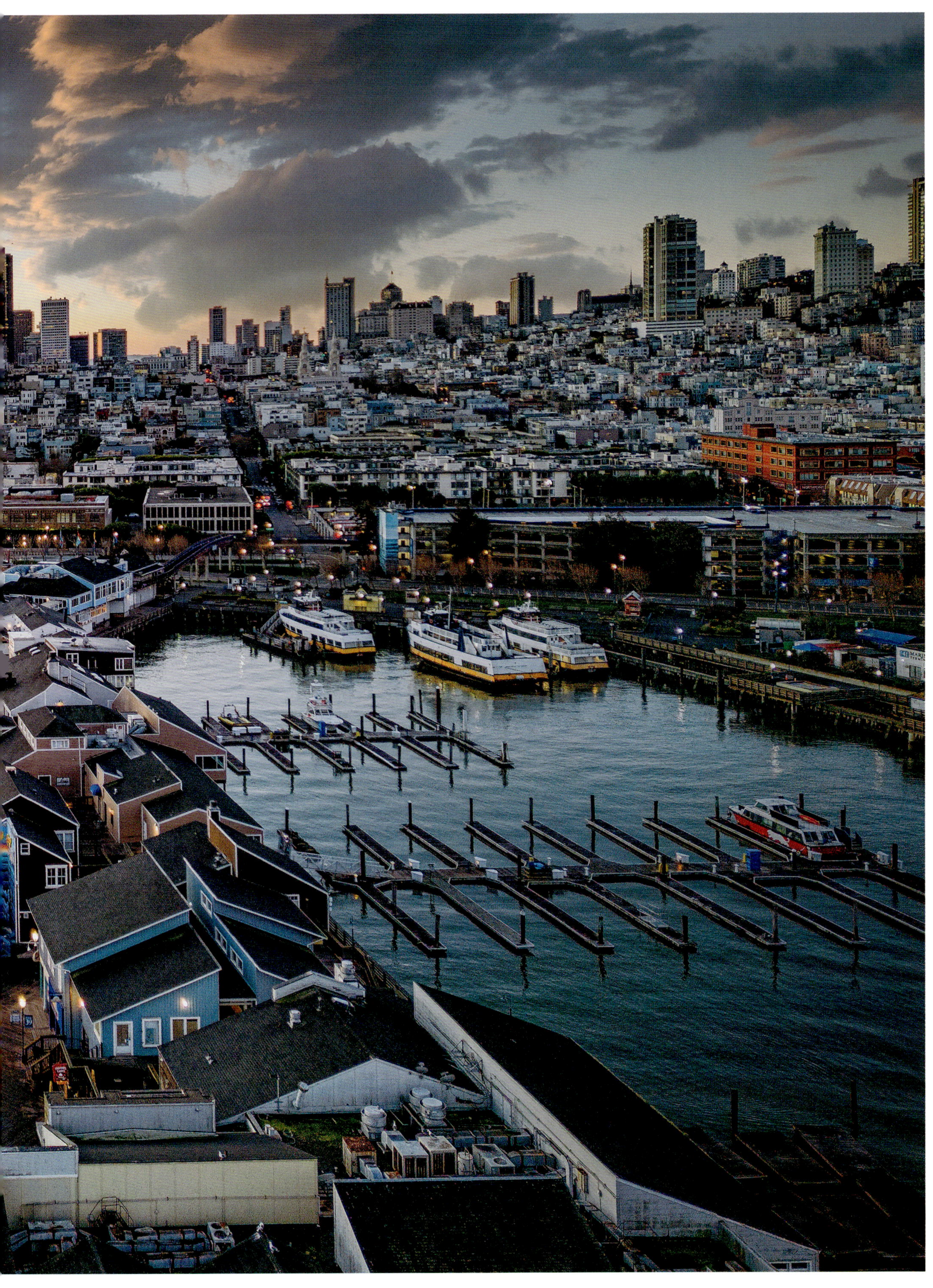

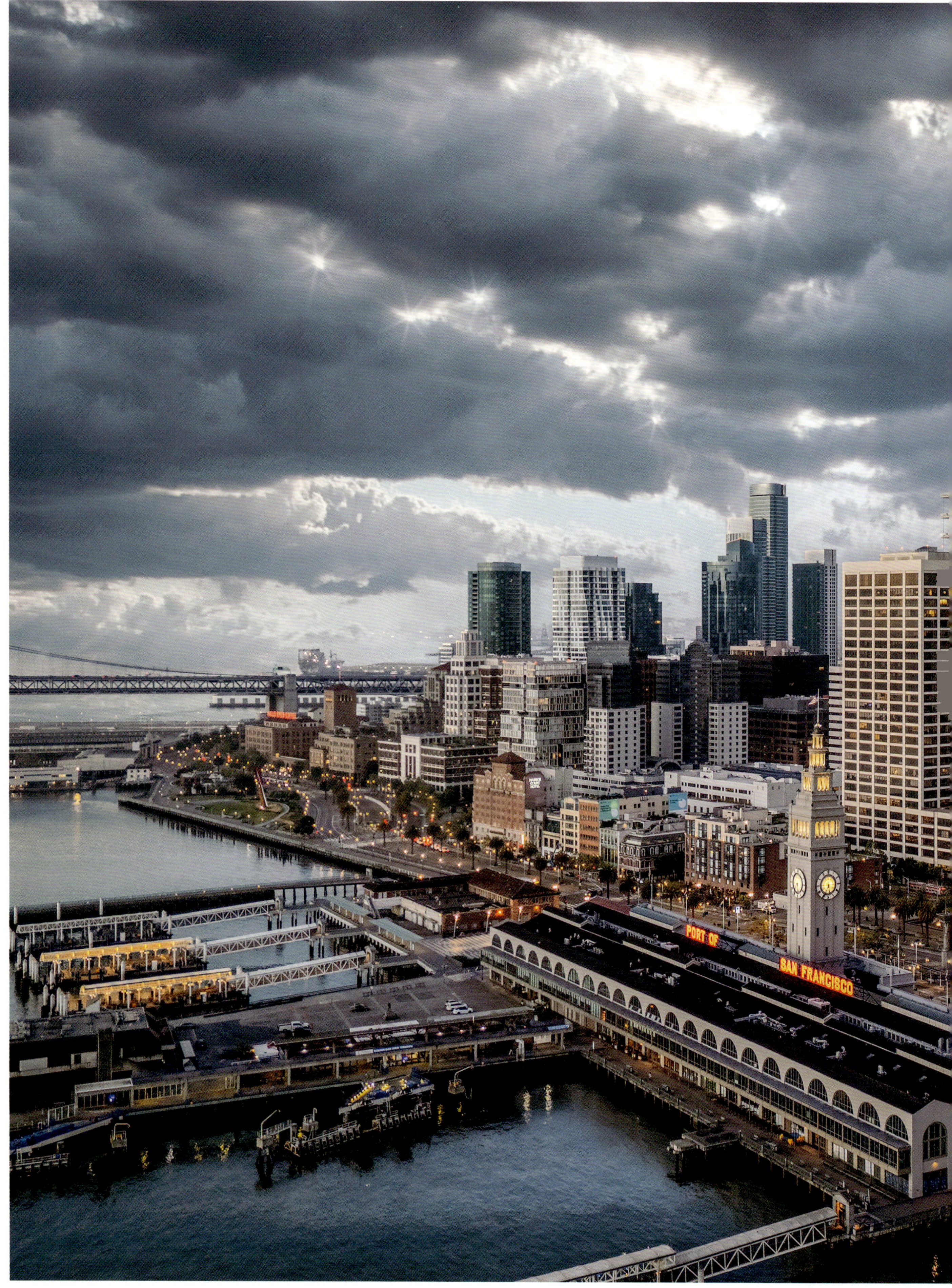
PORT OF
SAN FRANCISCO

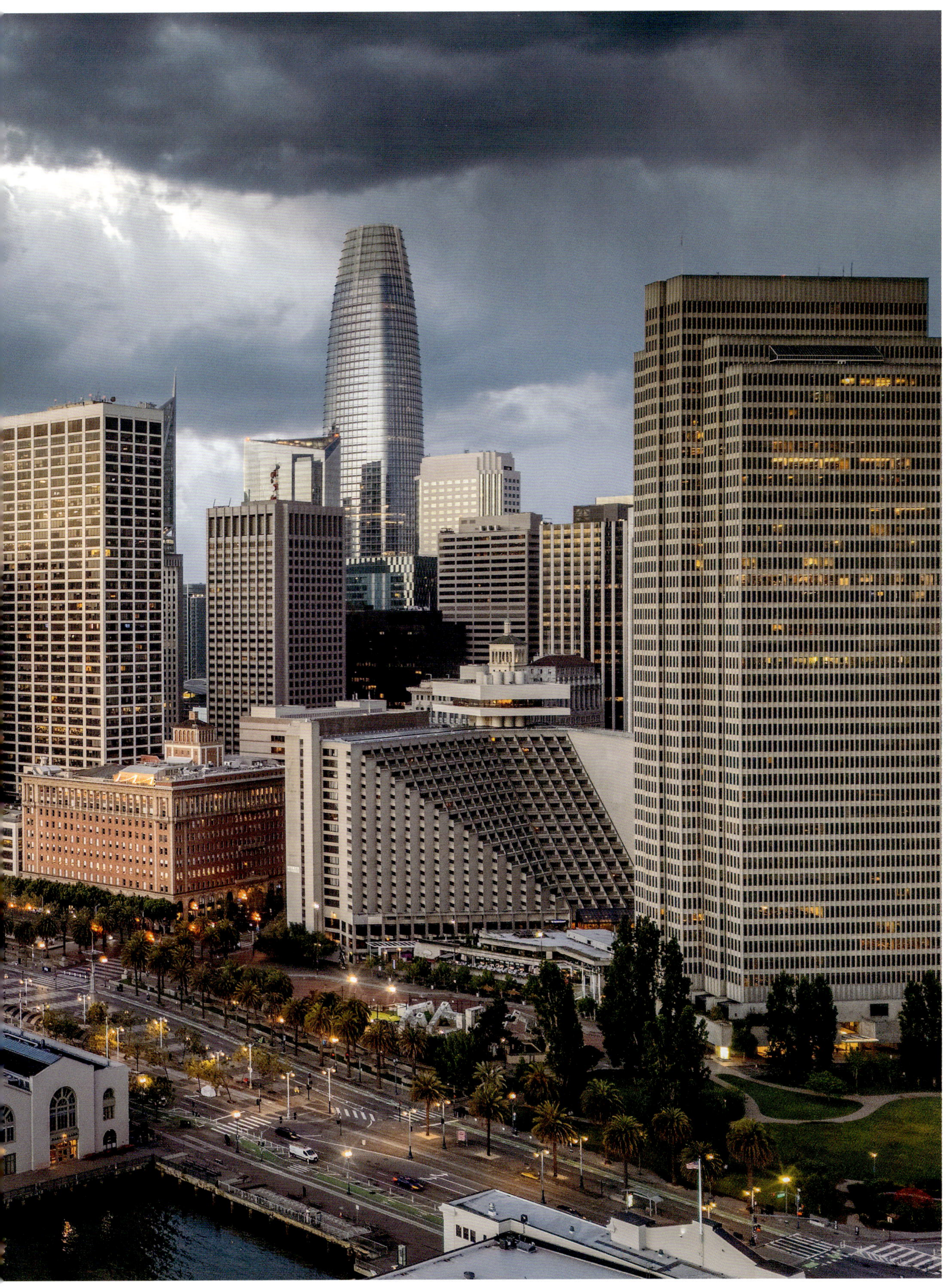

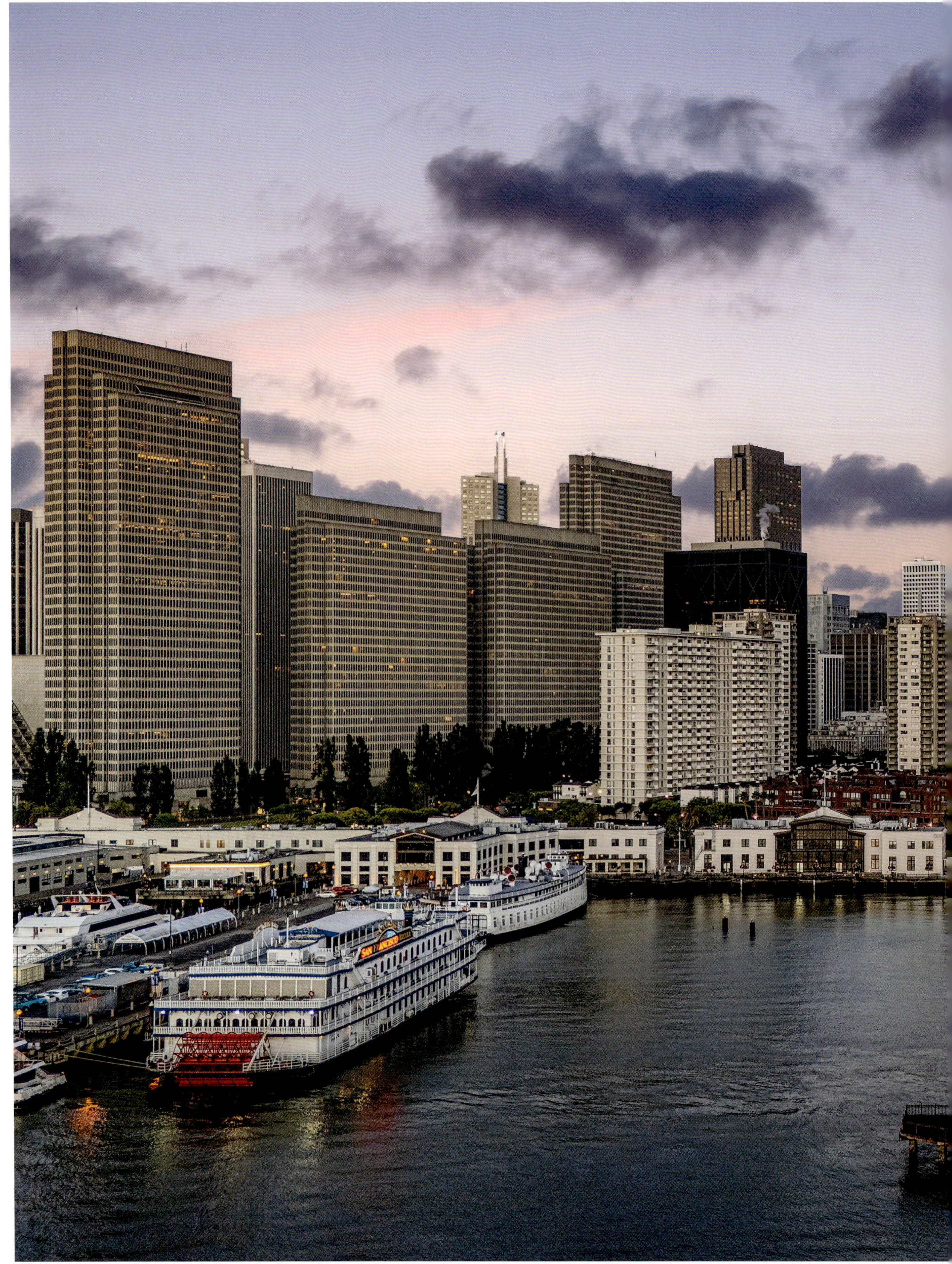
SAN FRANCISCO

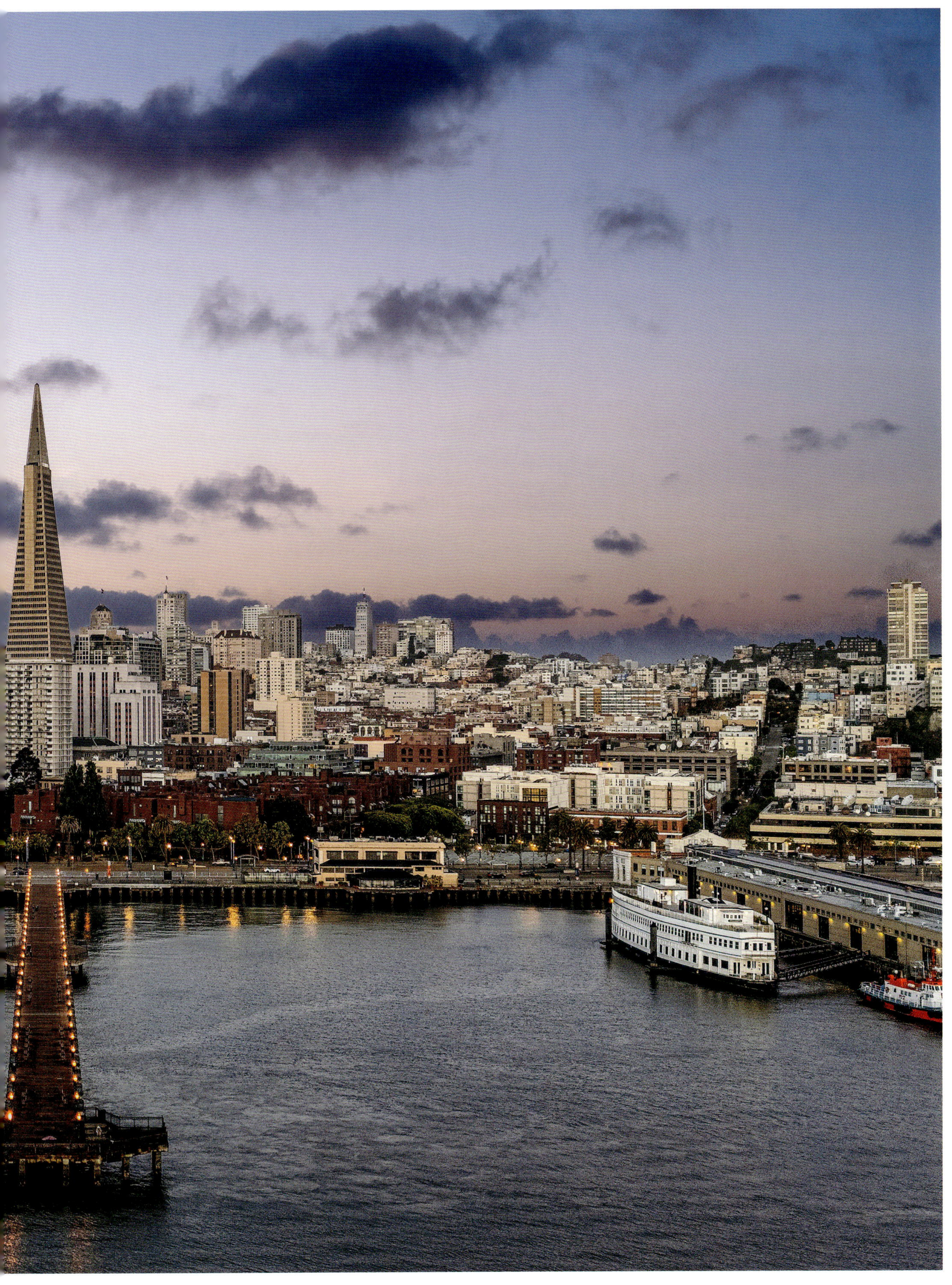

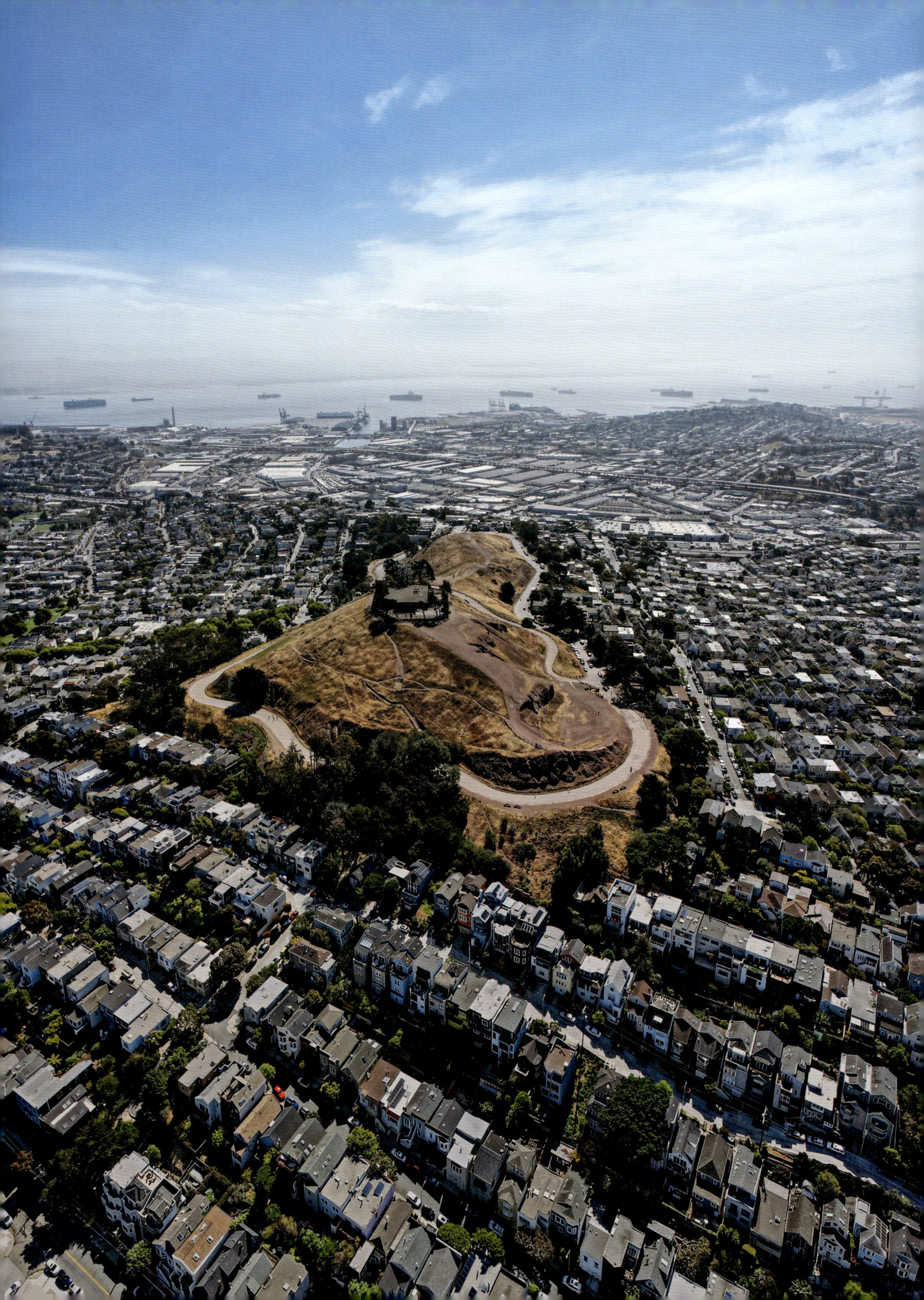

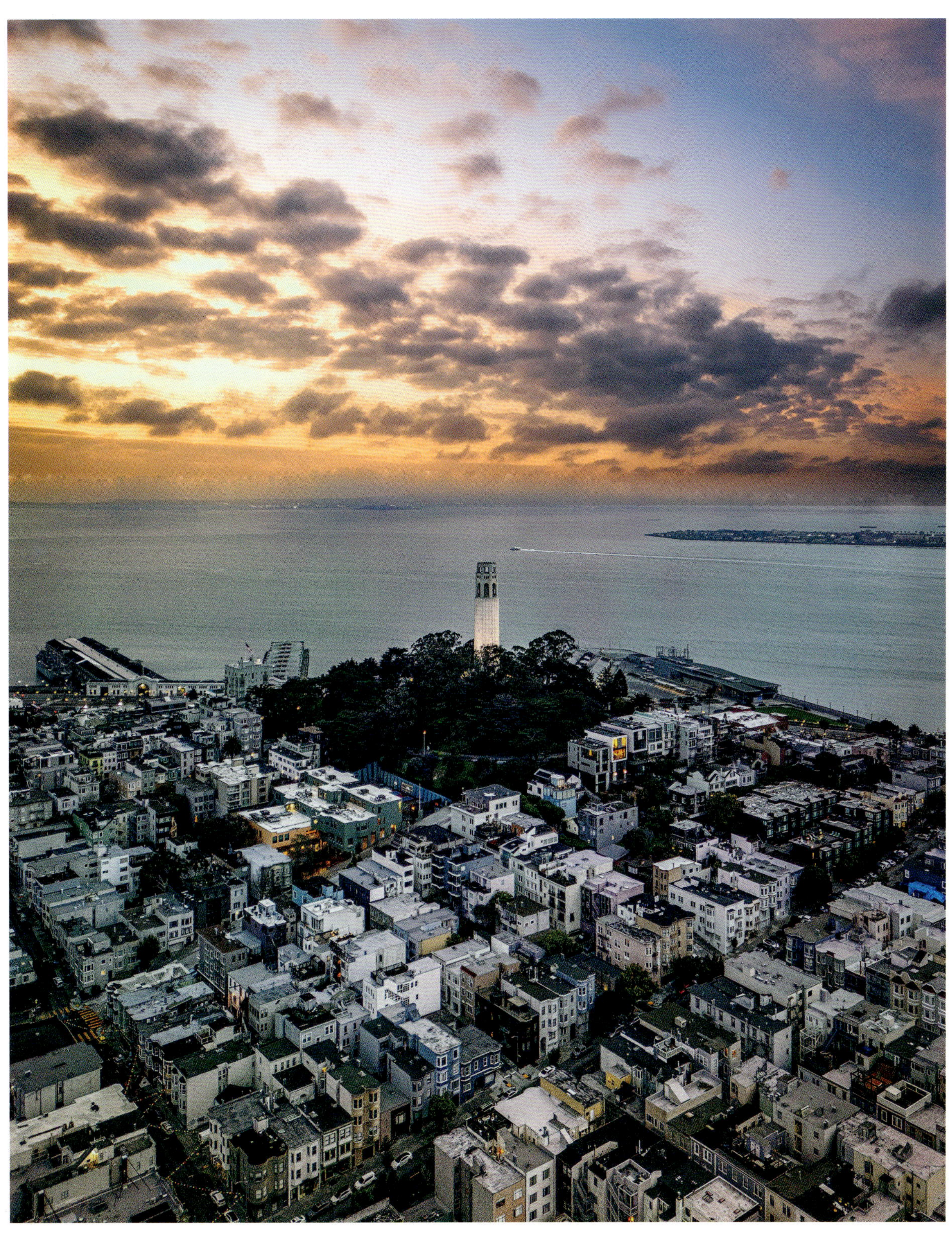

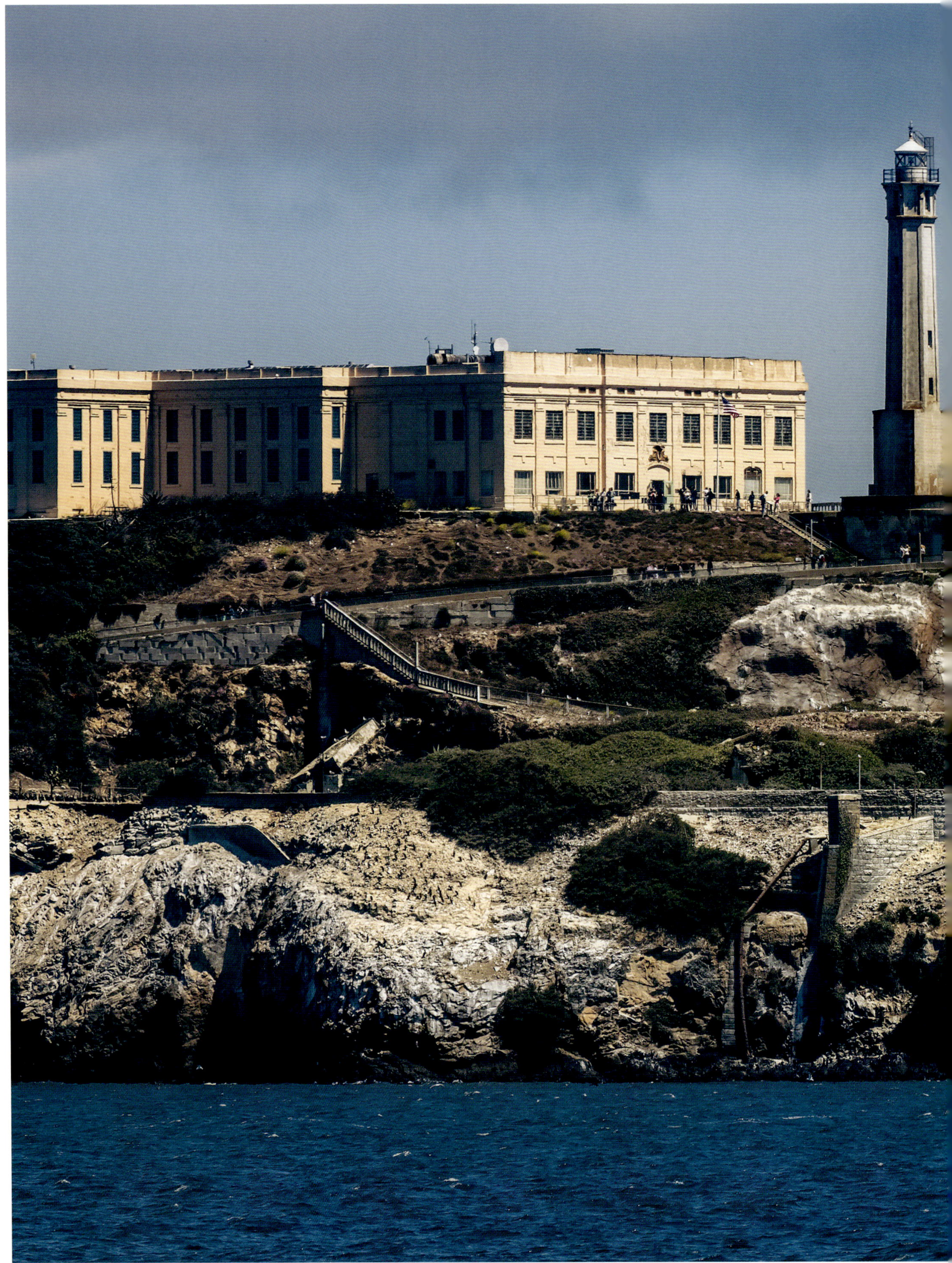

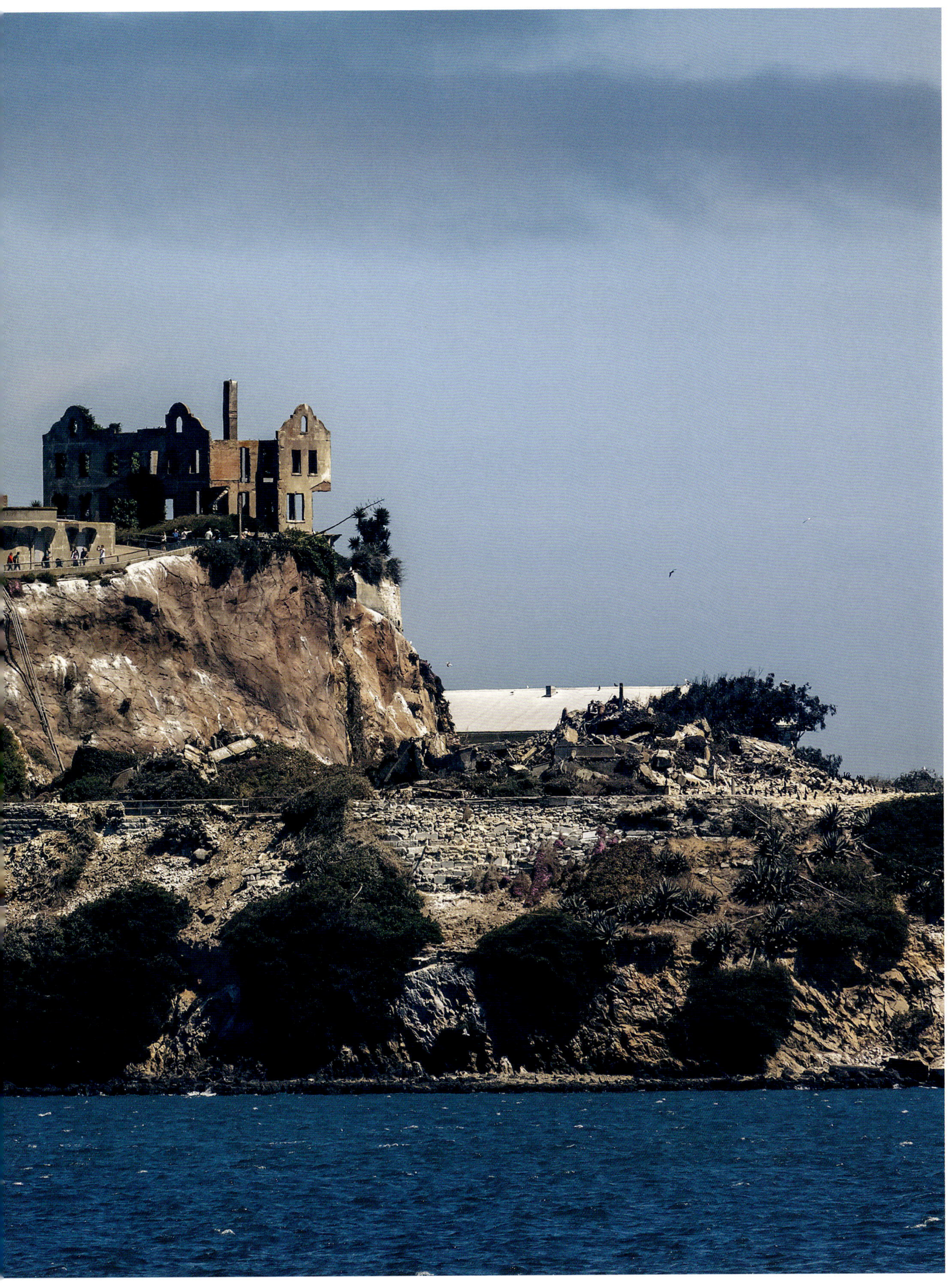

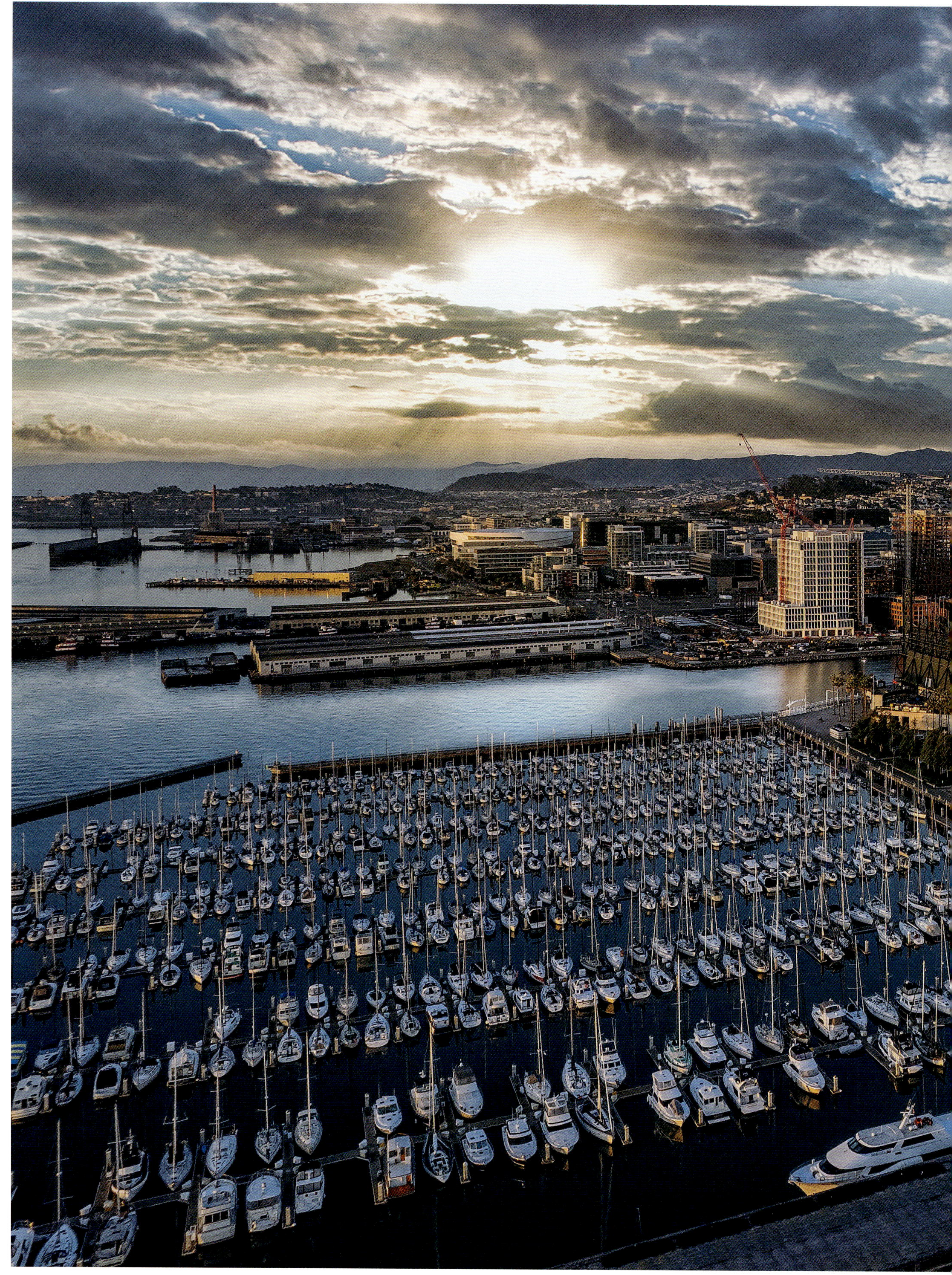

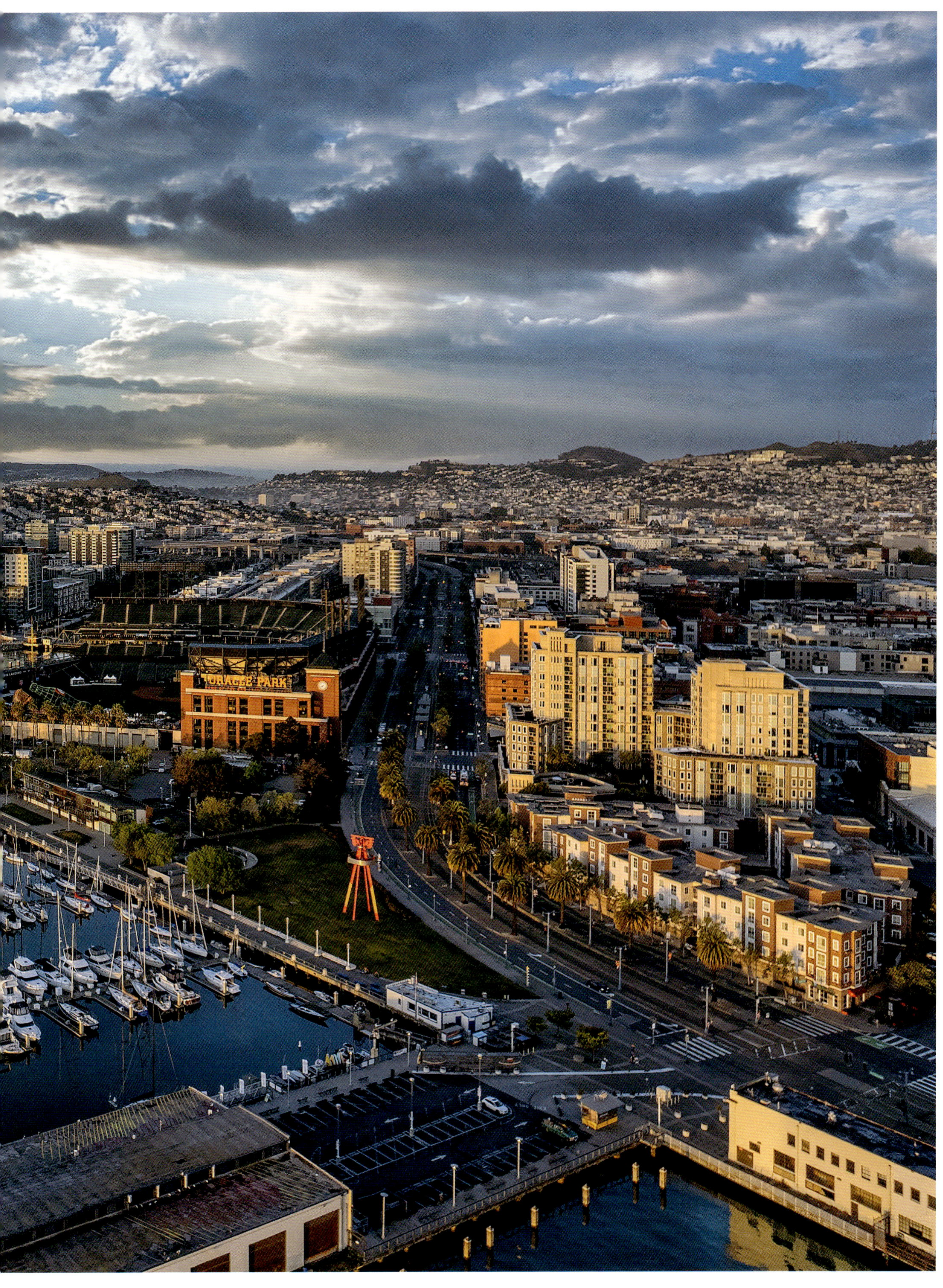
ORACLE PARK

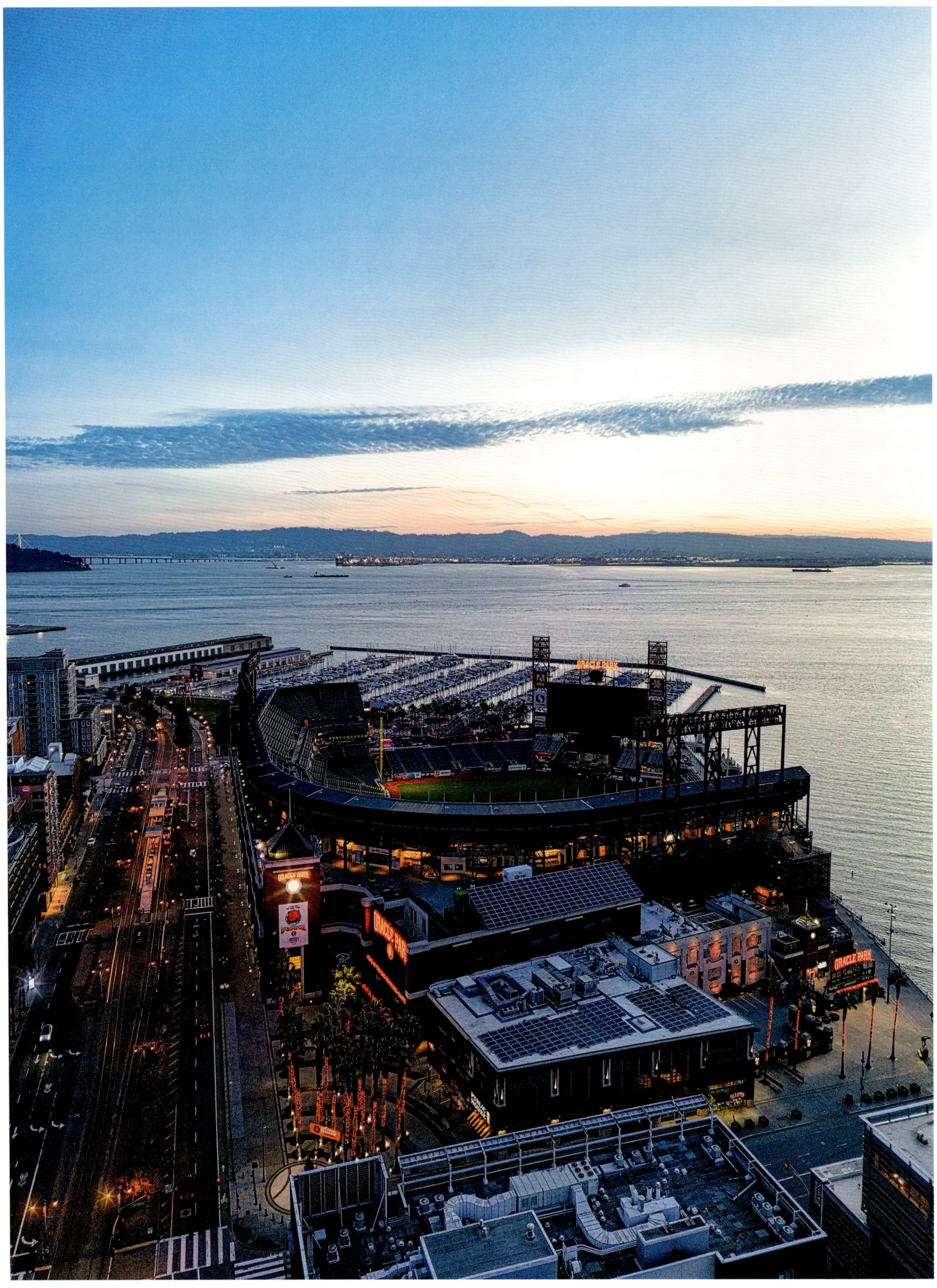

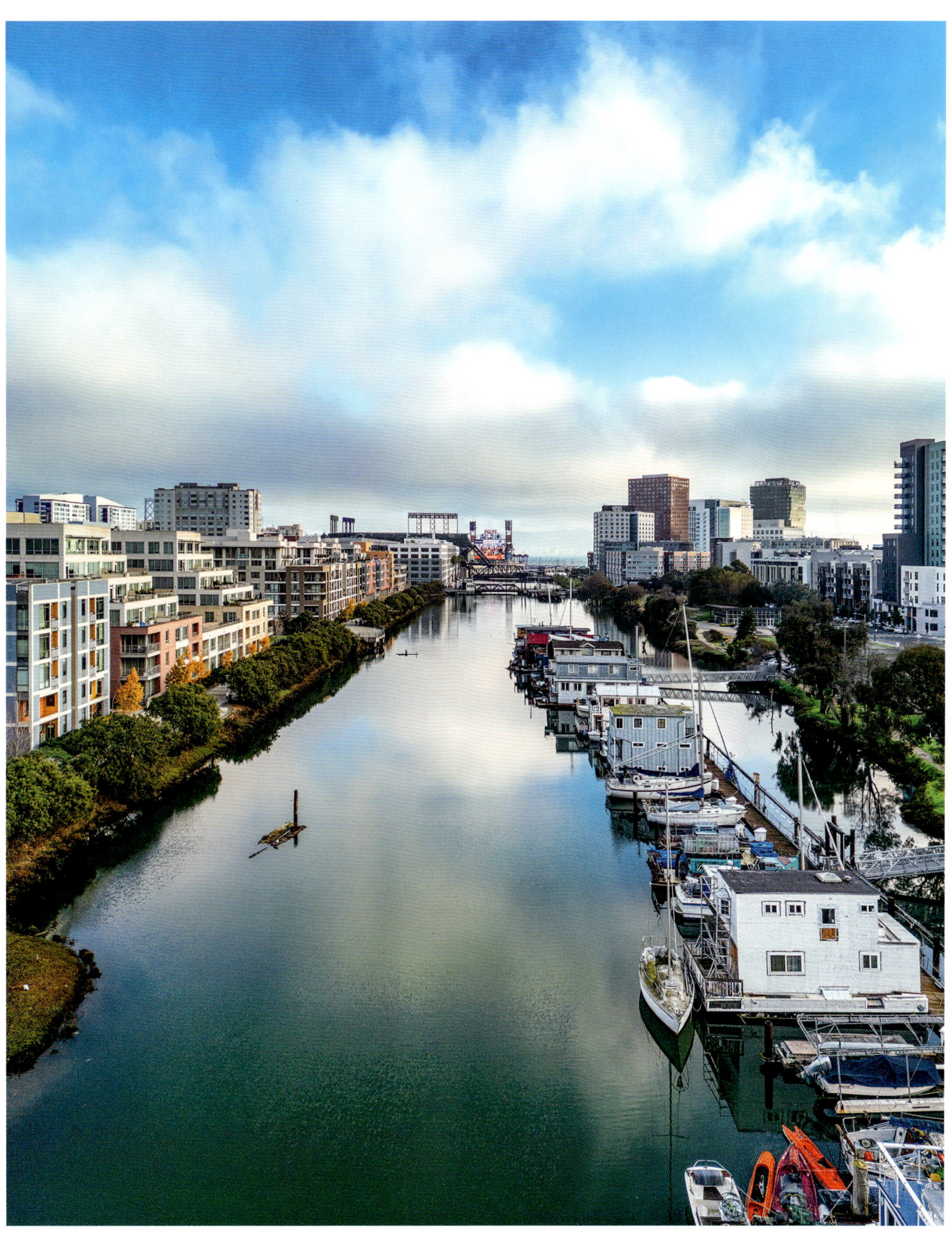

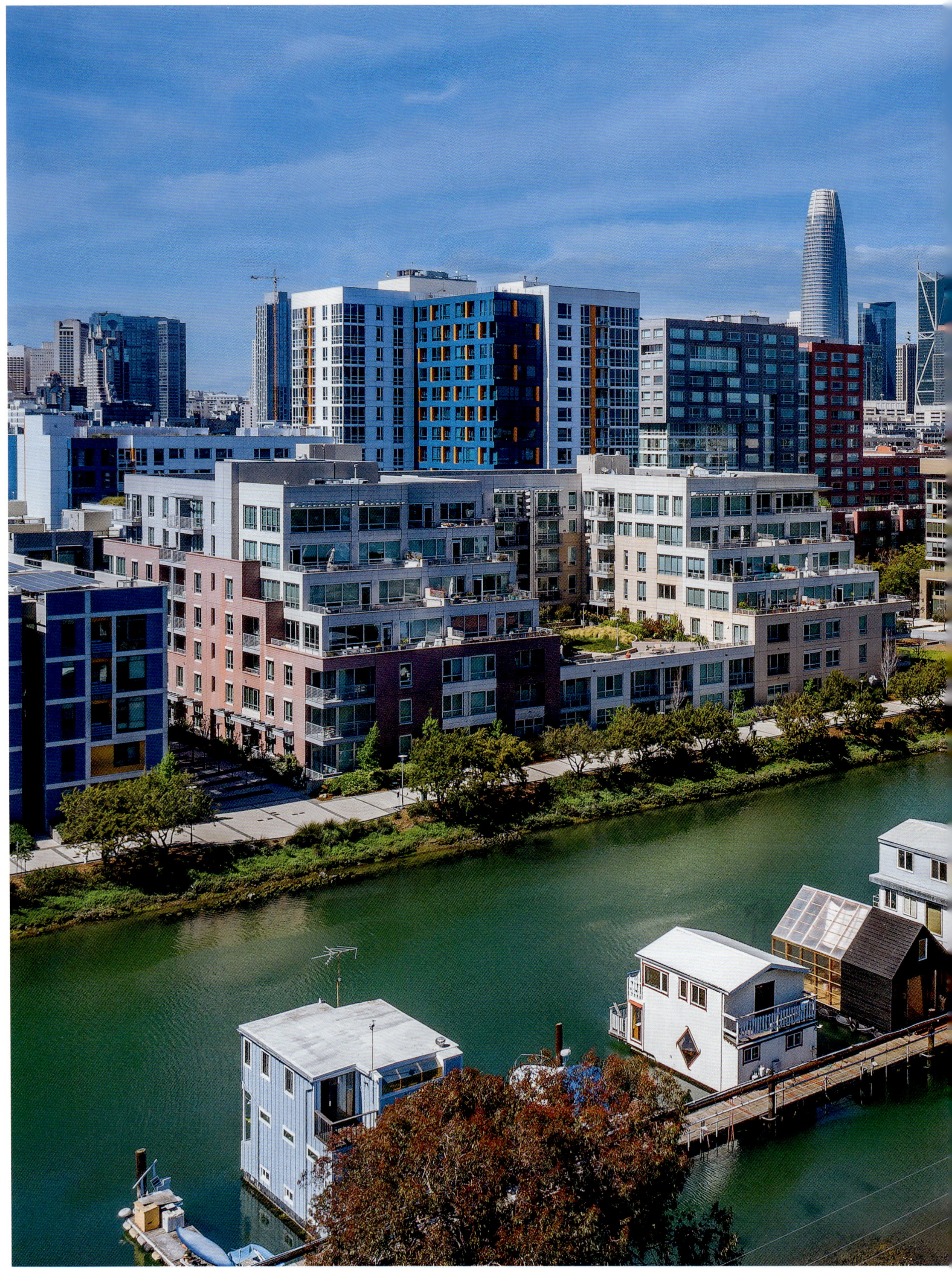

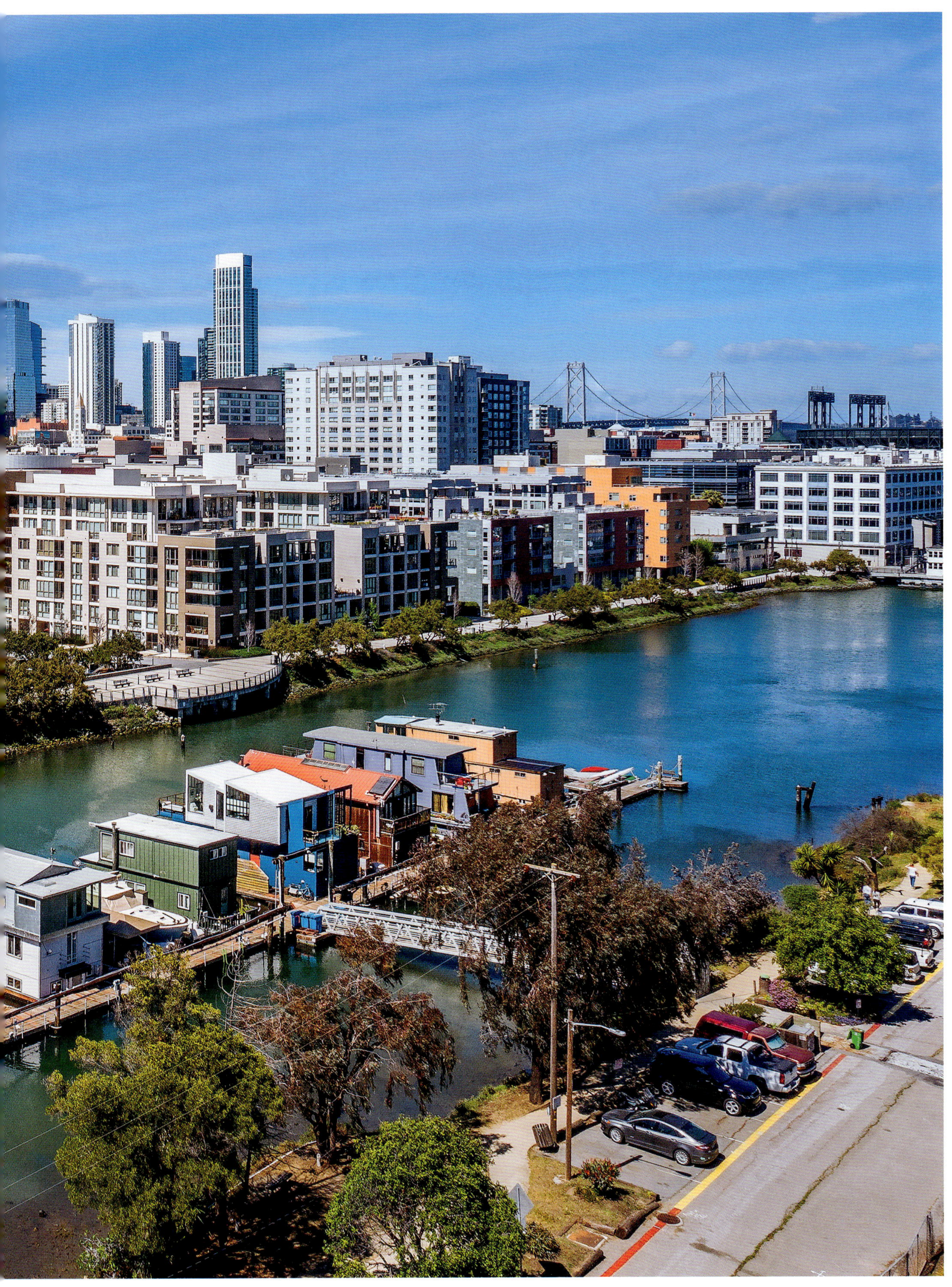

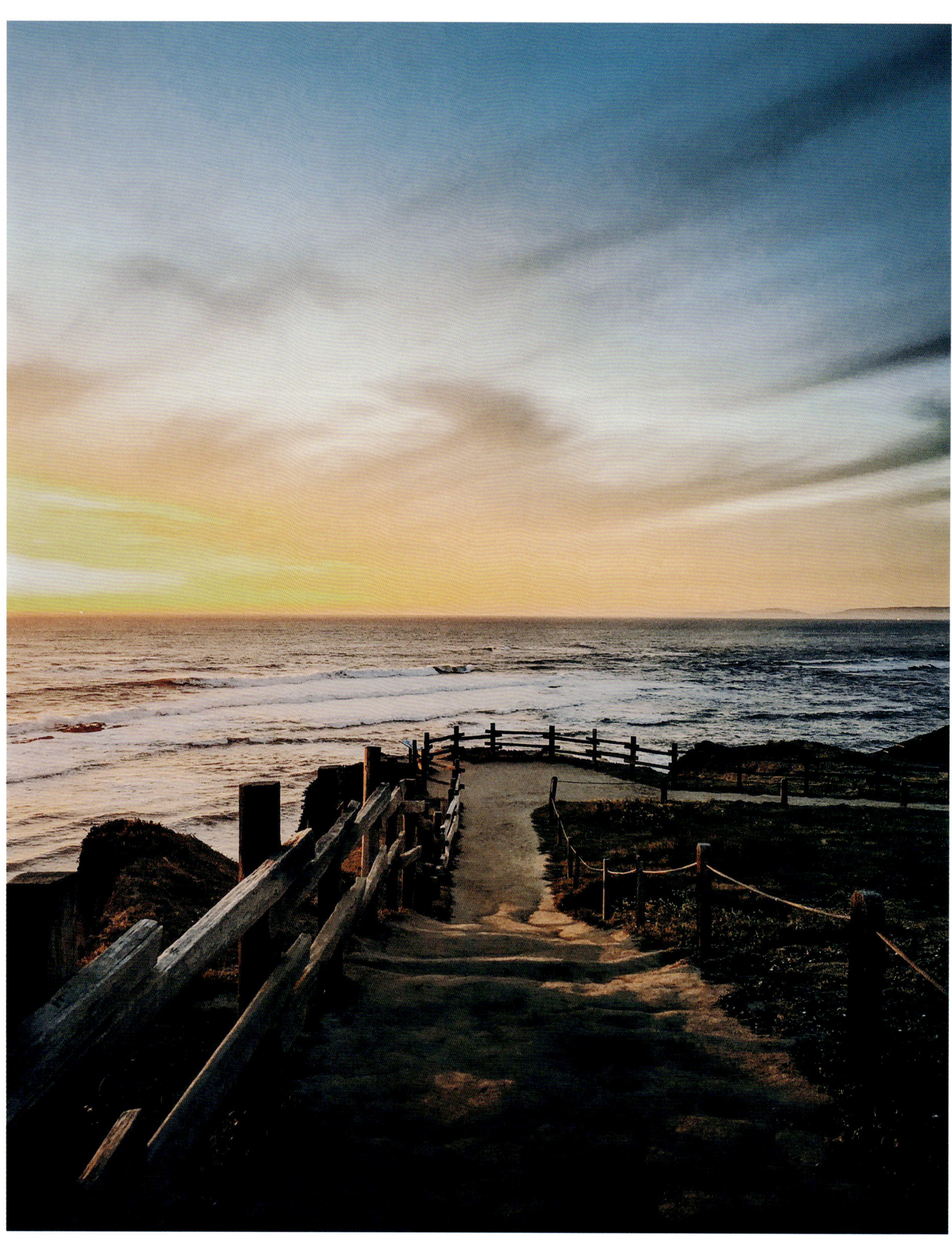

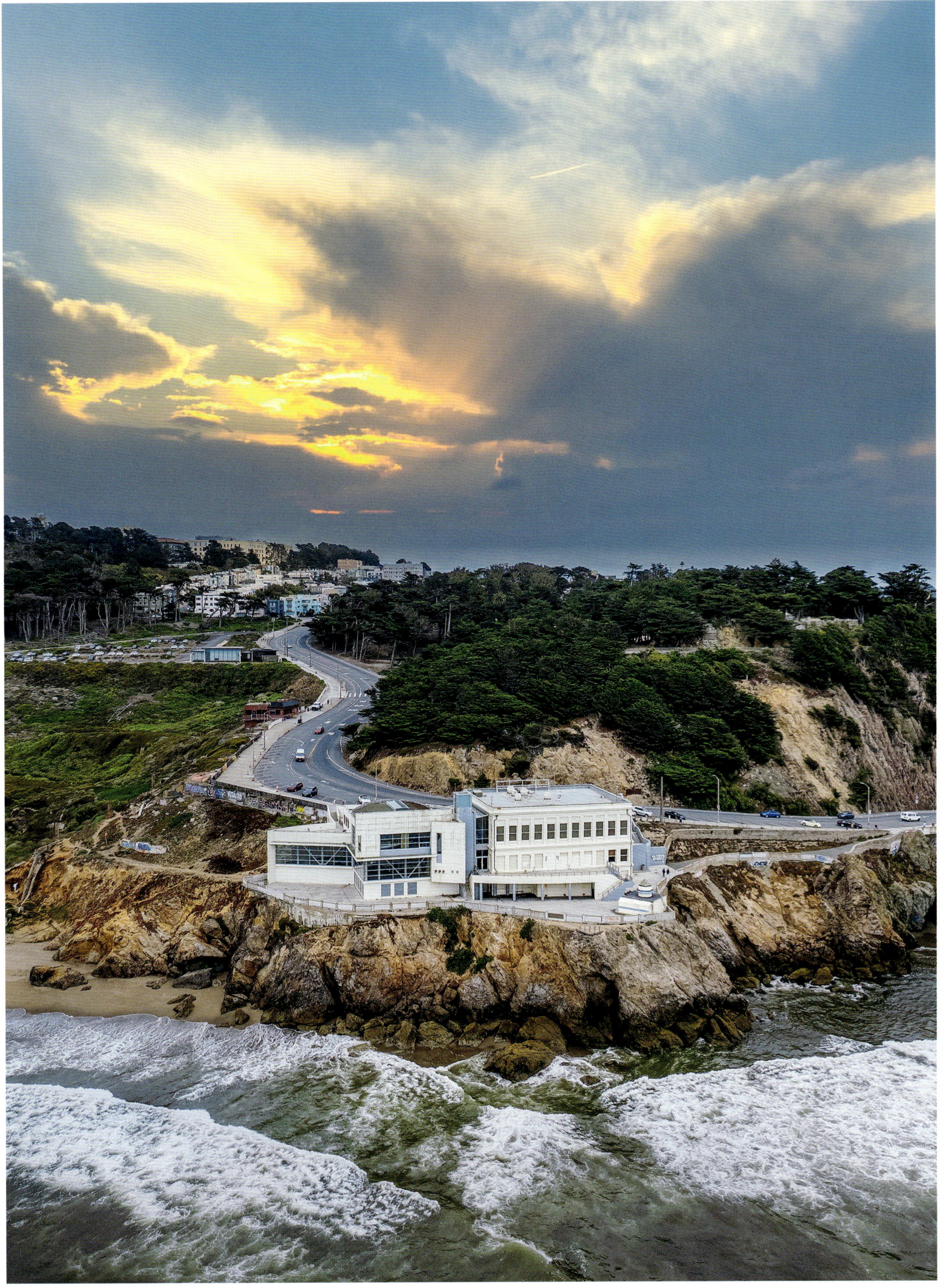

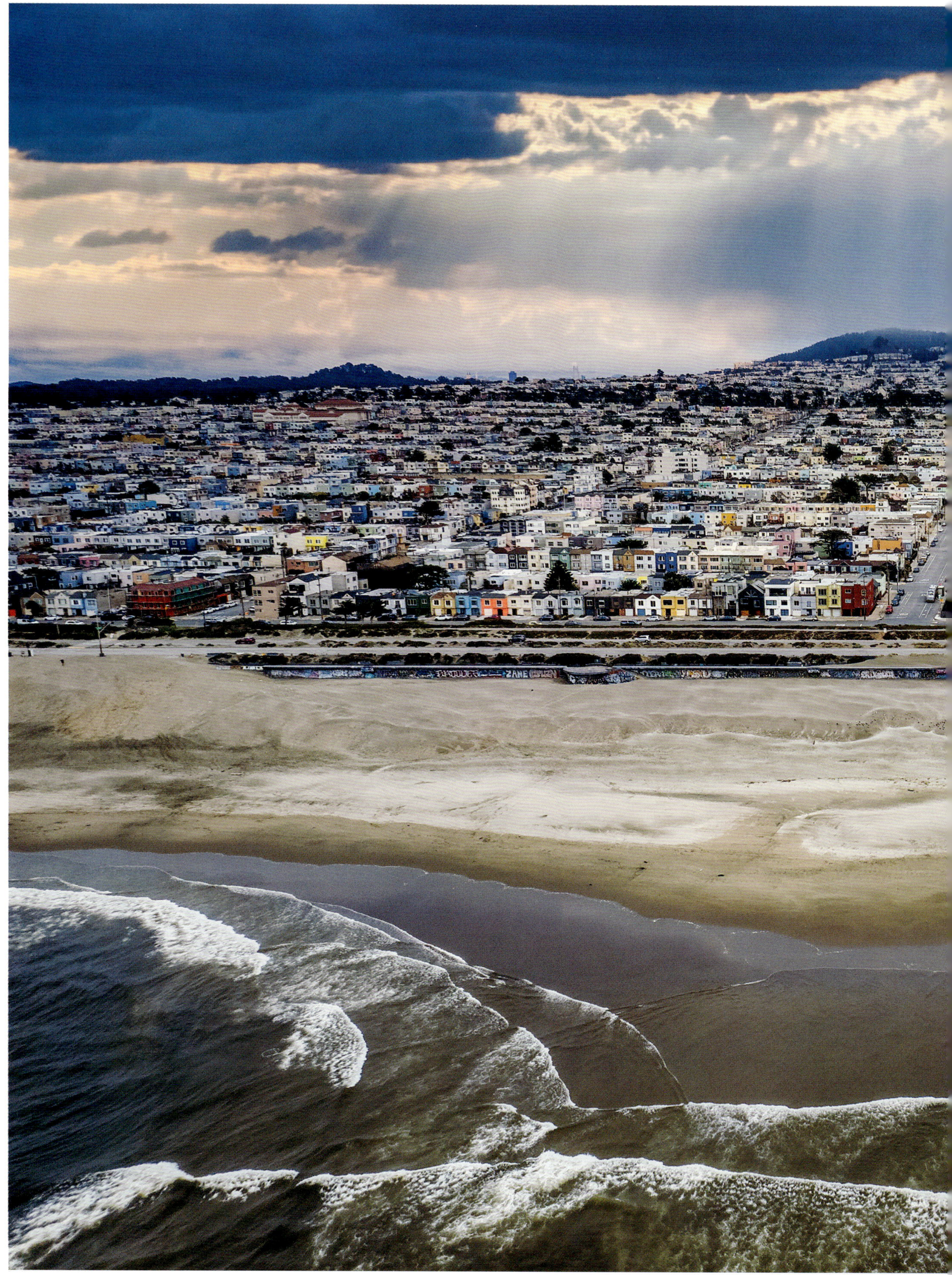

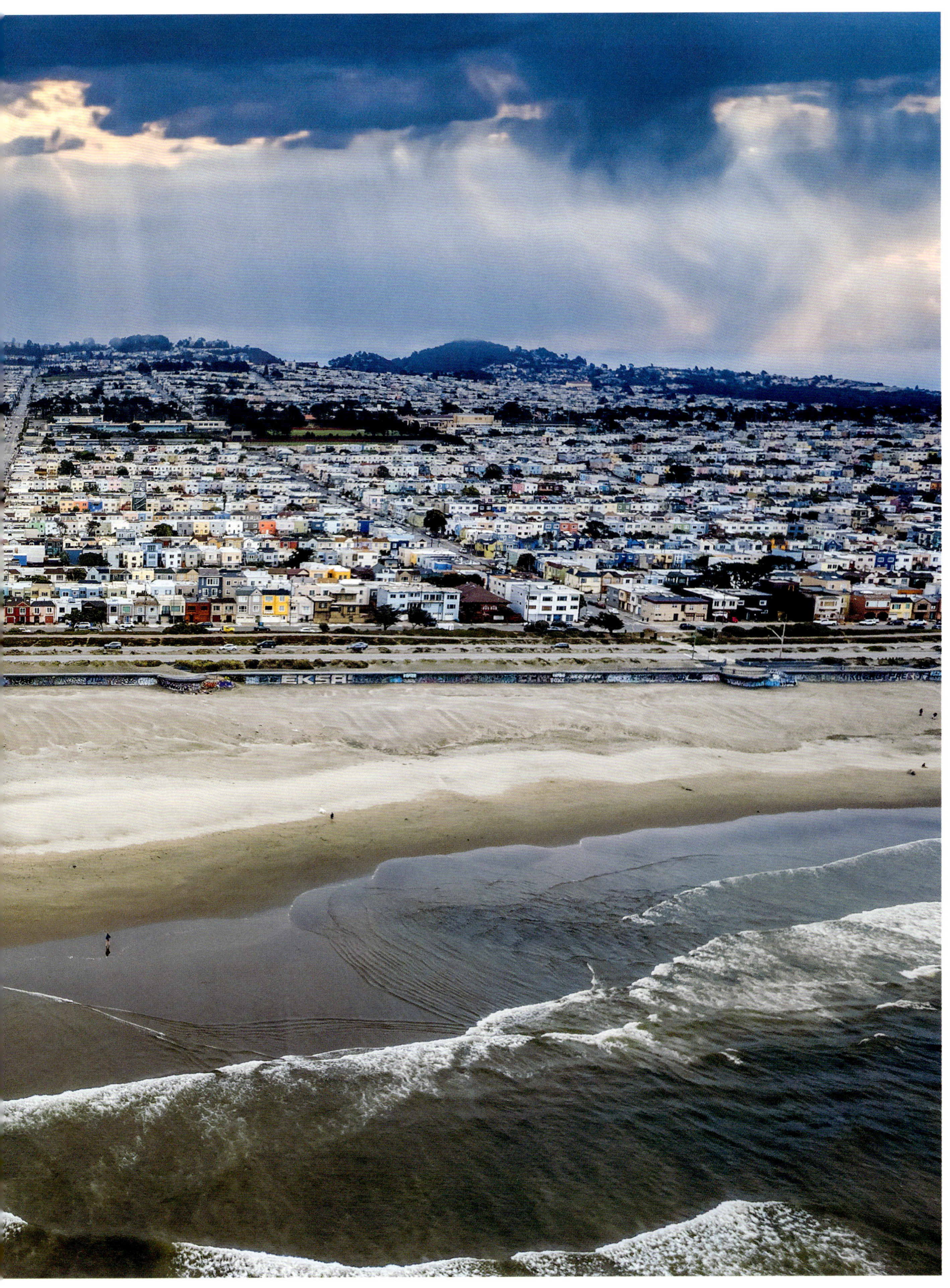

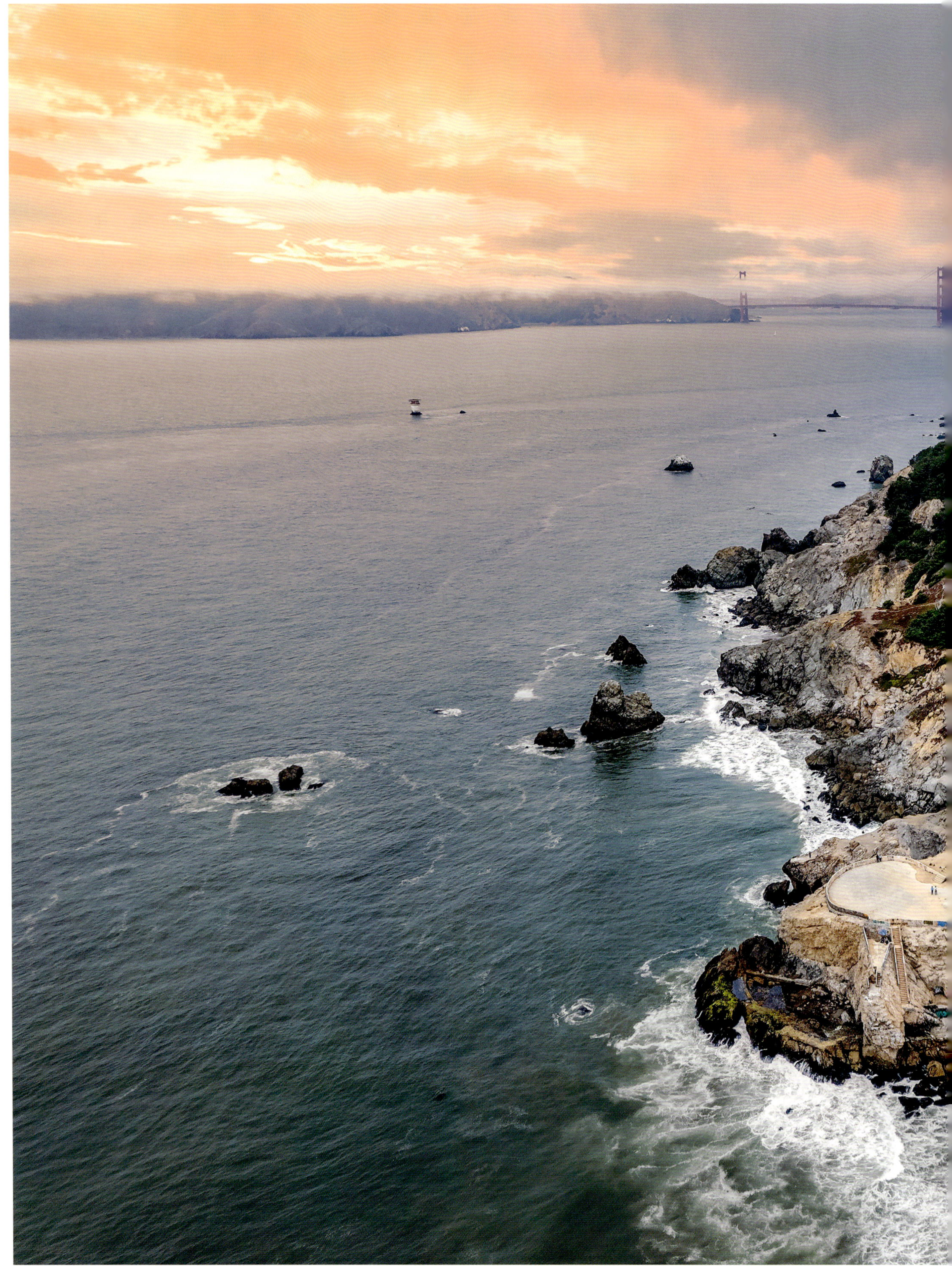

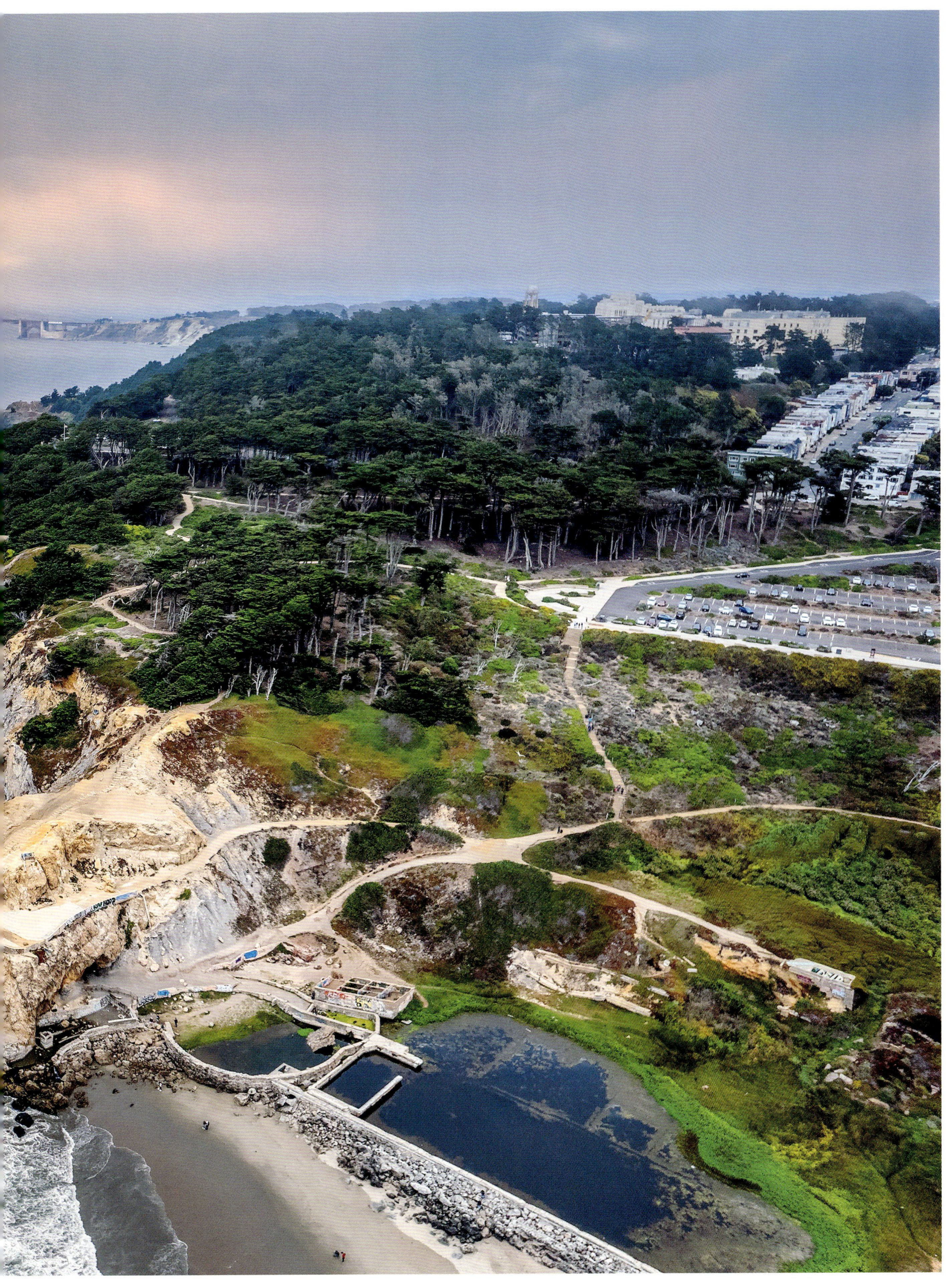

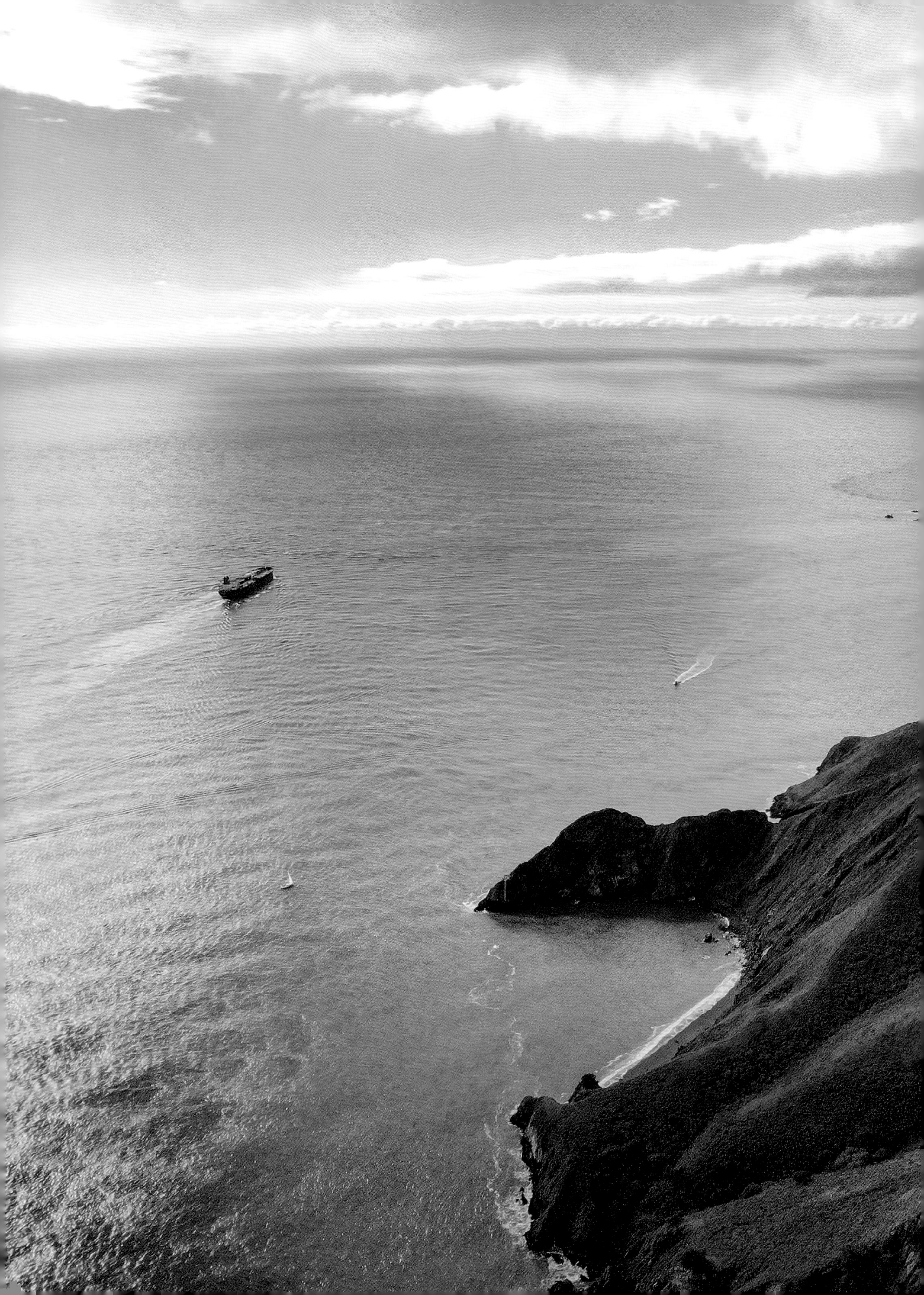

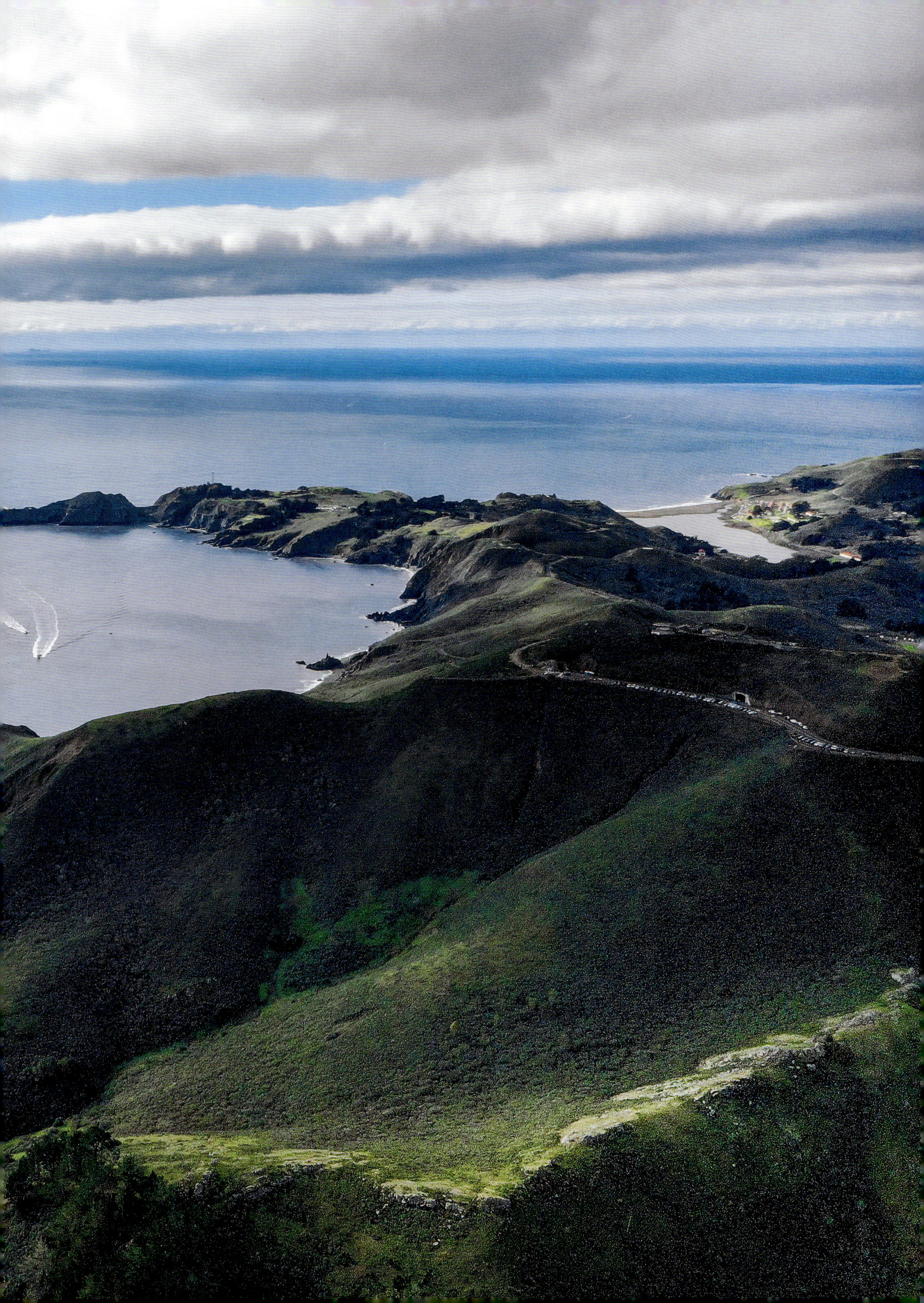

Resurrection ♦ When a devastating earthquake hit San Francisco on April 18, 1906, it lasted less than a minute but caused widespread destruction. Buildings collapsed, roads split open, and fires caused by ruptured gas lines ignited around the city. The fires raged for several days, causing more destruction than the earthquake itself, and an estimated 80% of the city was destroyed. San Francisco had no choice but to rebuild. ♦ This earthquake profoundly changed San Francisco's architecture, with a new emphasis on fireproof construction. Steel-framed buildings, more resistant to fire, became the norm. Stricter building codes were enacted to prevent another catastrophe and the city rapidly worked to reconstruct. ♦ Key buildings constructed in the post-earthquake period include The Hobart Building at 582 Market Street. Completed in 1914 and an iconic example of early 20th-century high-rise design, the building remains a San Francisco landmark with its curving structure reflecting the Beaux-Arts style with its narrow, curving structure, elaborate detailing, and classical influences. The Pacific Telephone Building, completed in 1925 and now called 140 New Montgomery, was once the tallest building in San Francisco and the city's first skyscraper development. Situated in the SoMa neighborhood, the building's Art Deco architecture is notable for its terra cotta detailing and setbacks on its higher floors that provide a tiered effect. ♦ More recent skyscrapers, including the Transamerica Pyramid, perhaps the most iconic building in San Francisco, and the modernist skyscraper at 555 California Street, once known as the Bank of America Building, were built to reflect the international style of architecture focused on minimalism and functionality. These glass-and-steel structures, free from ornamentation, dominate the San Francisco skyline. Salesforce Tower, now the tallest building in San Francisco, was completed in 2018 and embodies sleek modernity with its curved glass façade.

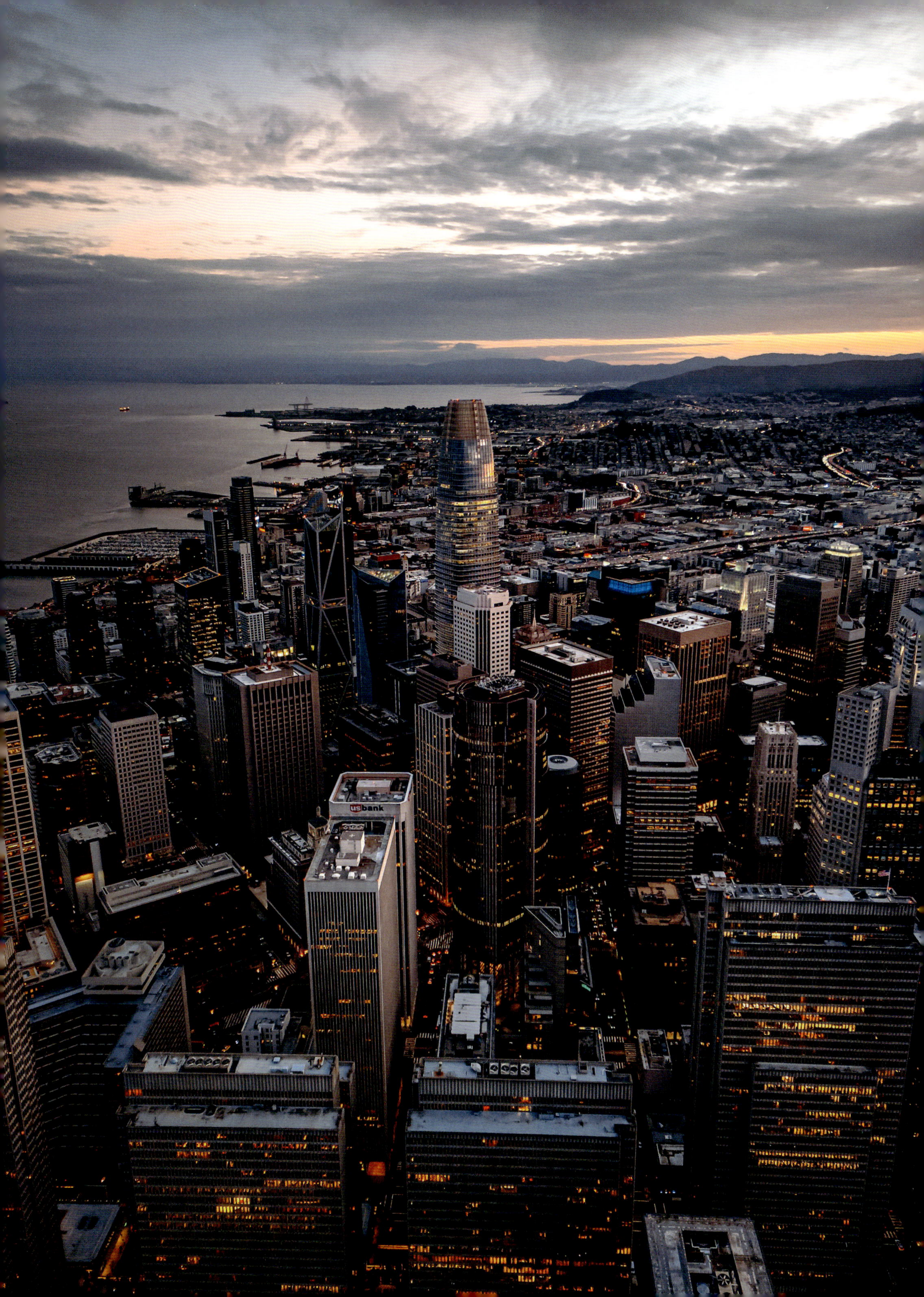

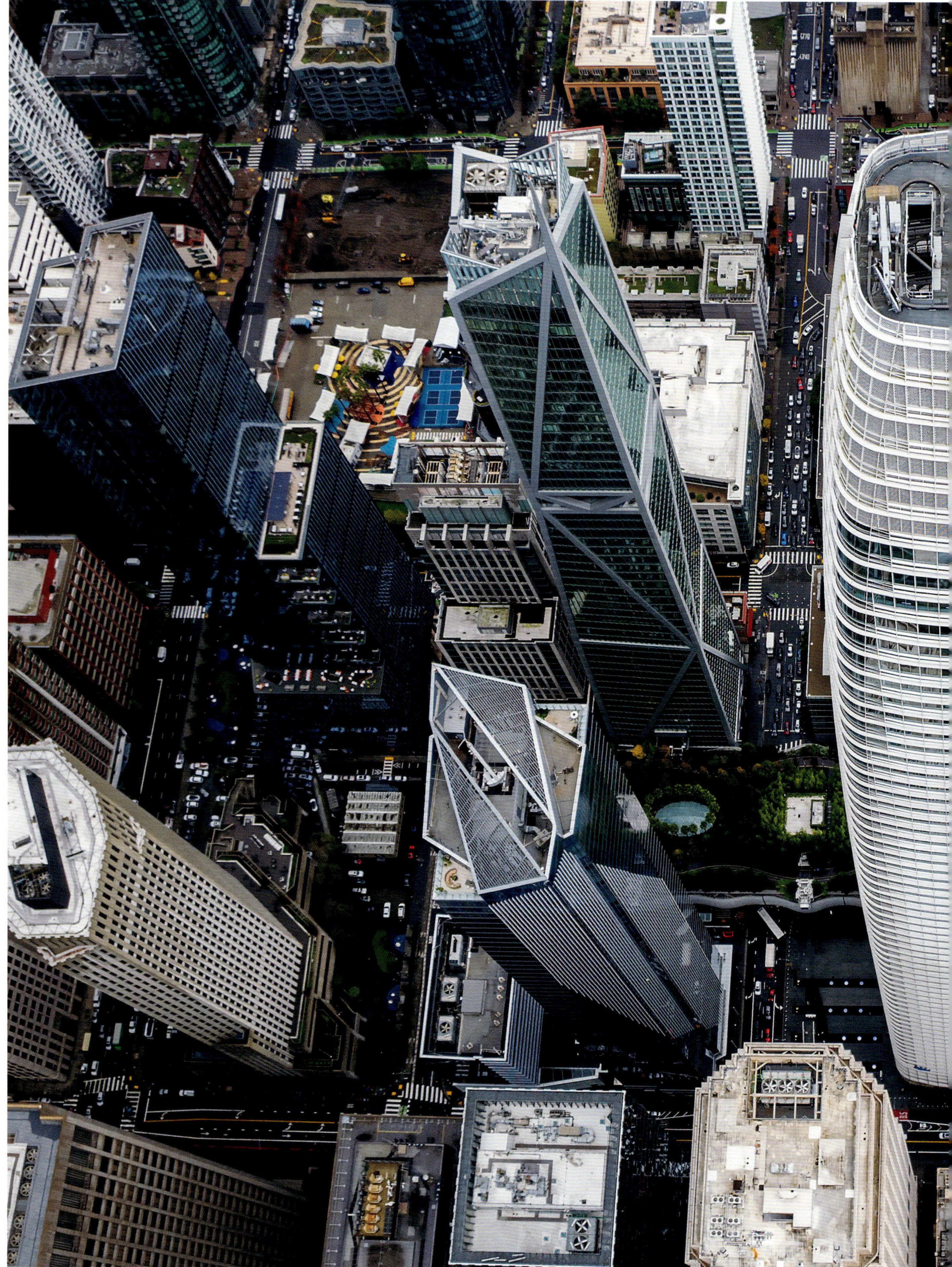

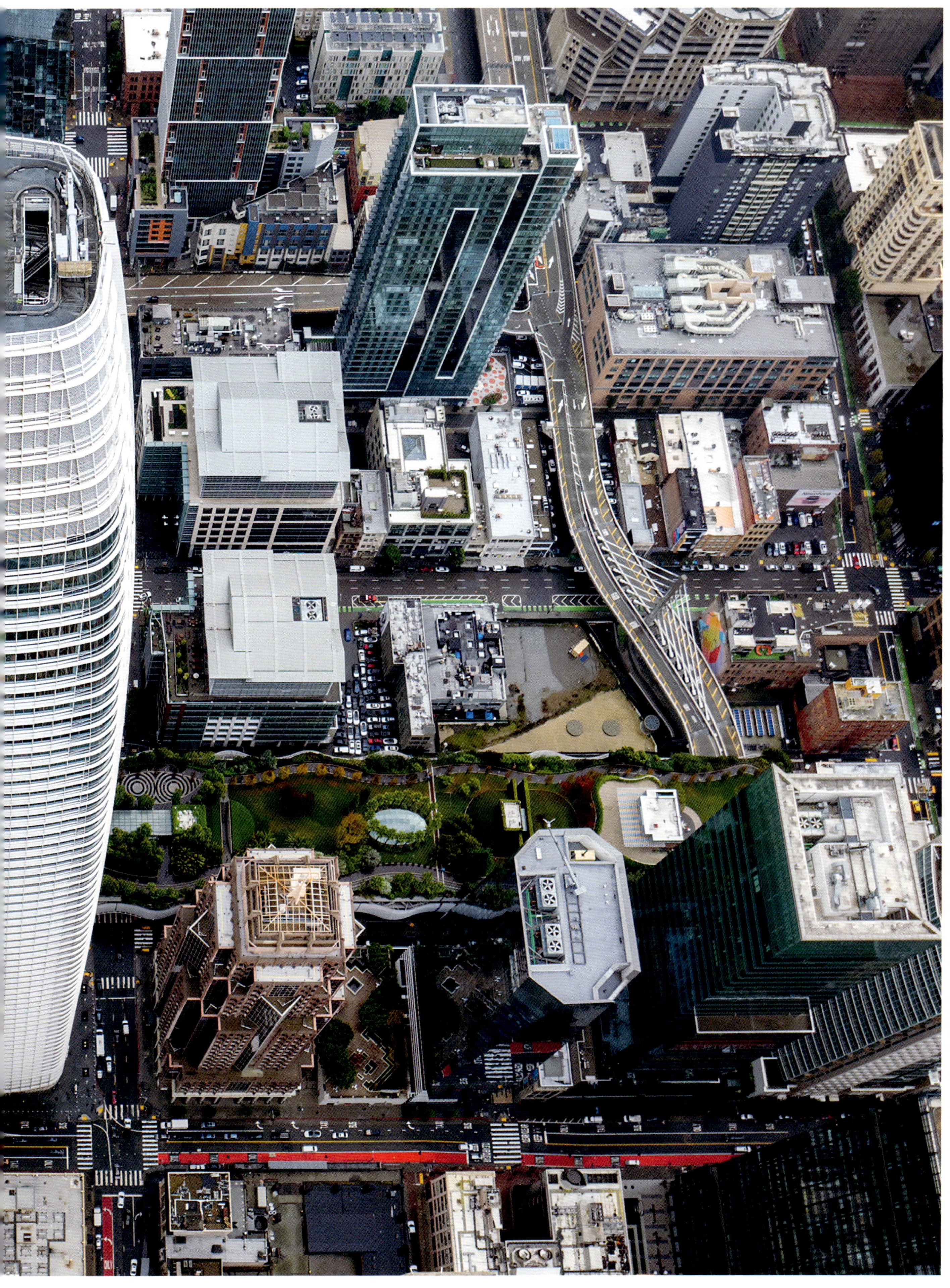

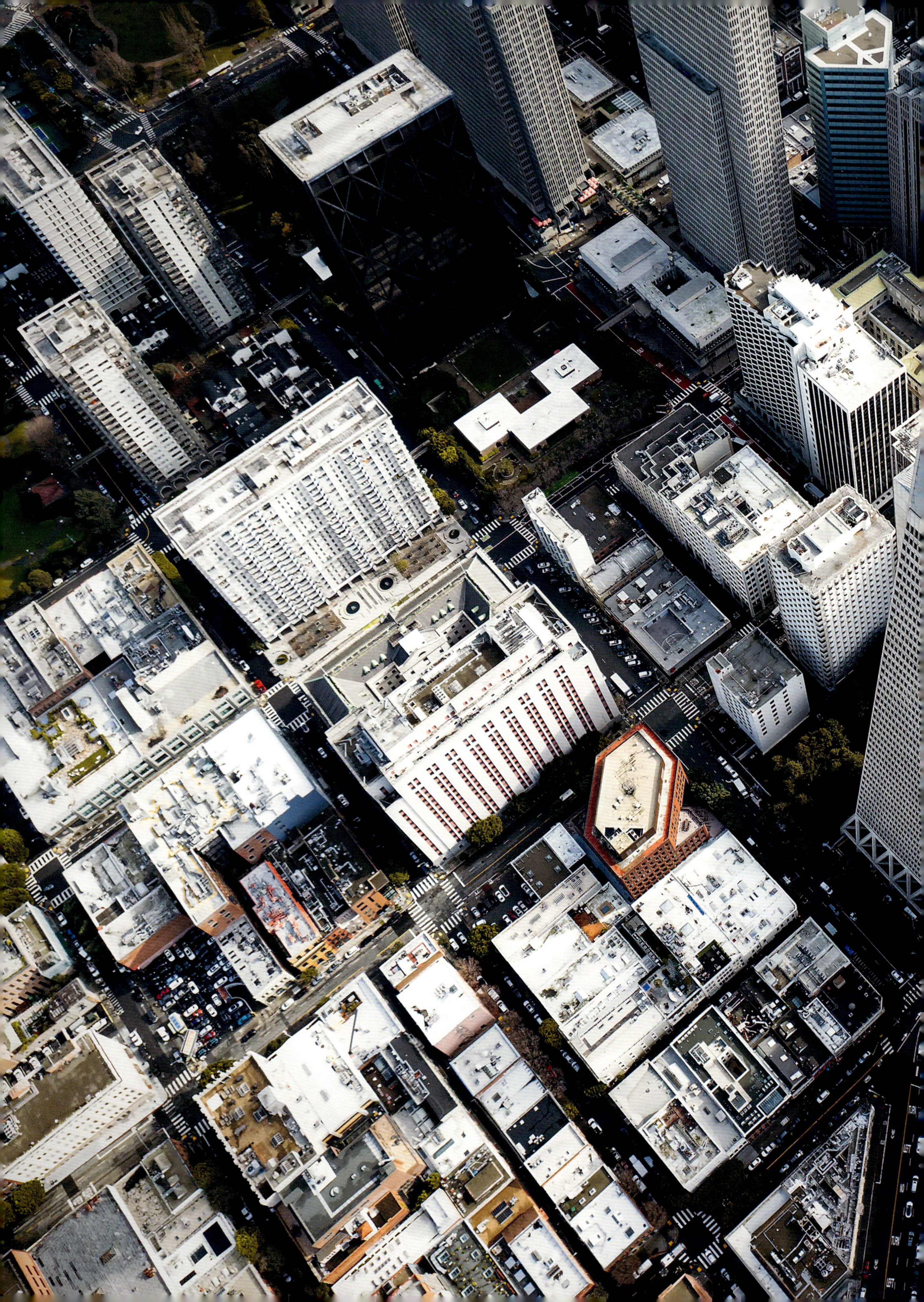

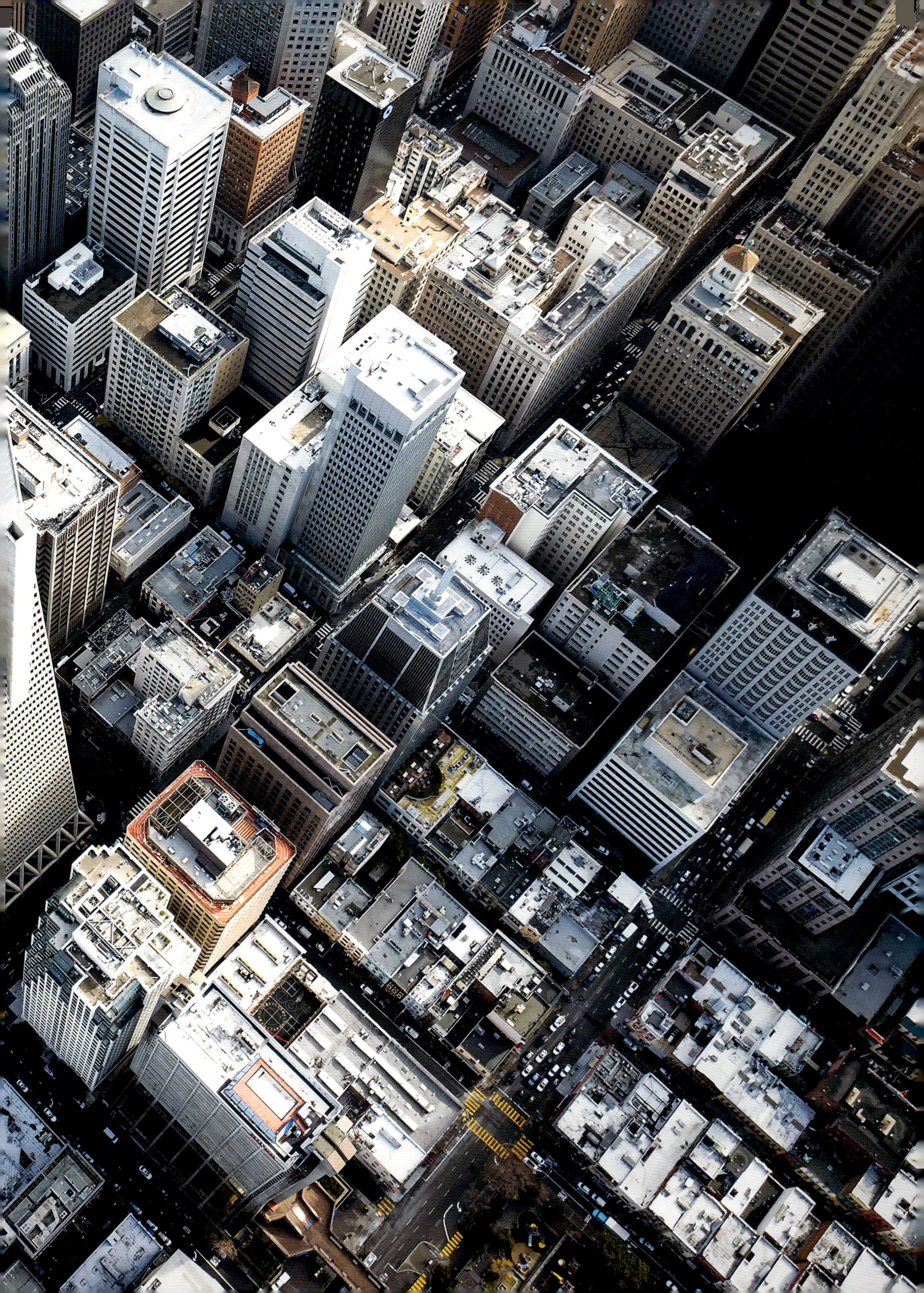

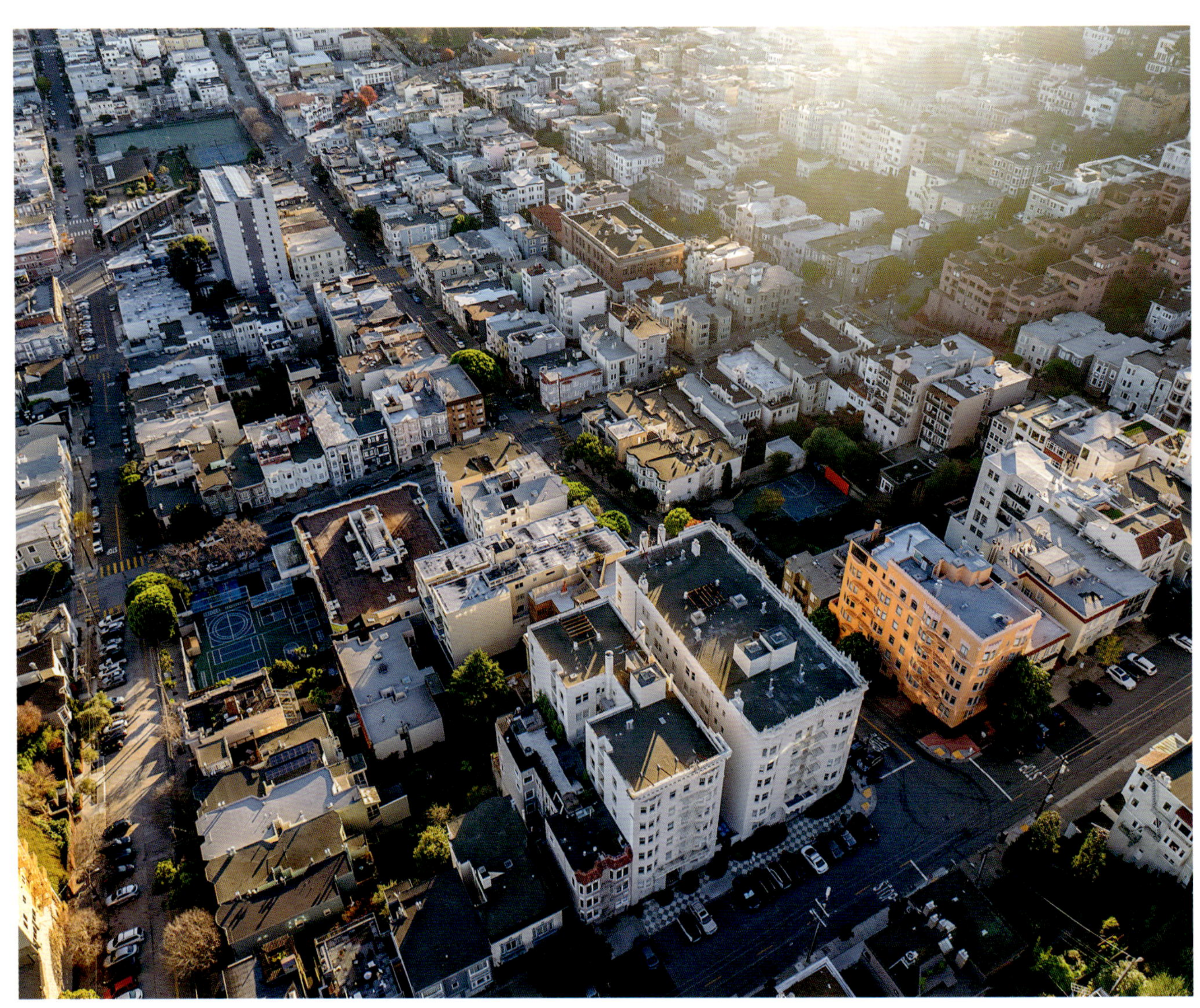

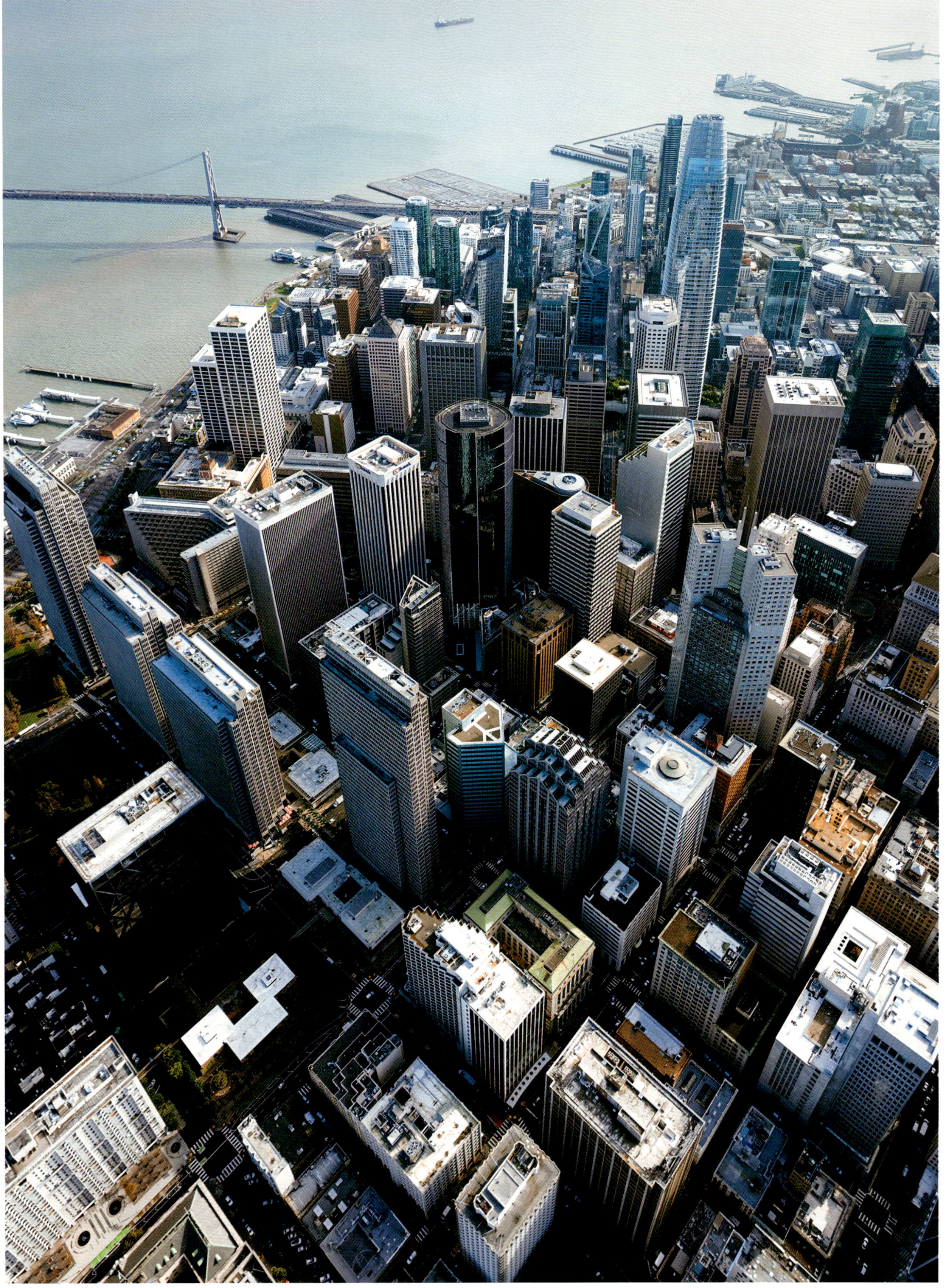

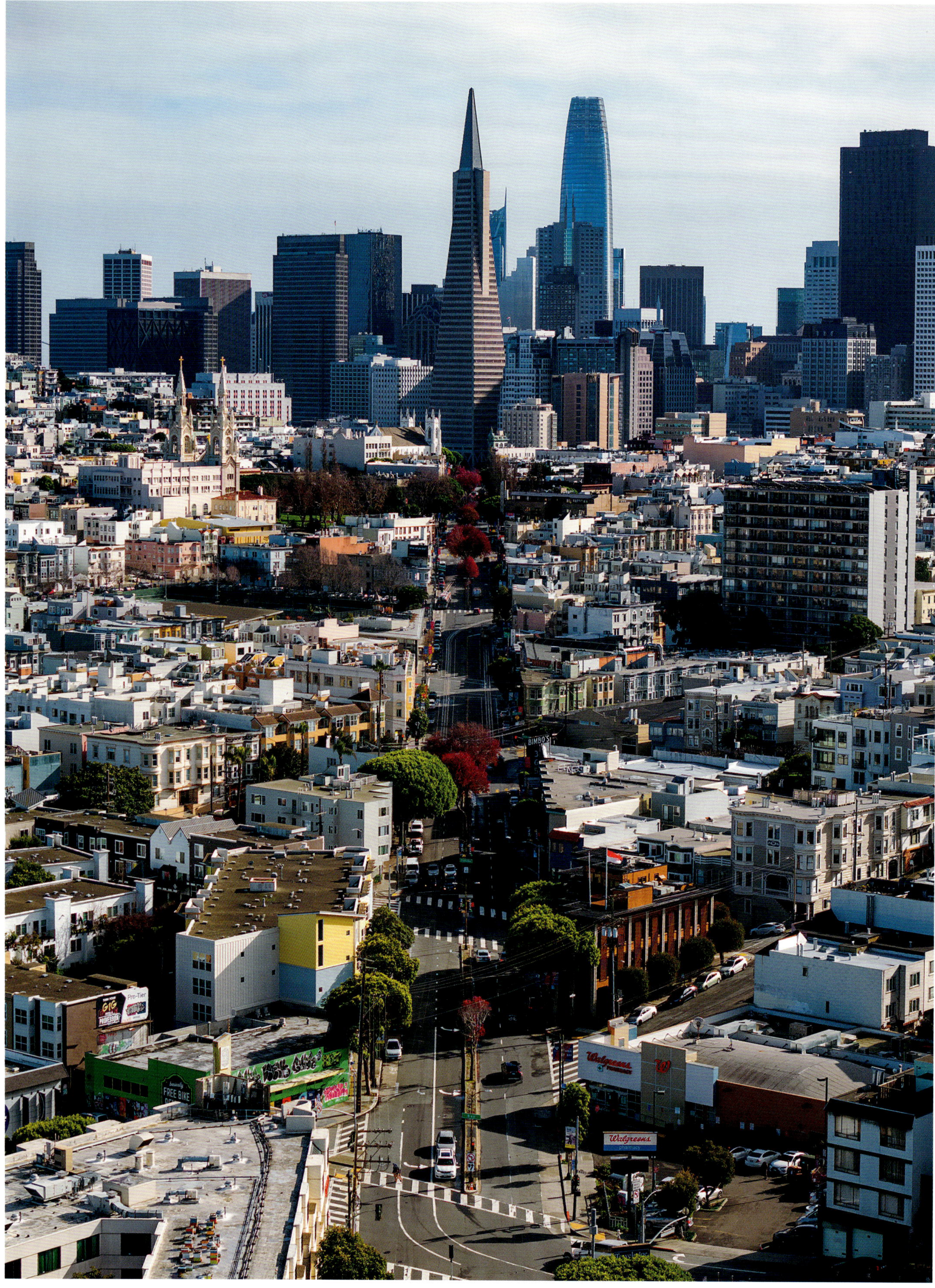

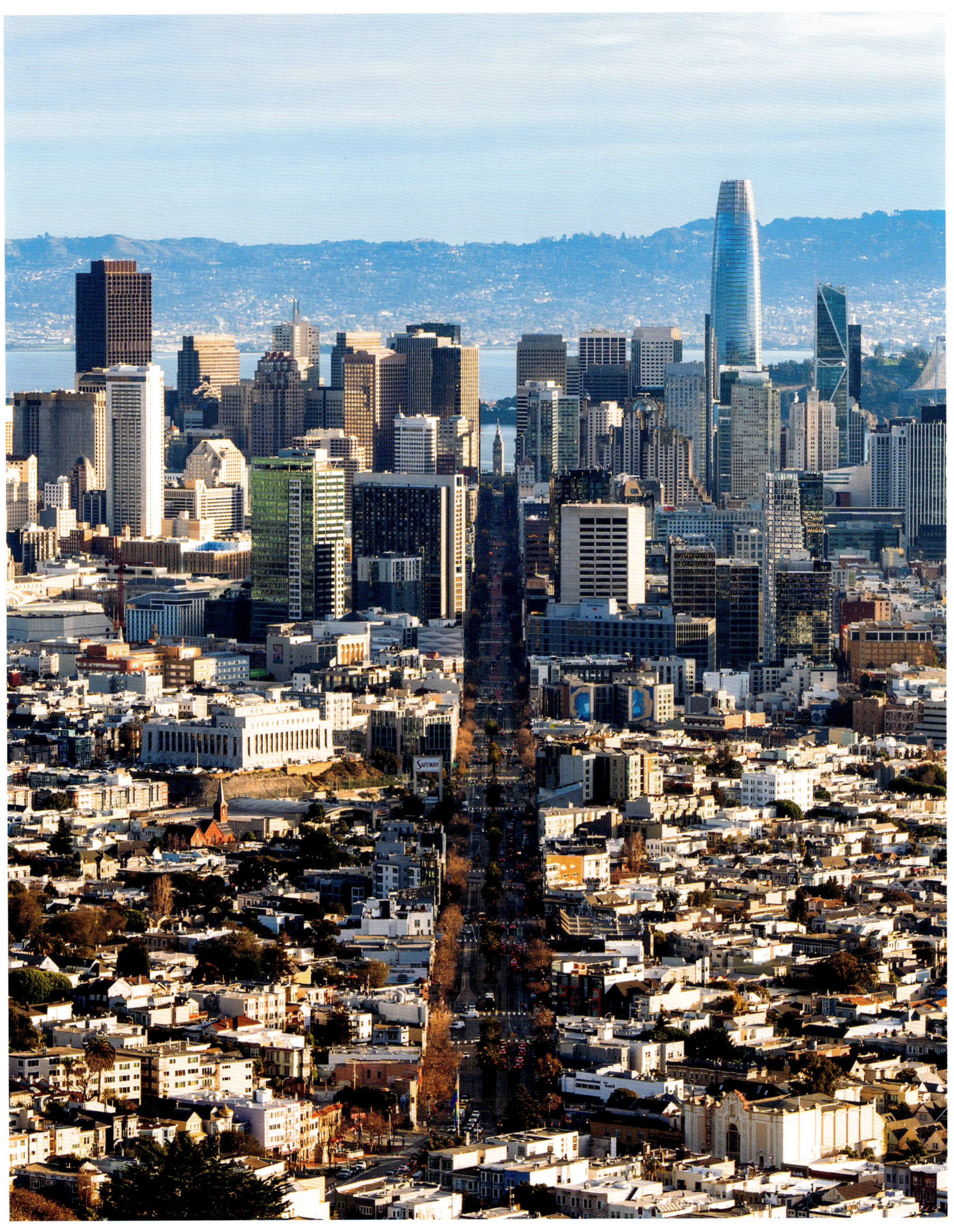

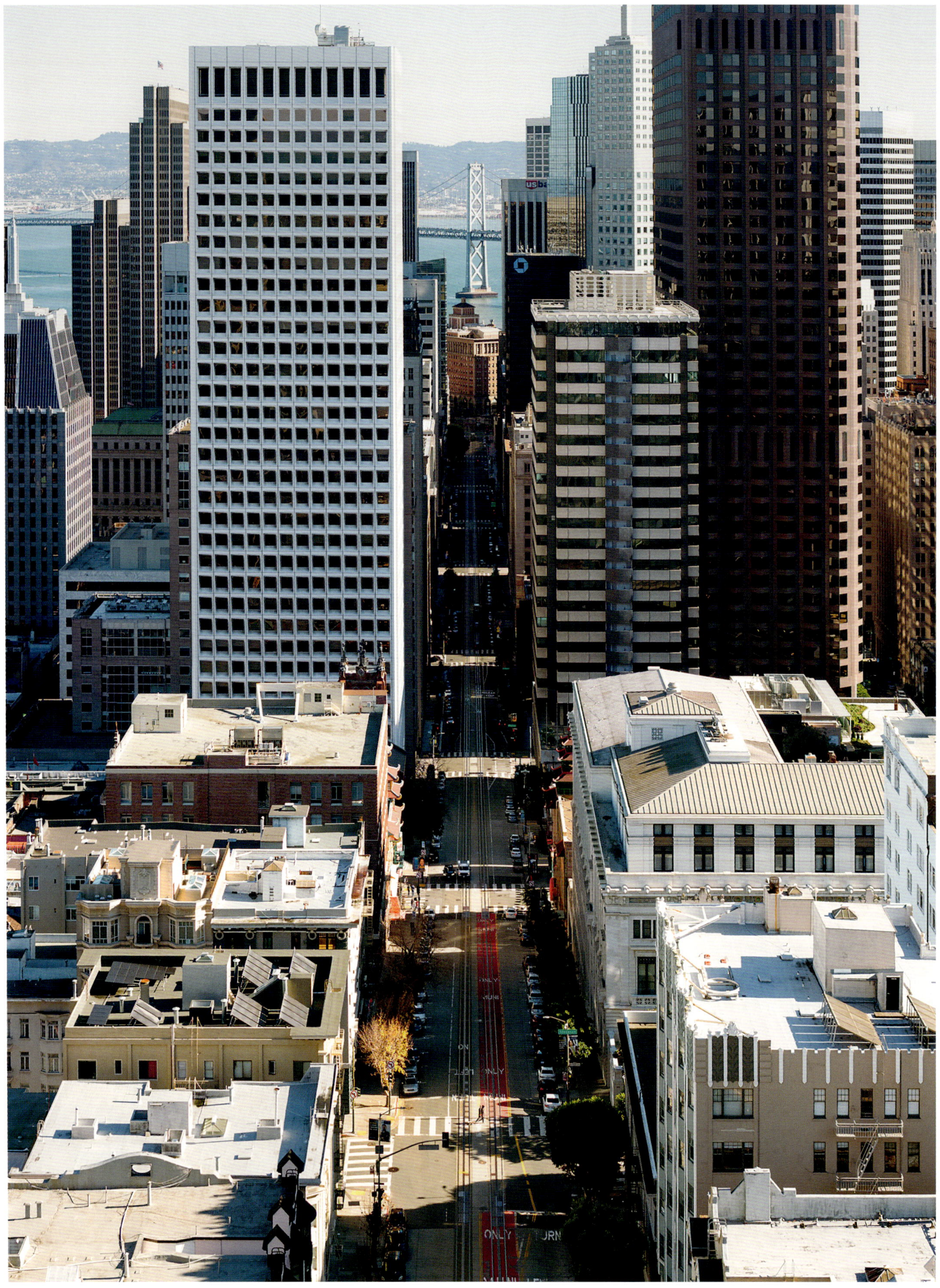

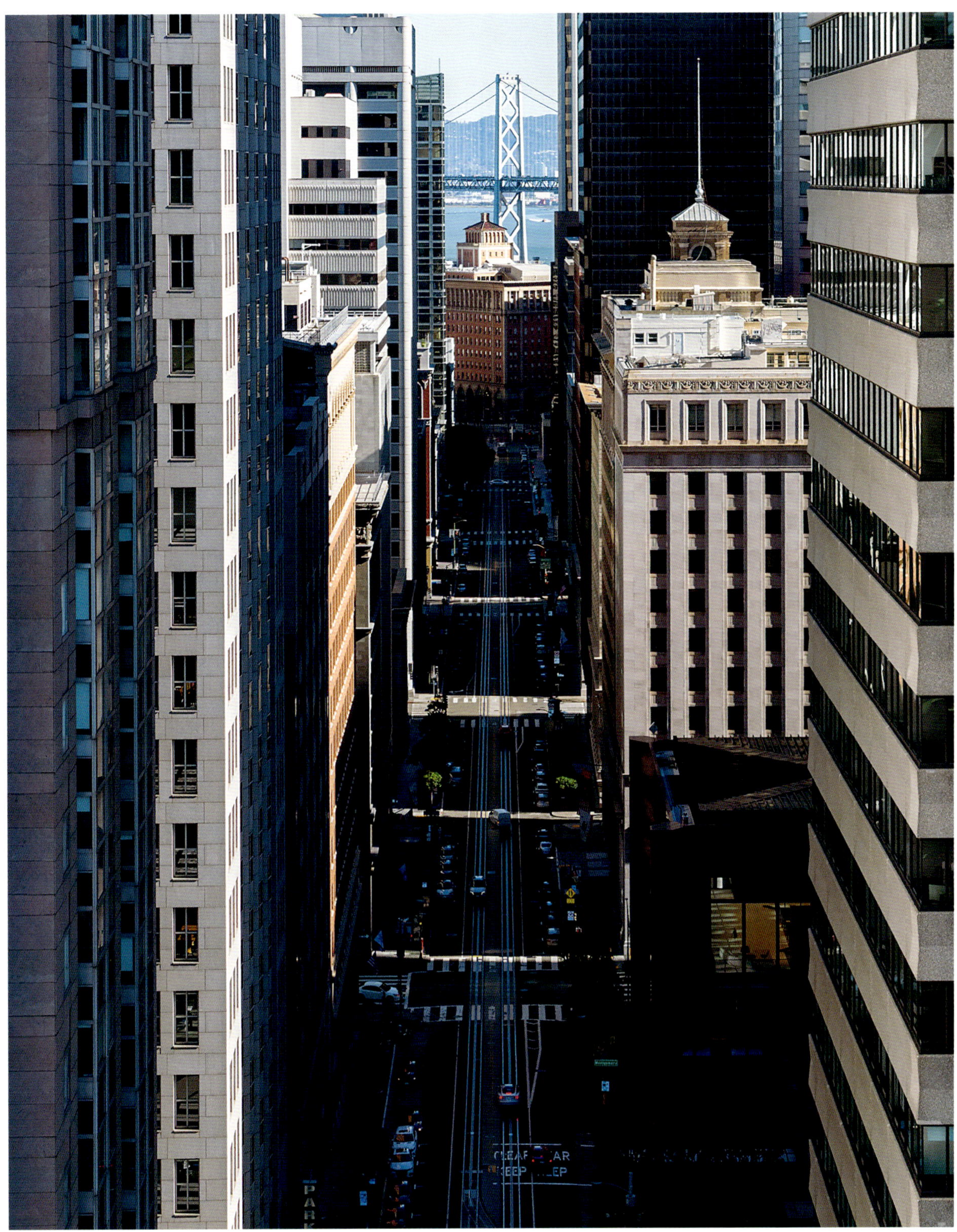

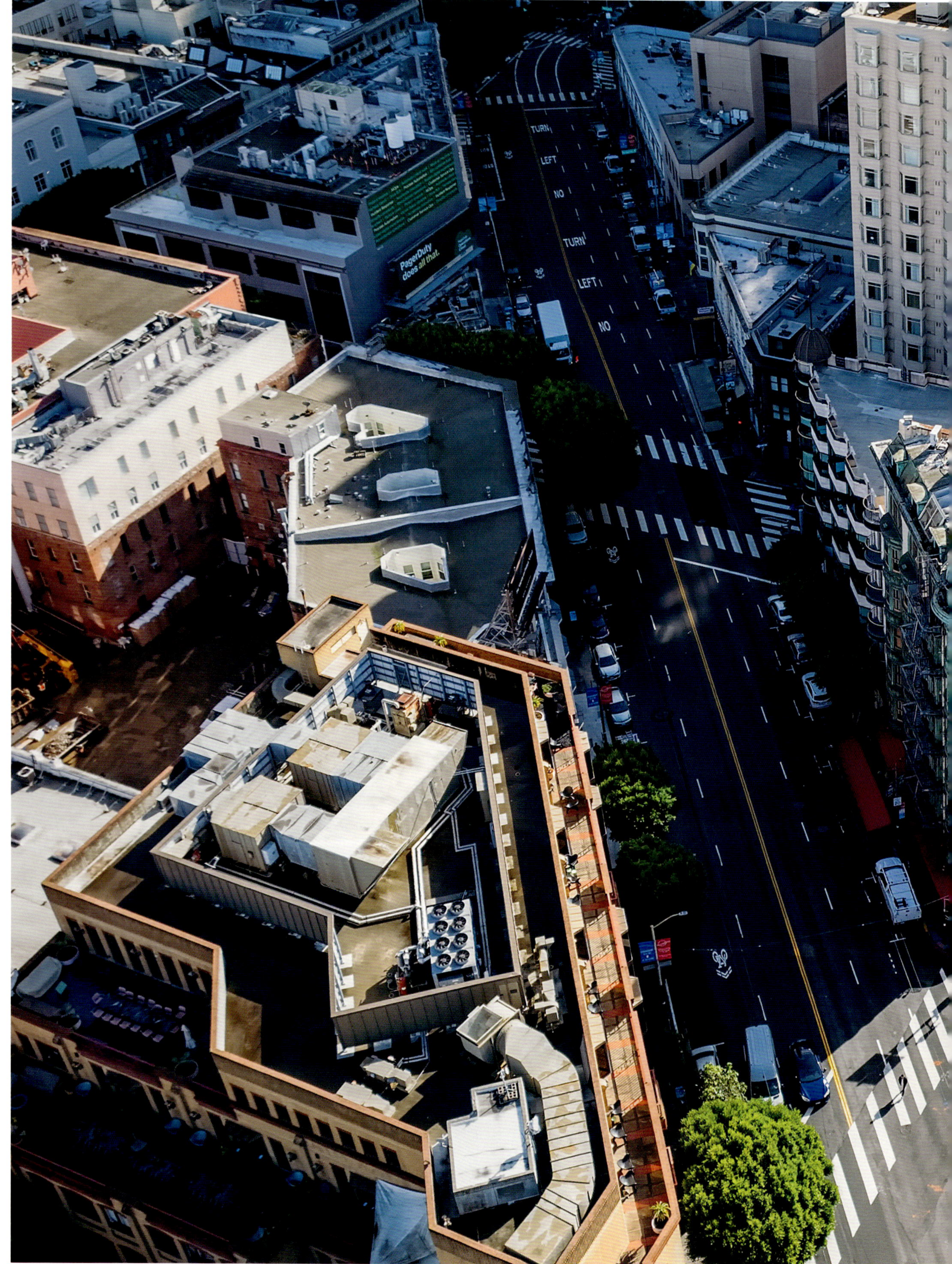

PagerDuty
does all that.
TURN
LEFT
NO
TURN
LEFT
NO

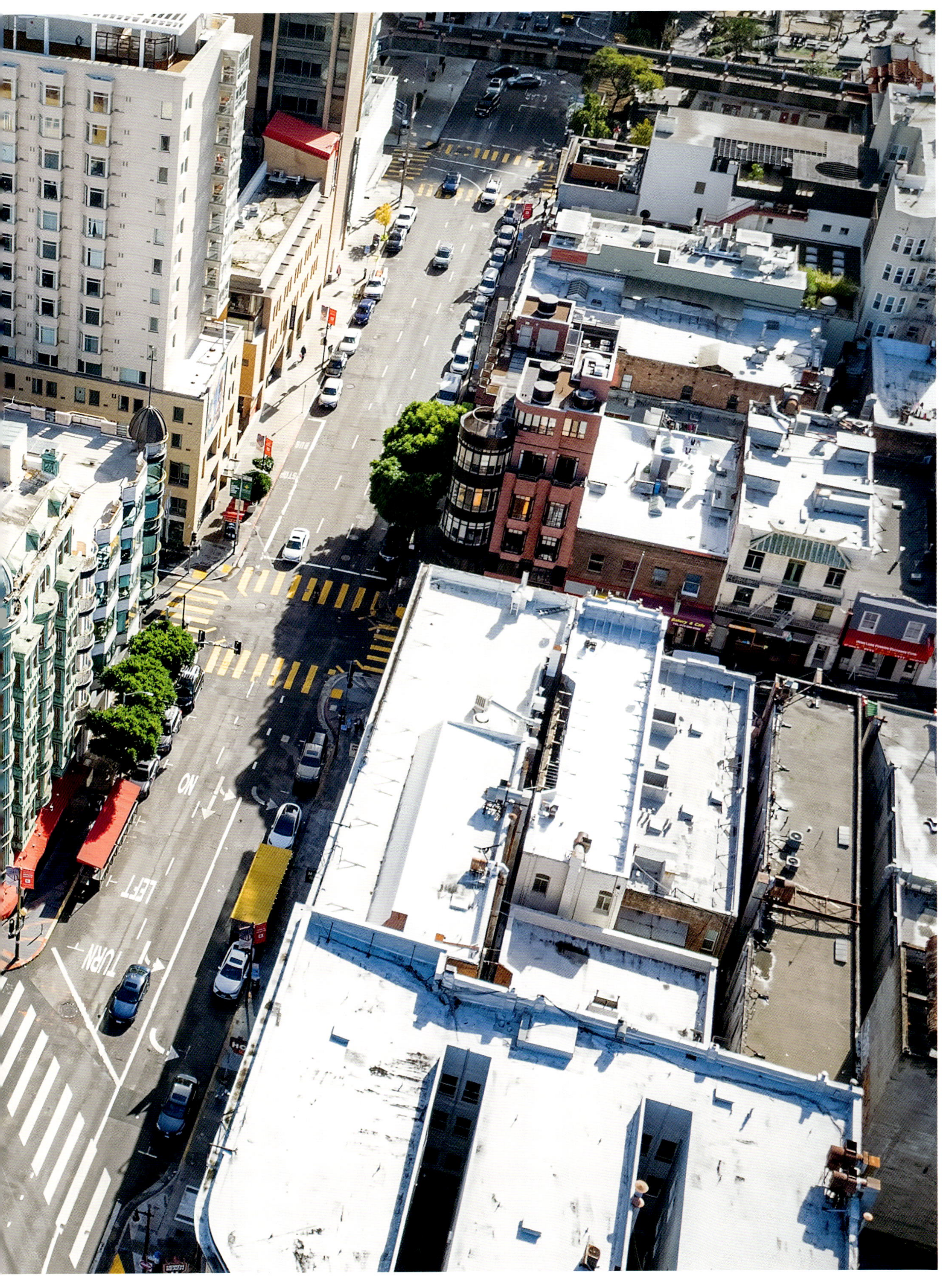
ONE WAY
LEFT
TURN
Bakery & Cafe

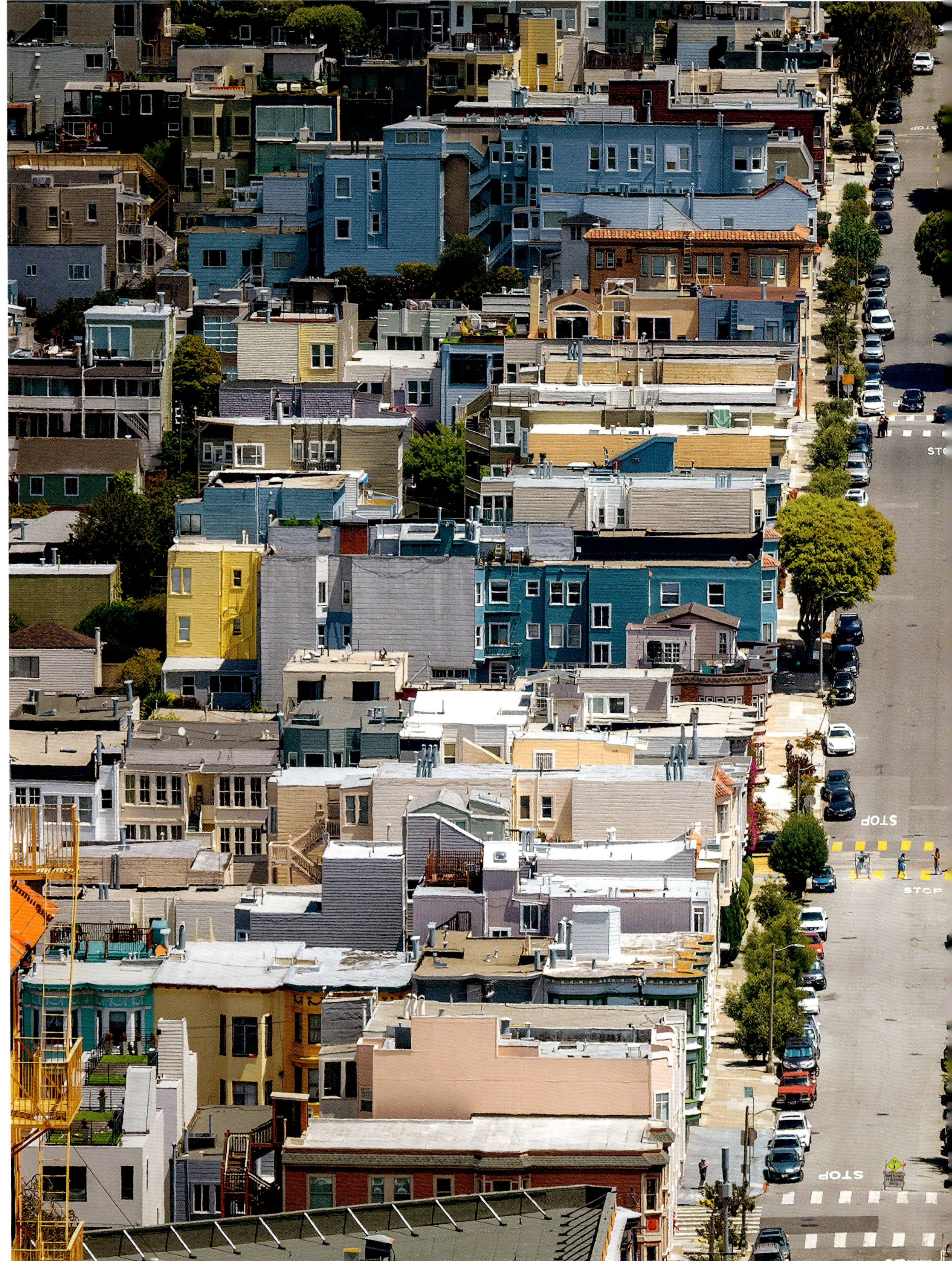

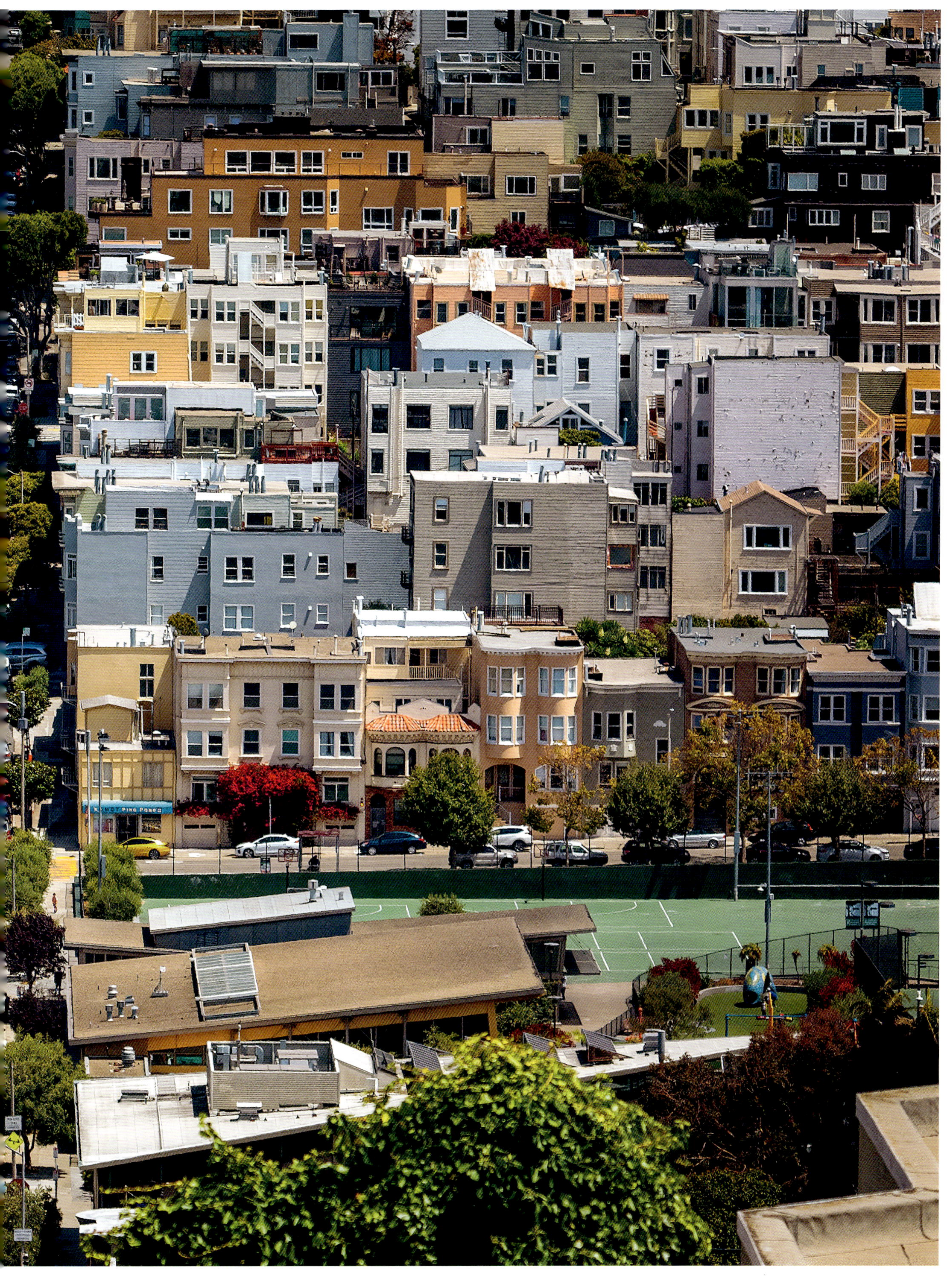

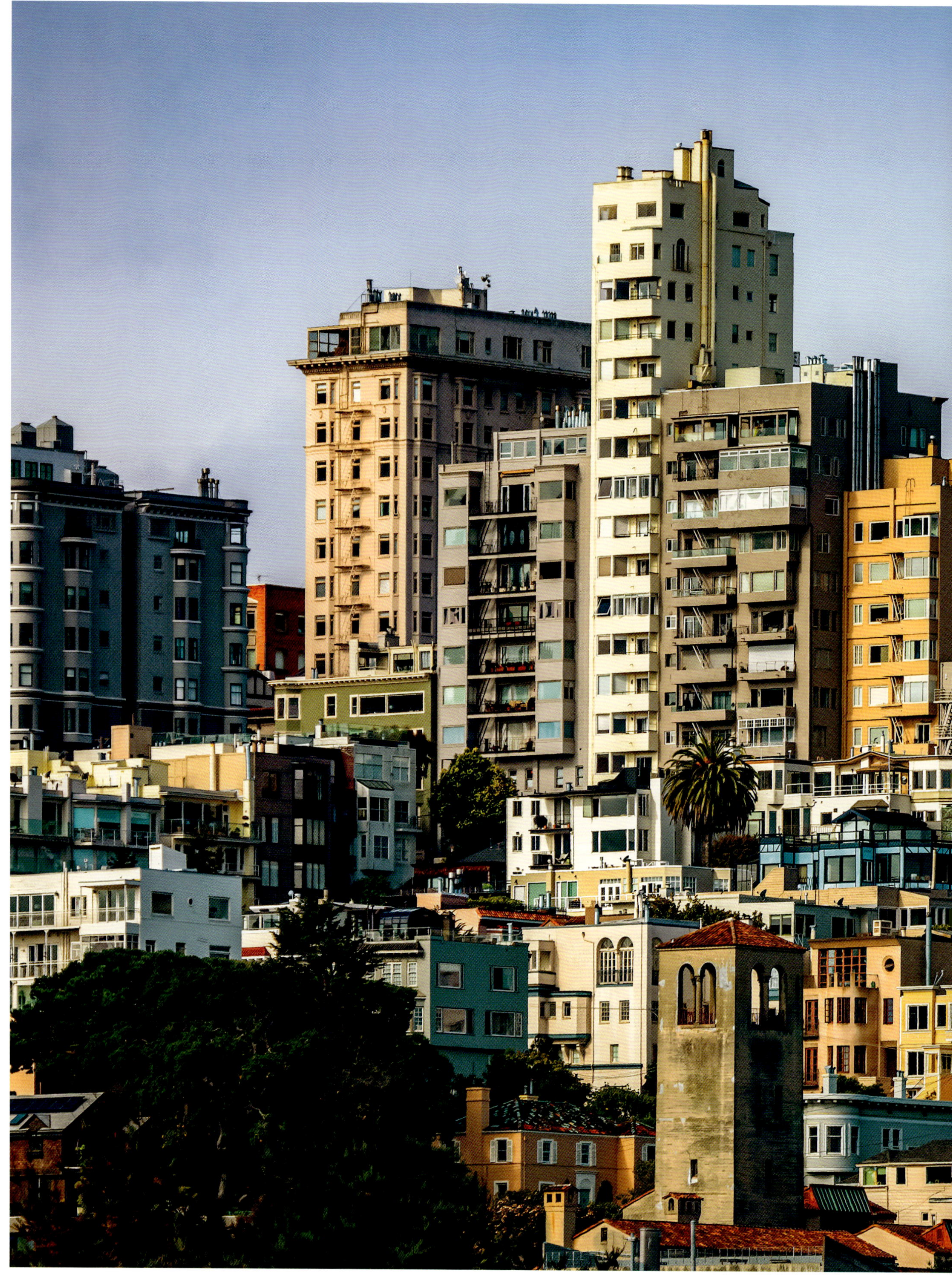

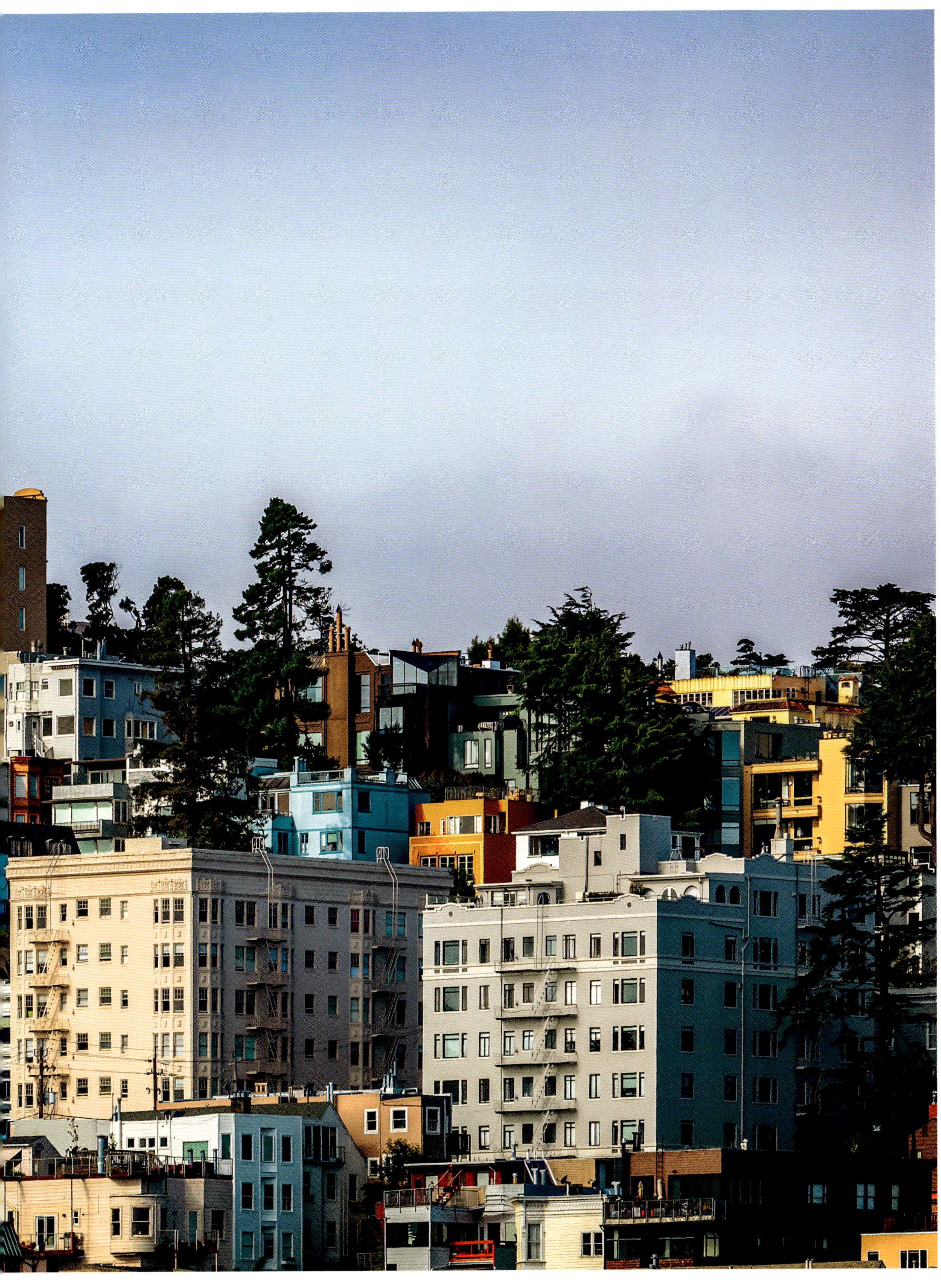

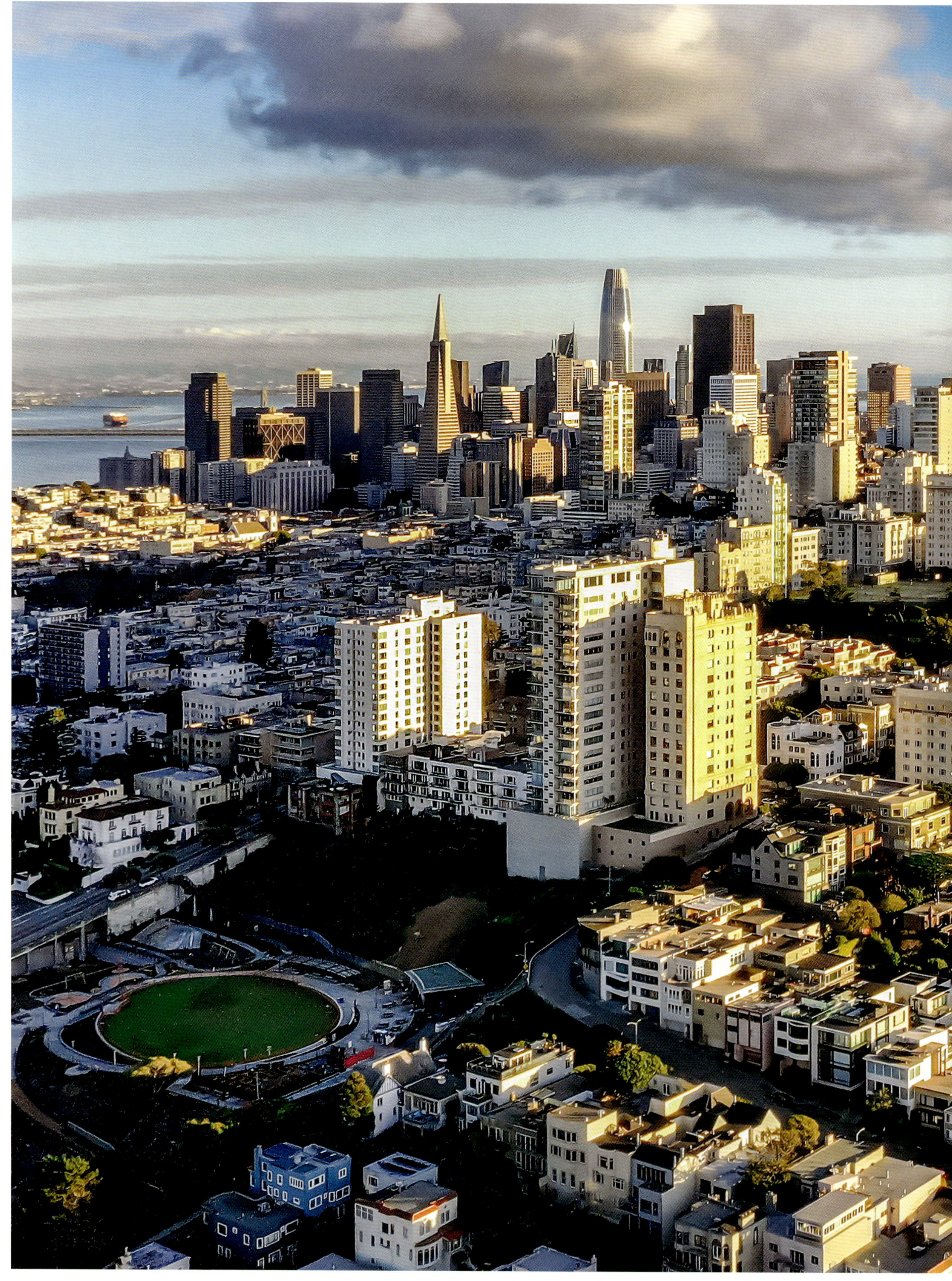

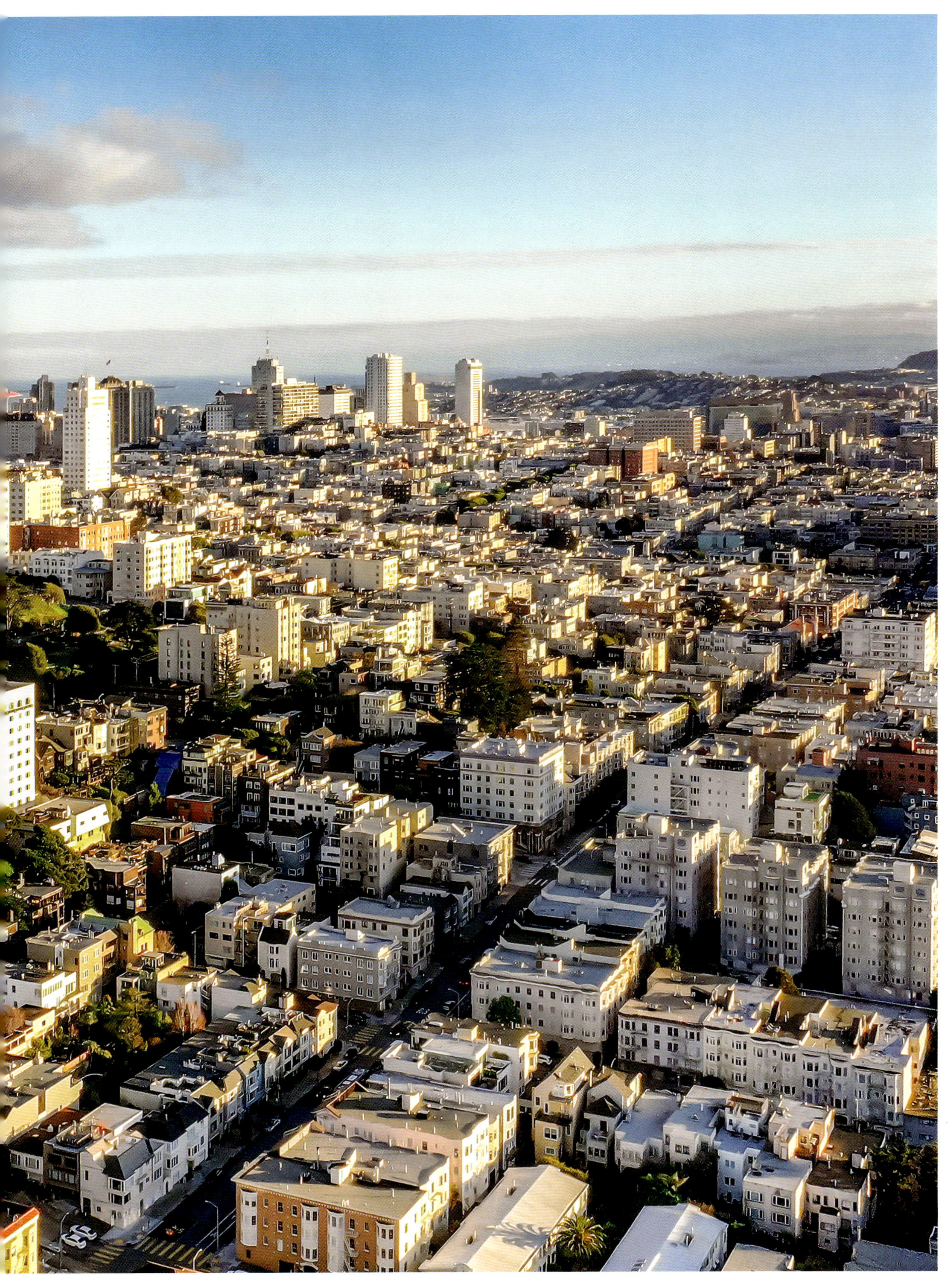

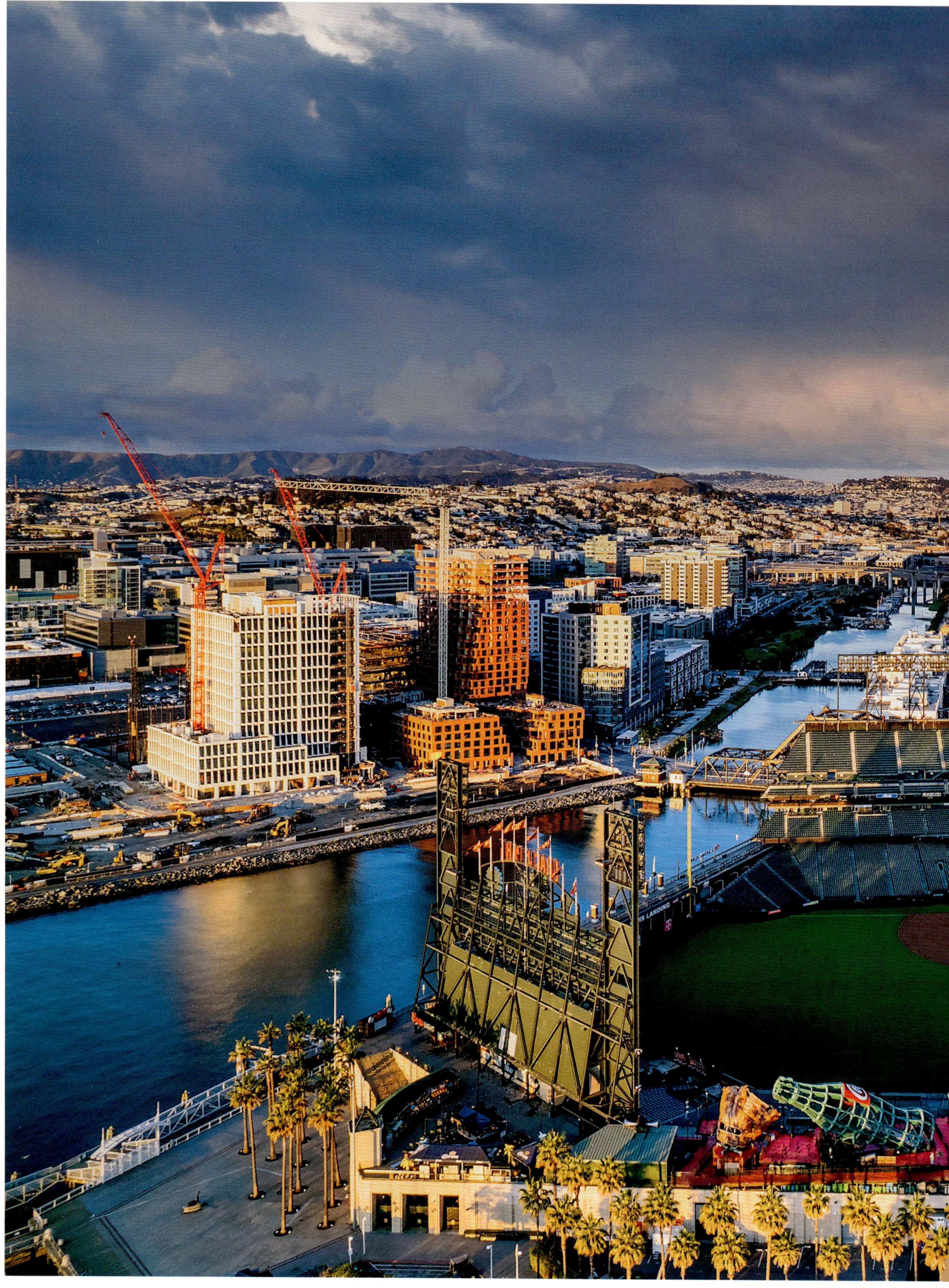

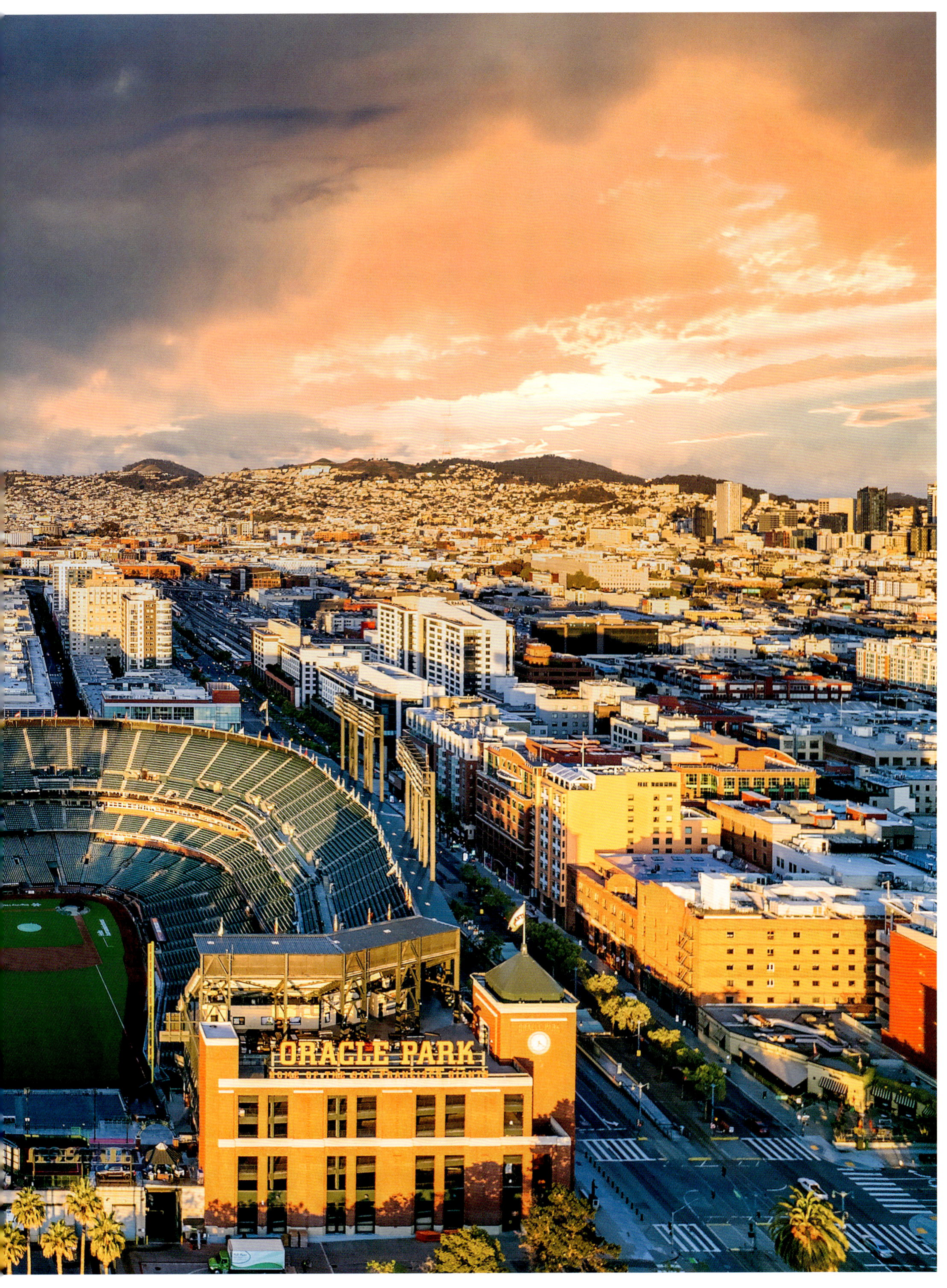
ORACLE PARK
HOME OF THE SAN FRANCISCO GIANTS
ORACLE PARK

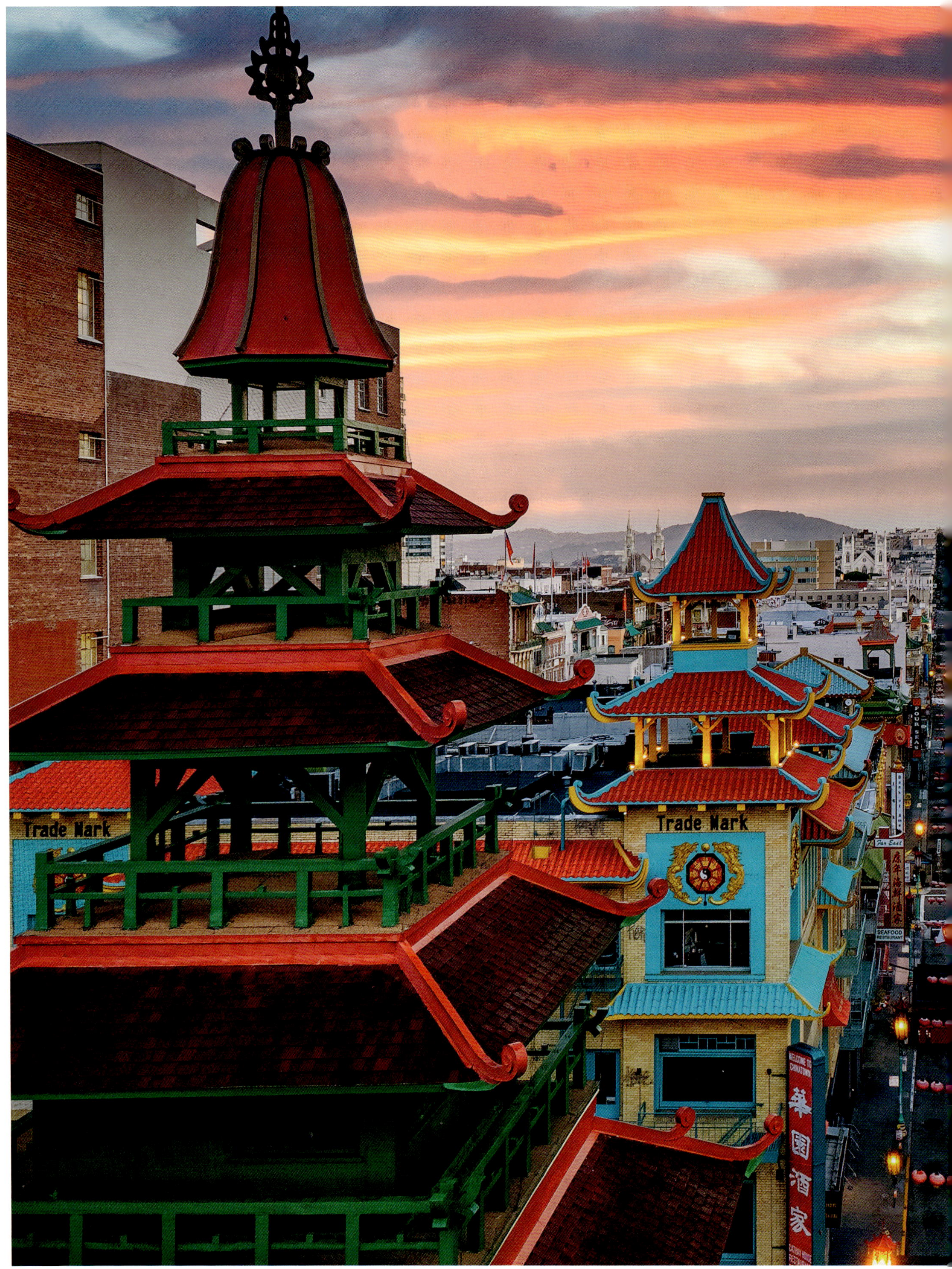
Trade Mark
Trade Mark
WELCOME TO
CHINATOWN
華
園
酒
家
Far East
SEAFOOD
RESTAURANT
FOUR SEAS

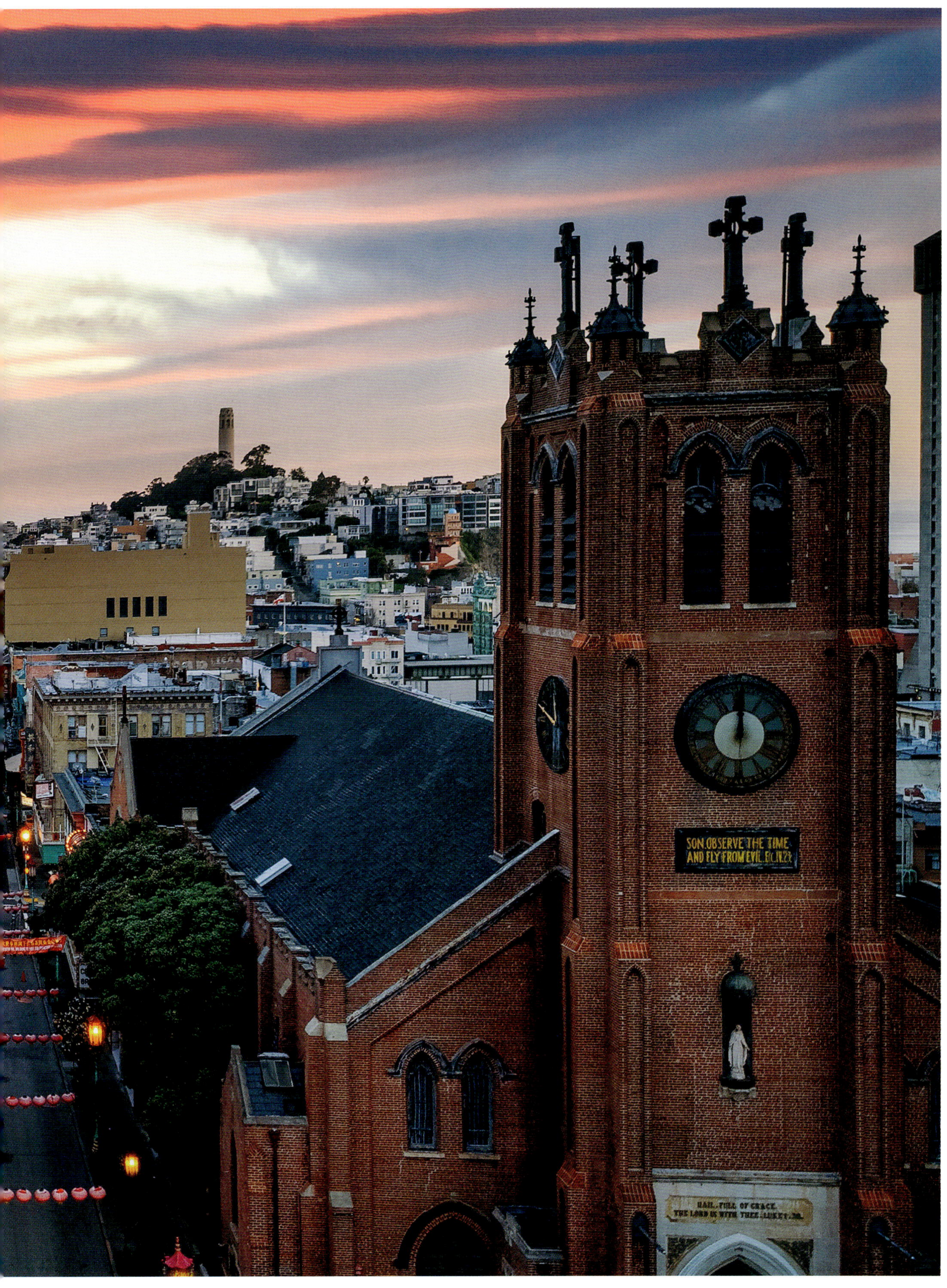
SON. OBSERVE THE TIME
AND FLY FROM EVIL. ECII.28
HAIL, FULL OF GRACE.
THE LORD IS WITH THEE. LUKE I. 28.

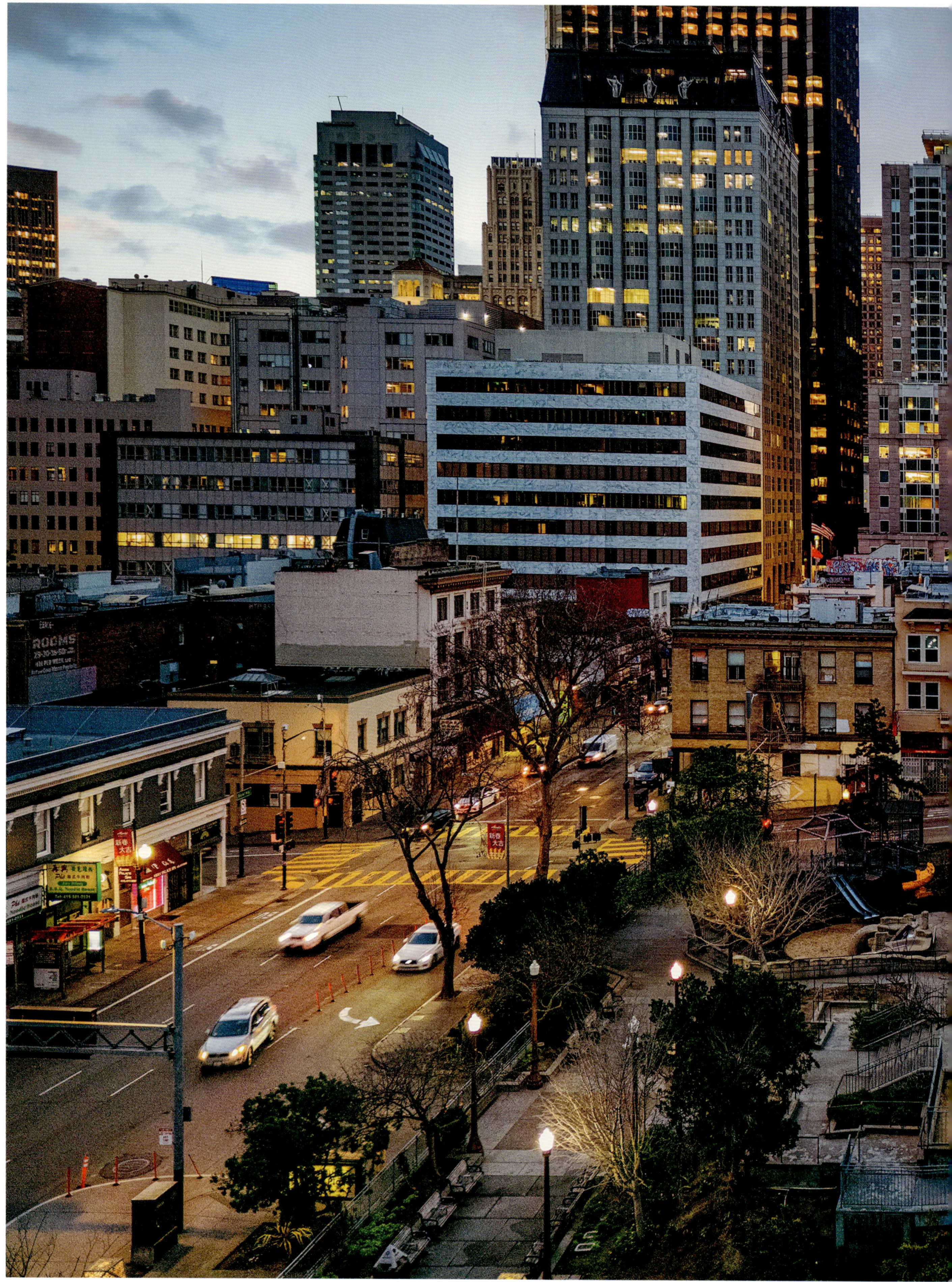

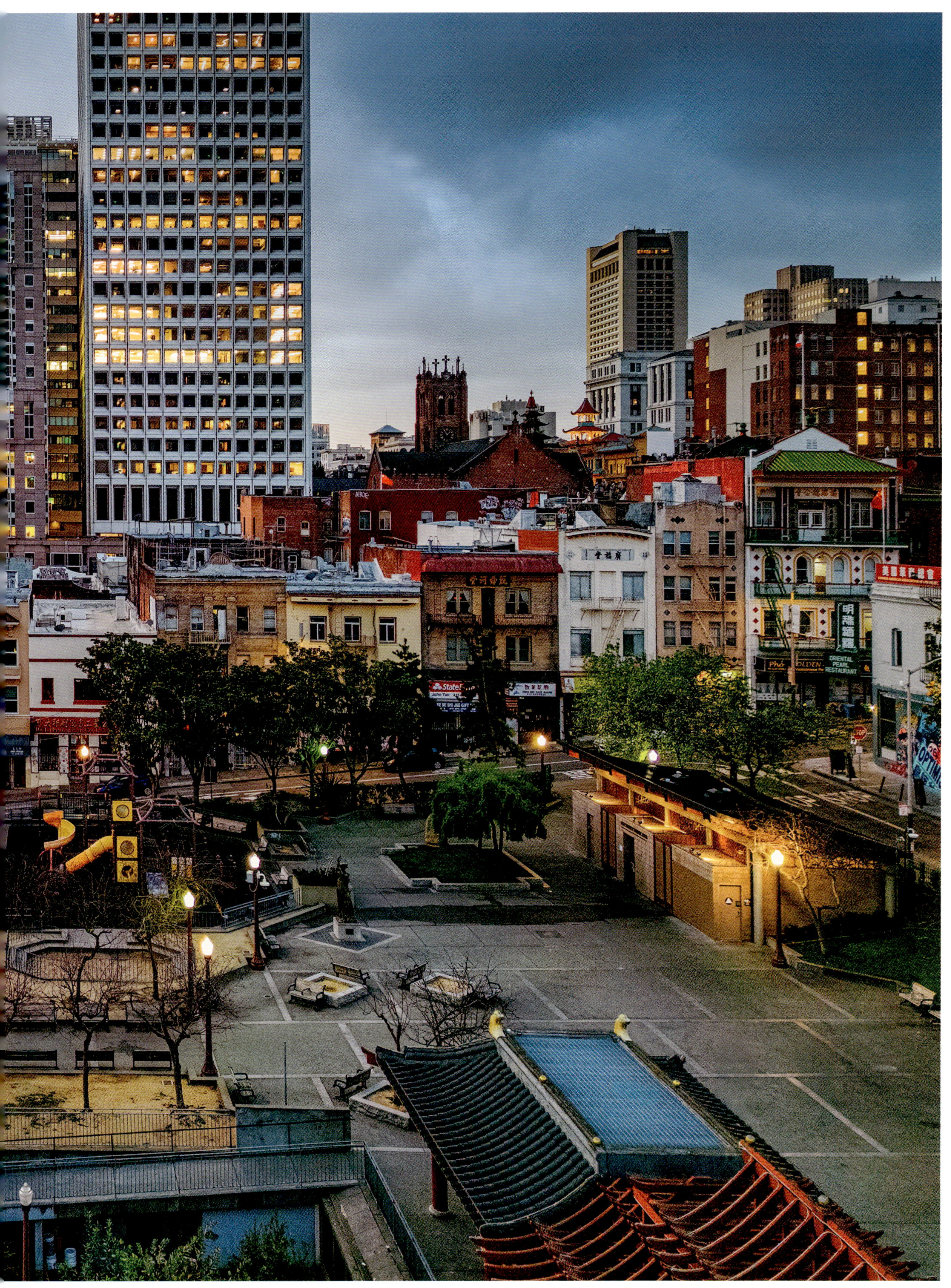

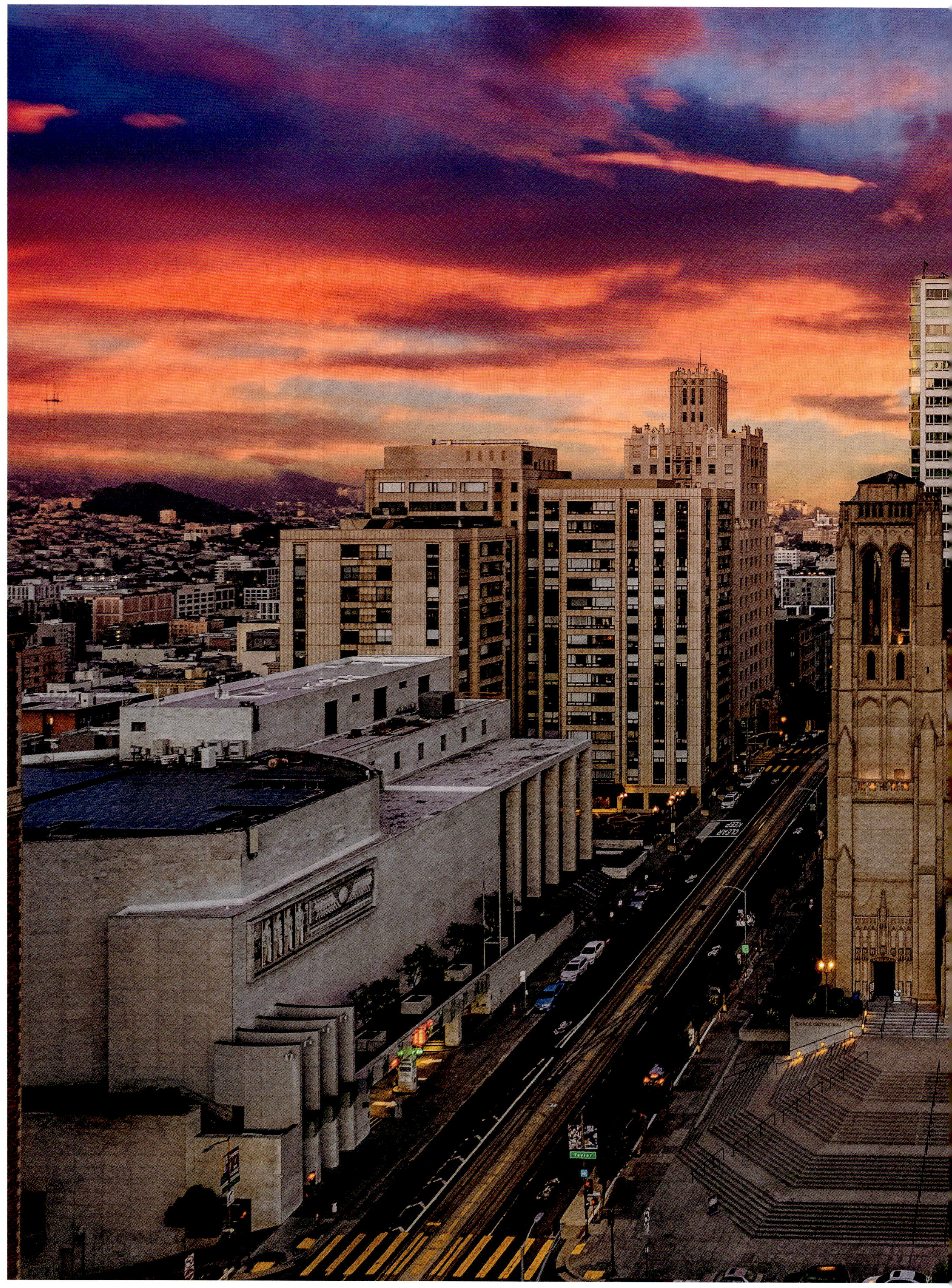

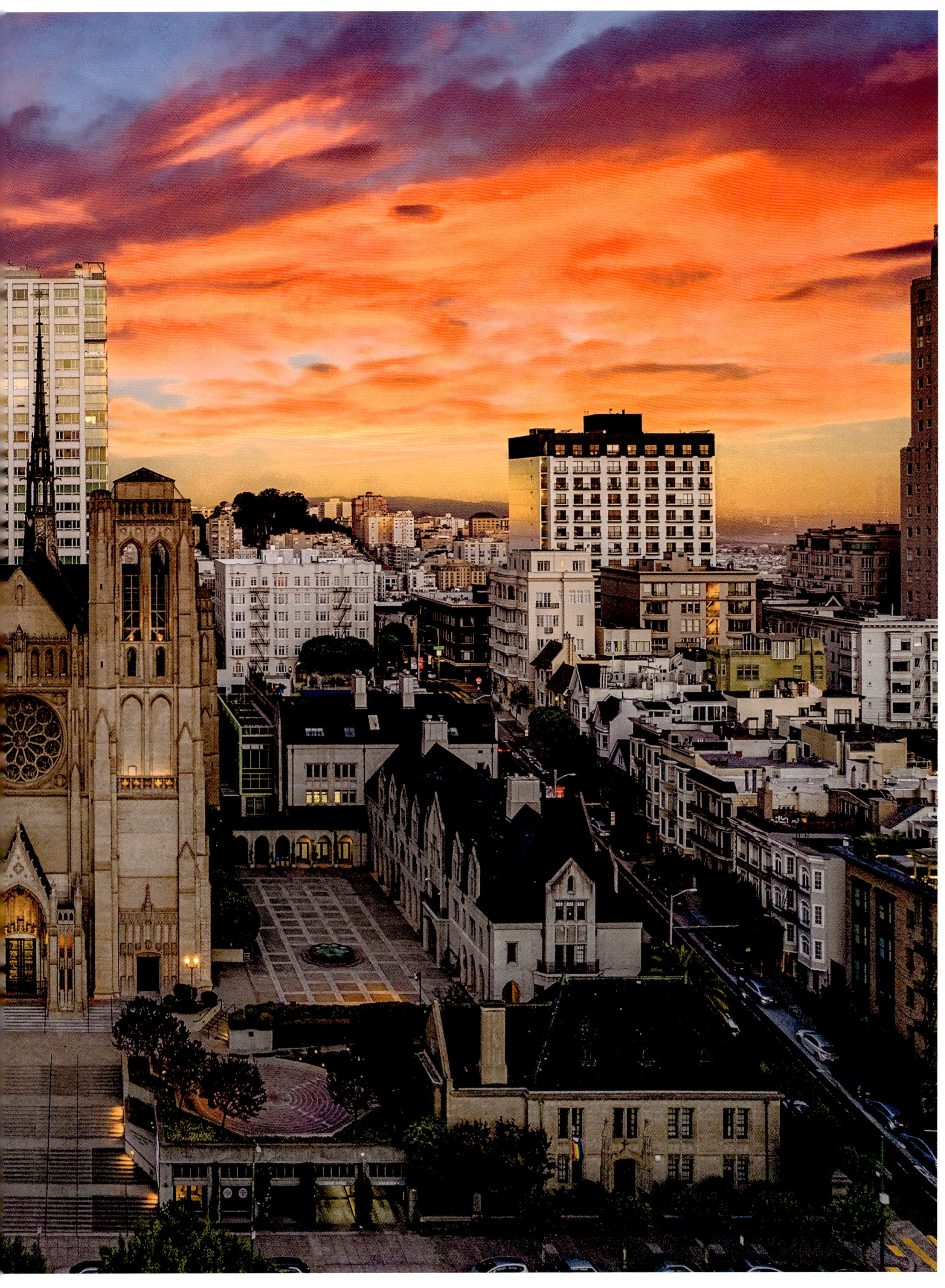

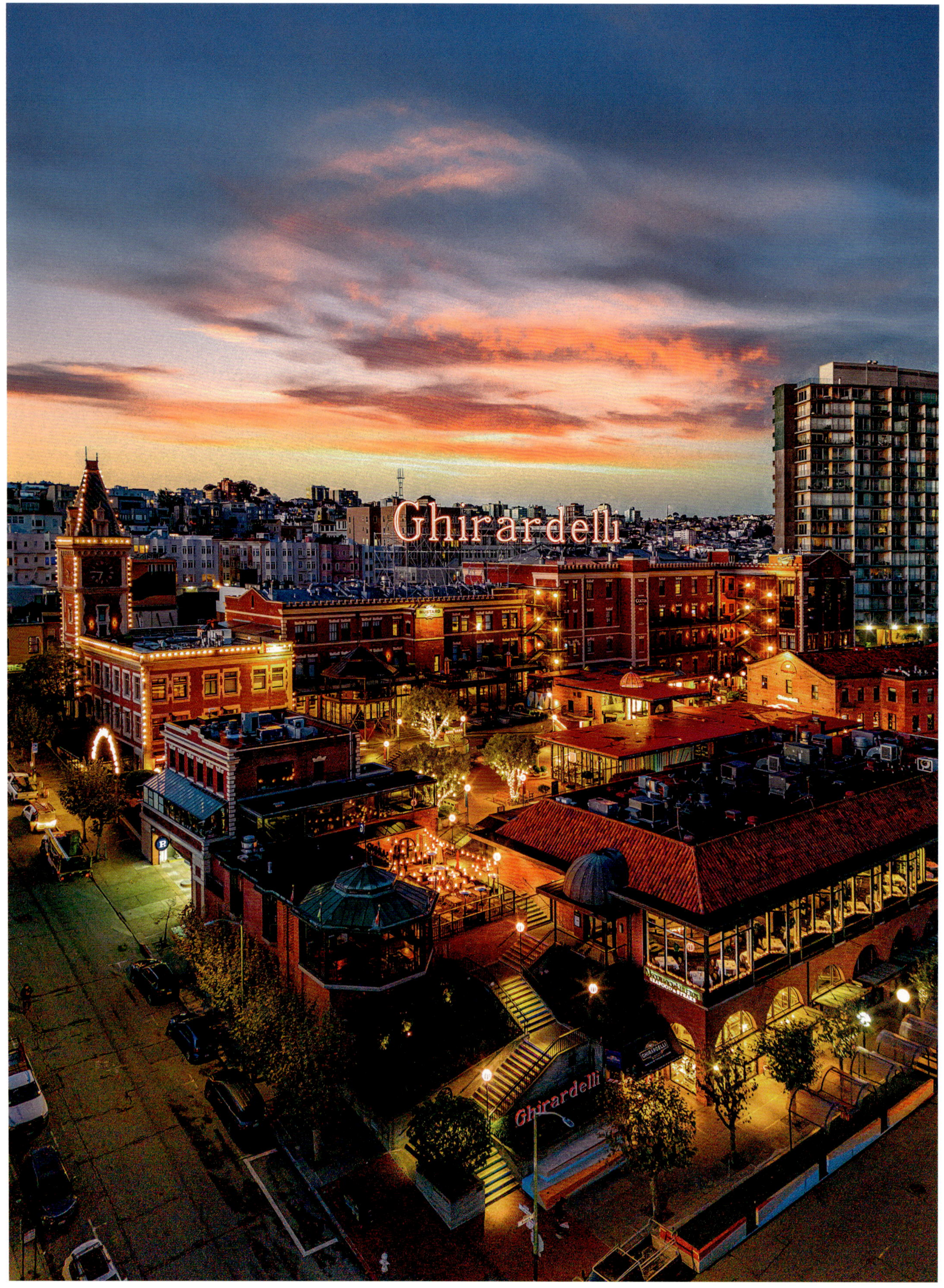

Ghirardelli
Ghirardelli

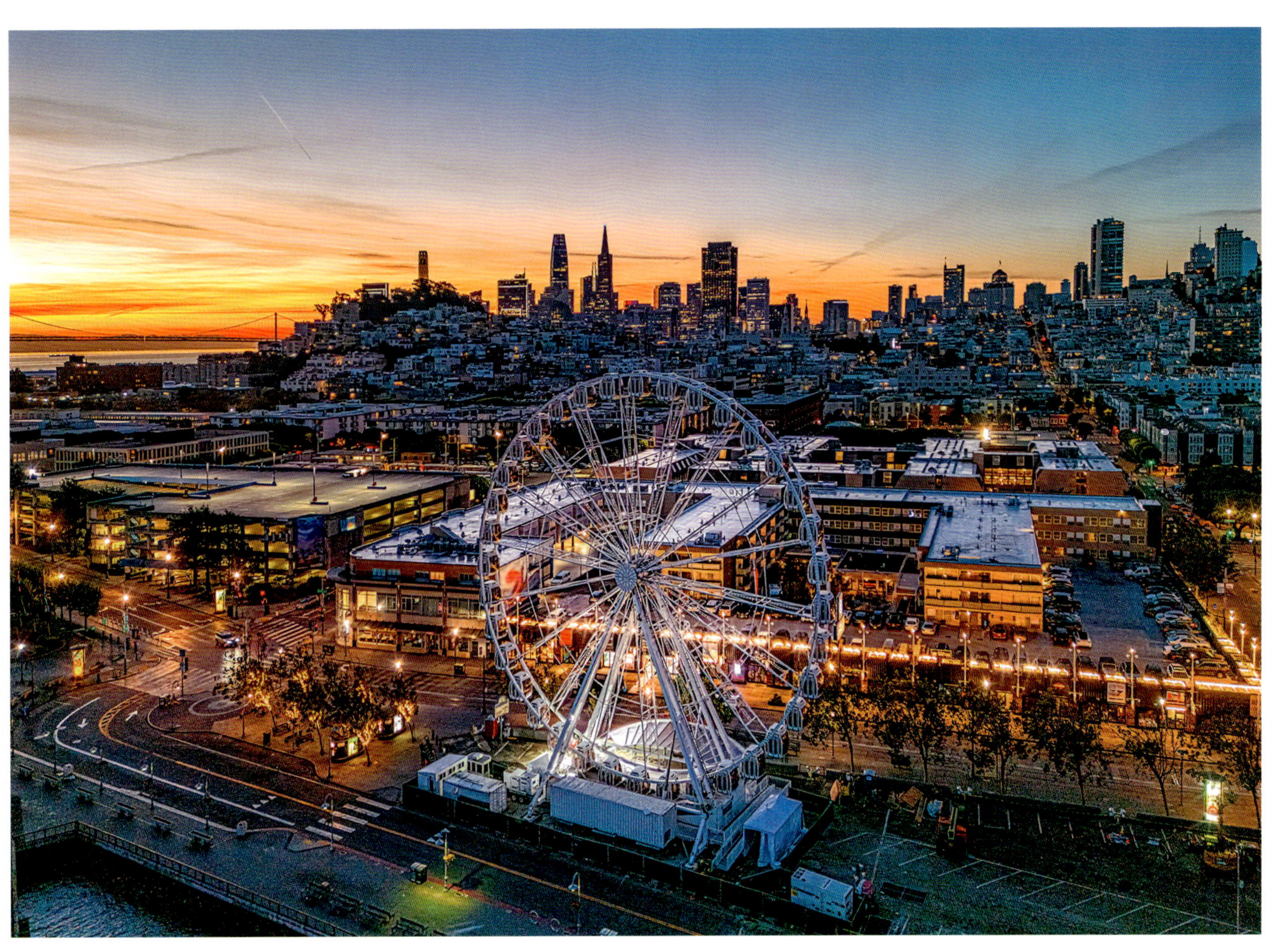

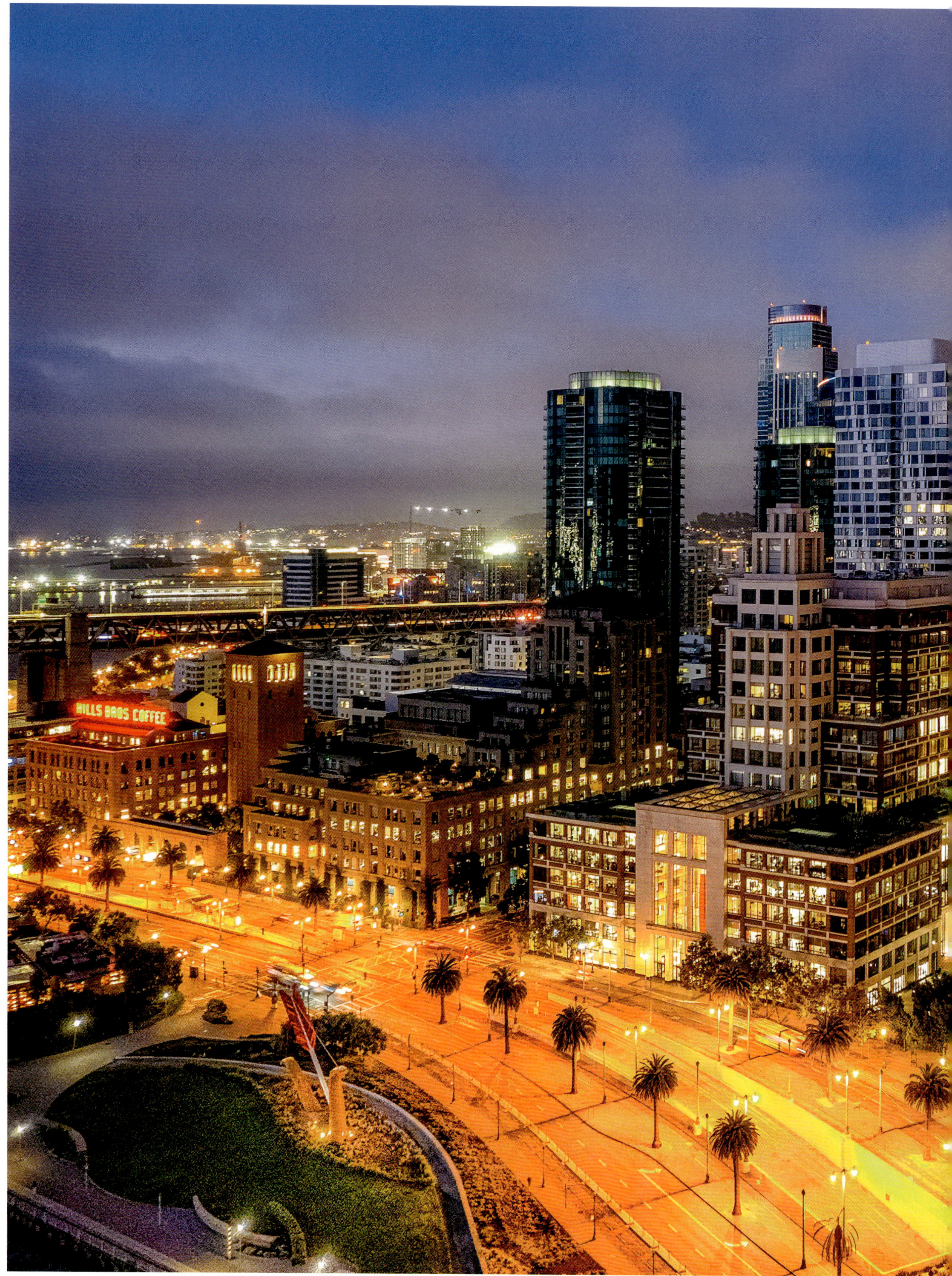

HILLS BROS COFFEE

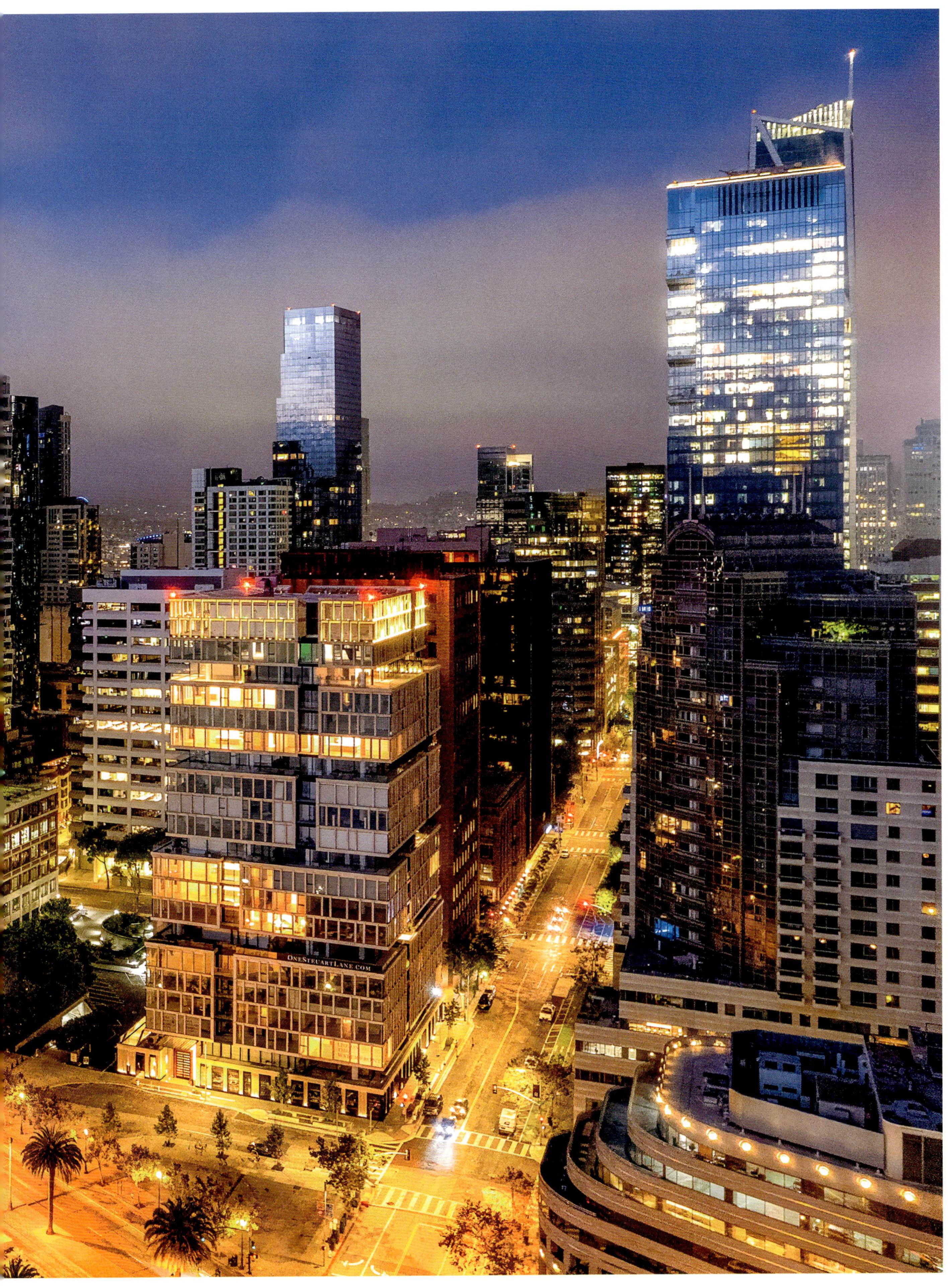
ONESTEUARTLANE.COM

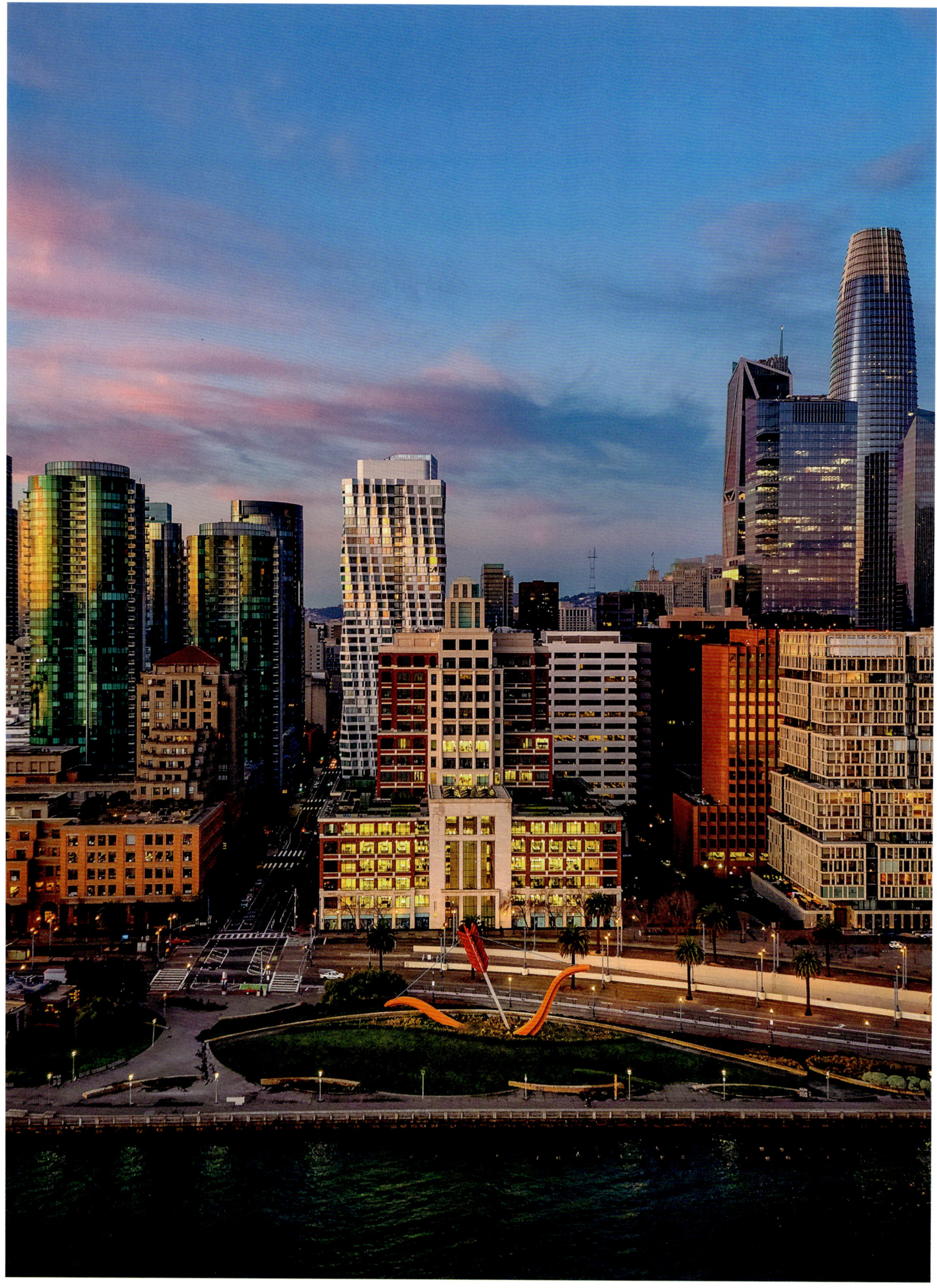

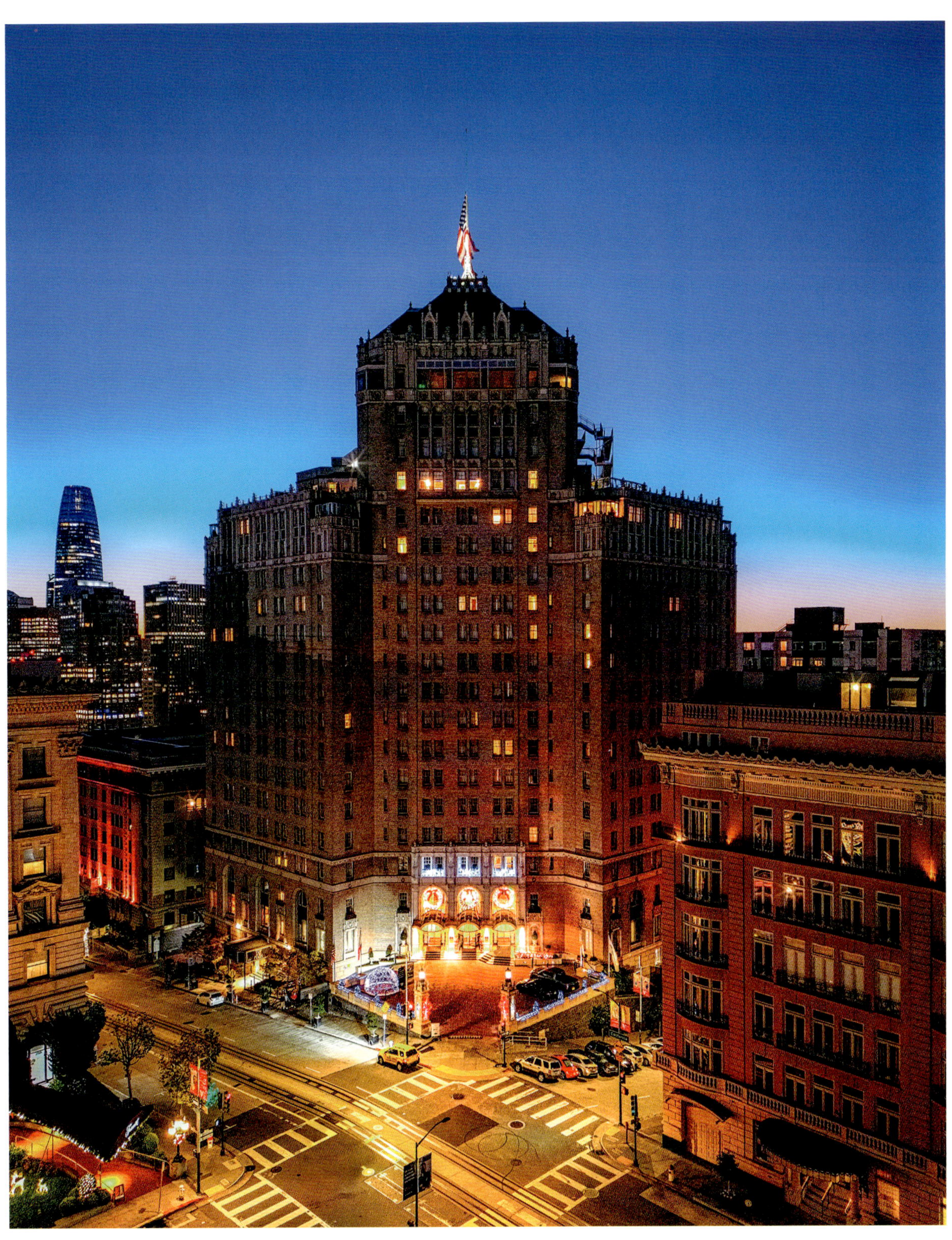

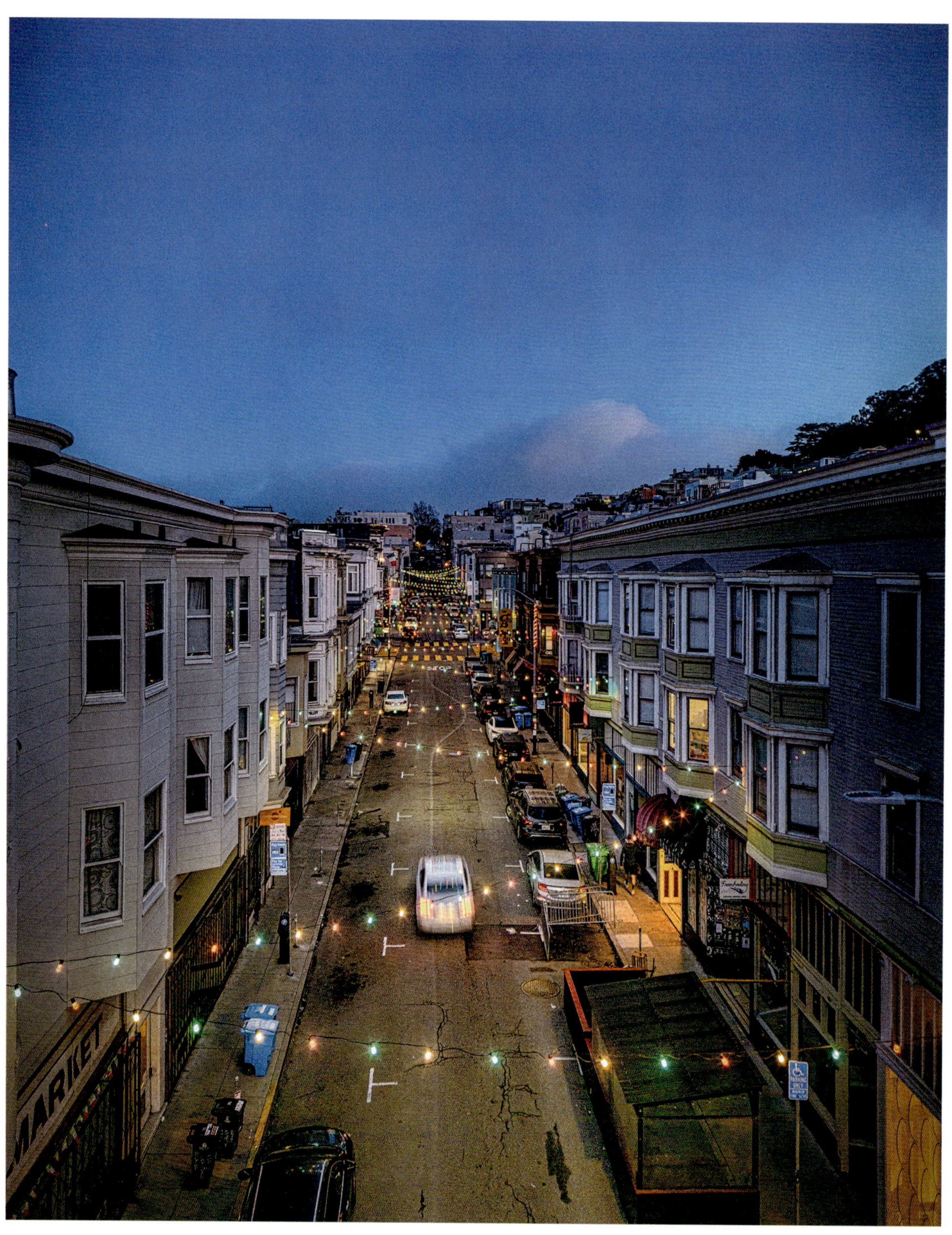

MARKET

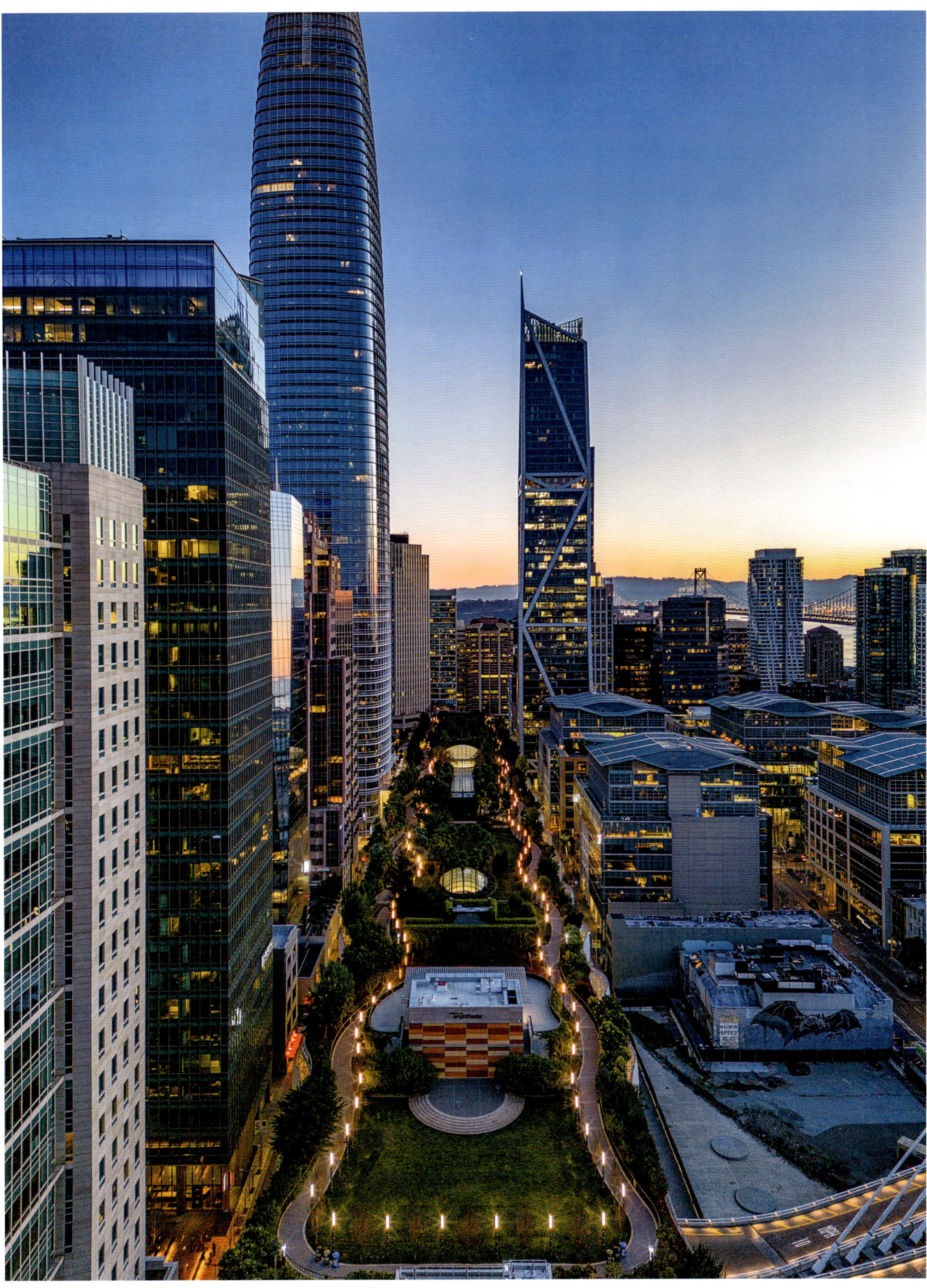

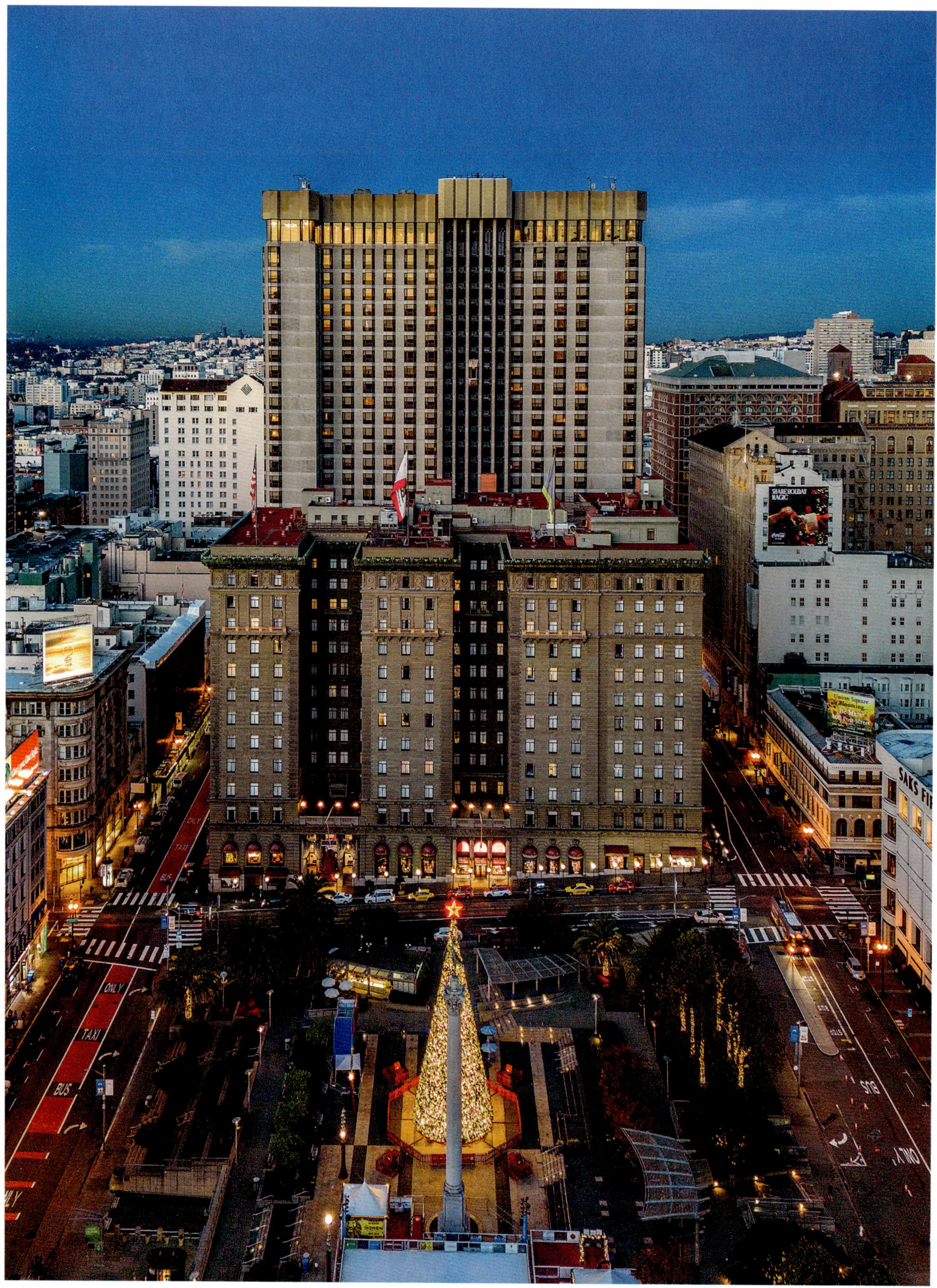

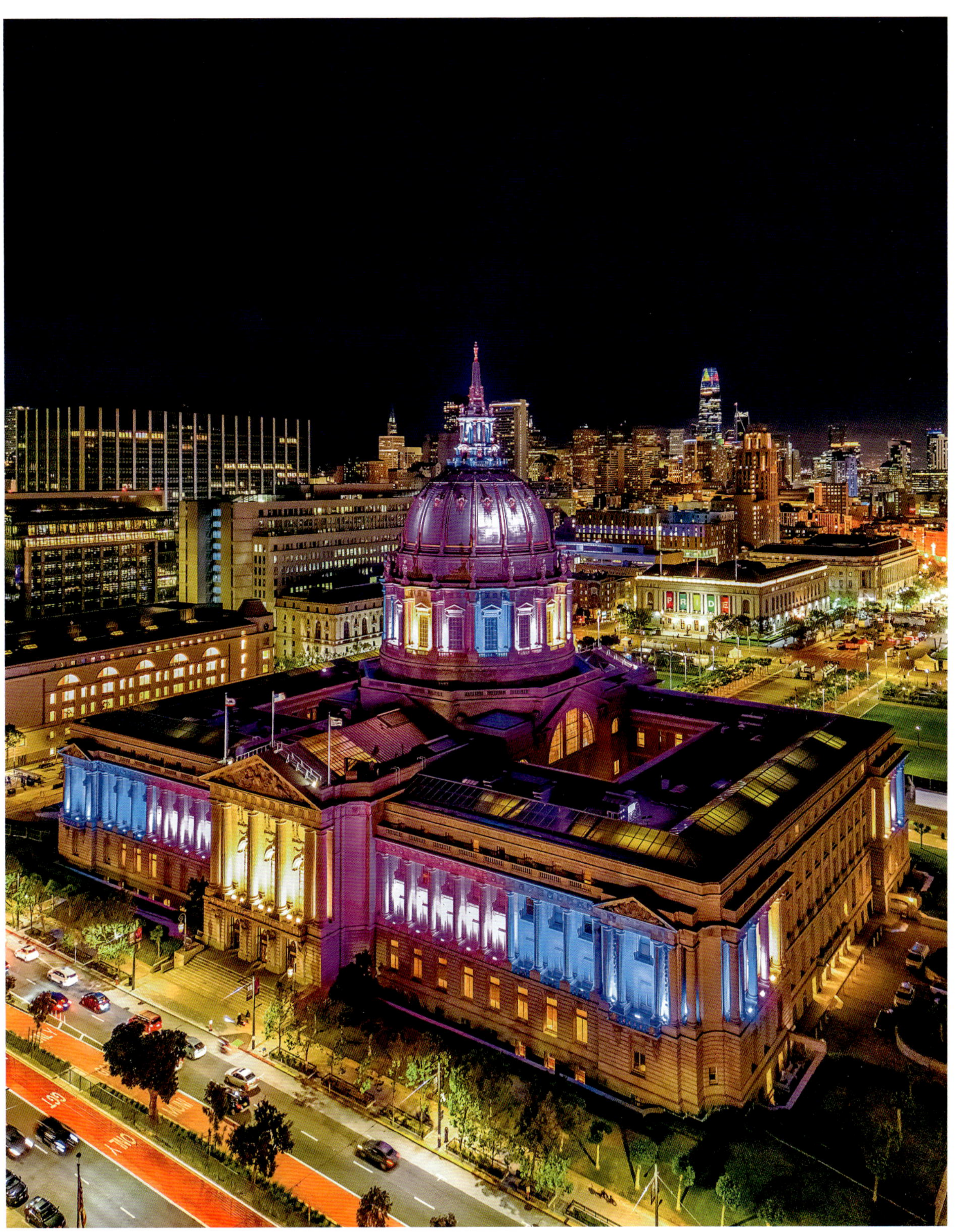

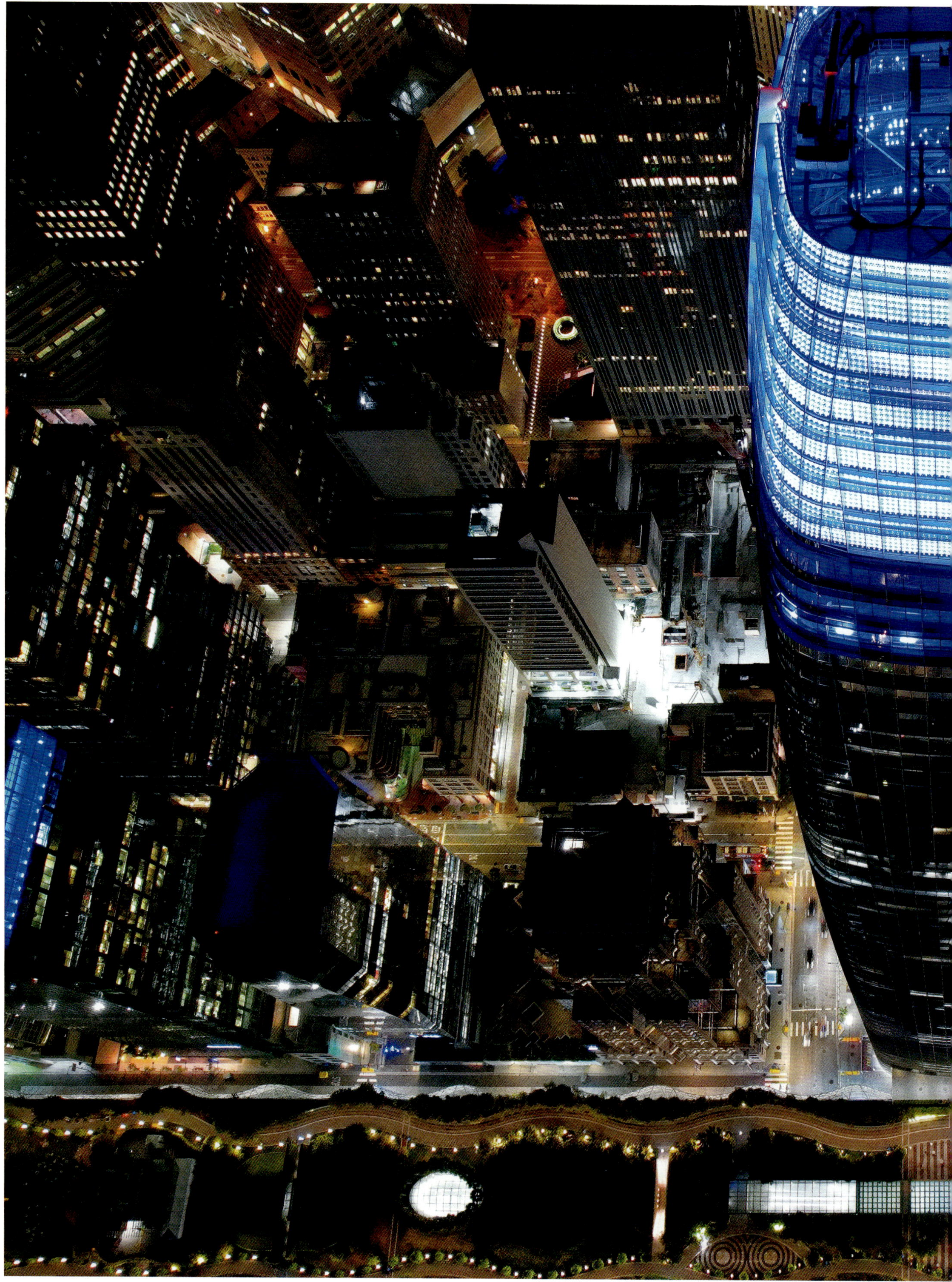

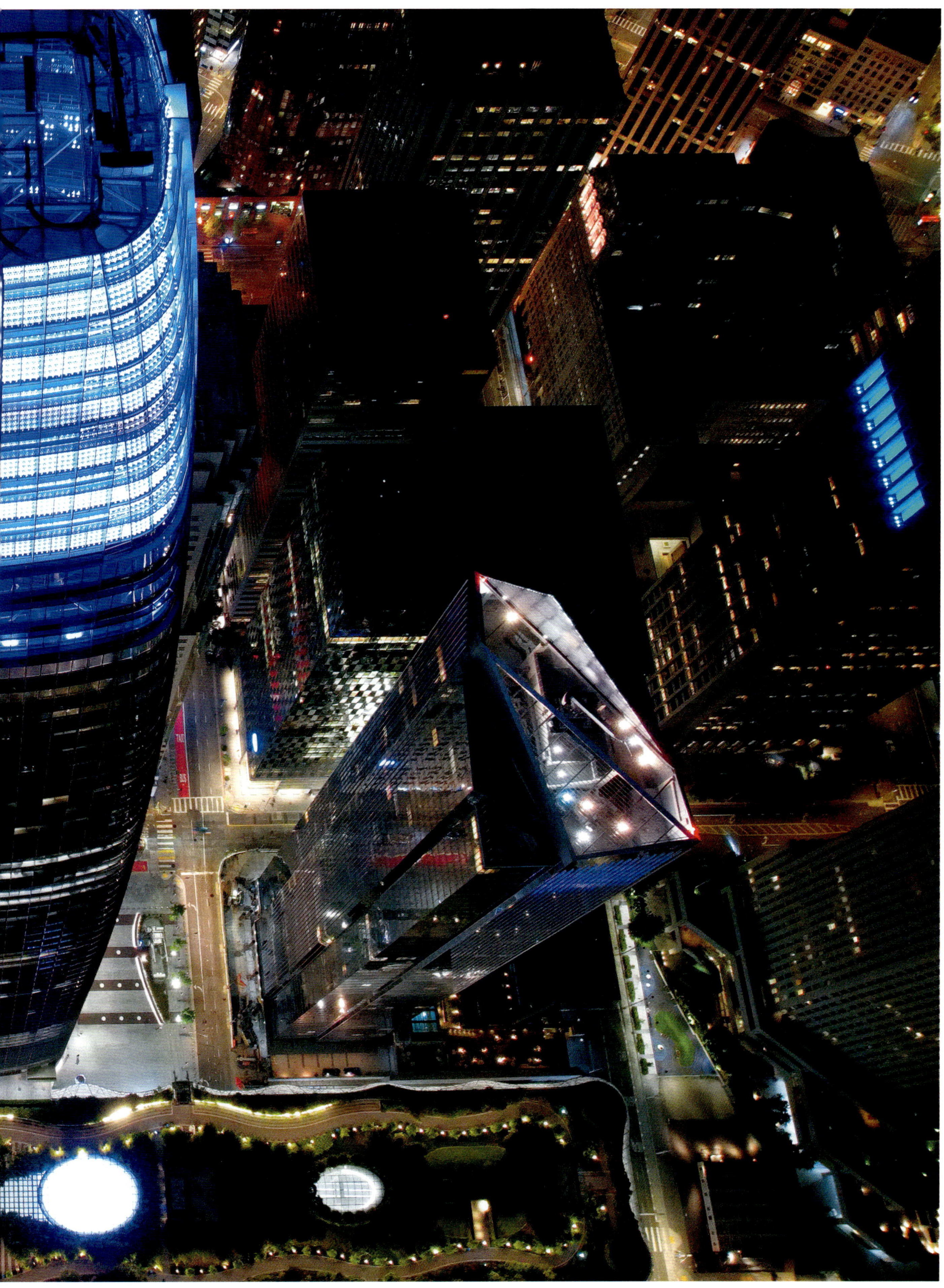

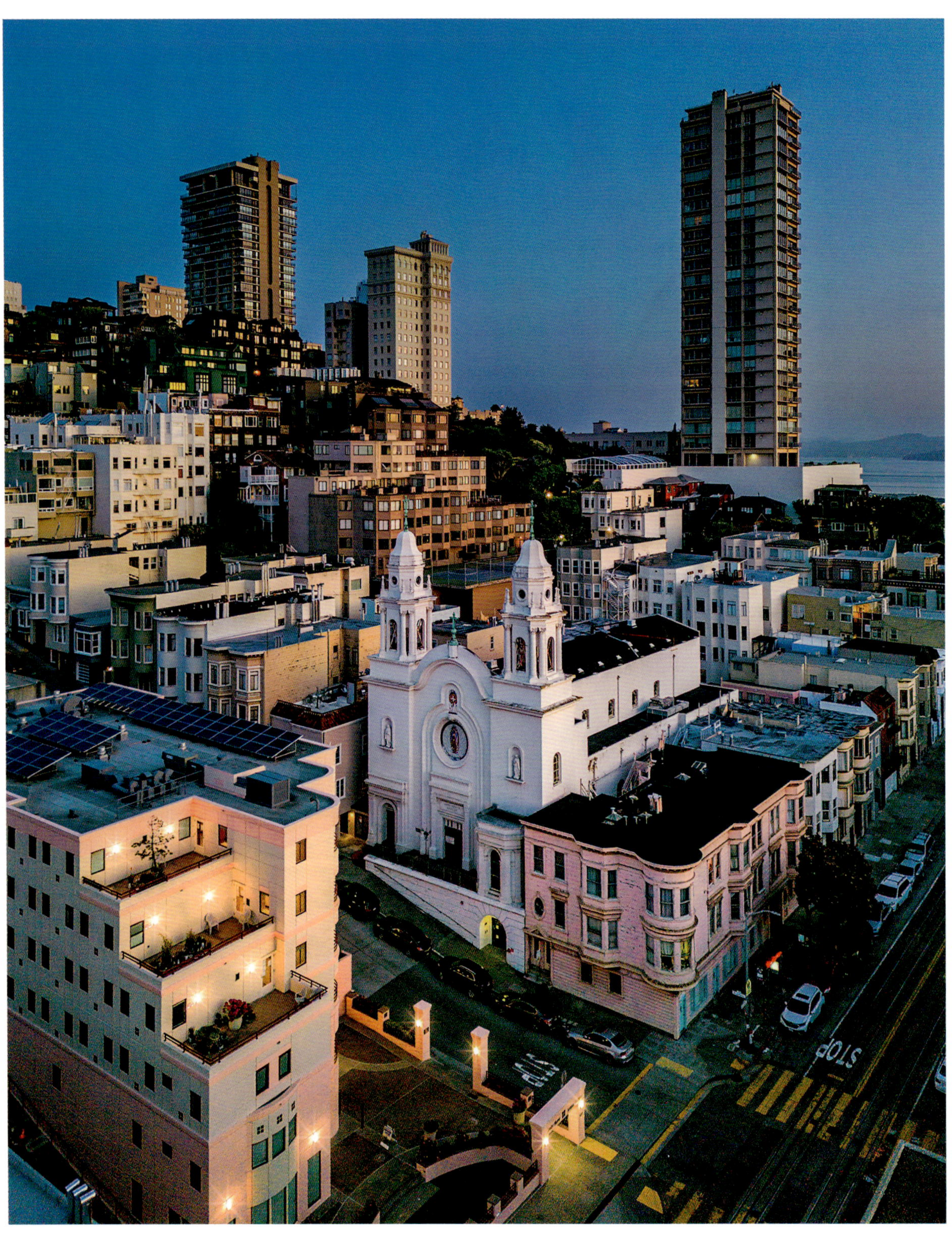

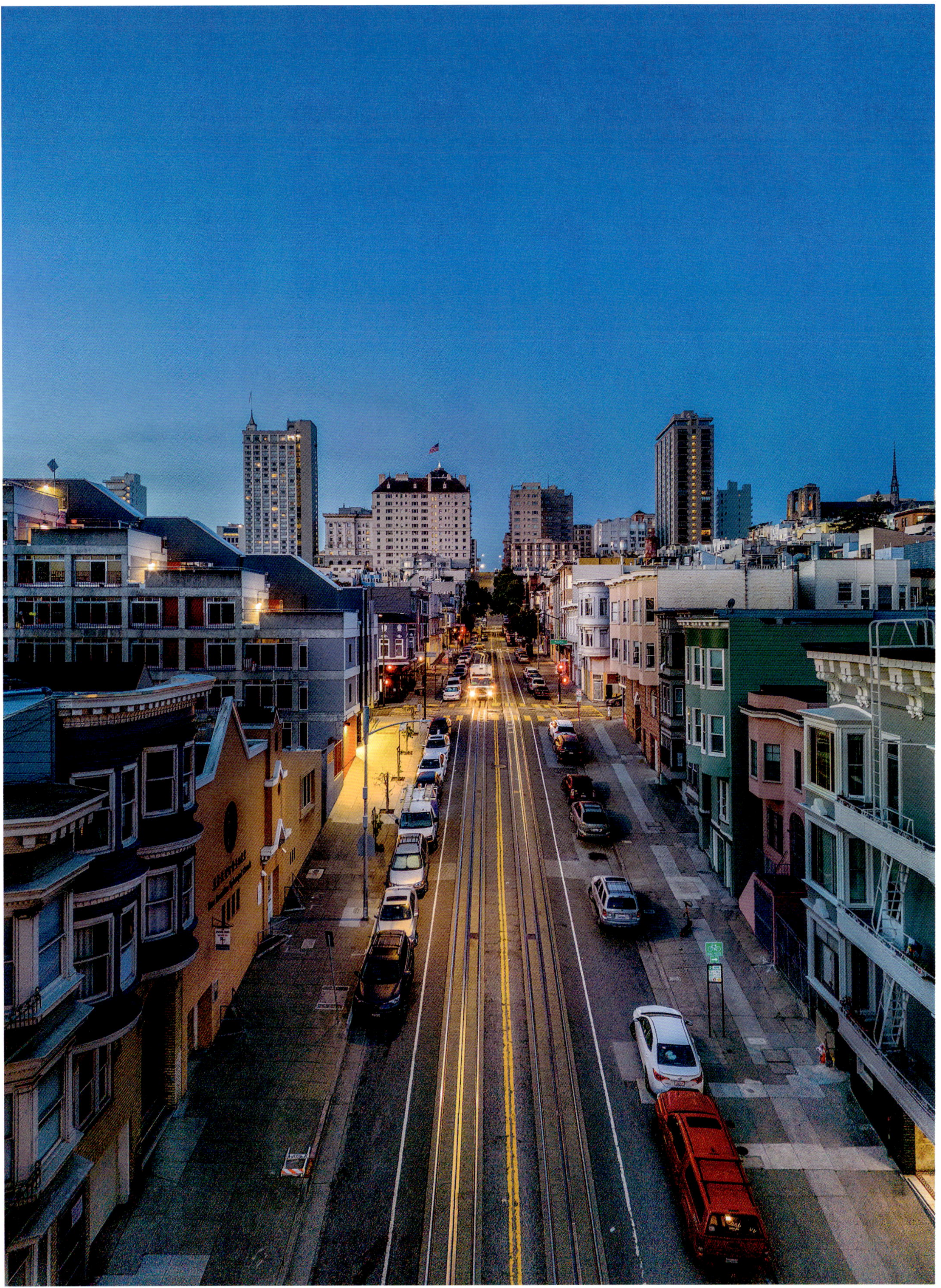

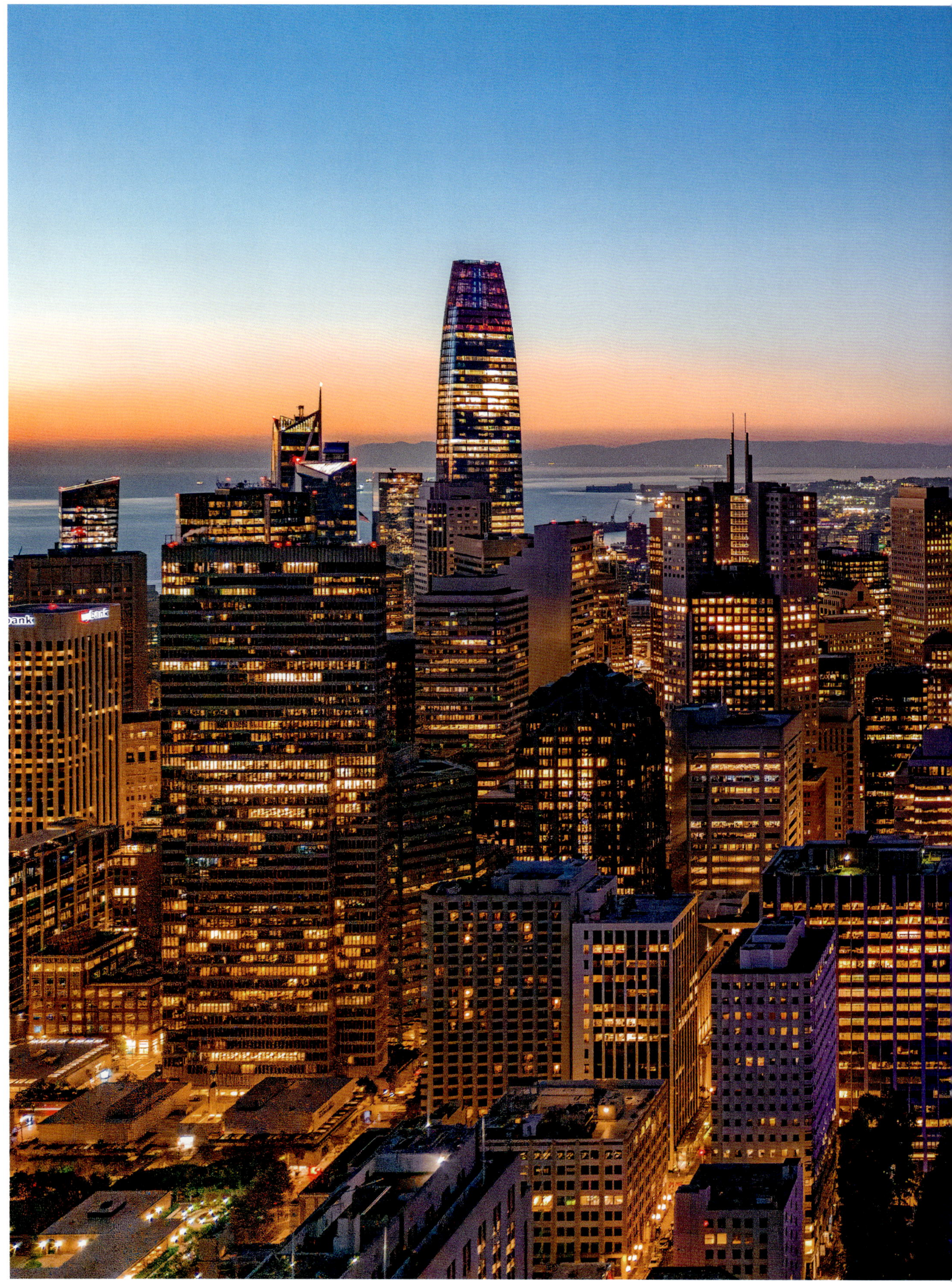

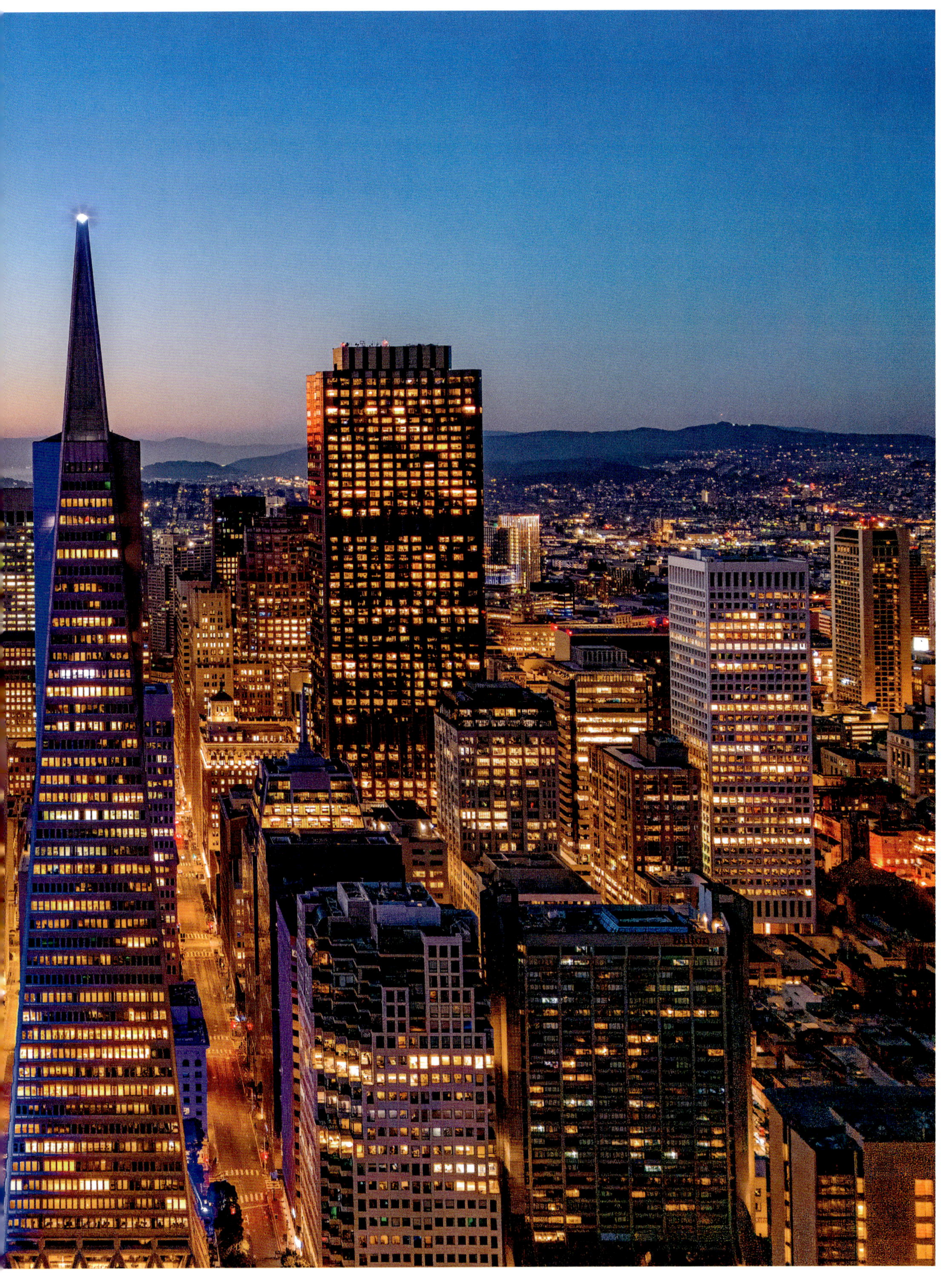

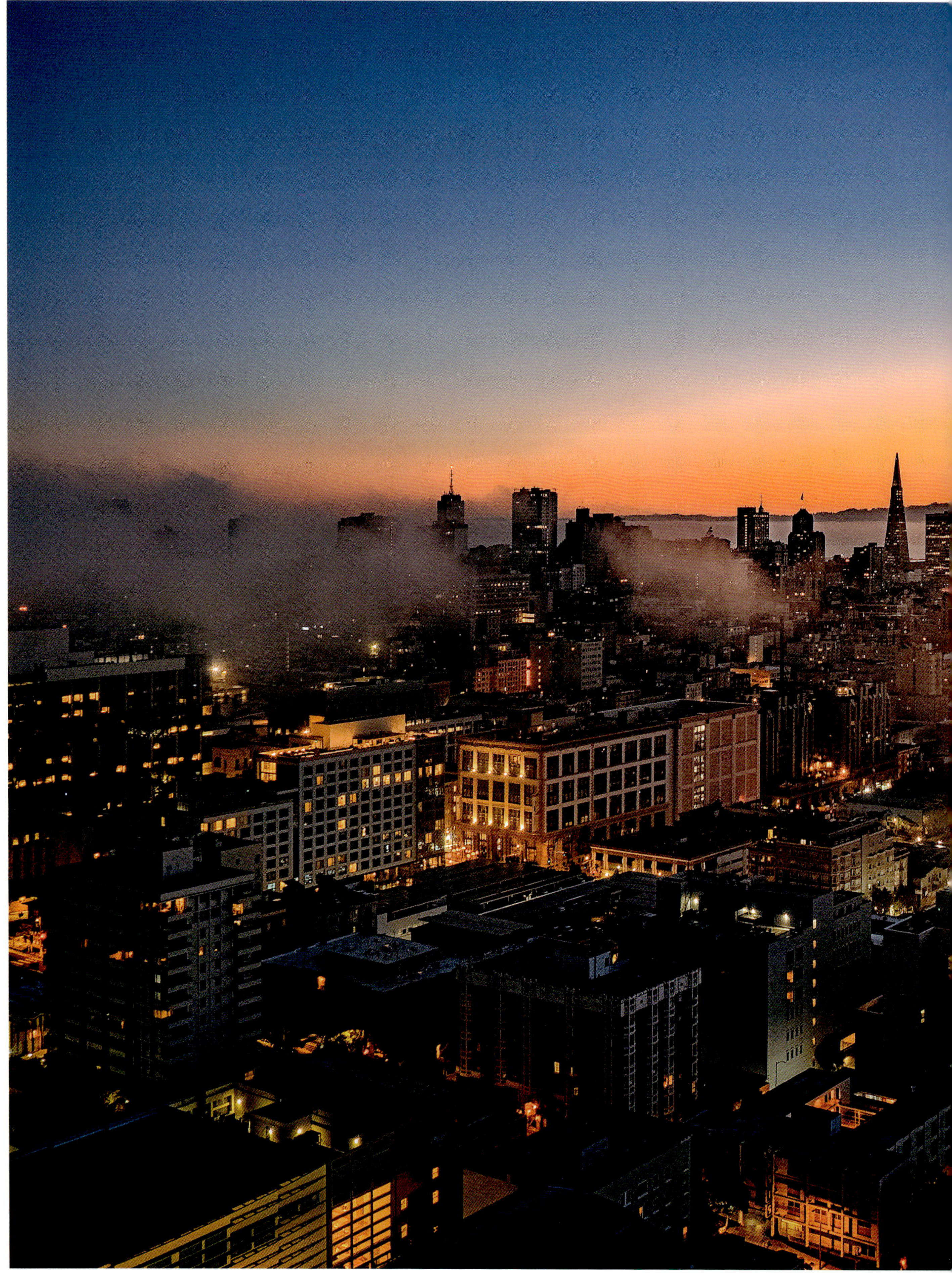

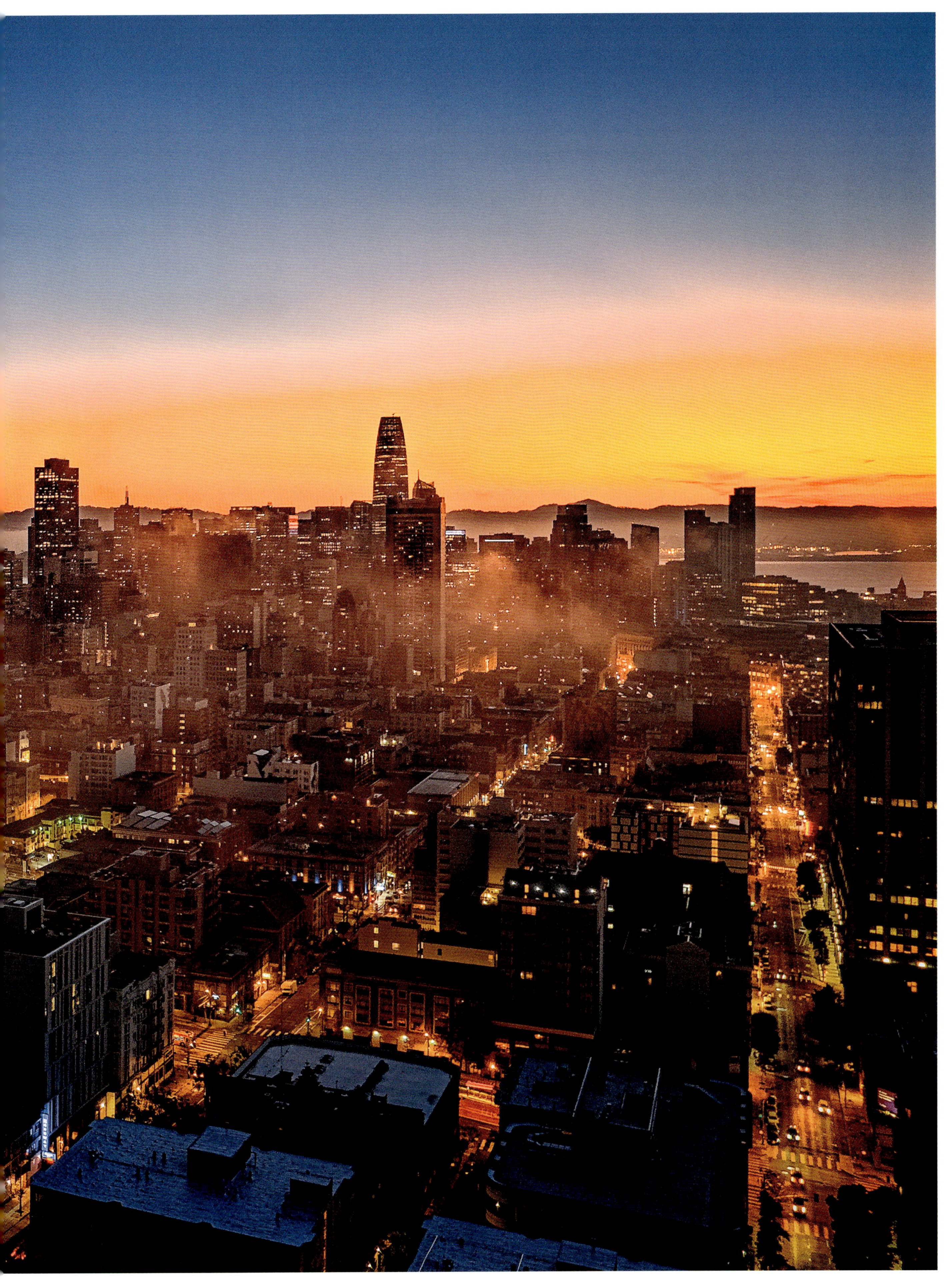

Getting Outside ♦ San Francisco is famous for its hills. And while they contribute to the city's charm and make for striking vistas of the city and the bay, they can also be physically challenging for the unaccustomed. The steep hills are notoriously difficult to traverse. Historically, traditional horse-drawn carriages and streetcars proved impractical. In the late 19th century, cable cars were introduced to connect neighborhoods across the hills, making the movement of people and goods far easier. Despite modern transit options, San Francisco's cable car system remains an integral part of the city's transit system, and in 1964, received designation as a National Historic Landmark. ♦ San Francisco has more than 40 named hills within the city limits. Telegraph Hill is home to the historic Coit Tower. Built between 1932 and 1933, Coit Tower stands 210 feel tall and offers panoramic views of San Francisco. Inside the tower, a collection of murals painted during the Great Depression depict scenes of California life, labor, and the city's cultural diversity. In Russian Hill, Lombard Street is one of the city's most famous streets, known for its tight, winding curves. Tourists in cars line up on Hyde Street at the top of the hill to take their turn navigating the street's unique pattern. ♦ Outdoor living is an important part of the San Francisco experience. Residents and tourists alike flock to the city's parks to enjoy the temperate climate. One of San Francisco's most famous outdoor spaces is Golden Gate Park. Established in 1871, it spans more than 1,000 acres and is larger than New York City's Central Park. Beyond its open green spaces, Golden Gate Park is home to the California Academy of Sciences, the de Young Museum, the San Francisco Botanical Garden, and the Japanese Tea Garden, making it a popular spot to relax and enjoy the sunshine or experience a cultural festival or event. ♦ A former military base turned national park, the Presidio is situated at the northern tip of the San Francisco Peninsula. The Presidio offers stunning views of the Golden Gate Bridge, the Pacific Ocean, and the San Francisco Bay, and is a hub for outdoor activities with hiking and biking trails, picnic areas, and spaces to enjoy the shoreline like Crissy Field and Baker Beach.

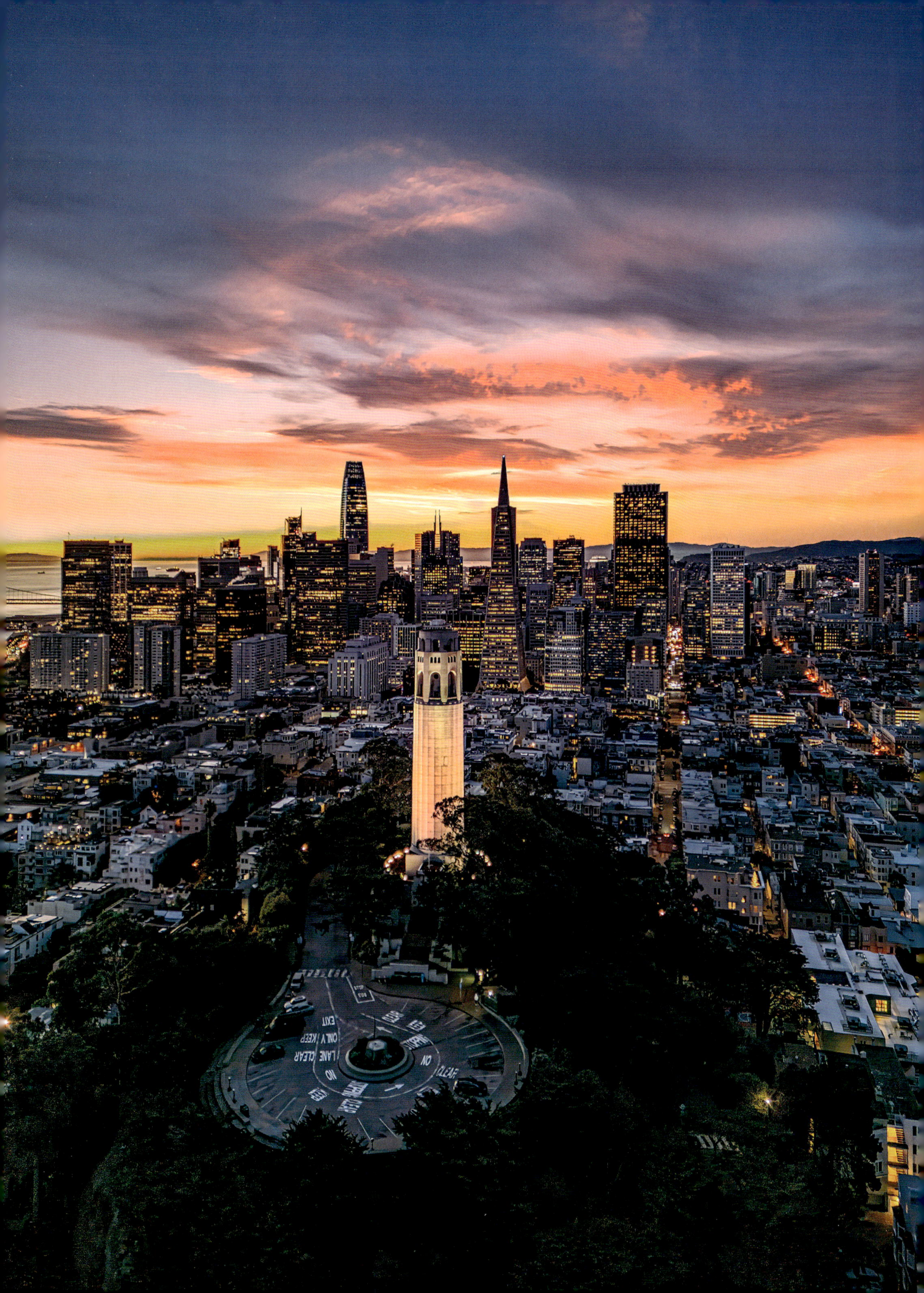
EXIT
ONLY / KEEP
LANE / CLEAR
NO
KEEP
KEEP CLEAR
ON
CLEAR
BUS
STOP

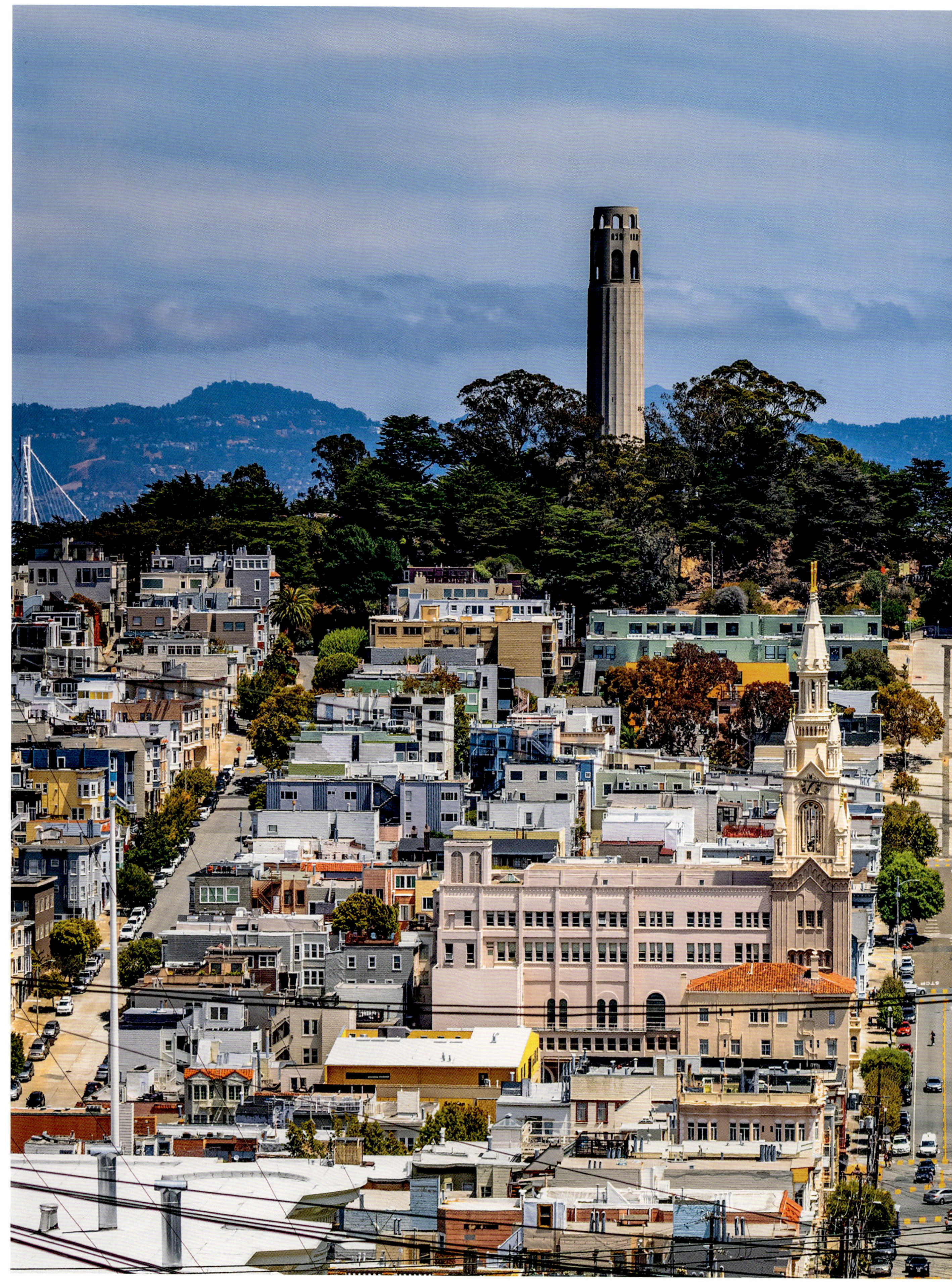

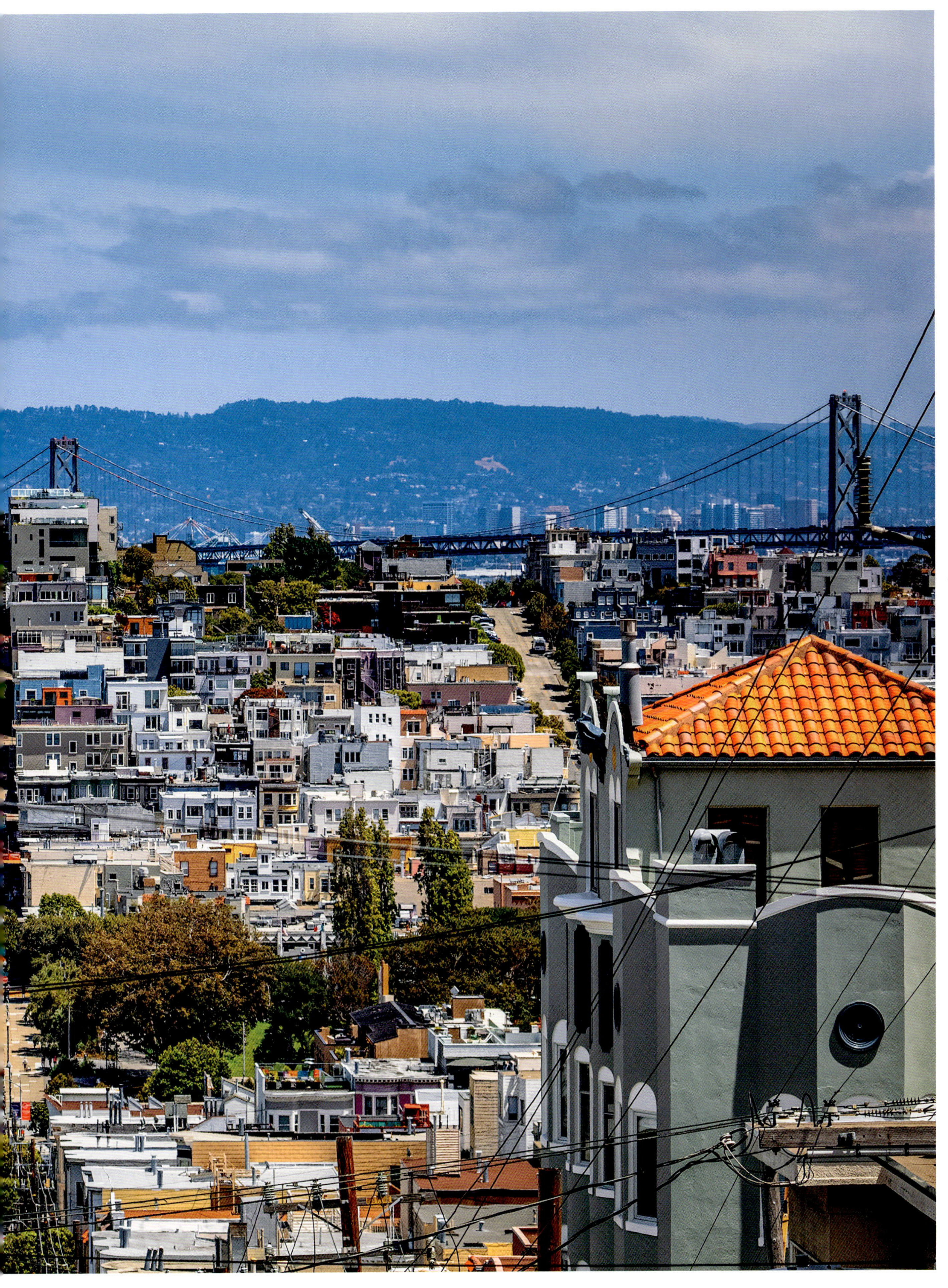

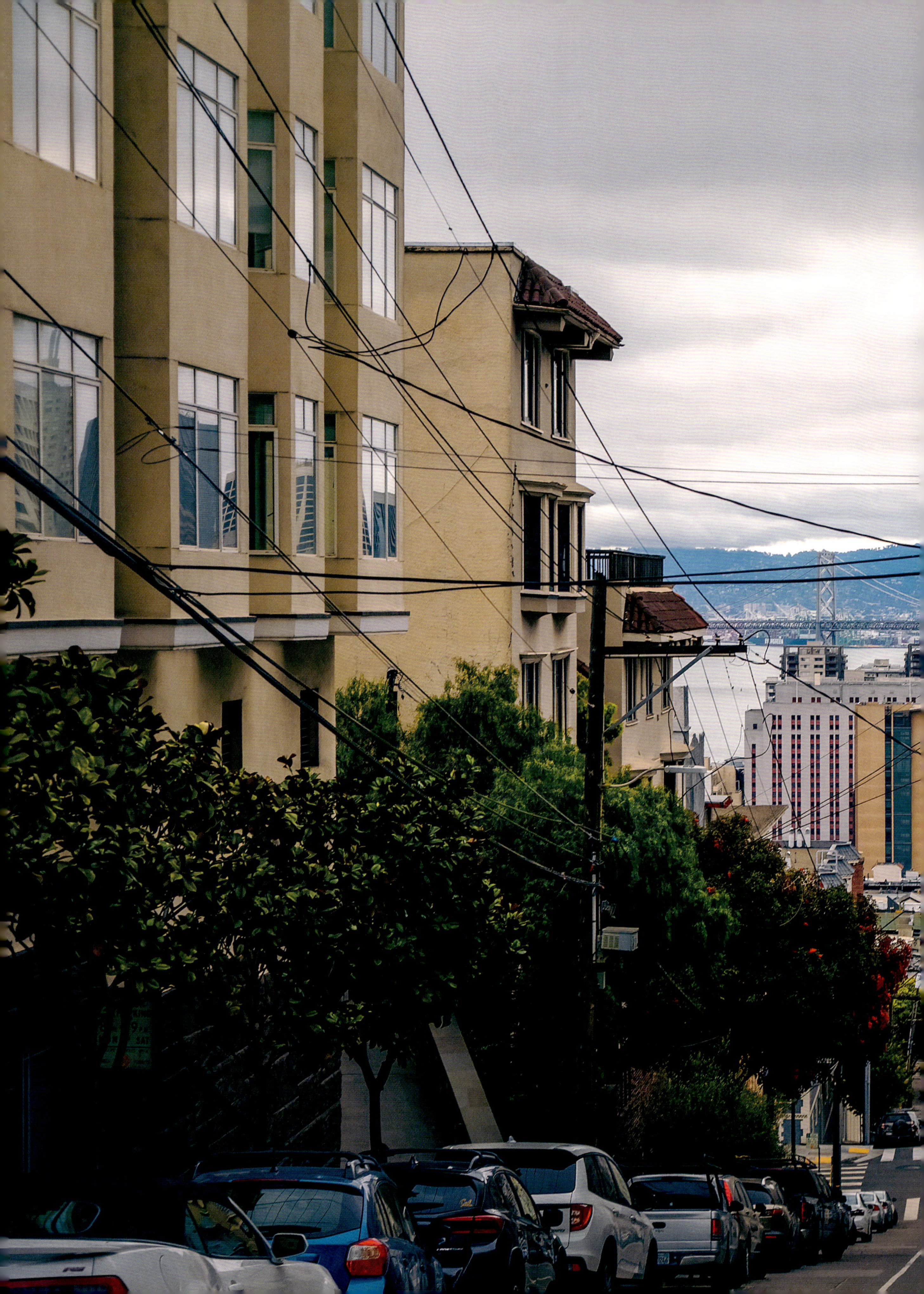

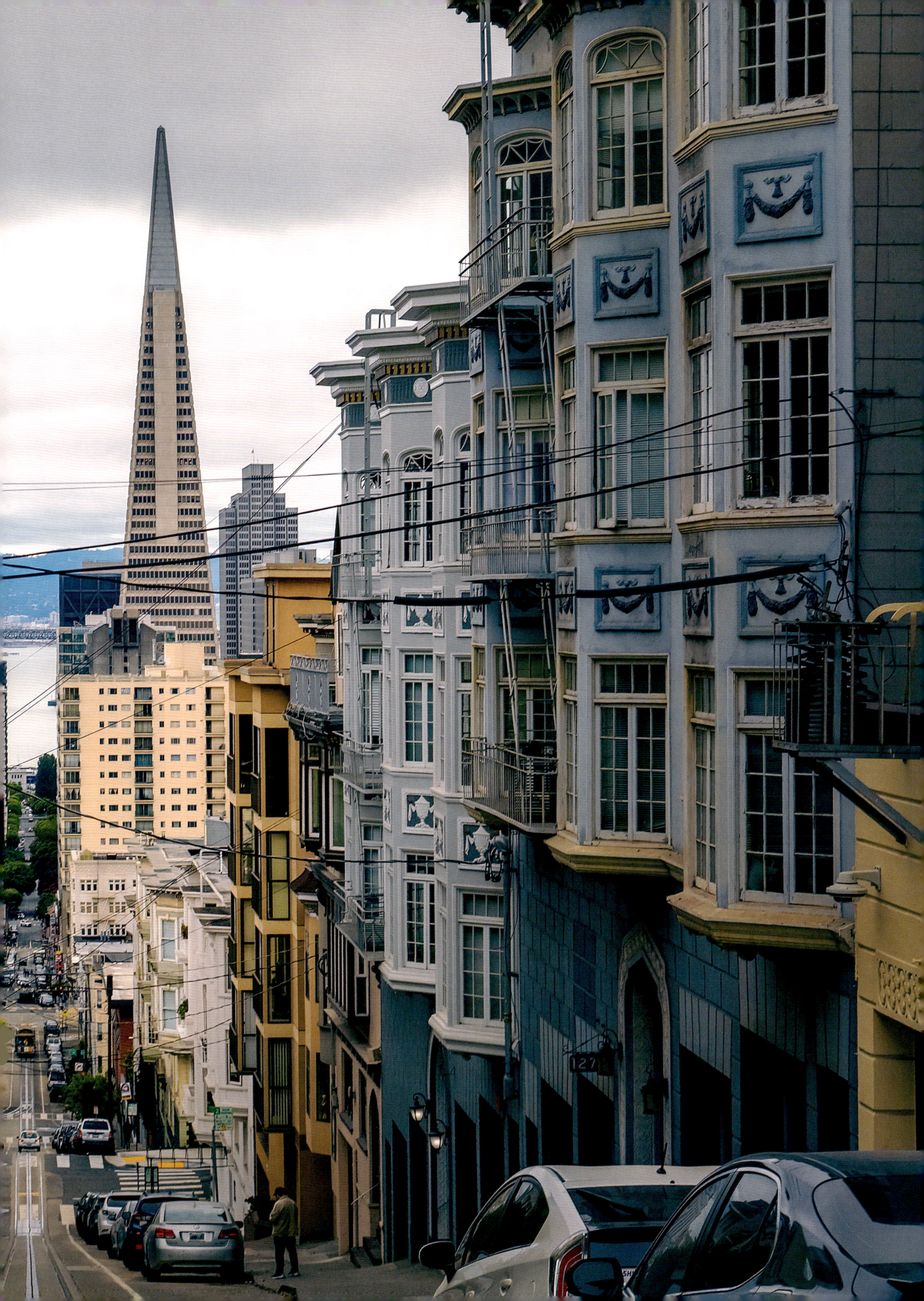

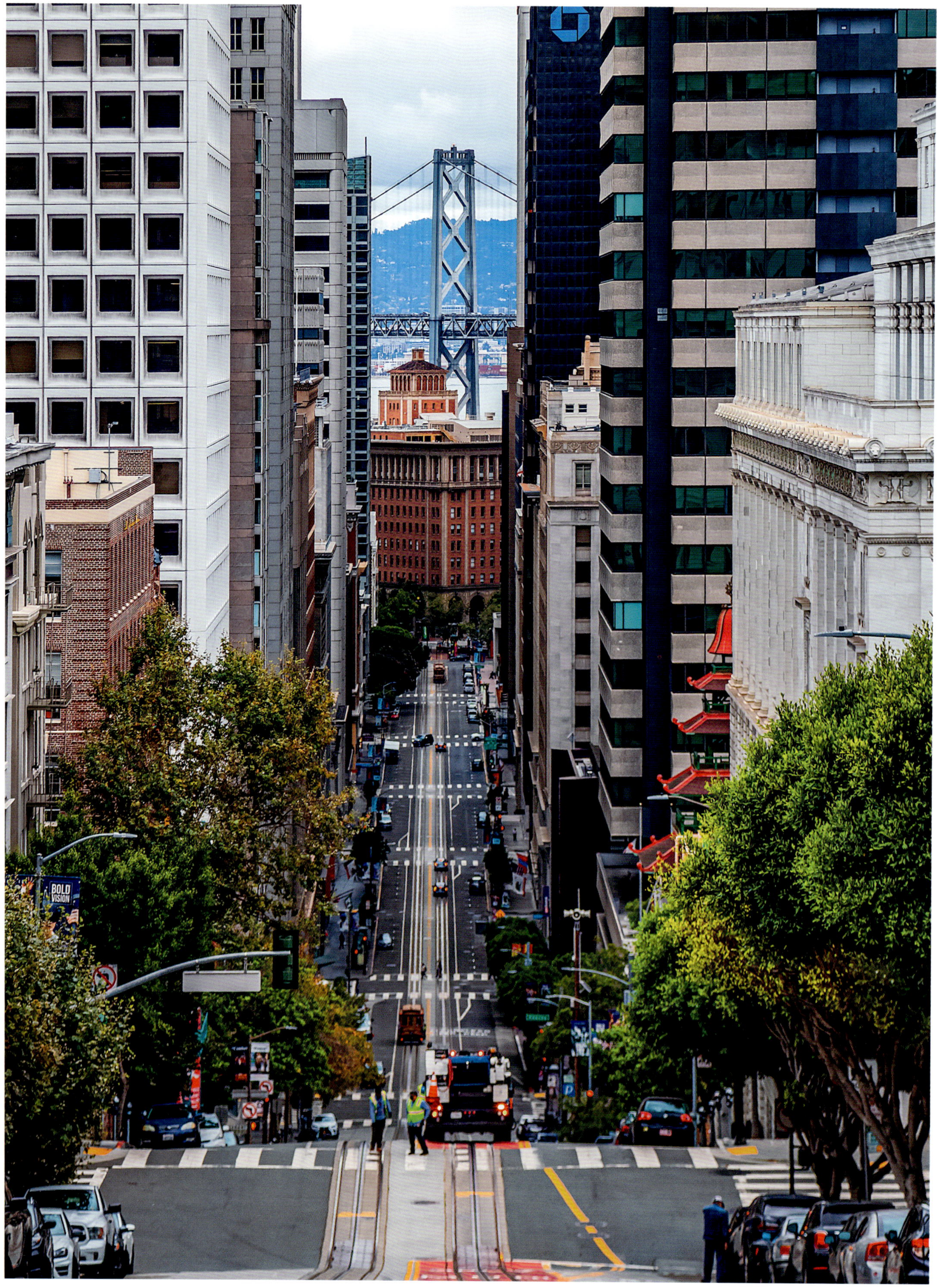

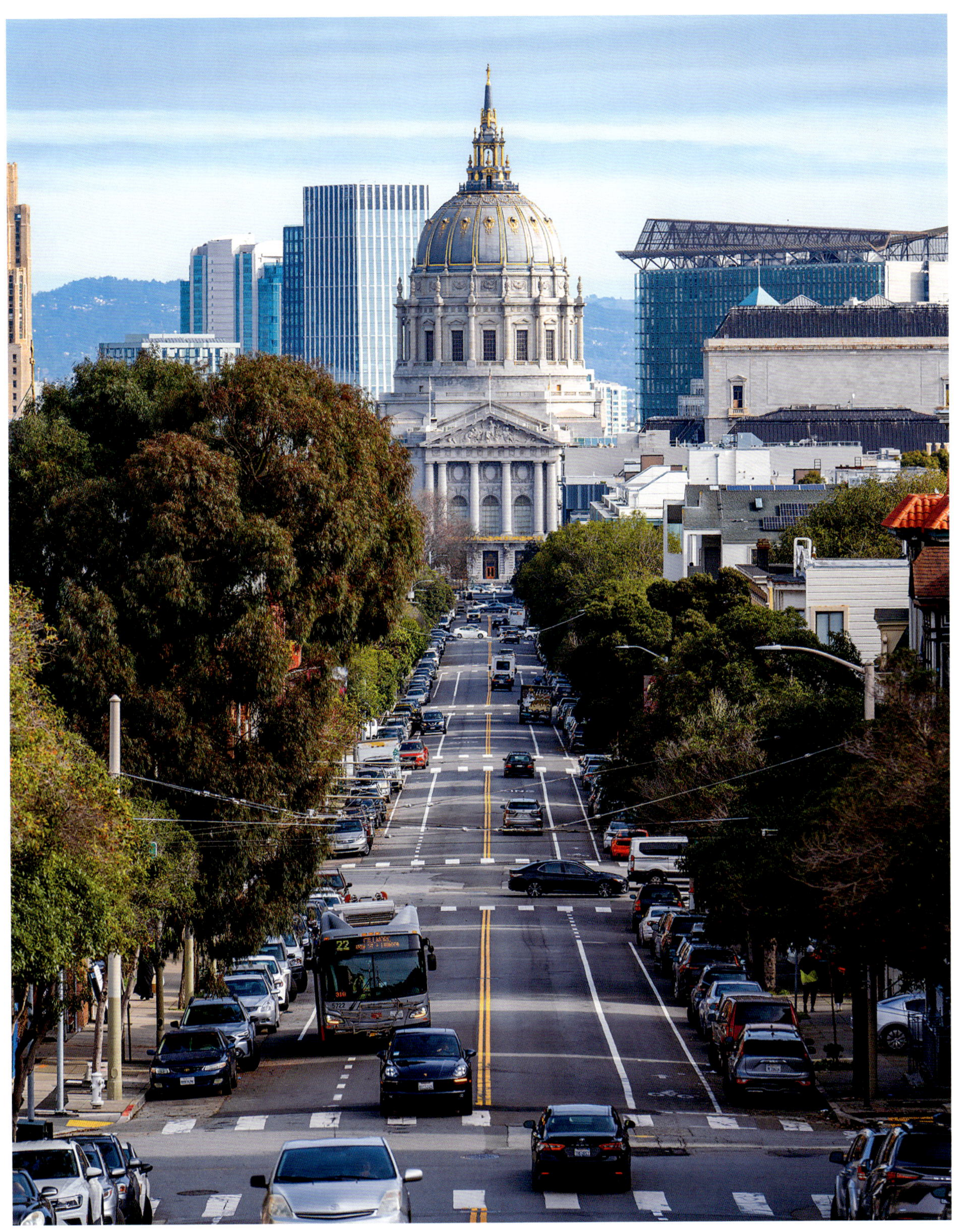

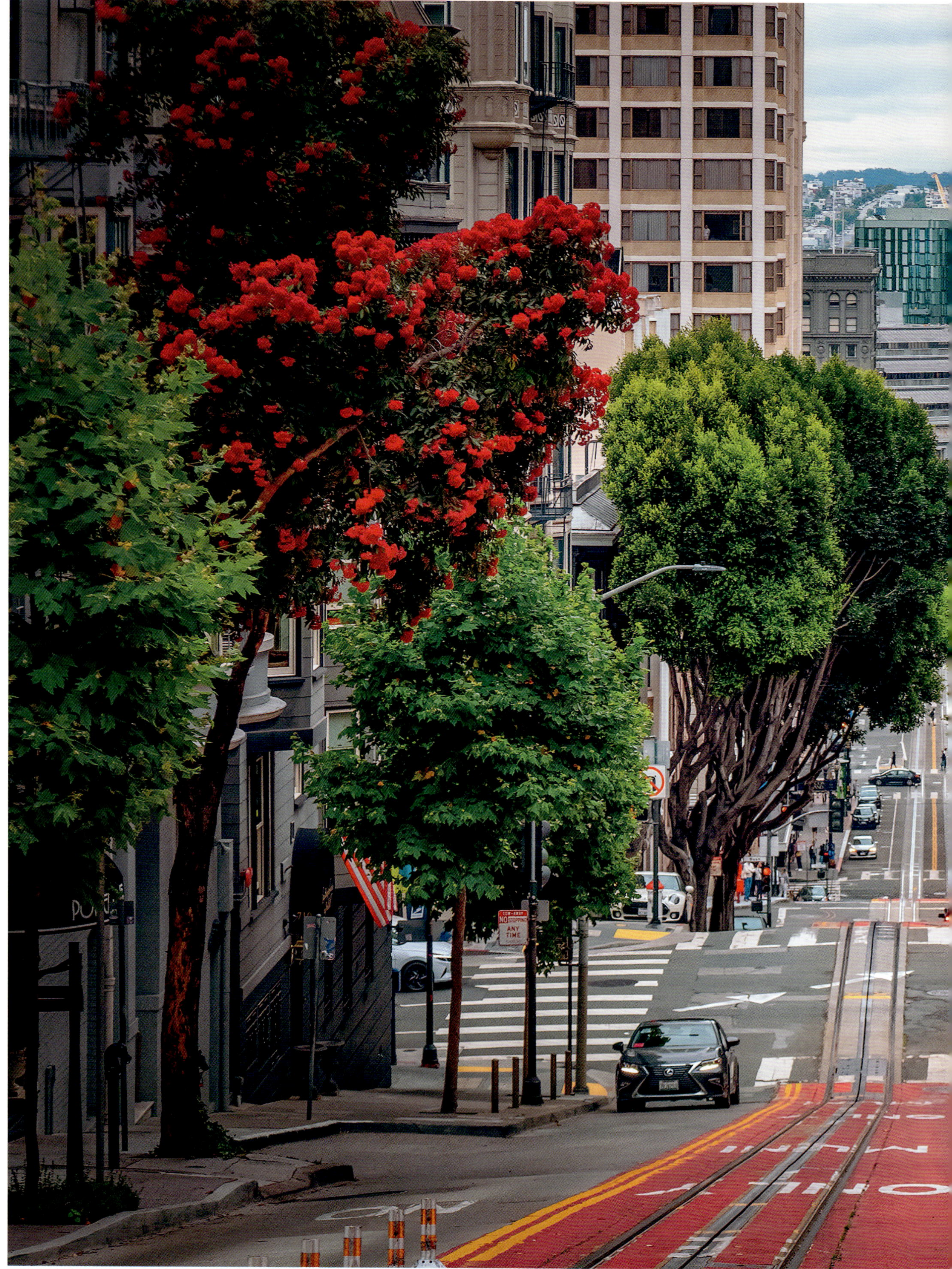

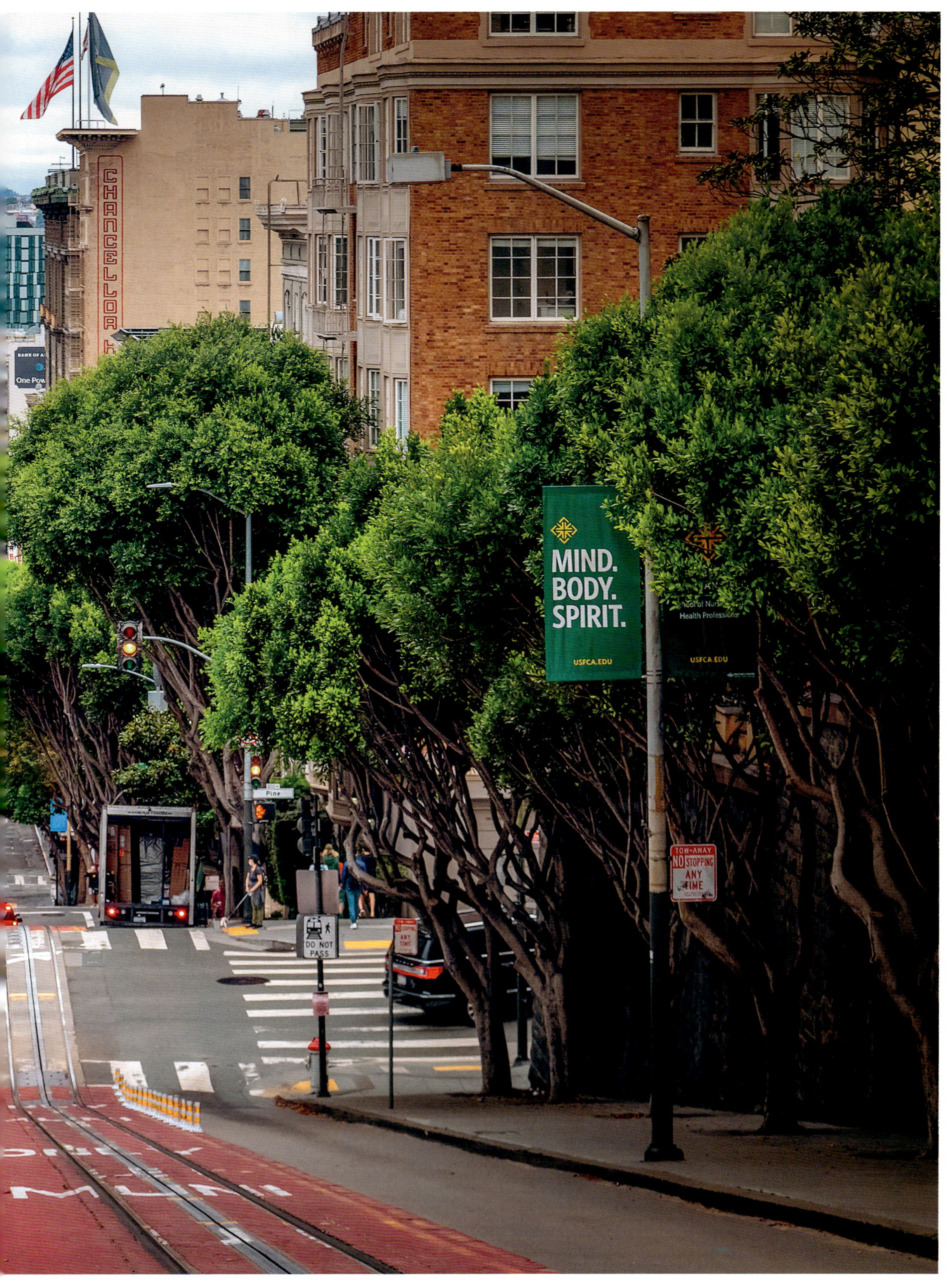

CHANCELLOR H
BANK OF A
One Pow
MIND.
BODY.
SPIRIT.
USFCA.EDU
School of Nursing and
Health Professions
USFCA.EDU
Pine
DO NOT
PASS
TOW-AWAY
NO STOPPING
ANY TIME
ANY
TIME

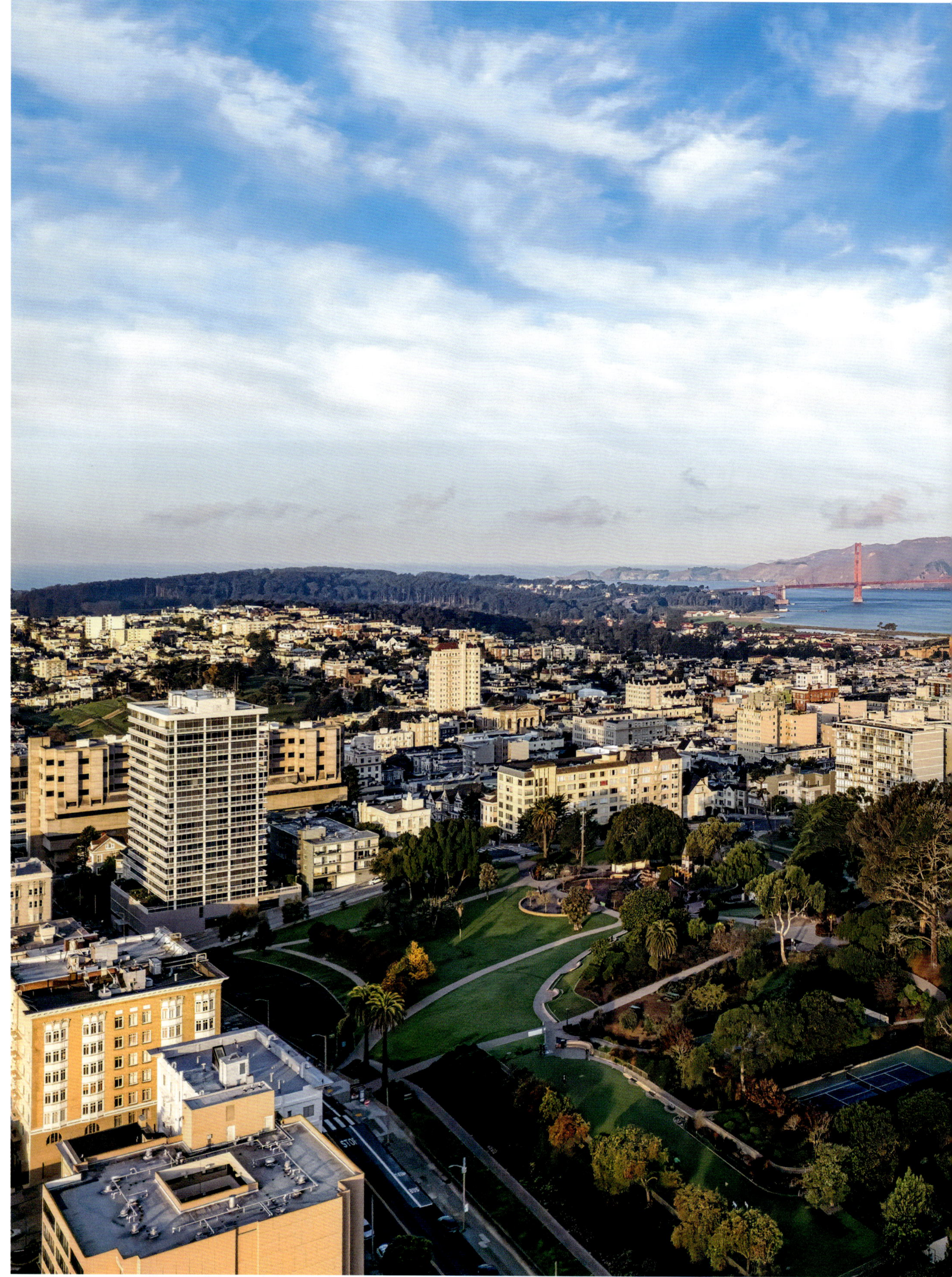

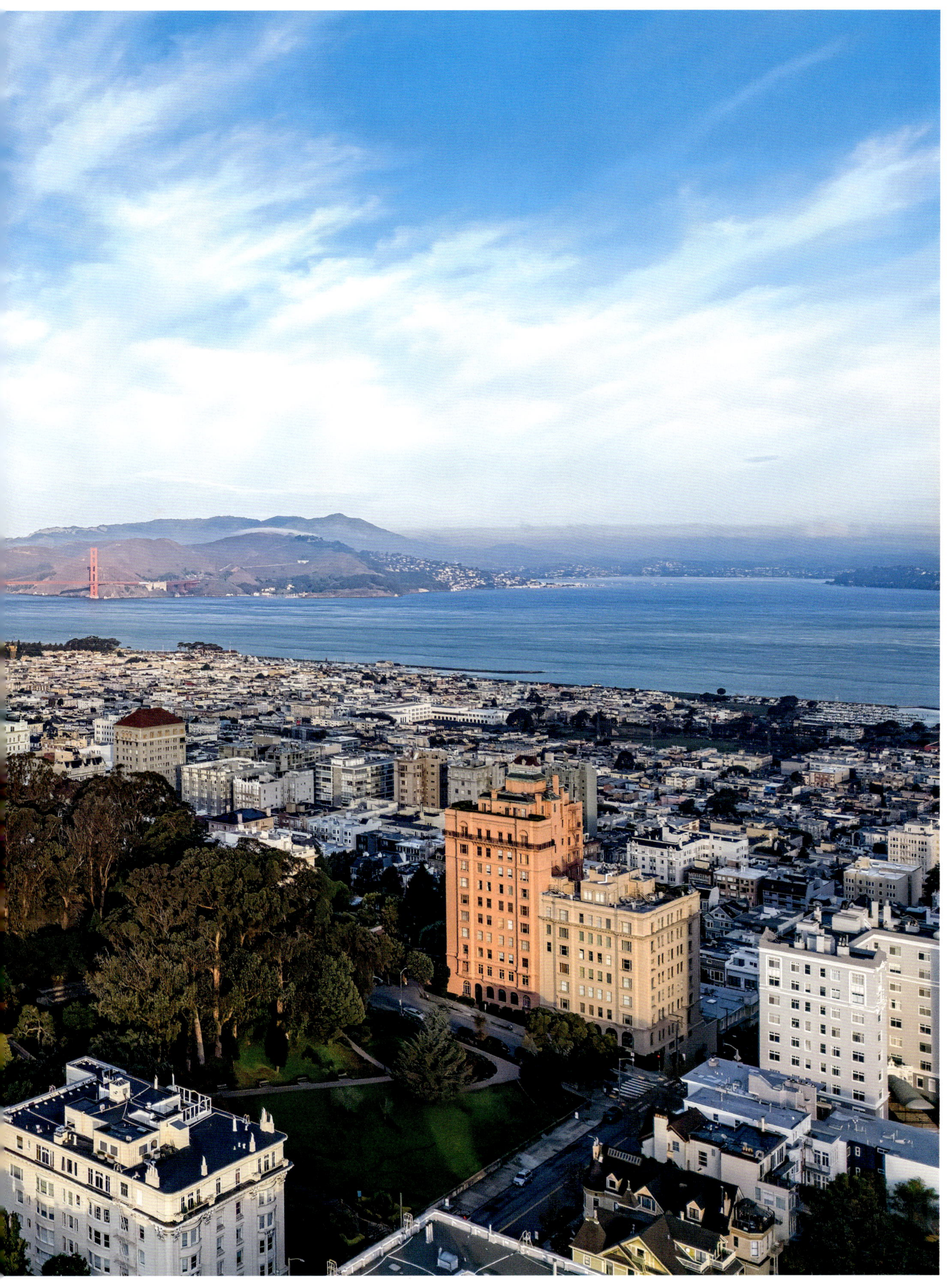

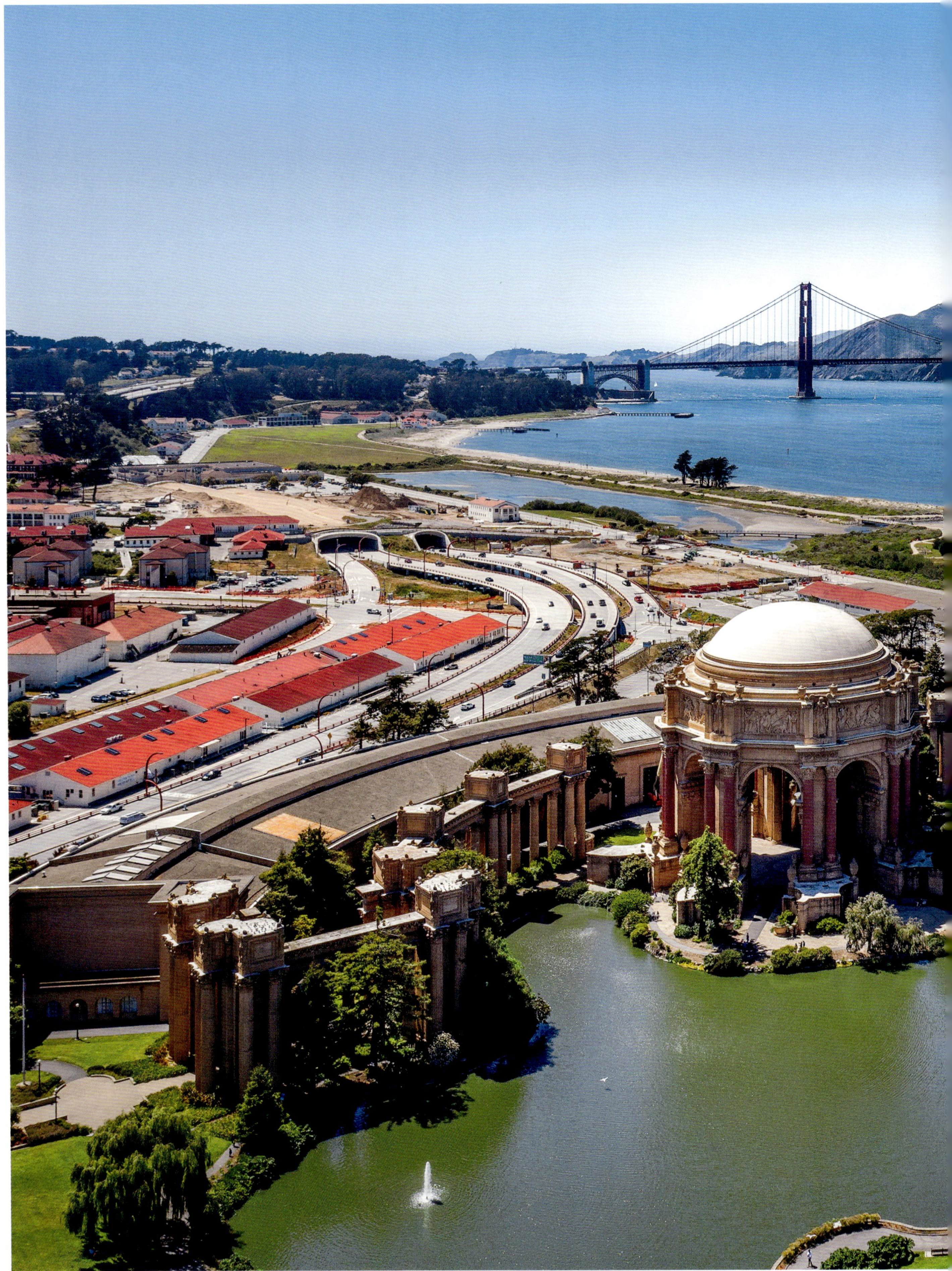

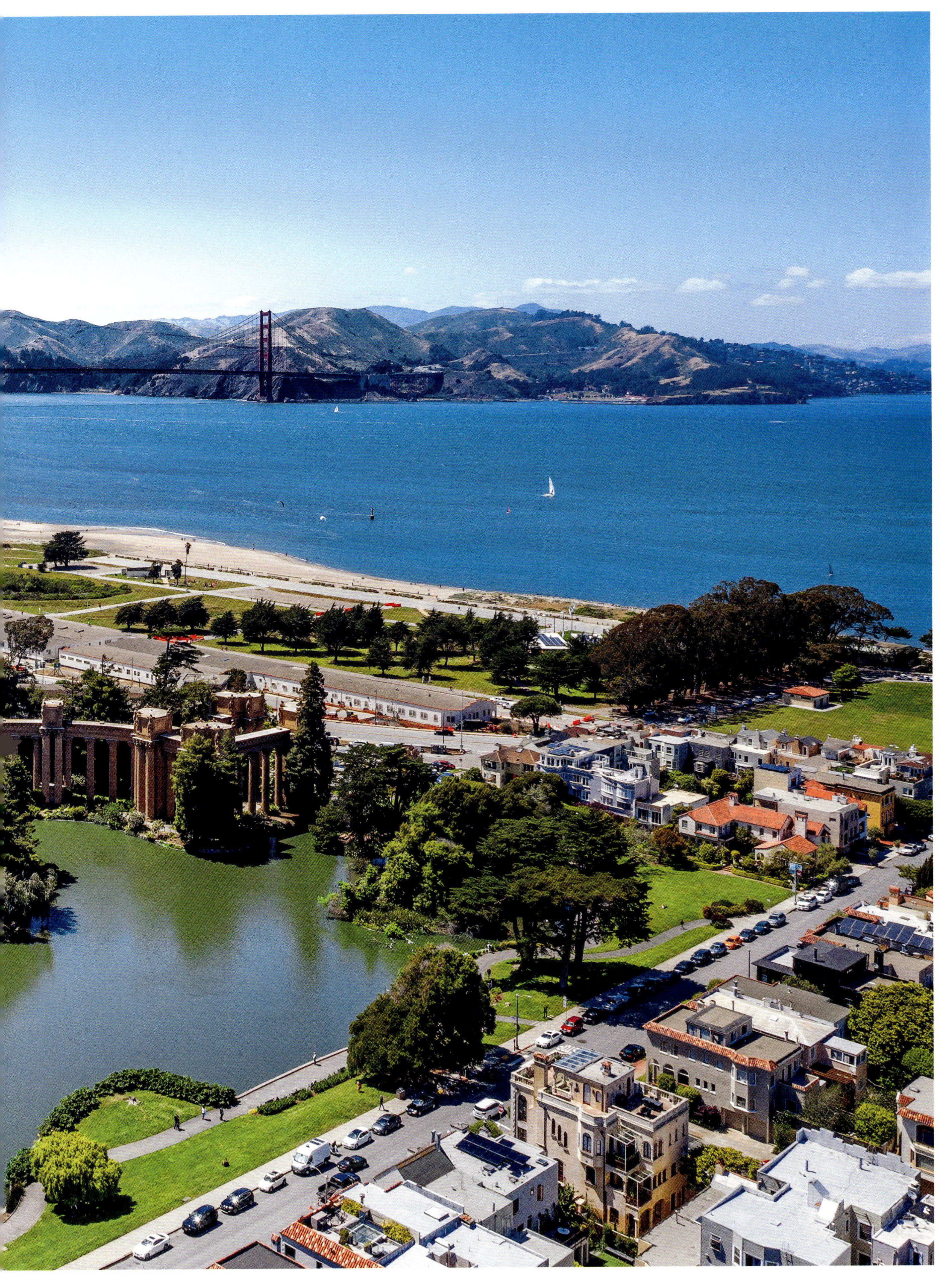

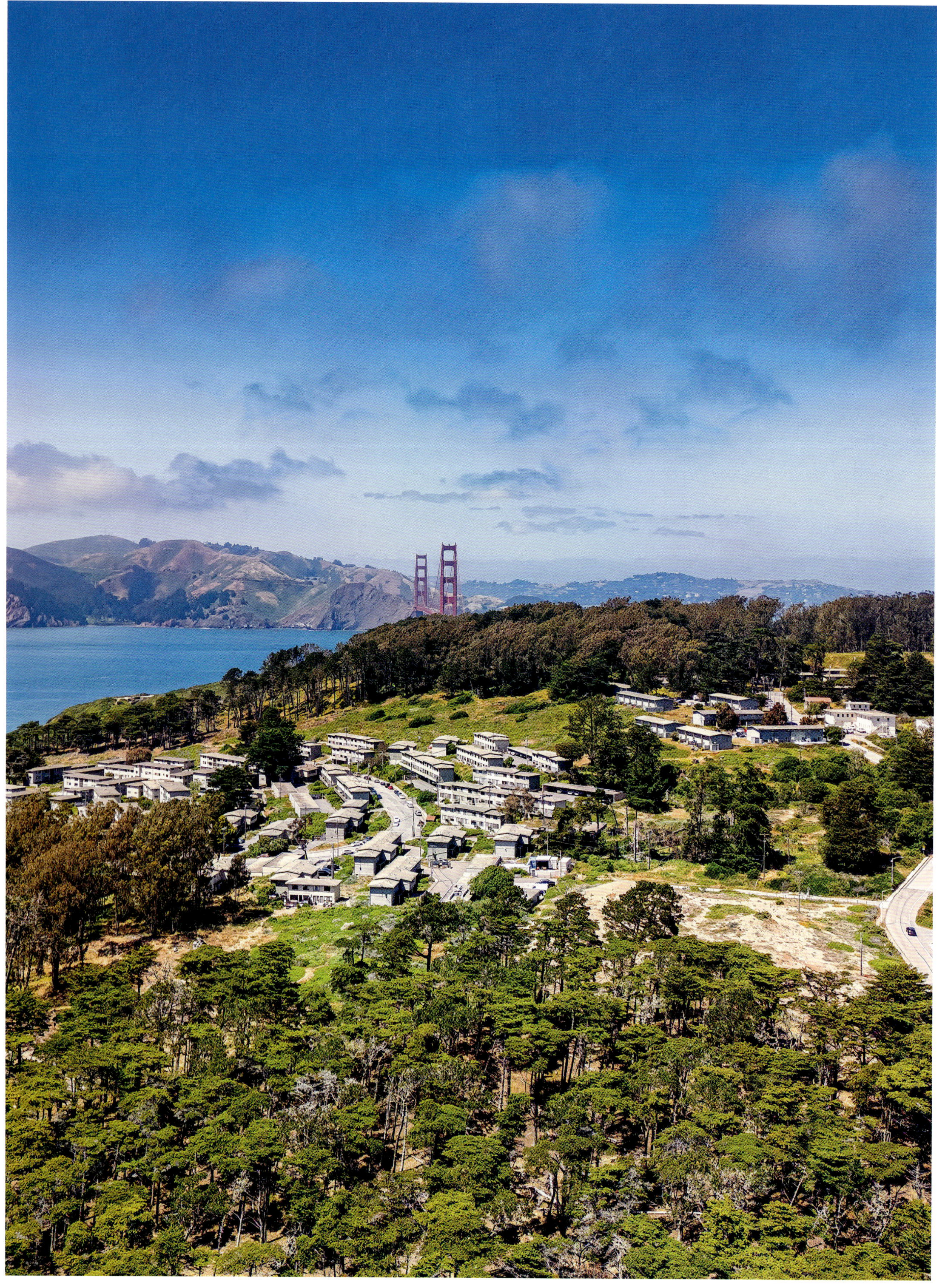

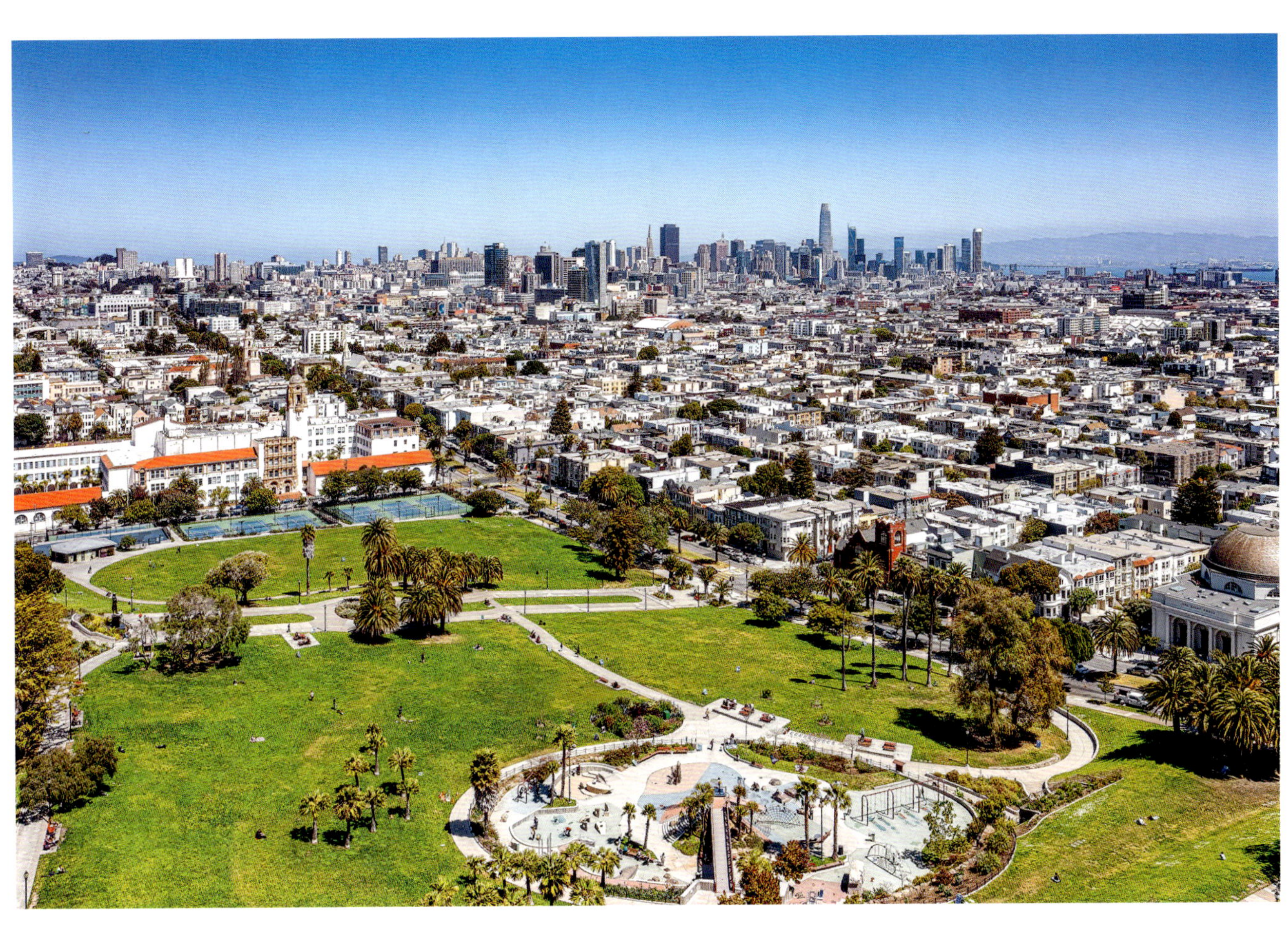

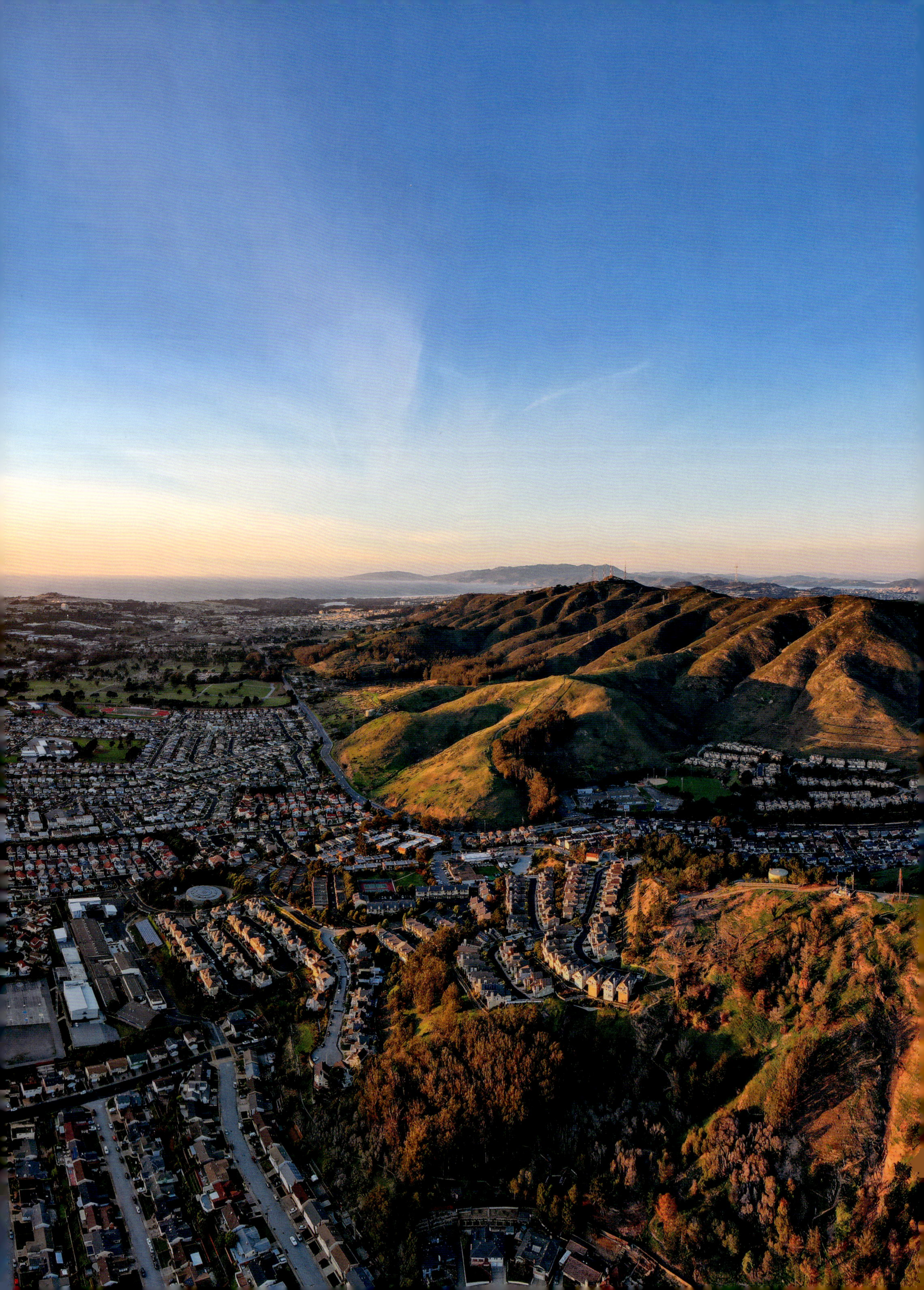

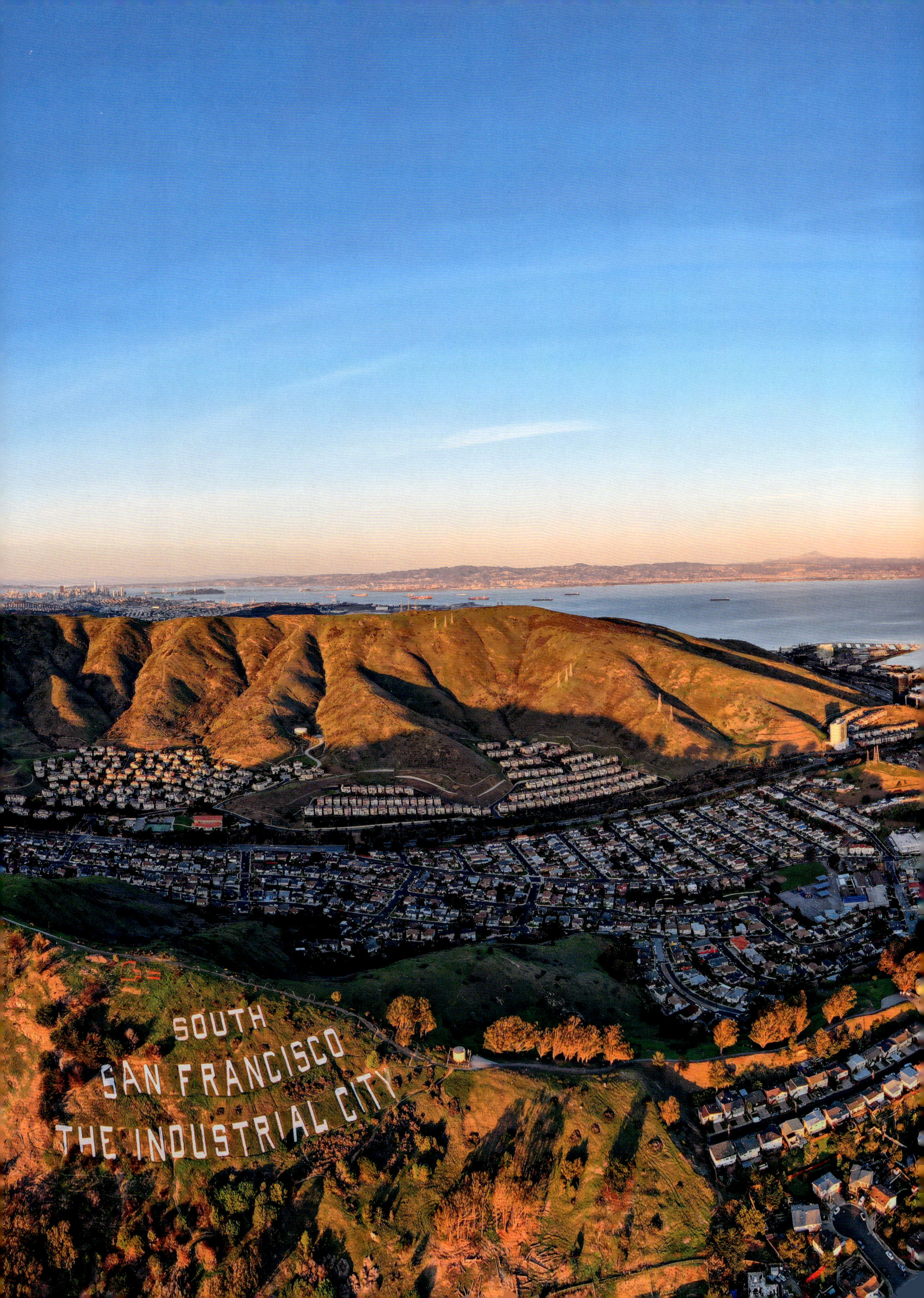

SOUTH
SAN FRANCISCO
THE INDUSTRIAL CITY

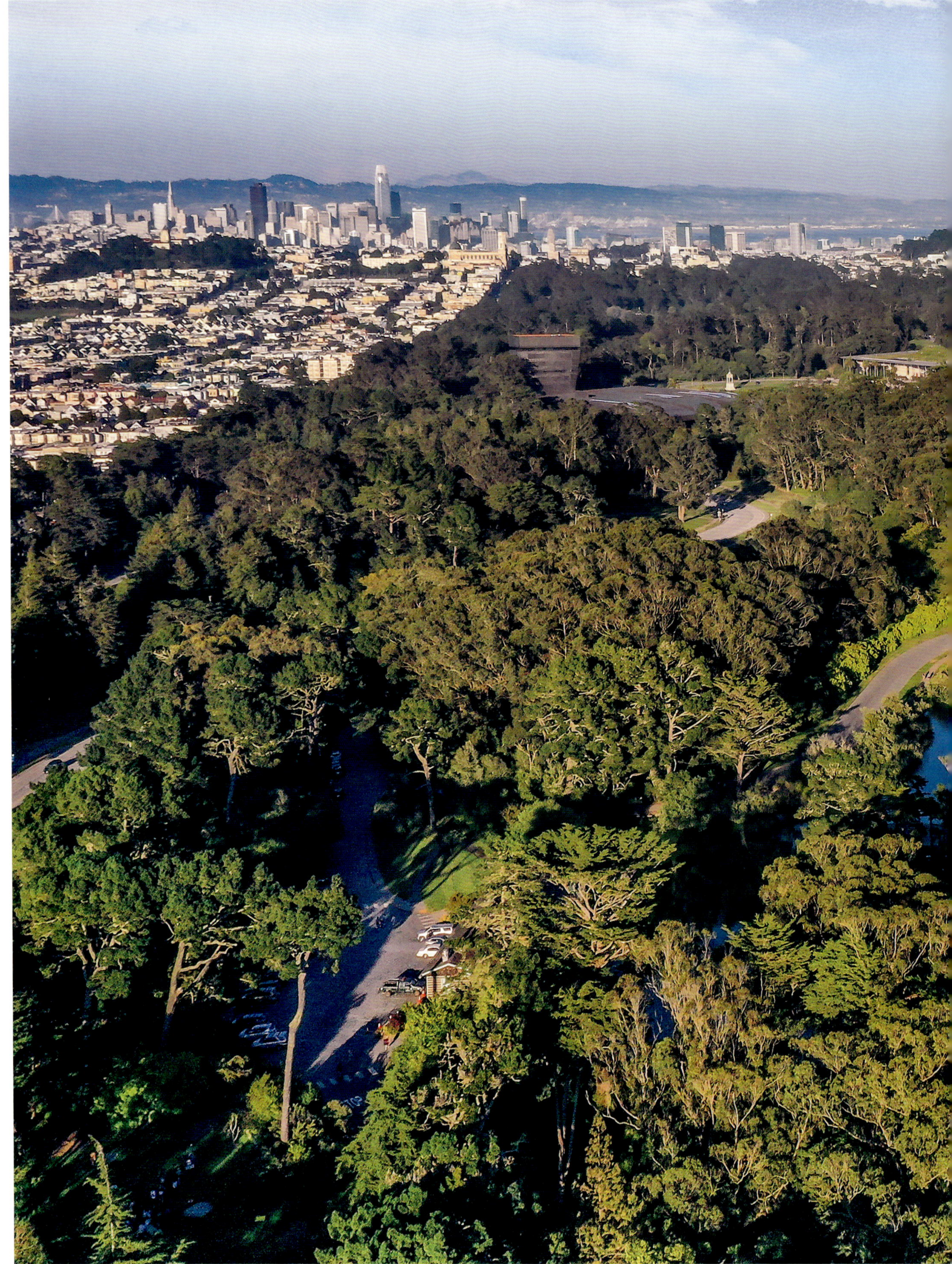

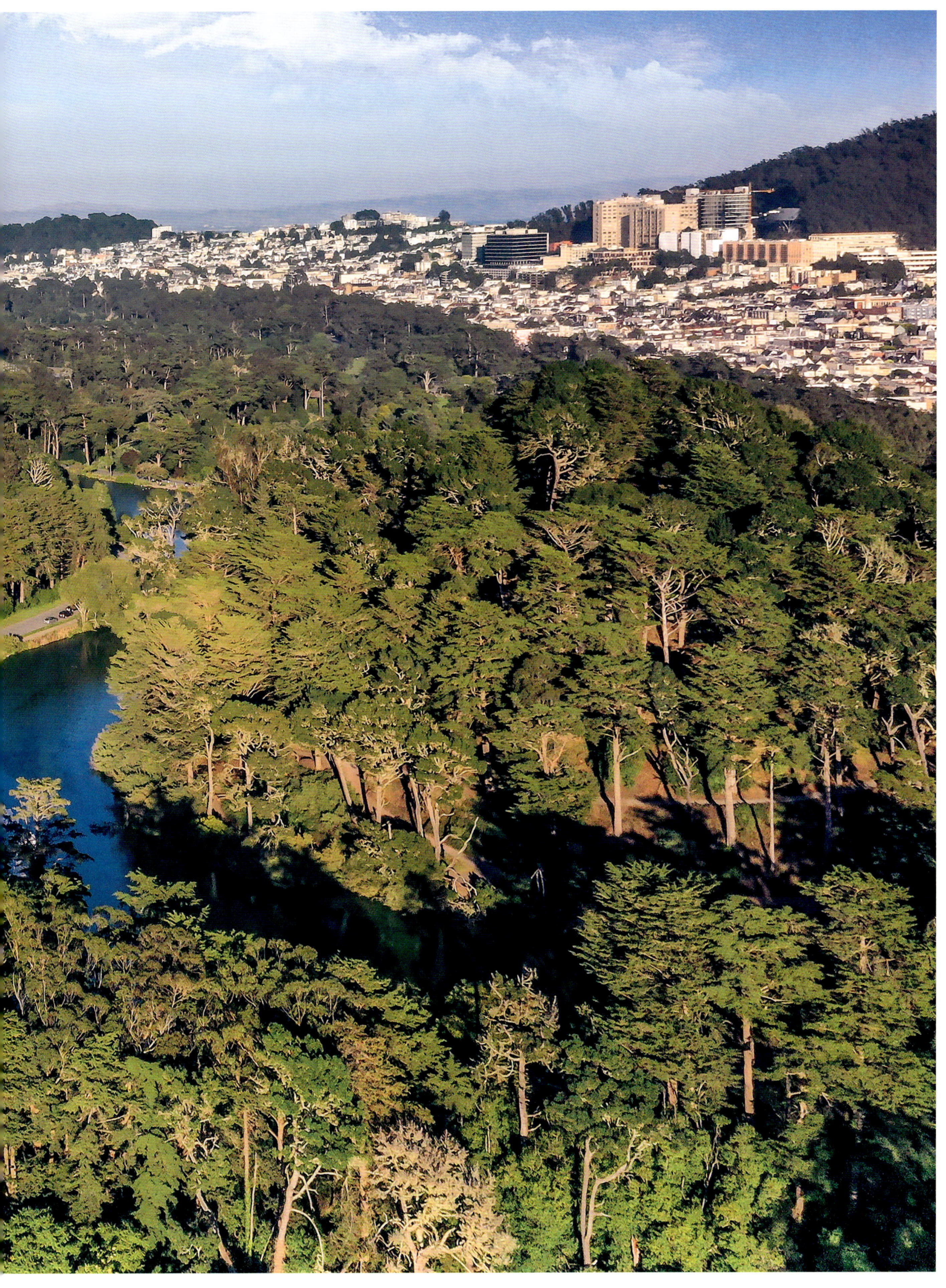

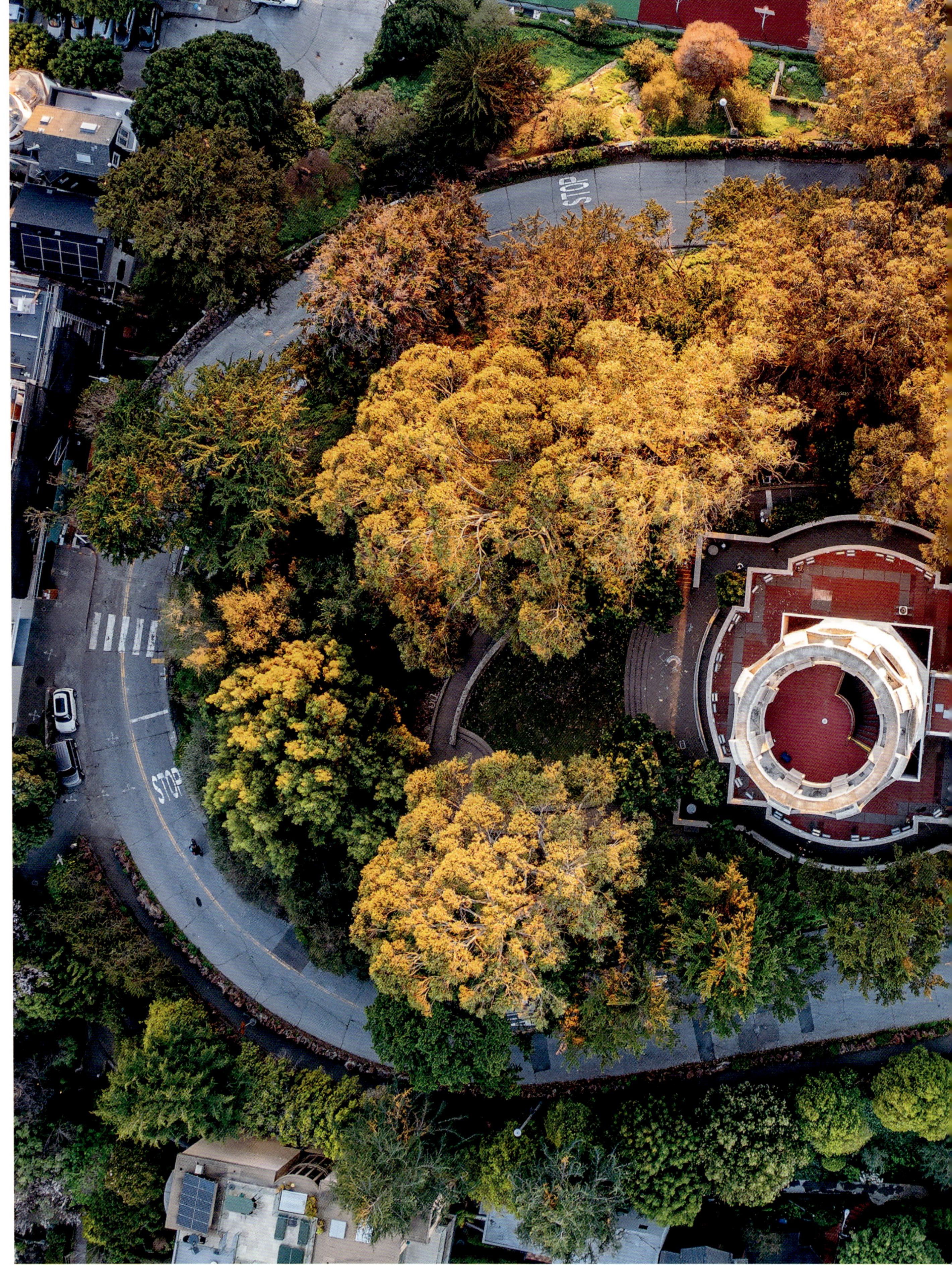

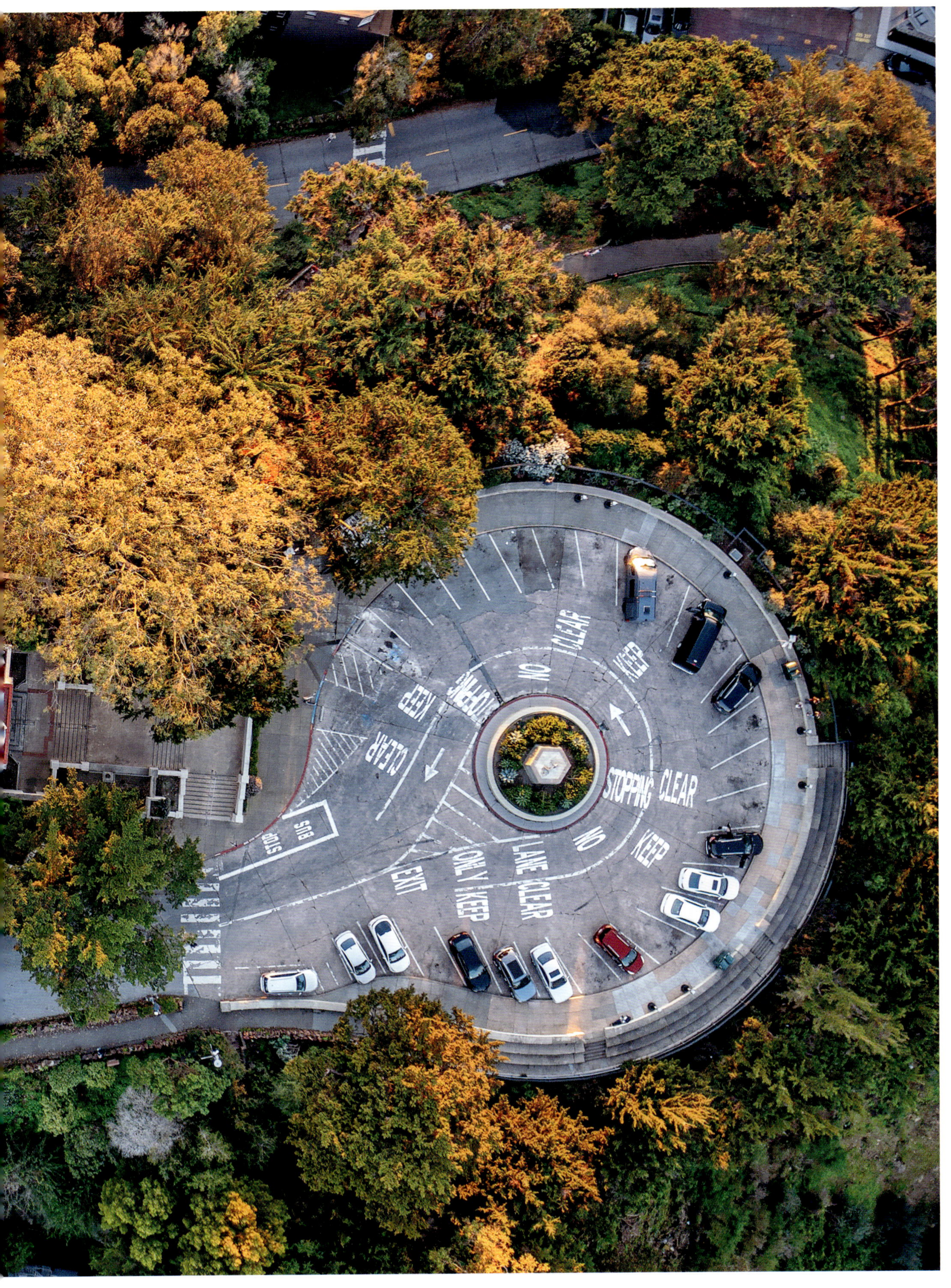

KEEP
CLEAR
NO
KEEP
CLEAR
STOPPING CLEAR
NO
KEEP
LANE CLEAR
ONLY KEEP
EXIT
BUS STOP

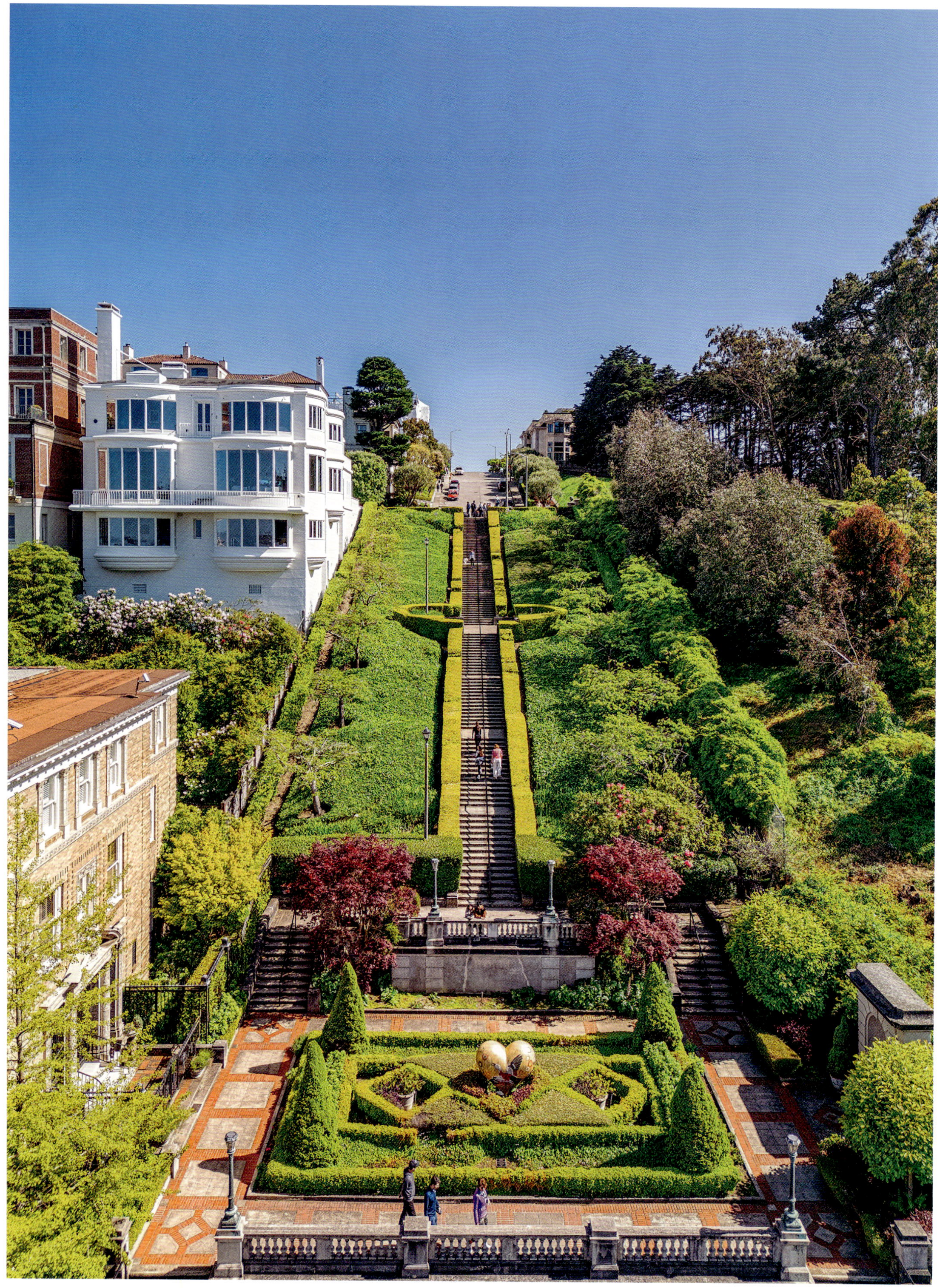

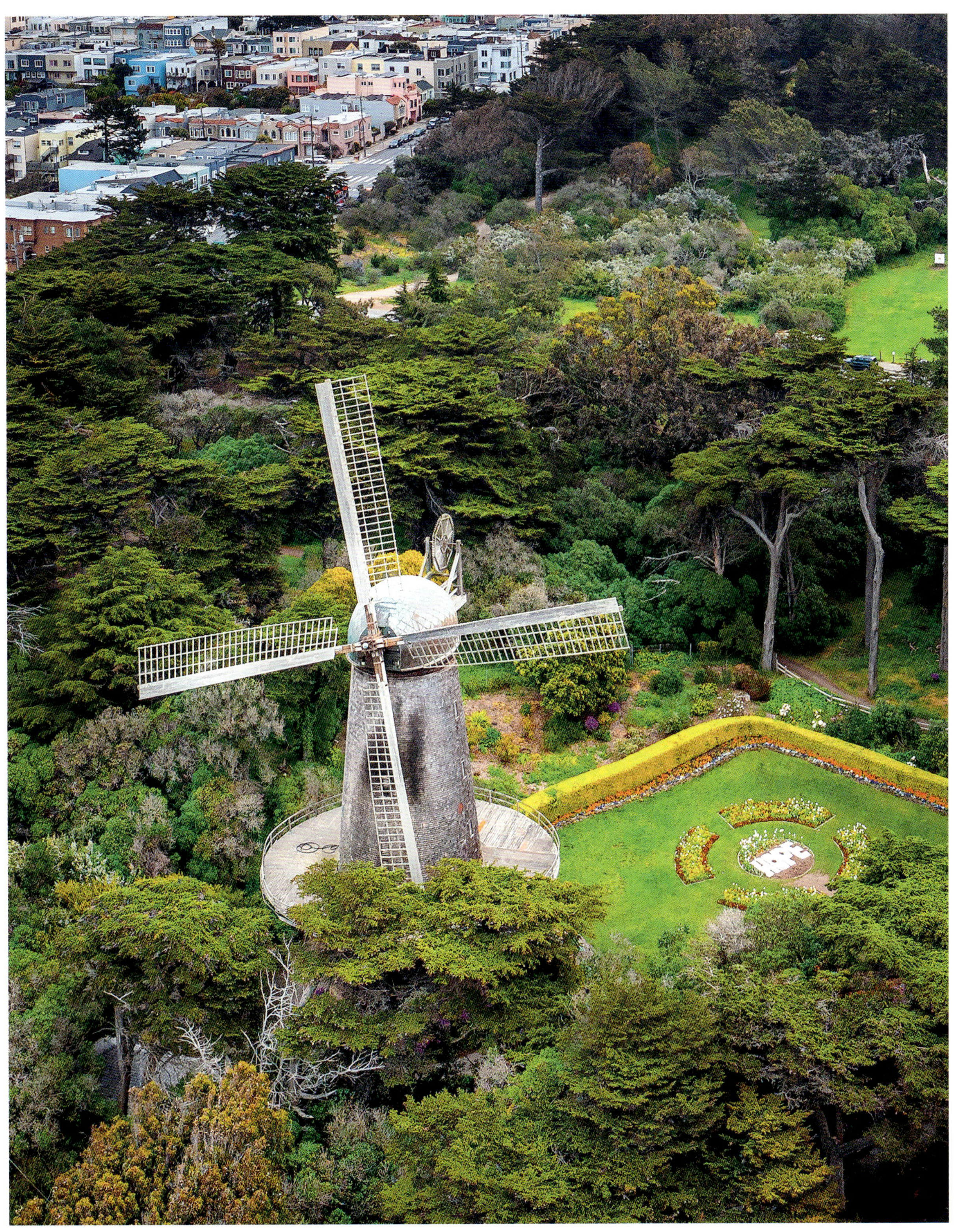

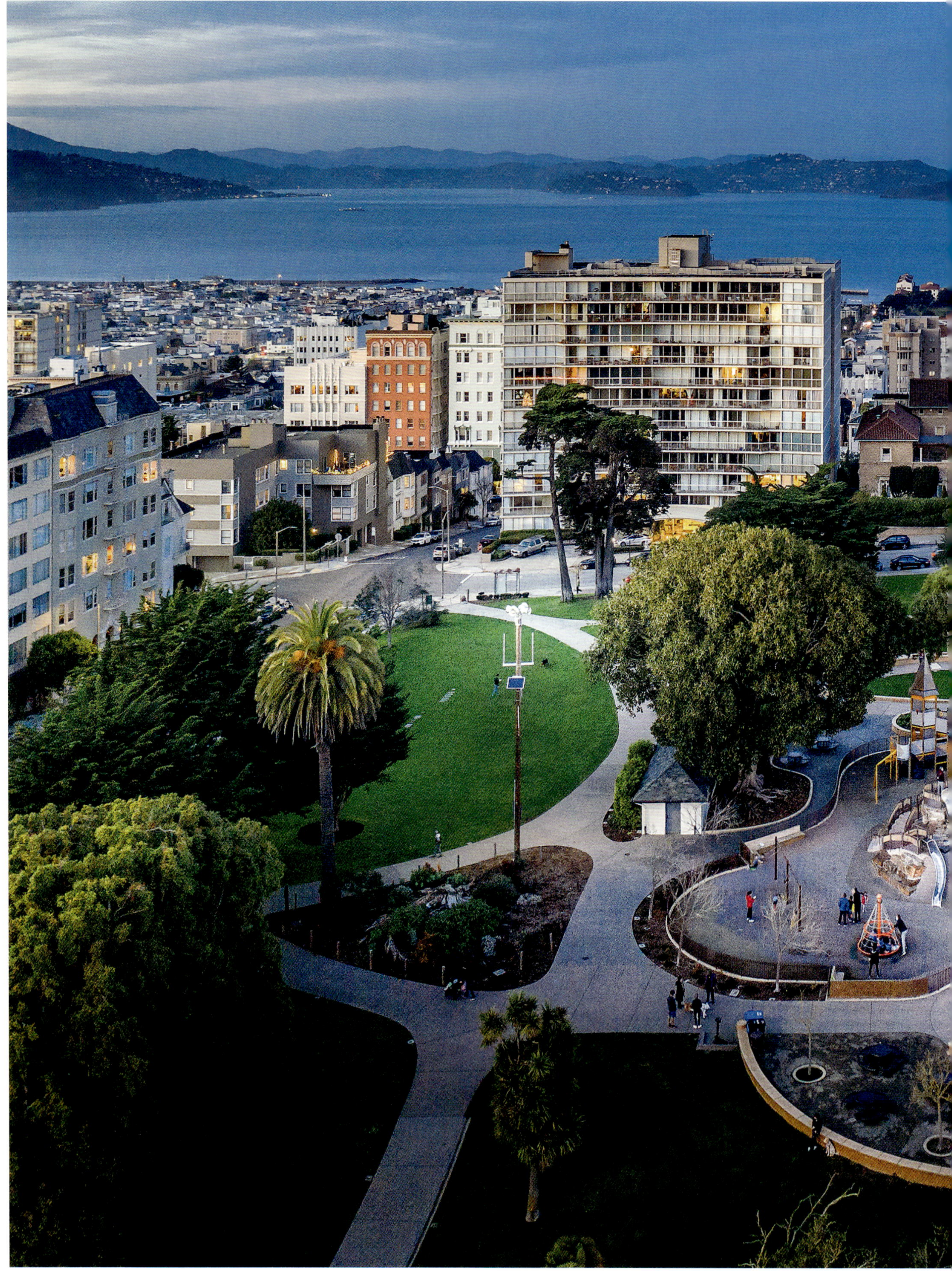

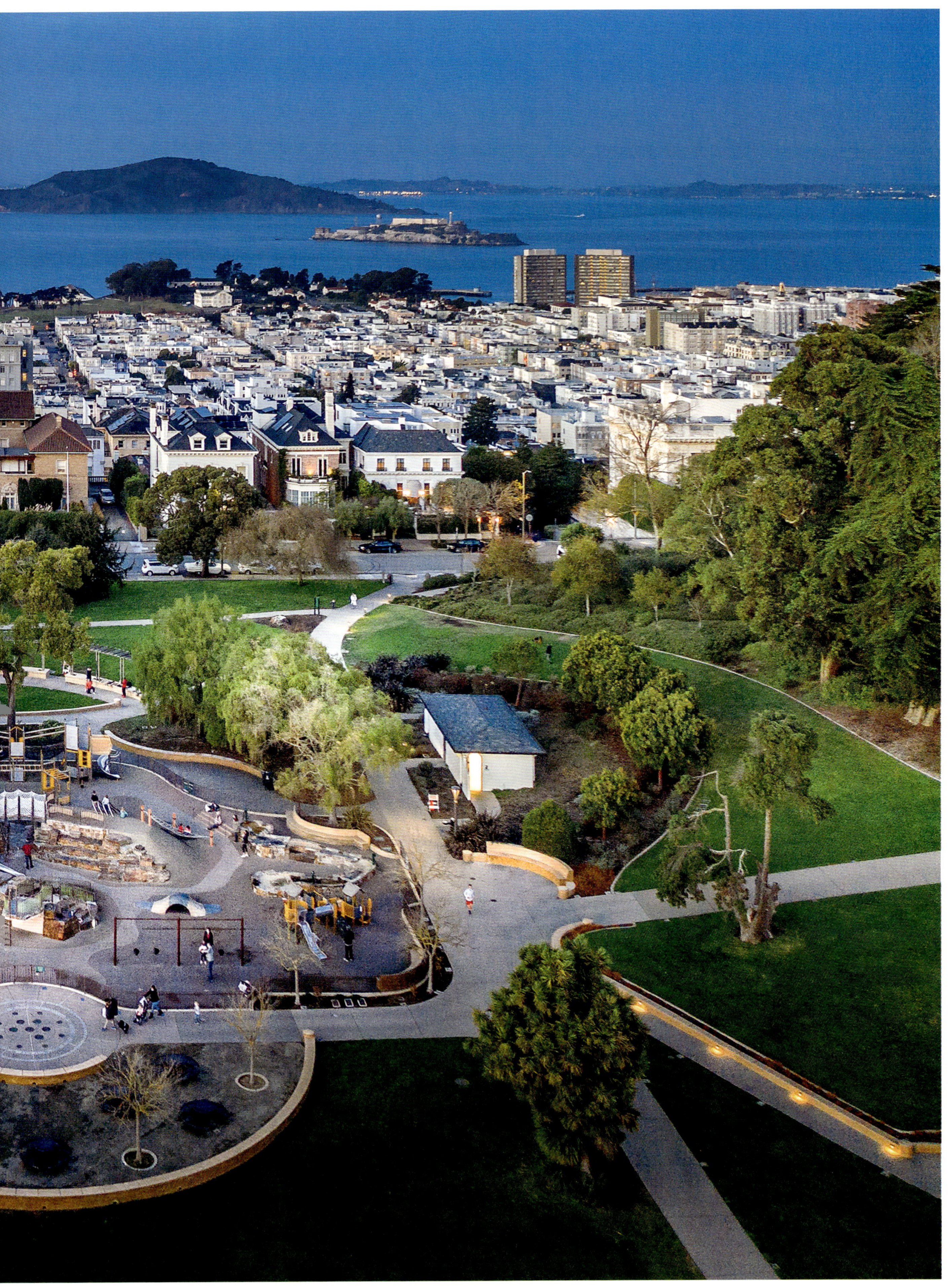

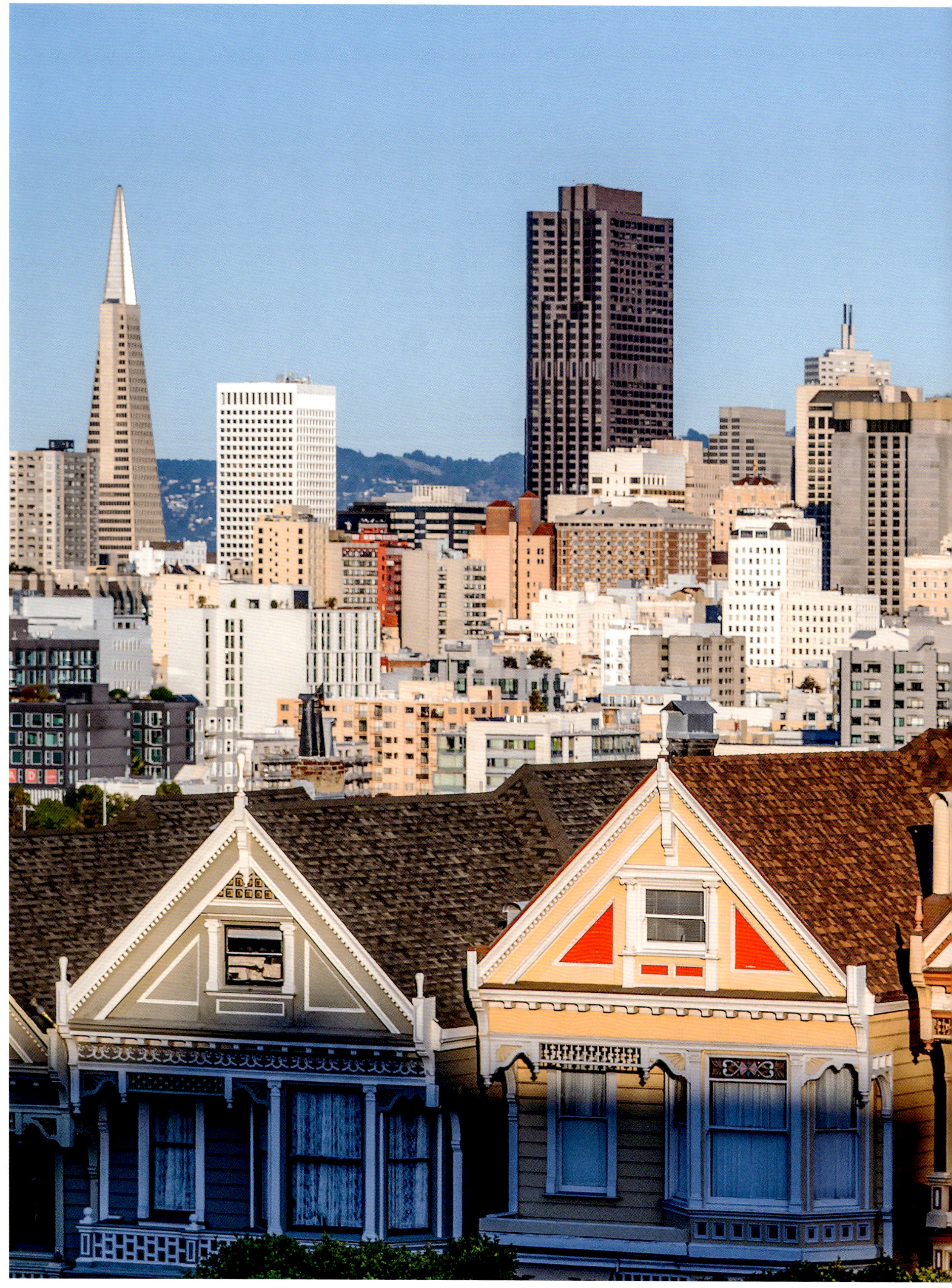

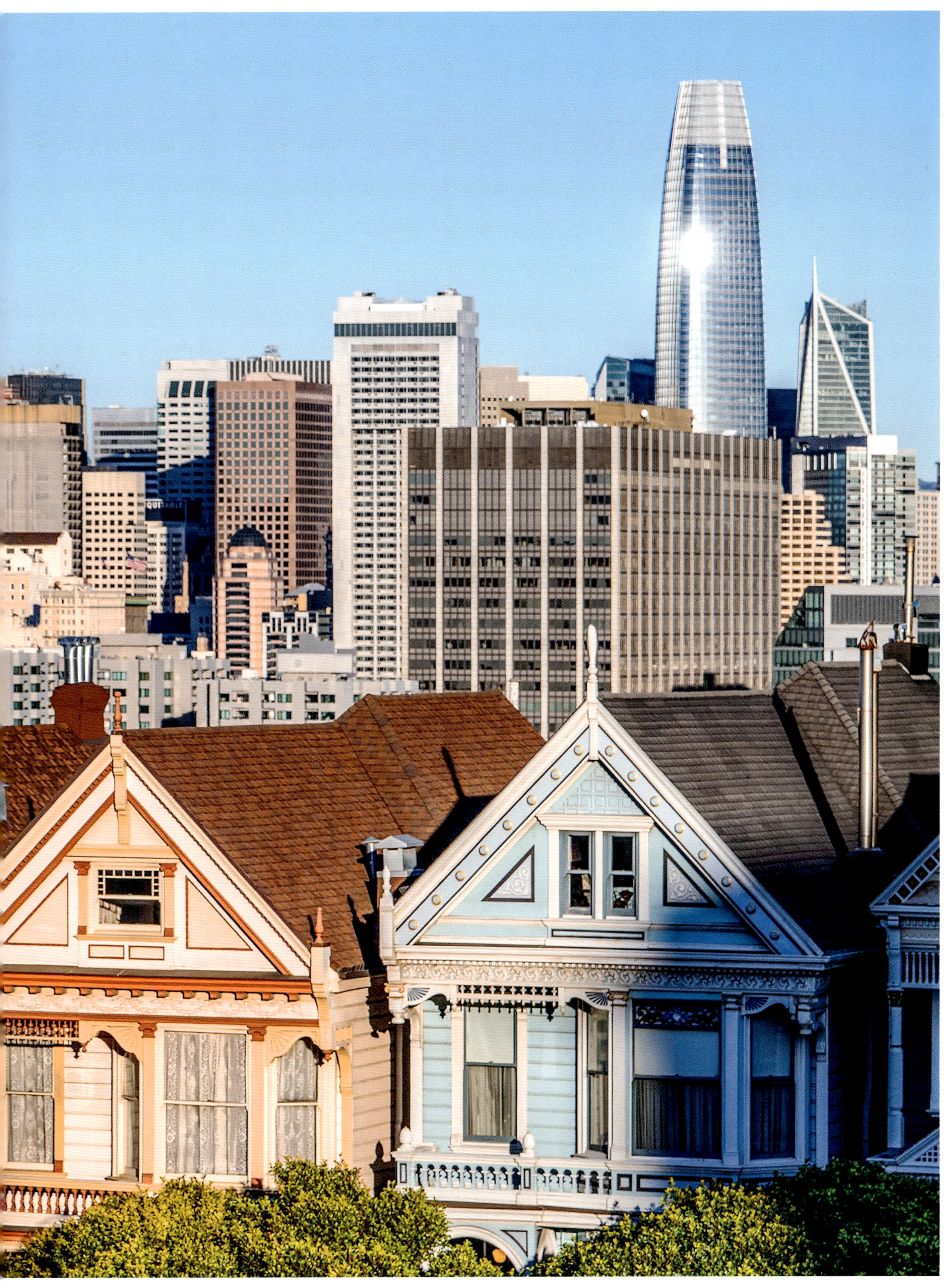

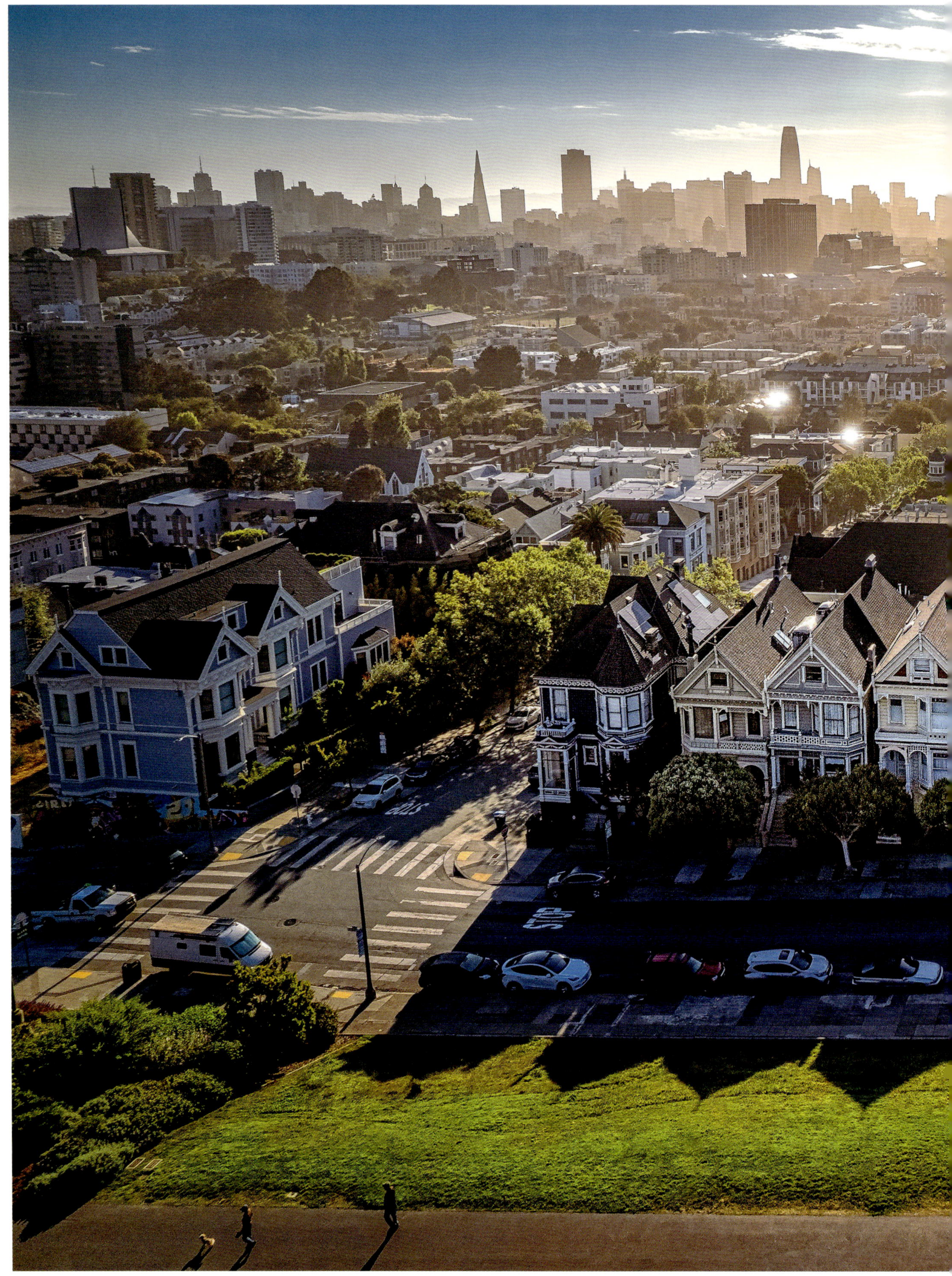

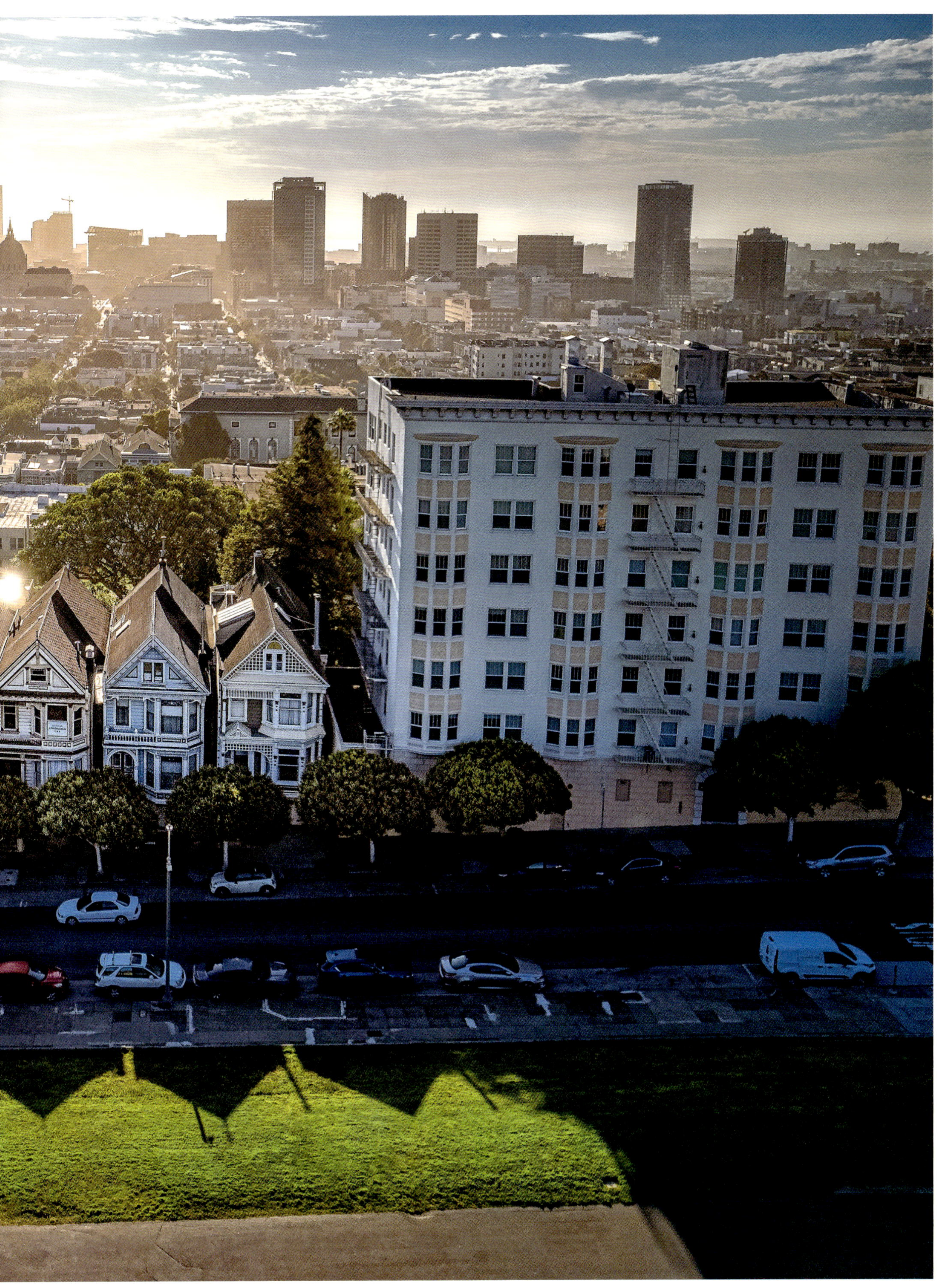

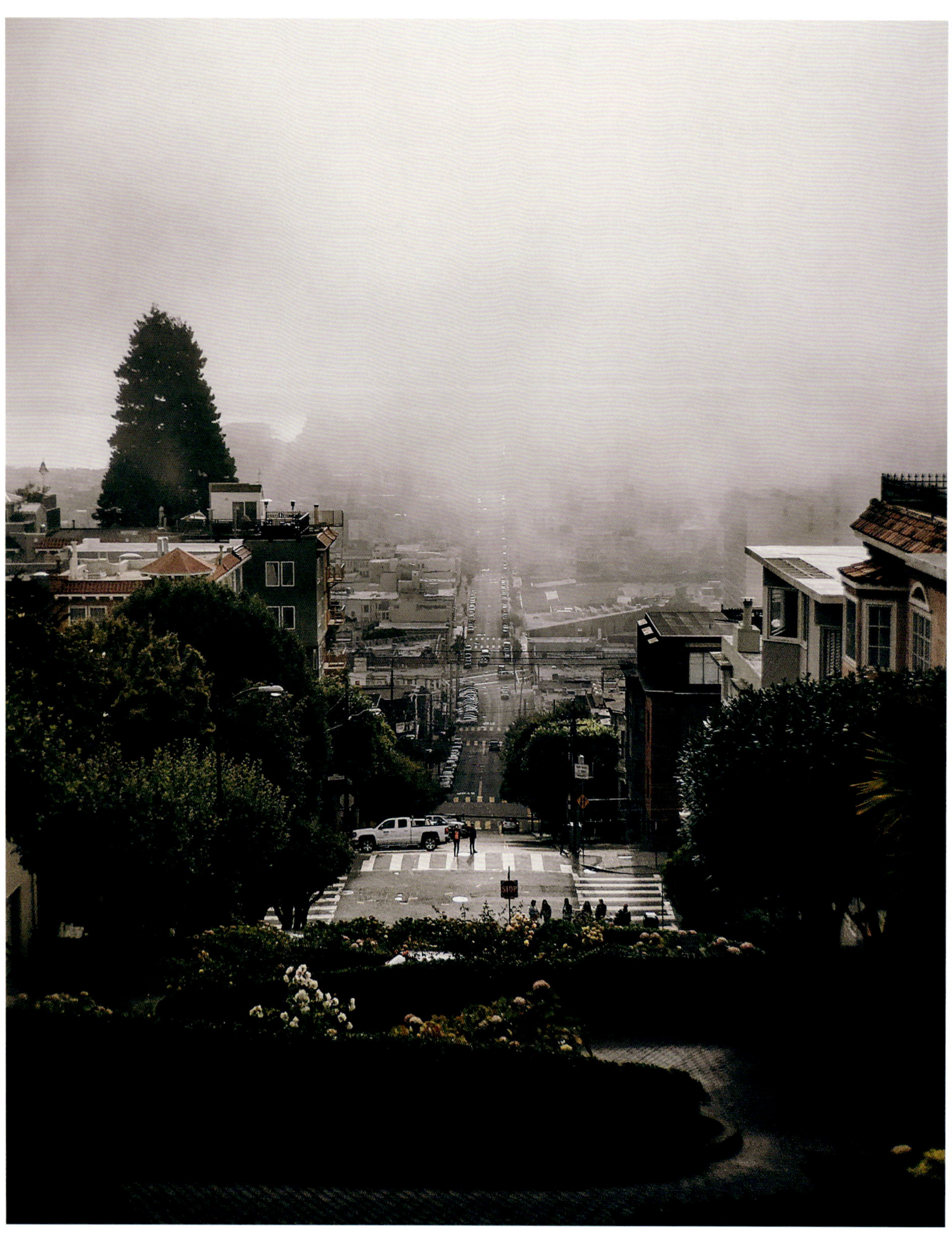

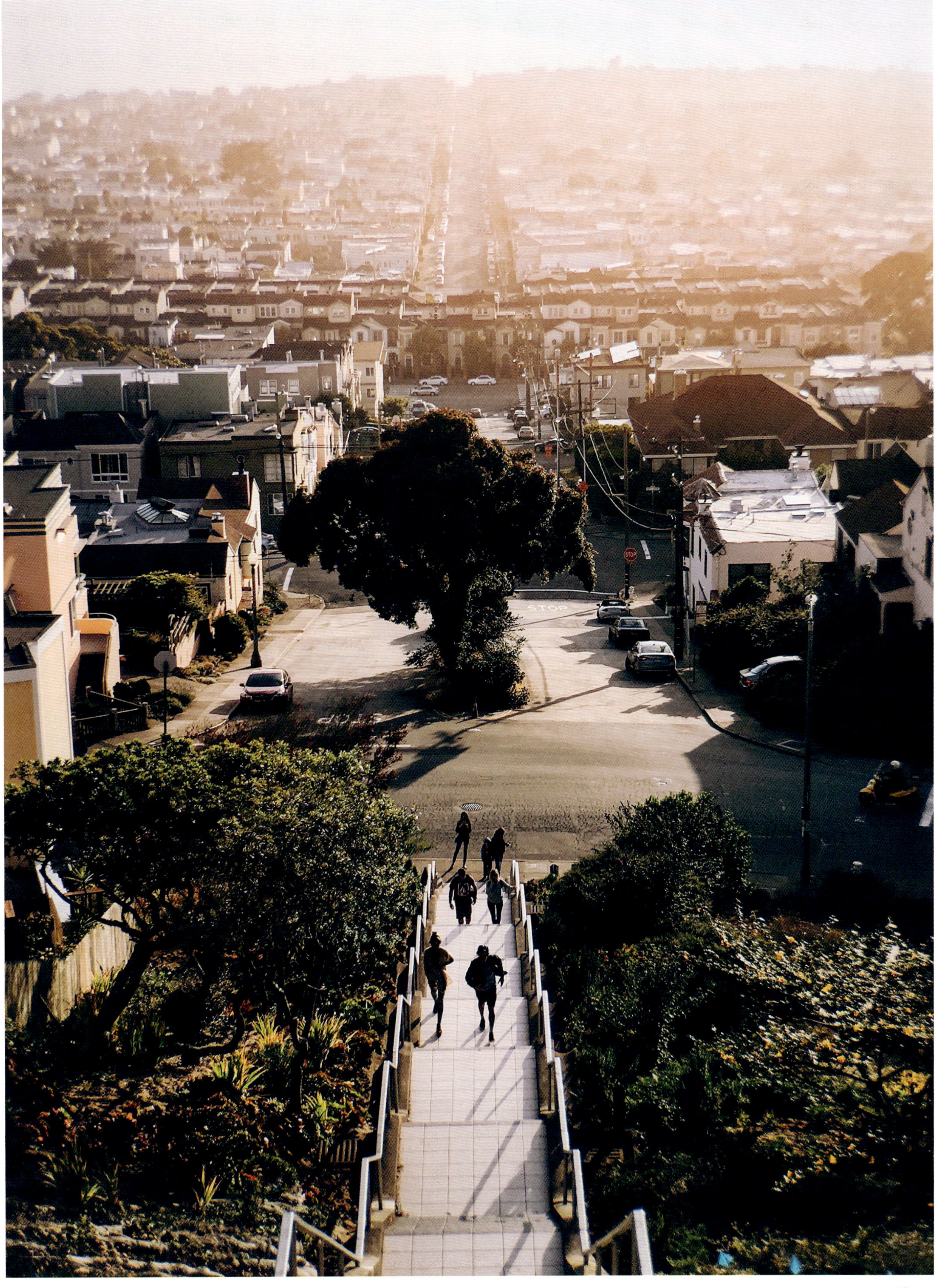

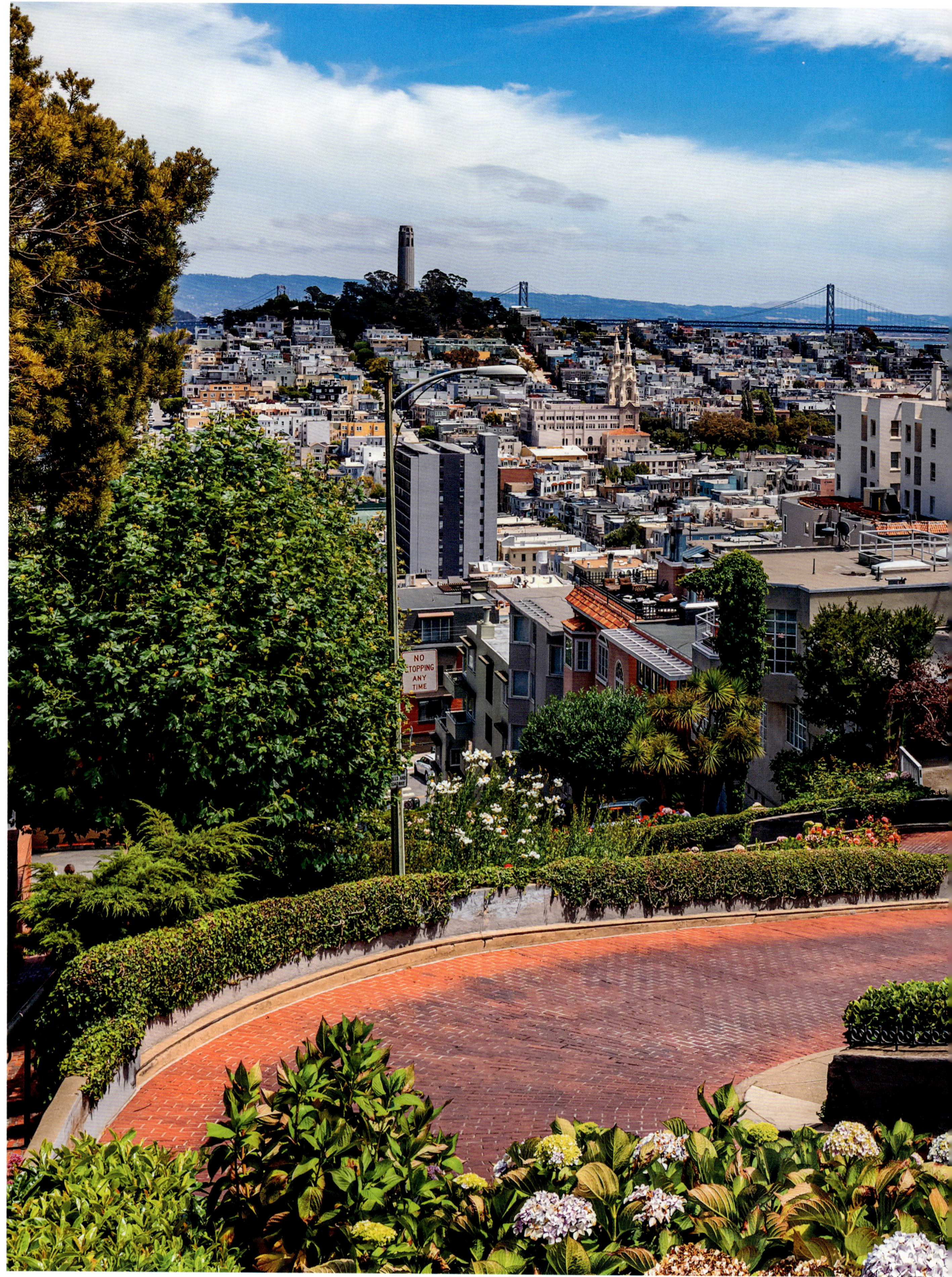

NO
STOPPING
ANY
TIME

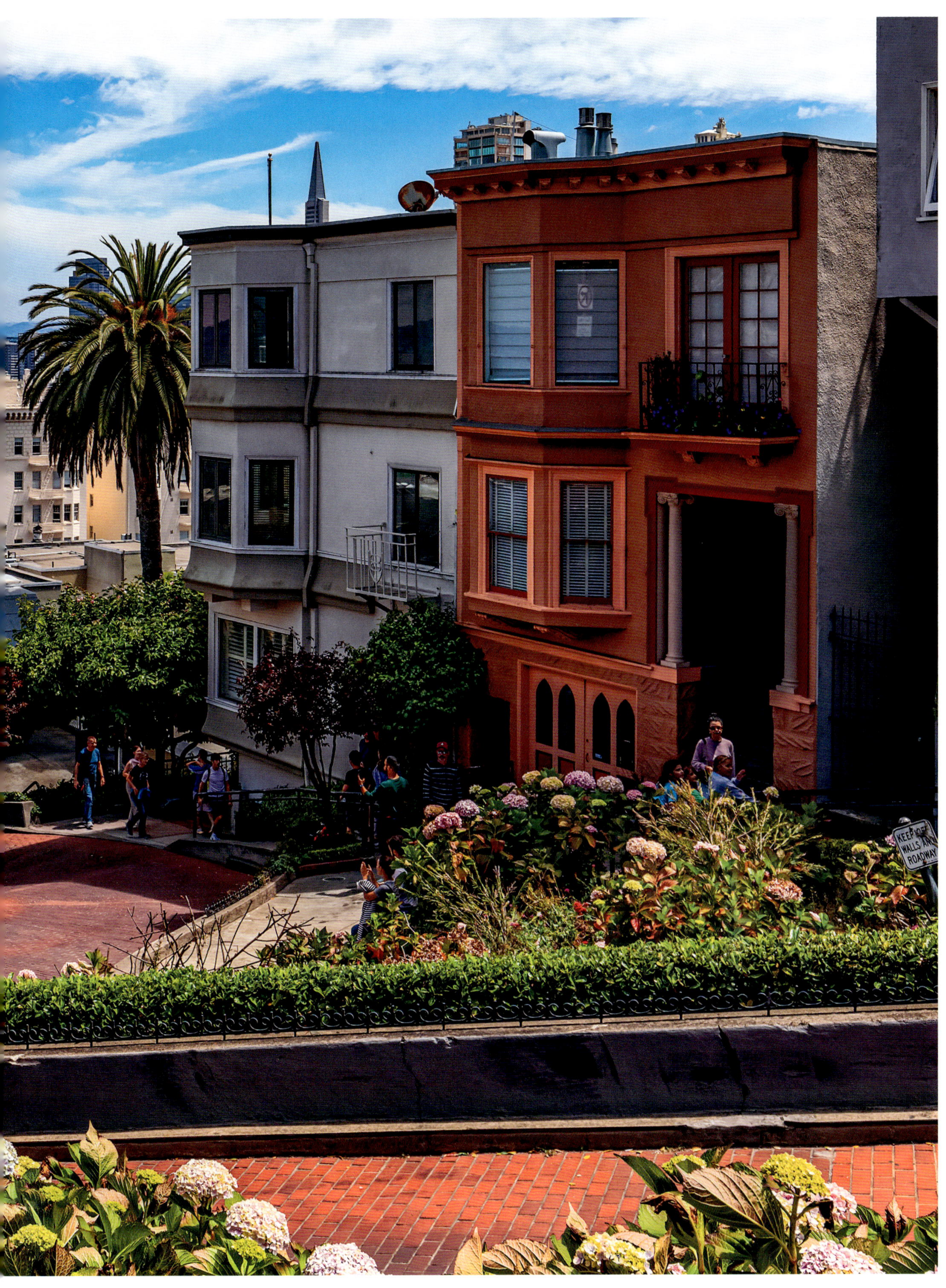

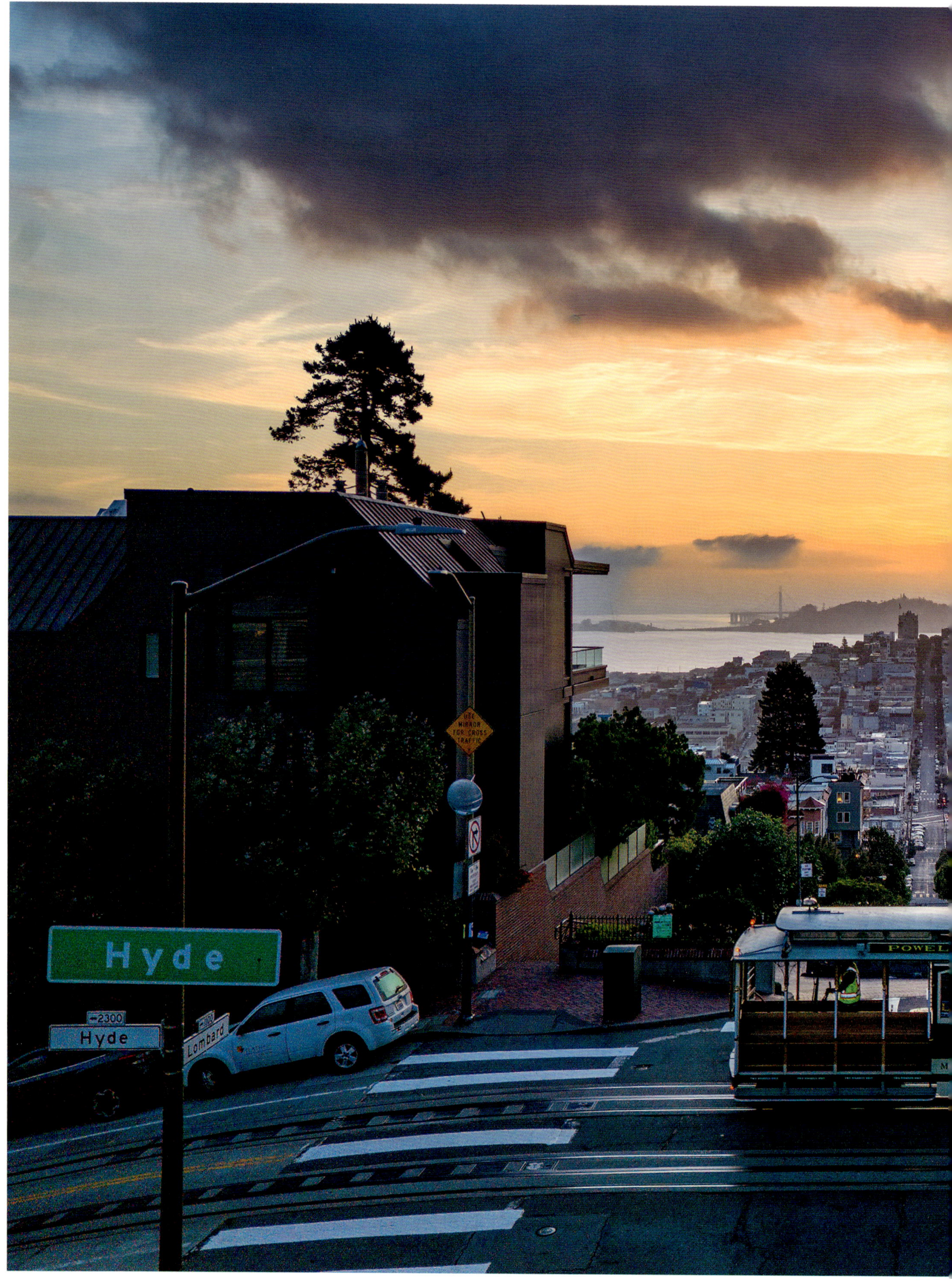

Hyde
2300
Hyde
Lombard
POWEL

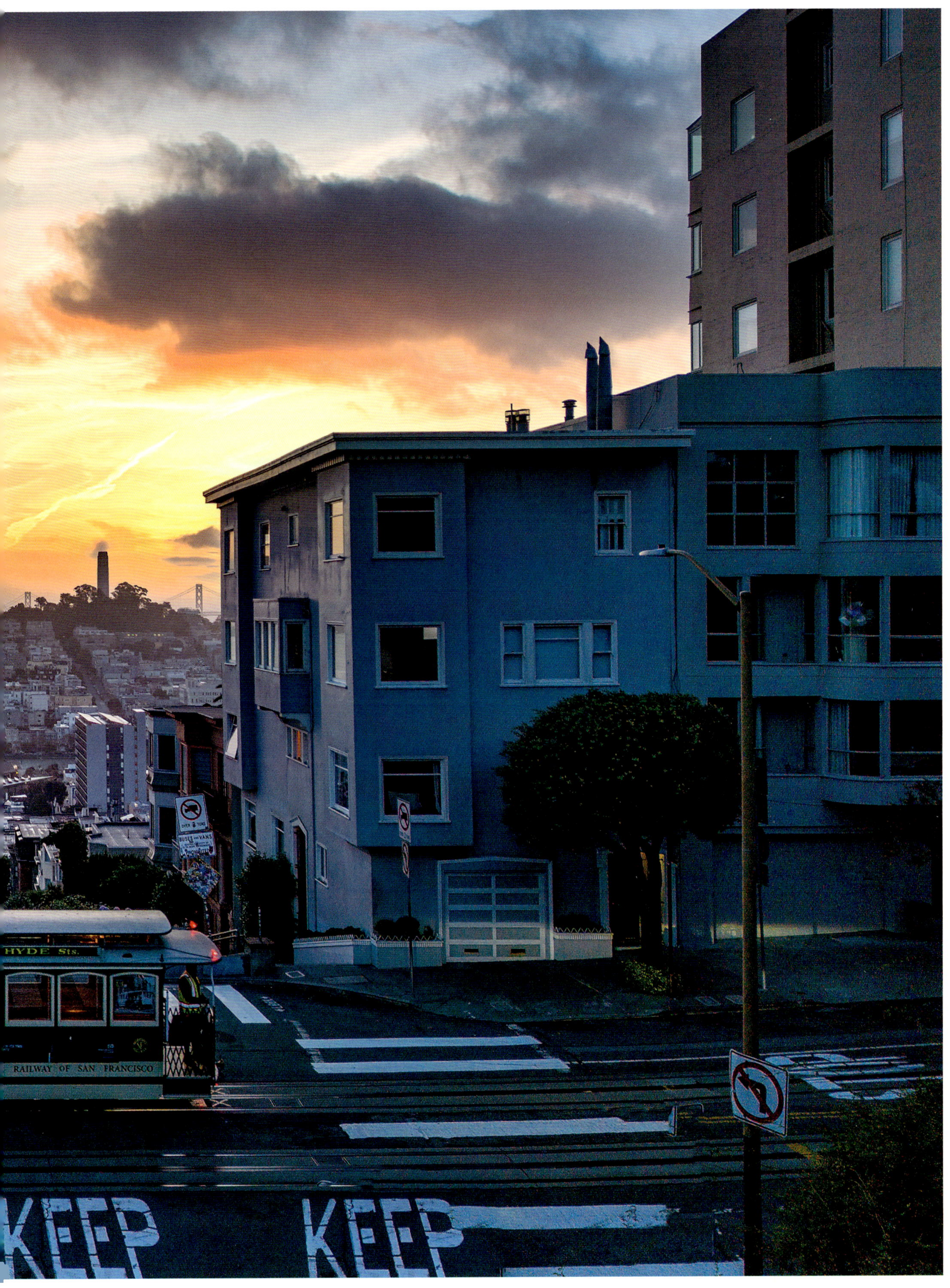
HYDE Sts
RAILWAY OF SAN FRANCISCO
KEEP
KEEP

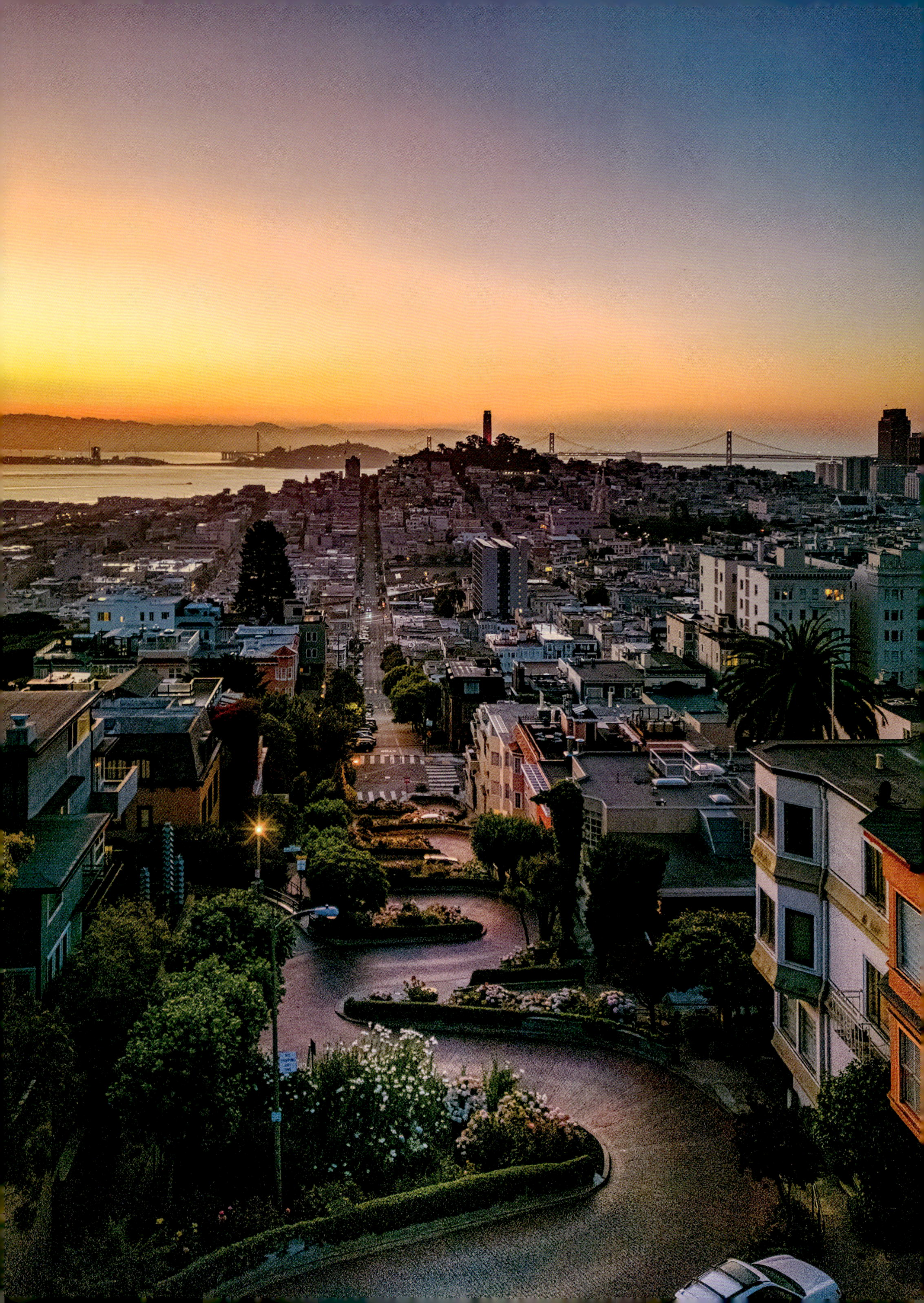

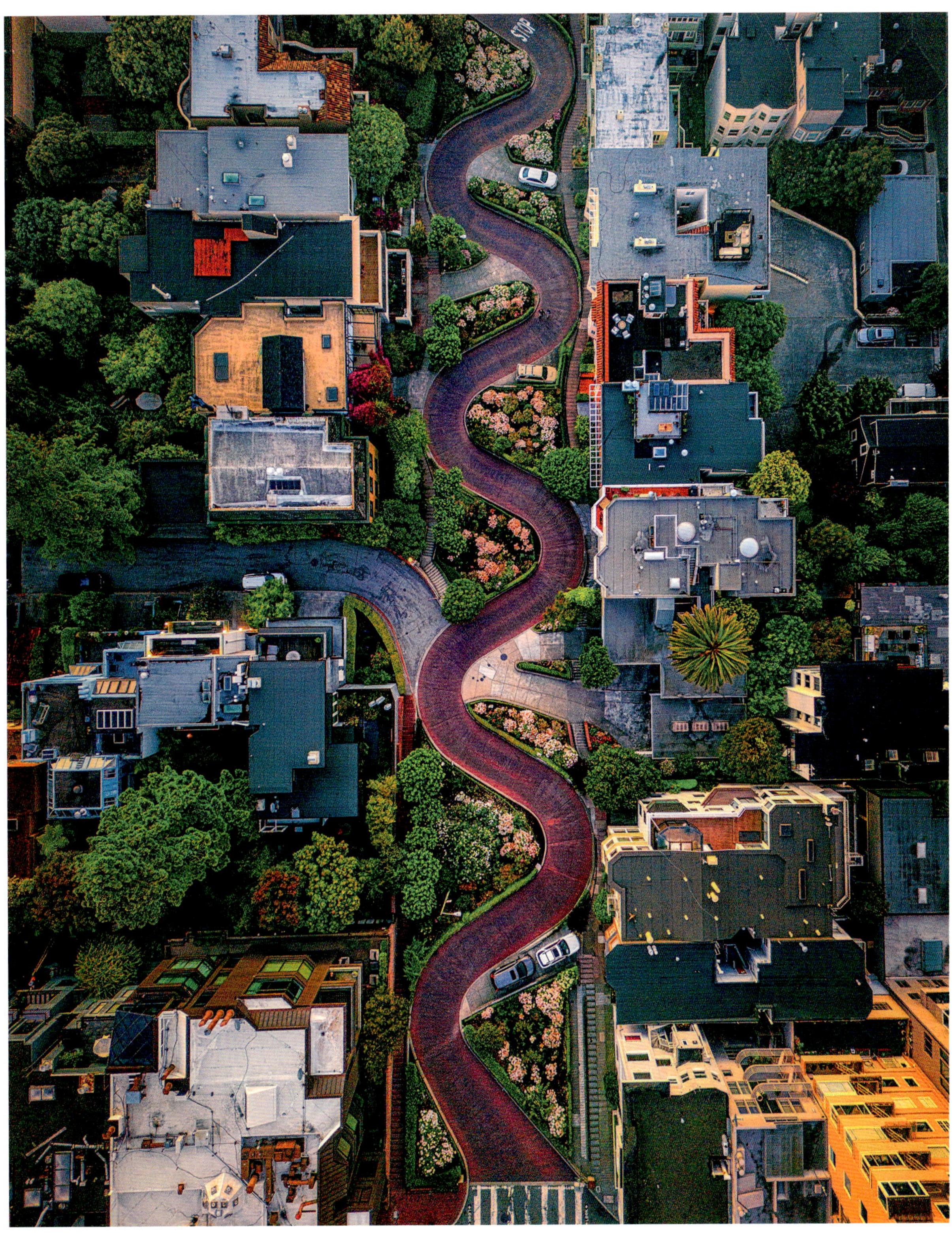

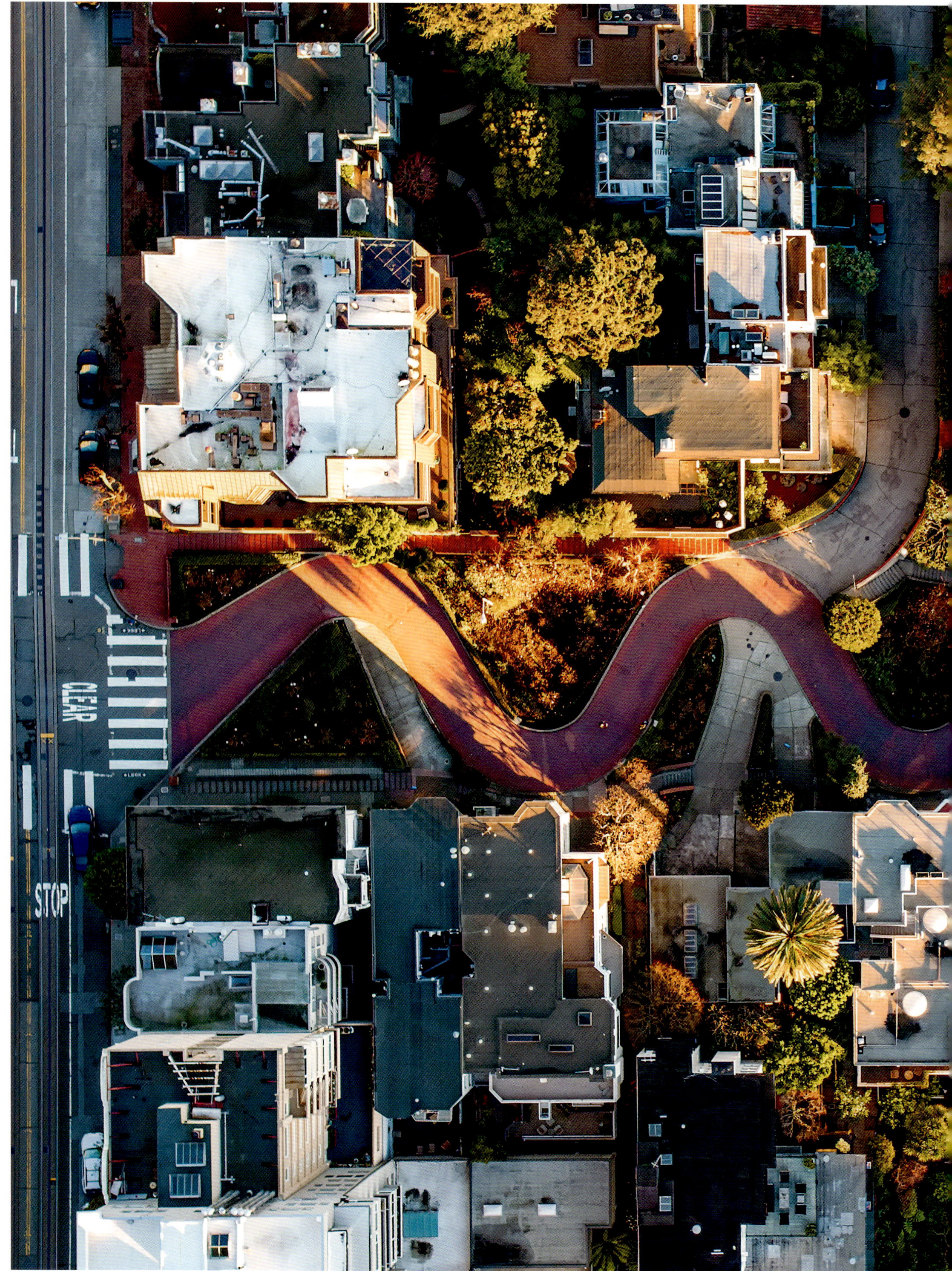
CLEAR
STOP

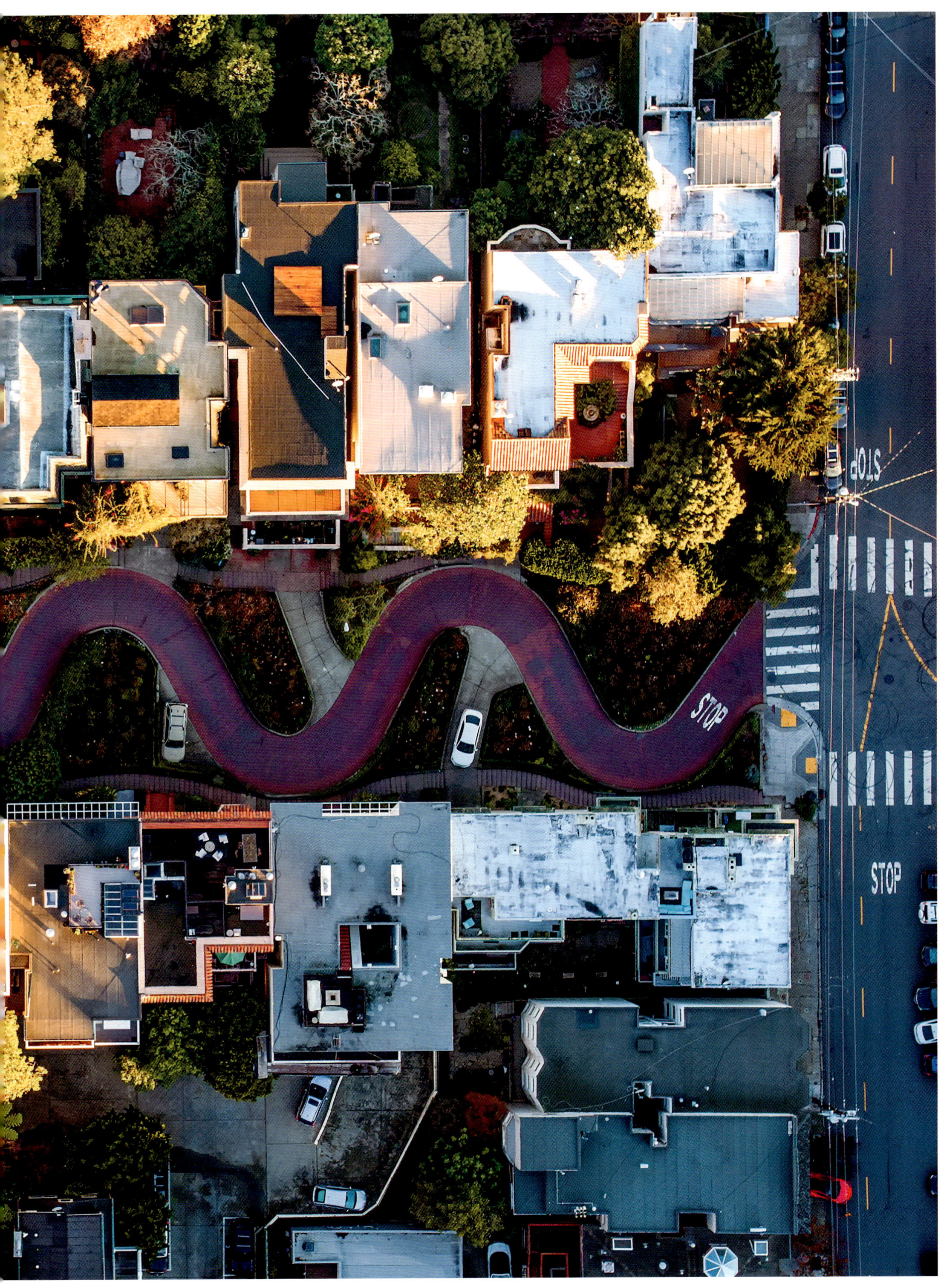

STOP
STOP
STOP

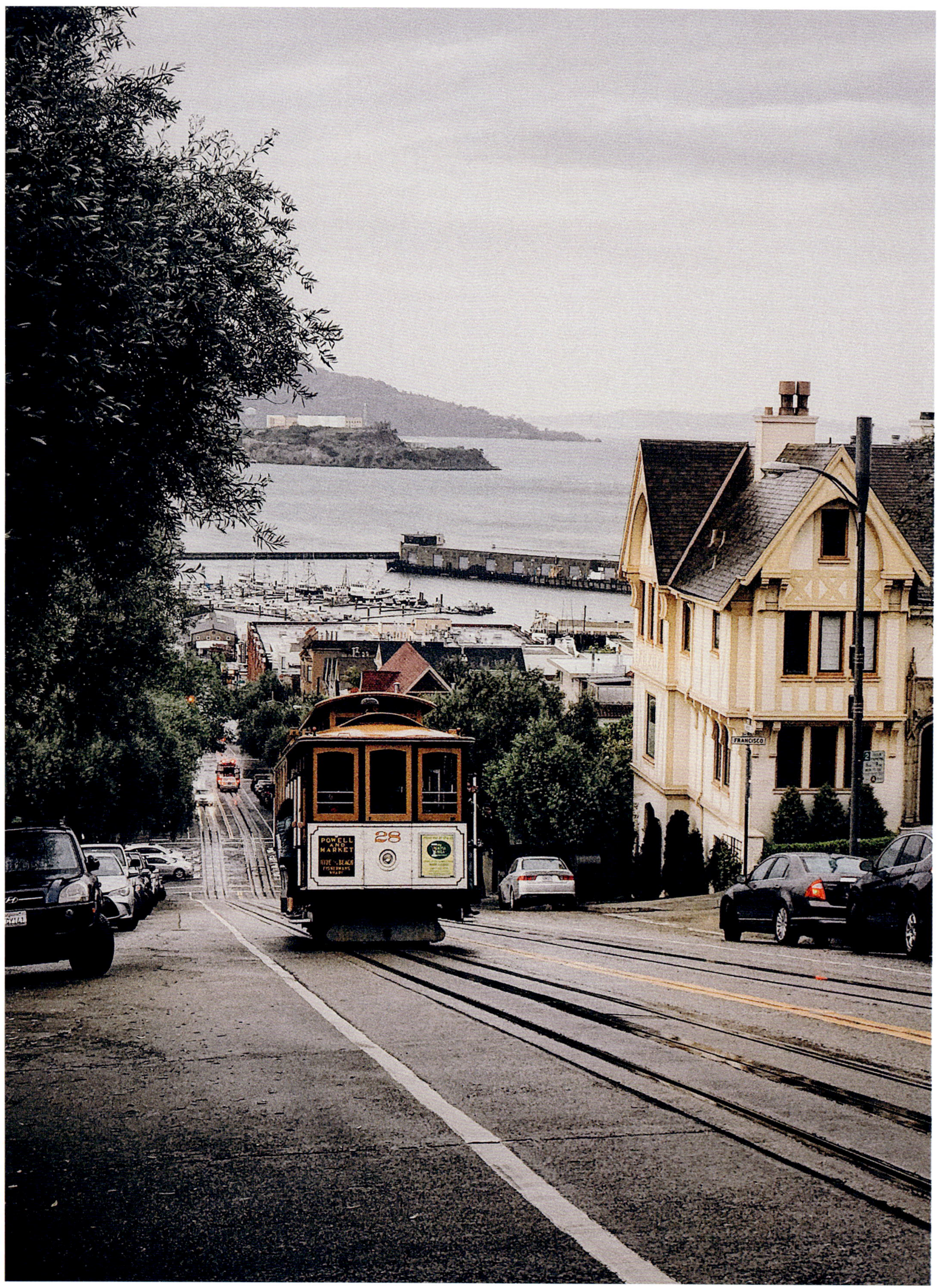

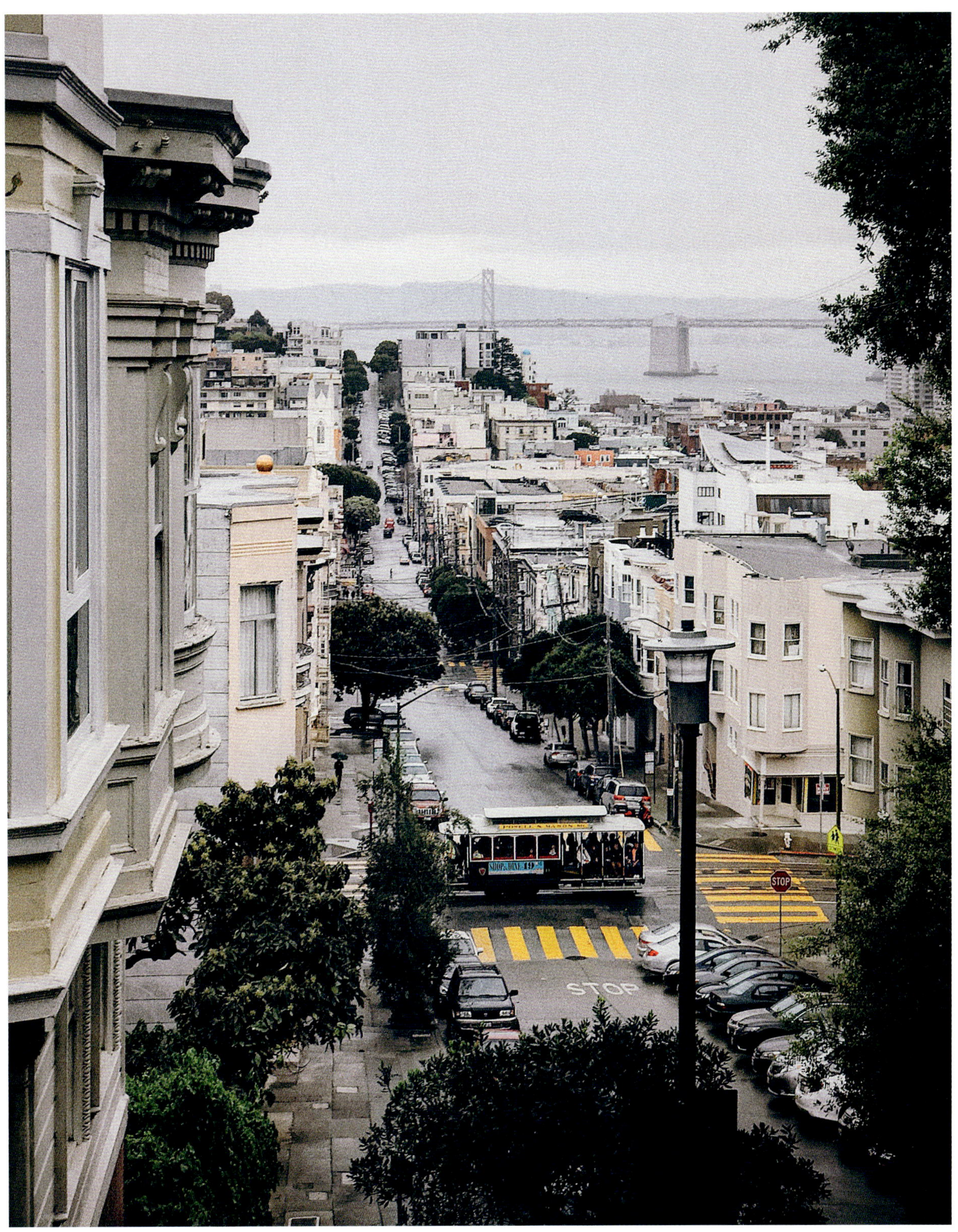

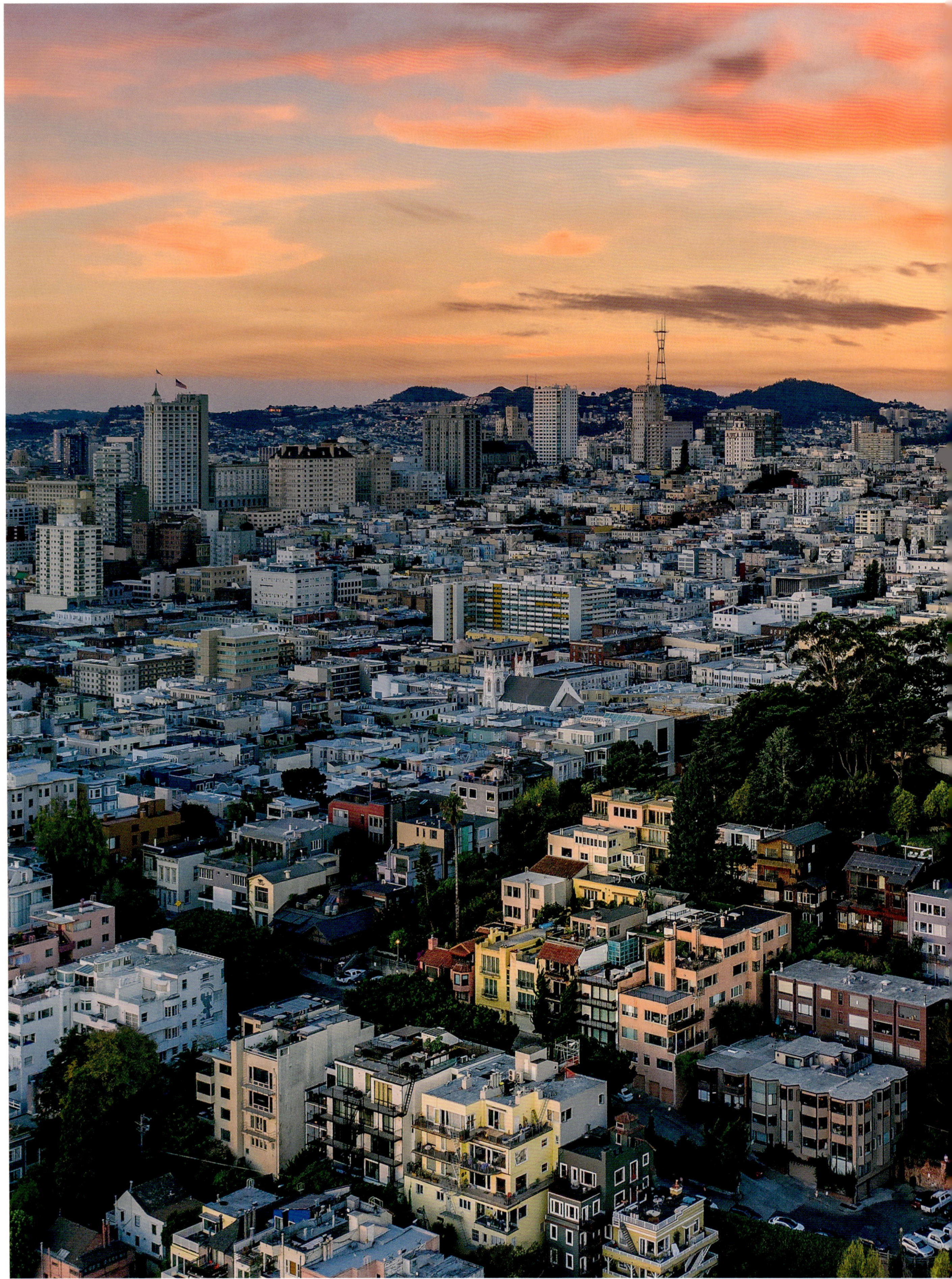

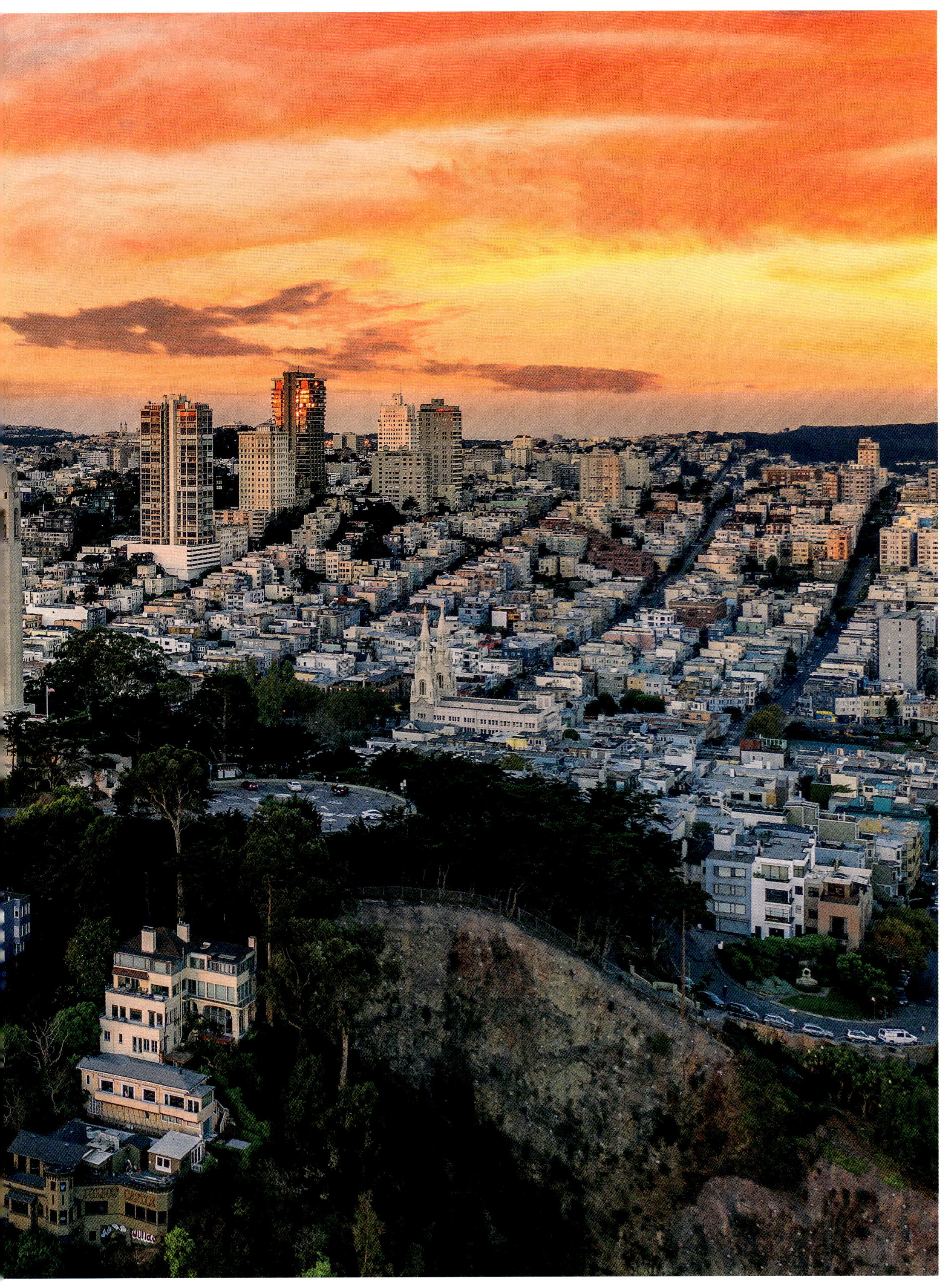

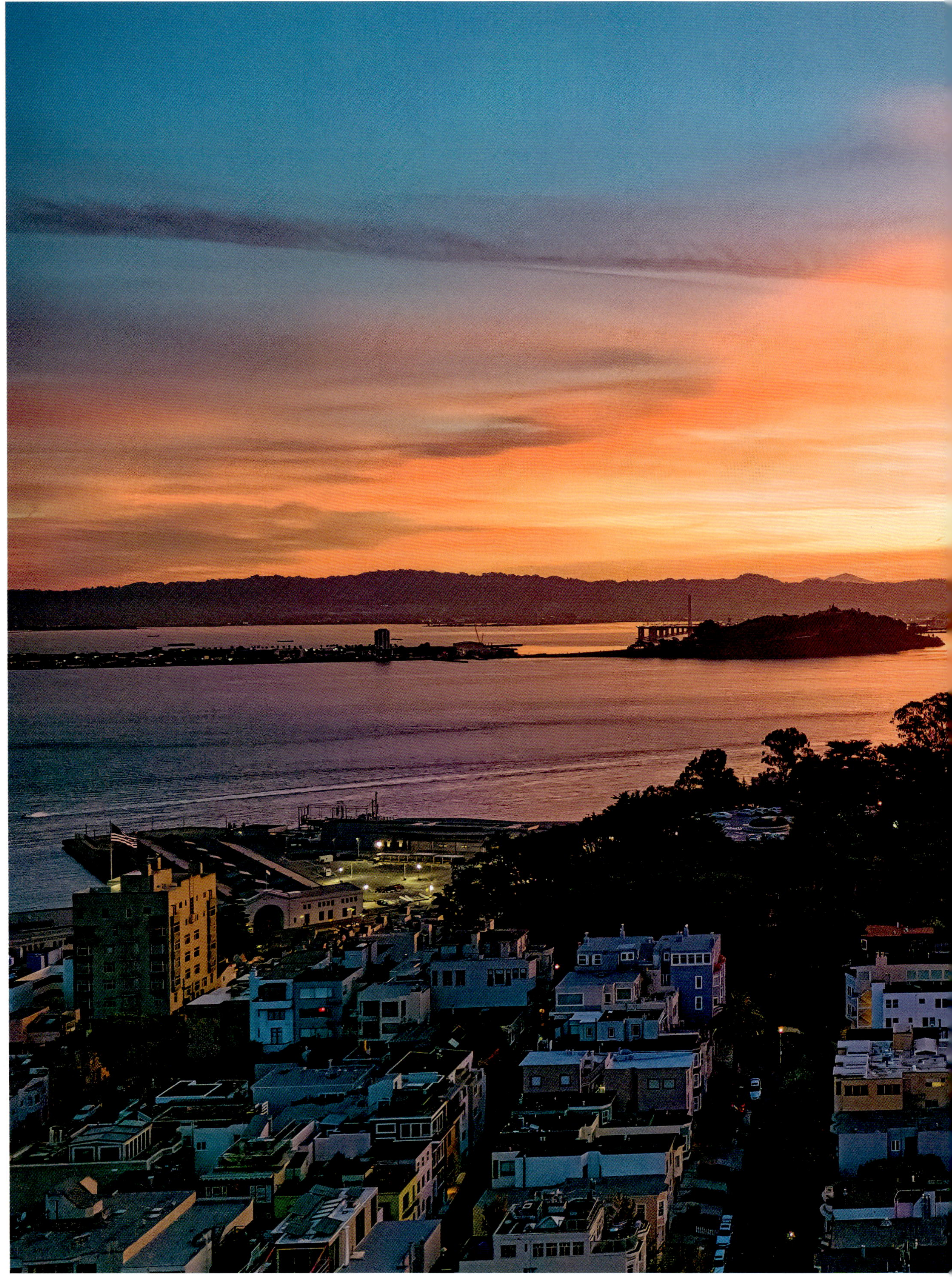

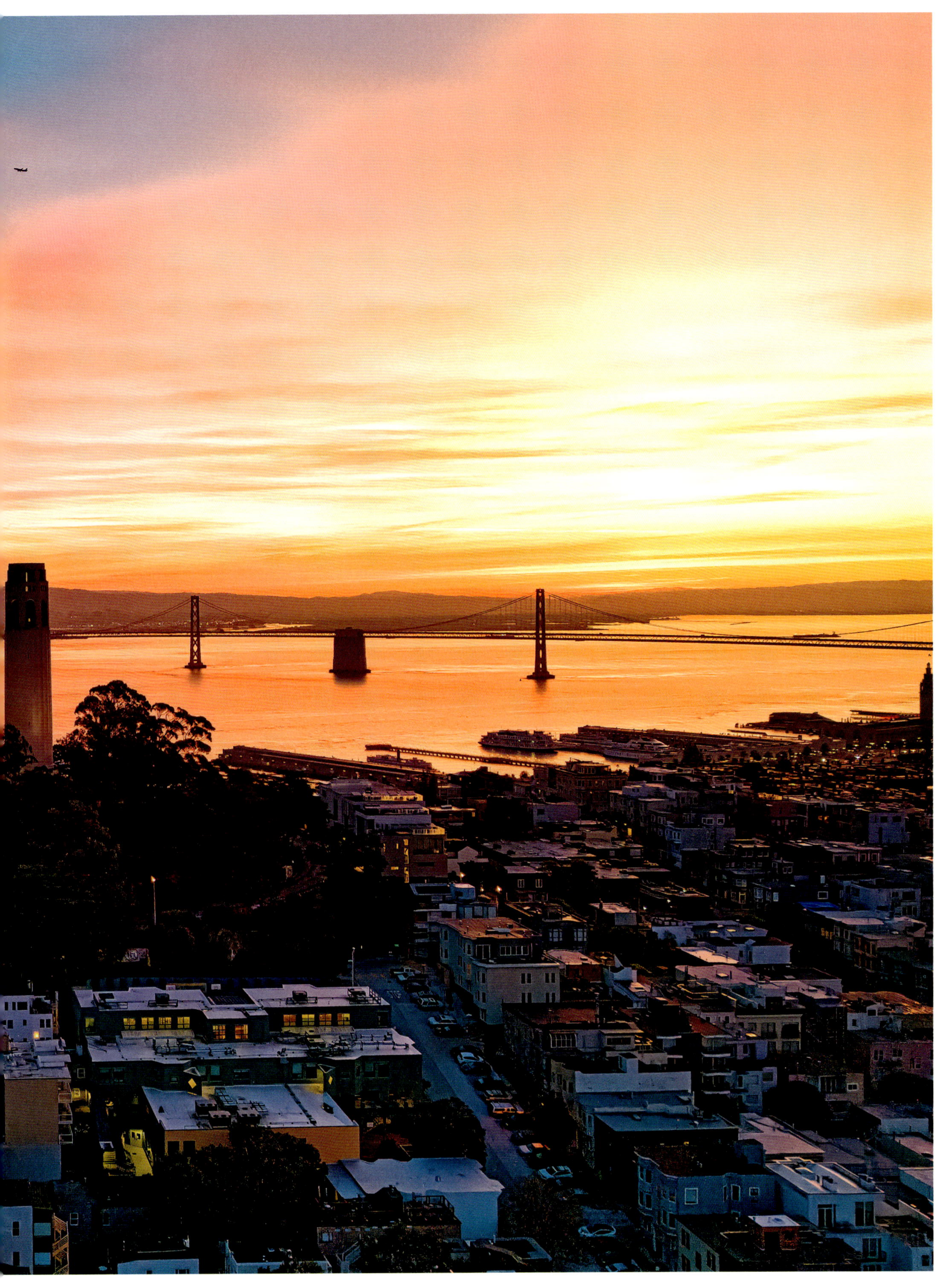

The Bridges ◆ The two bridges that connect San Francisco to other areas of northern California, the Golden Gate Bridge and the San Francisco-Oakland Bay Bridge, are both feats of modern engineering and design, as well as vital transportation connections. They shape the city's skyline and also serve the practical purpose of helping the city's hundreds of thousands of residents get where they need to go each day. ◆ The Golden Gate Bridge spans 1.7 miles across the Golden Gate Strait, the entrance to the San Francisco Bay from the Pacific Ocean, connecting San Francisco to Marin County in the north. Completed in 1937, the Golden Gate Bridge was the longest and tallest suspension bridge in the world when it was completed. Its two main towers rise 746 feet above the water. Featuring Art Deco elements, particularly in the design of its towers and walkways, the bridge is recognized worldwide for its distinctive color "International Orange" that was chosen not only for aesthetic appeal, but also to aid in visibility through the city's persistent fog. ◆ The San Francisco-Oakland Bay Bridge, typically referred to simply as the Bay Bridge, links San Francisco to Oakland in the east and the larger East Bay region. When the Bay Bridge was completed in 1936, it was the longest bridge of its kind in the world. Consisting of two major spans, a western span that runs from San Francisco to Yerba Buena Island, and an eastern span that stretches from Yerba Buena Island to Oakland, the Bay Bridge is 8.4 miles long in total, including its approaches, tunnels, and connectors. It remains one of the longest bridges in the world.

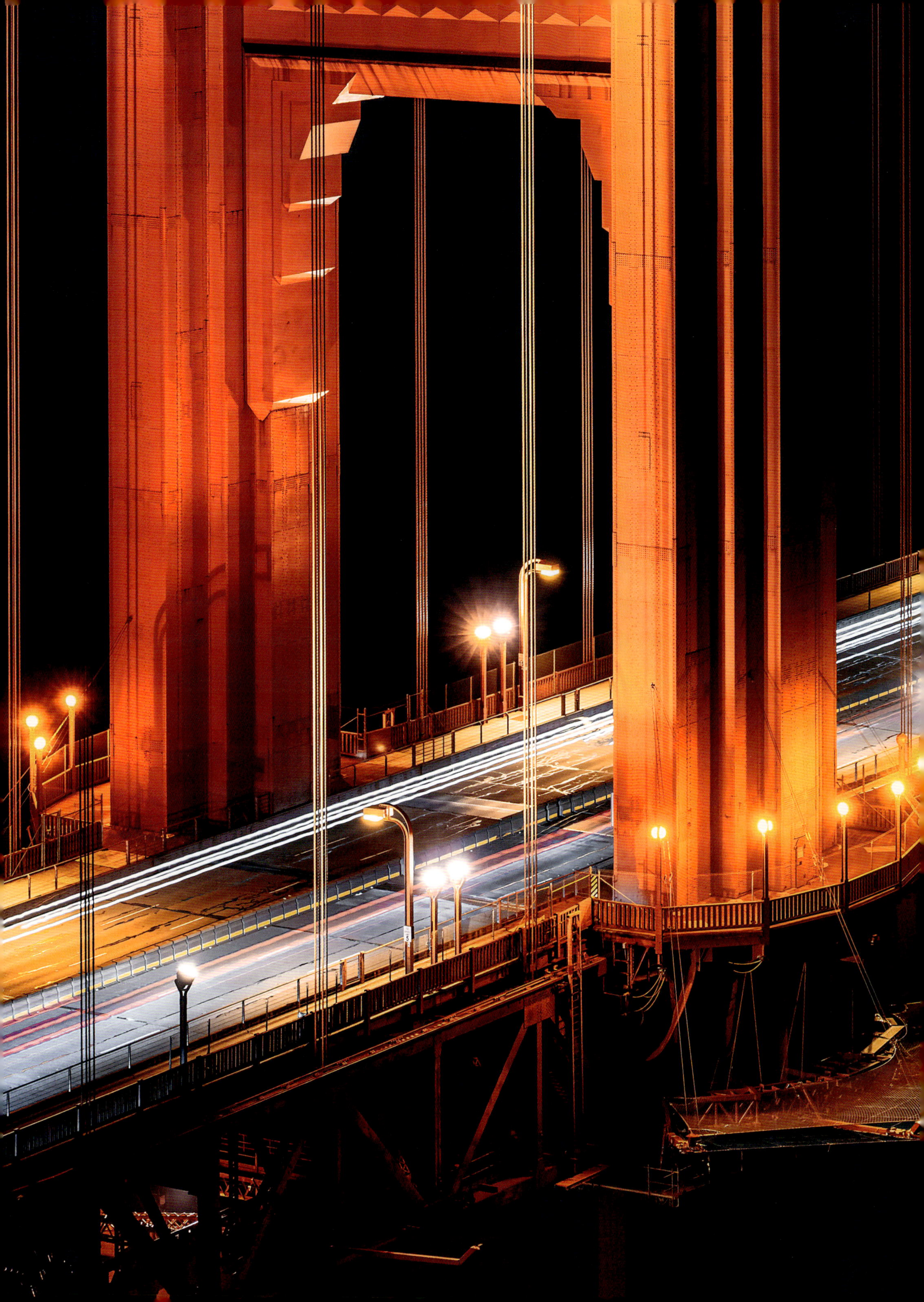

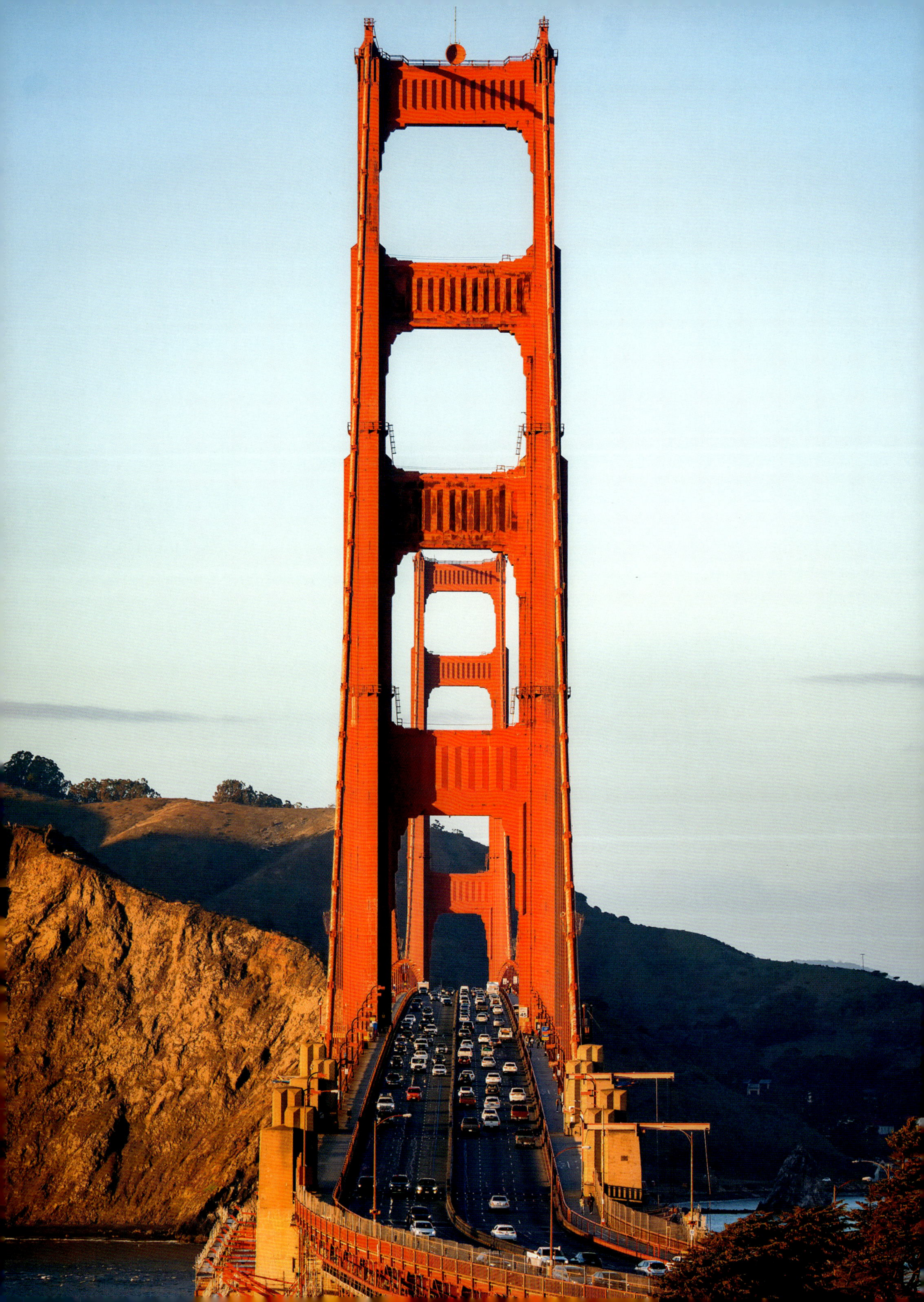

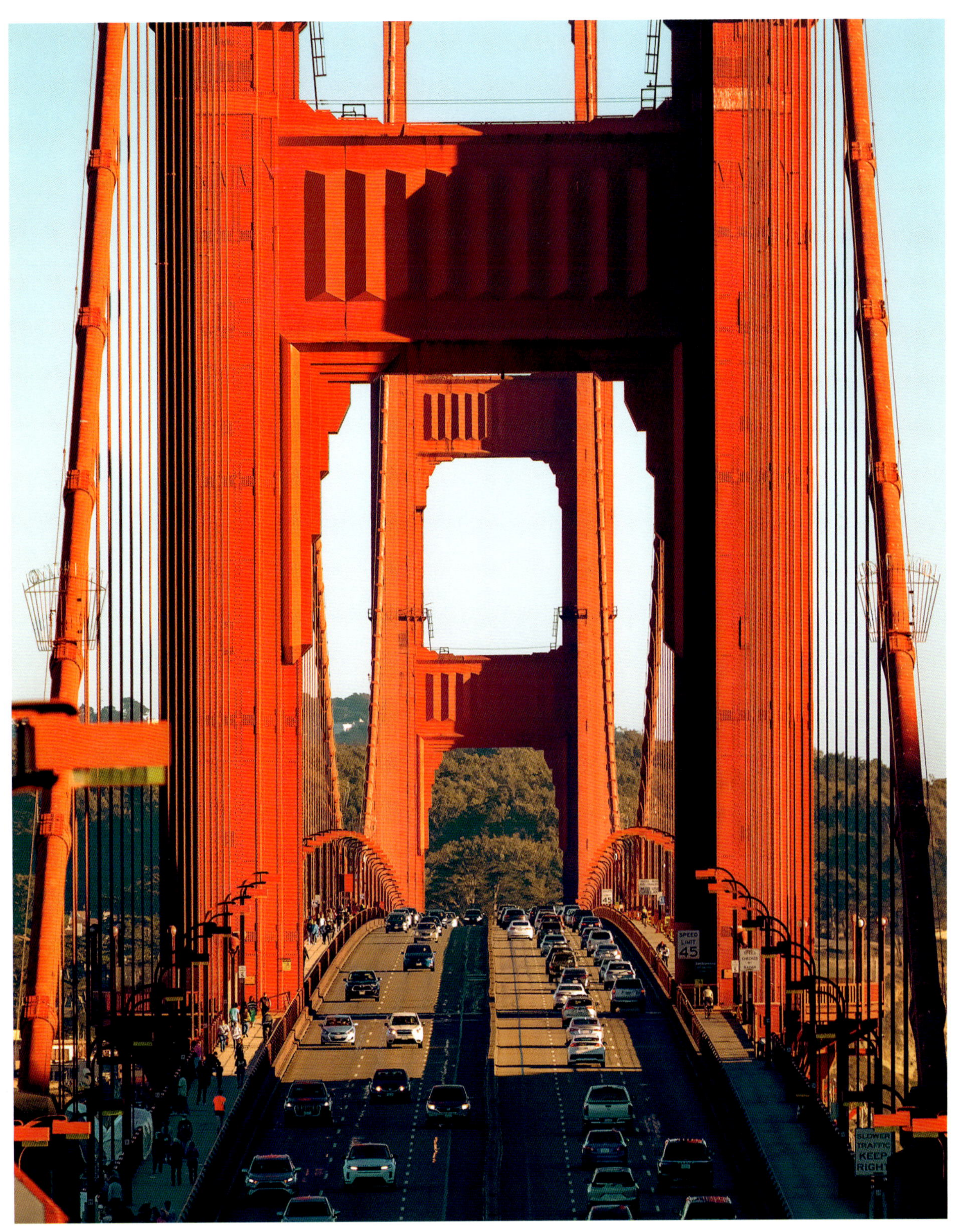

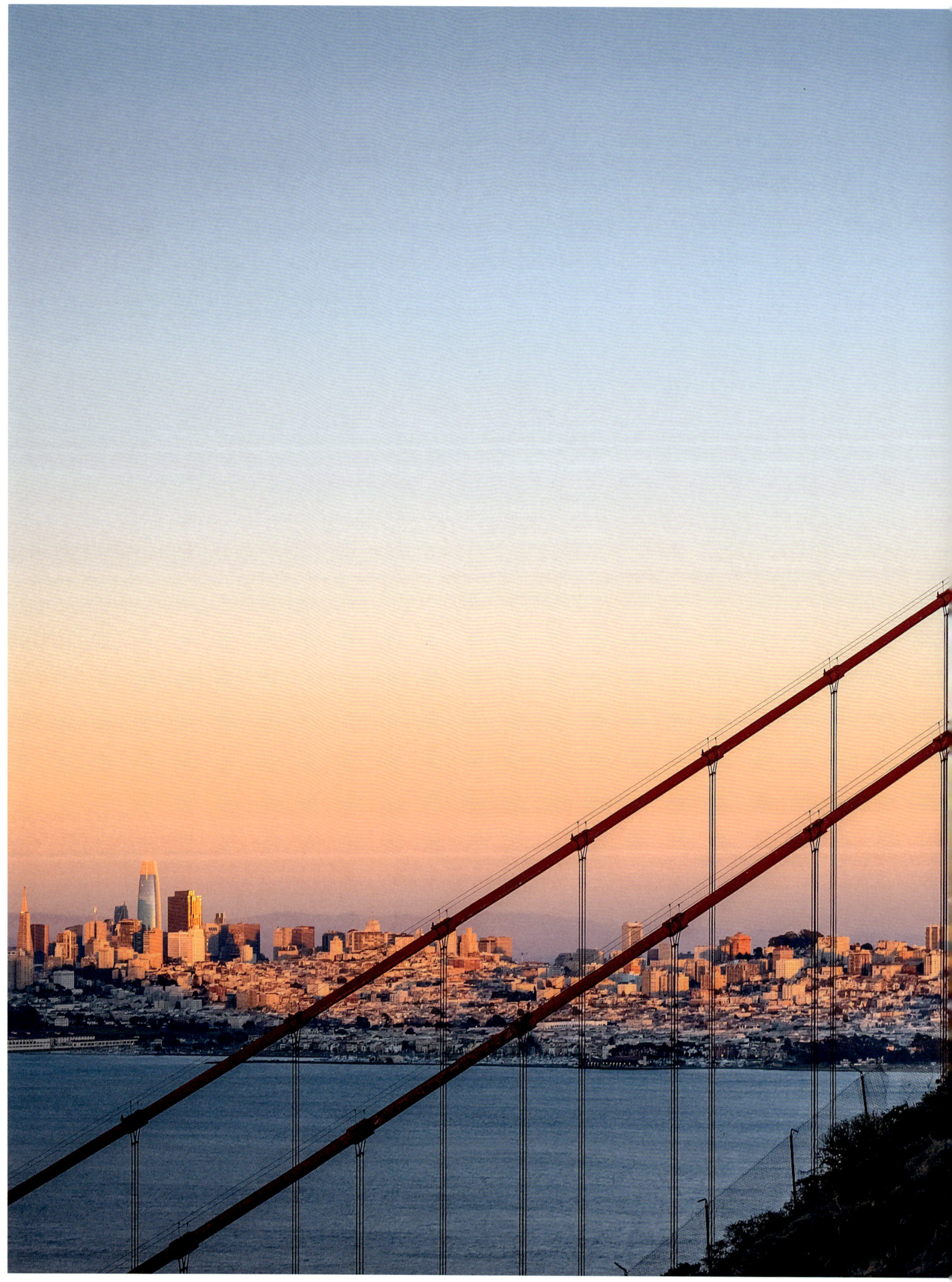

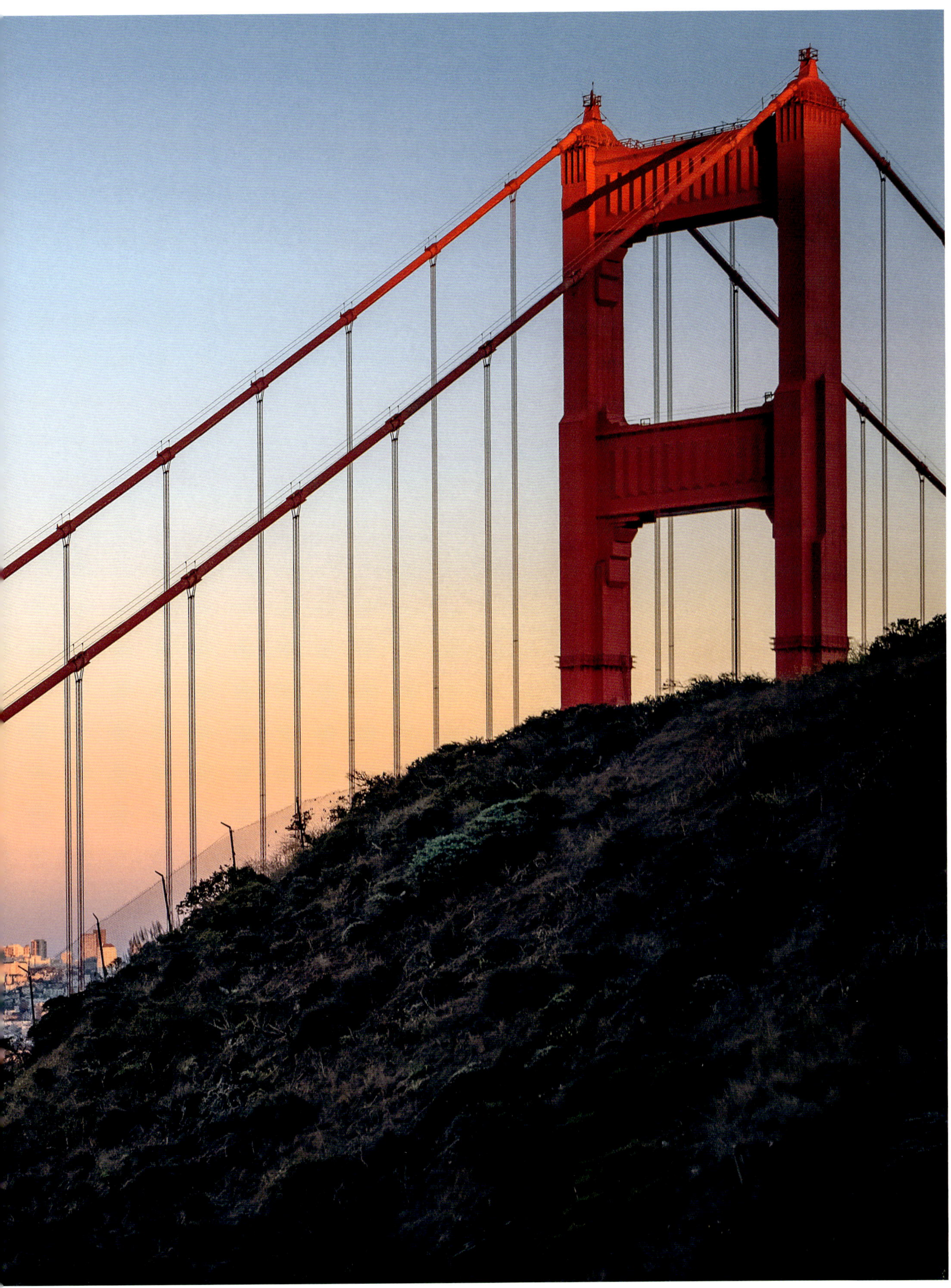

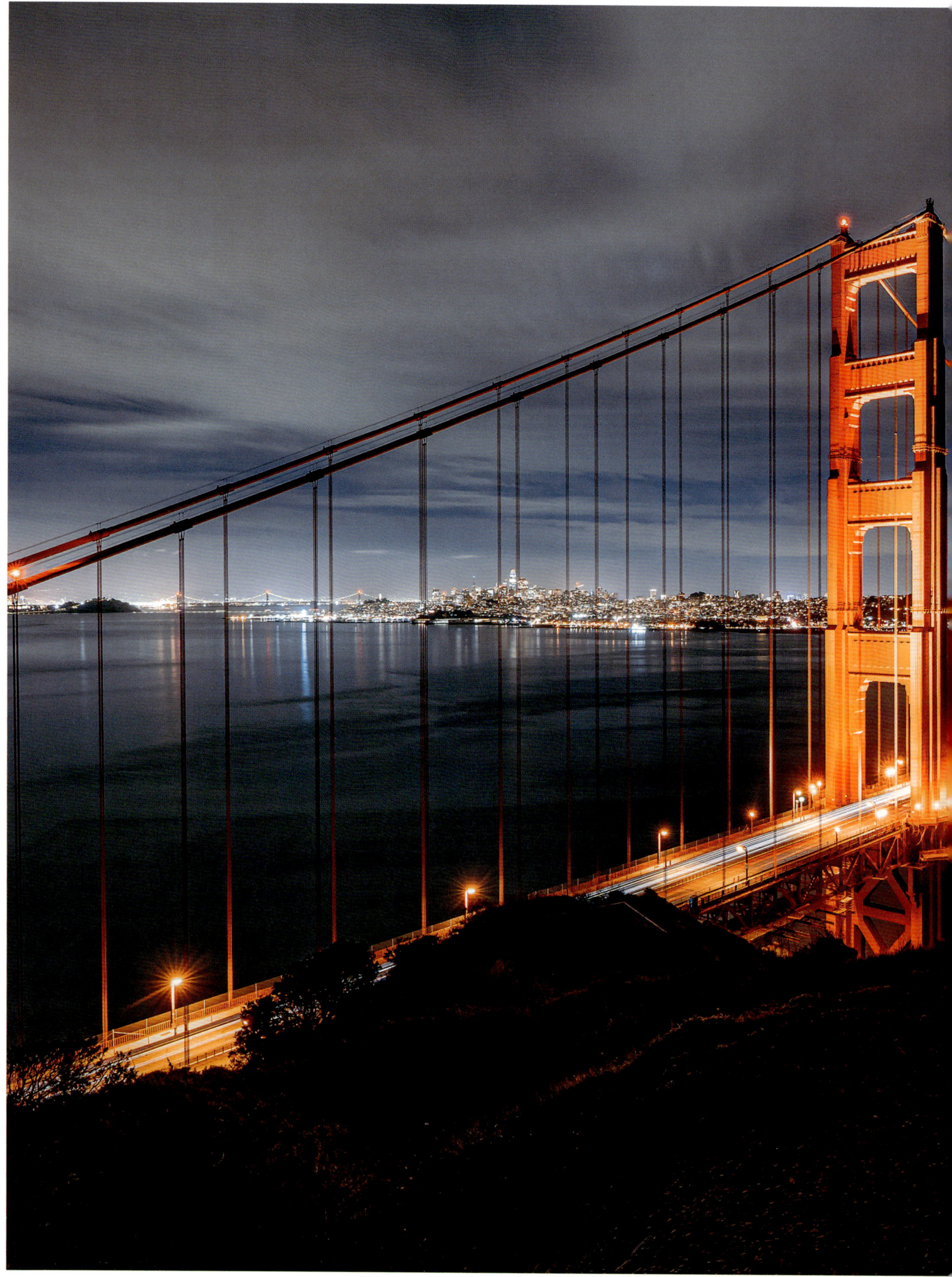

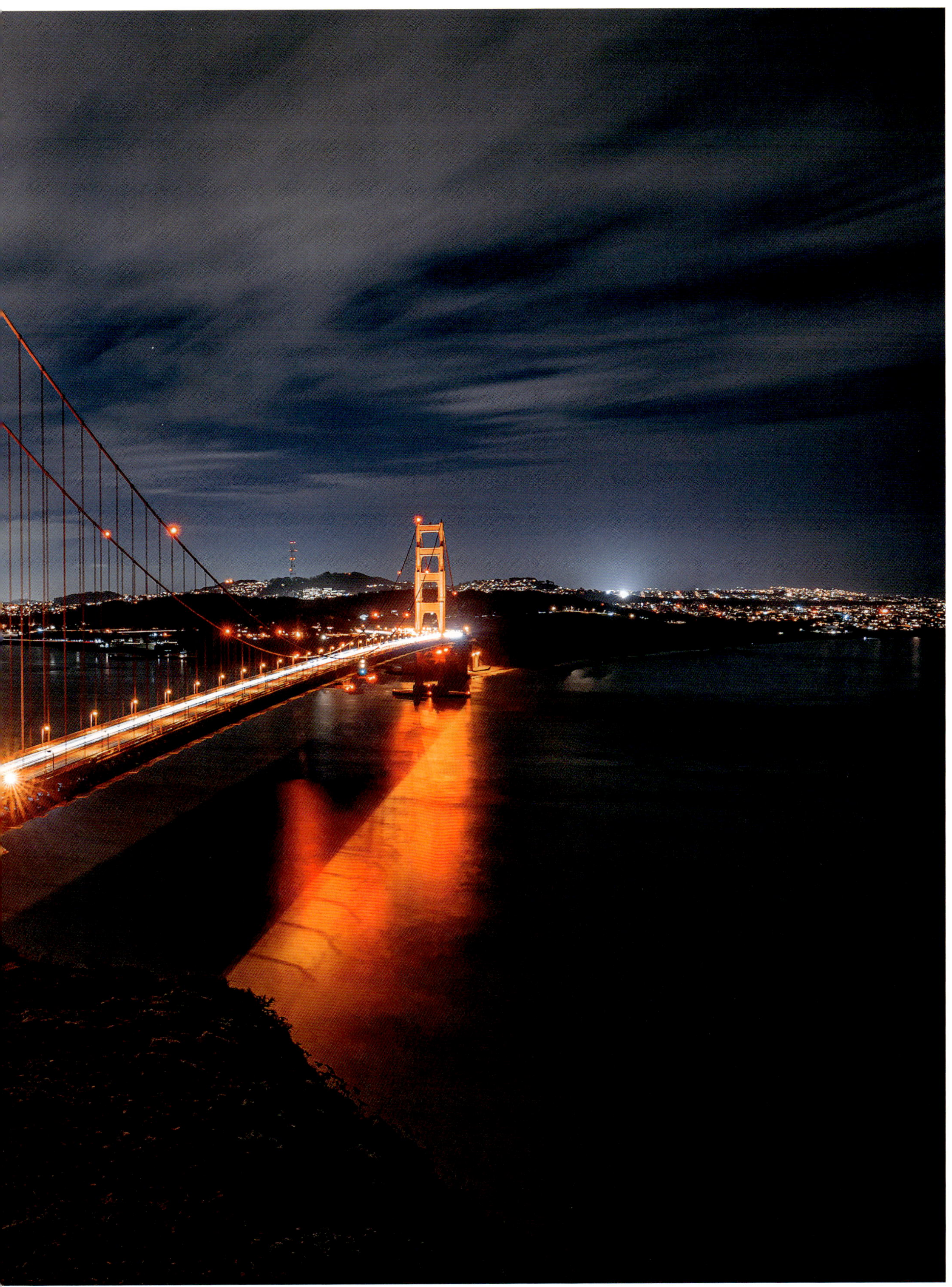

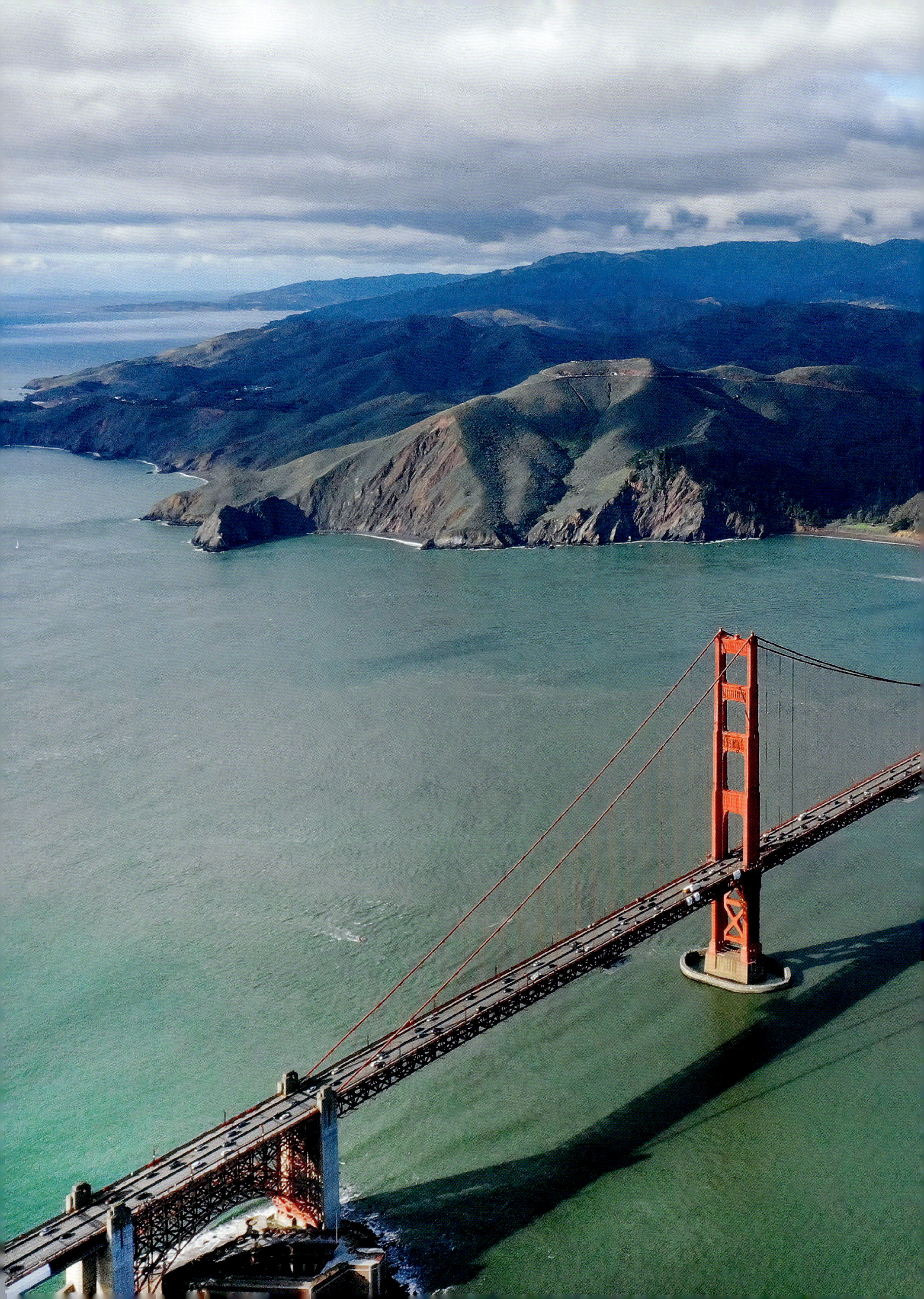

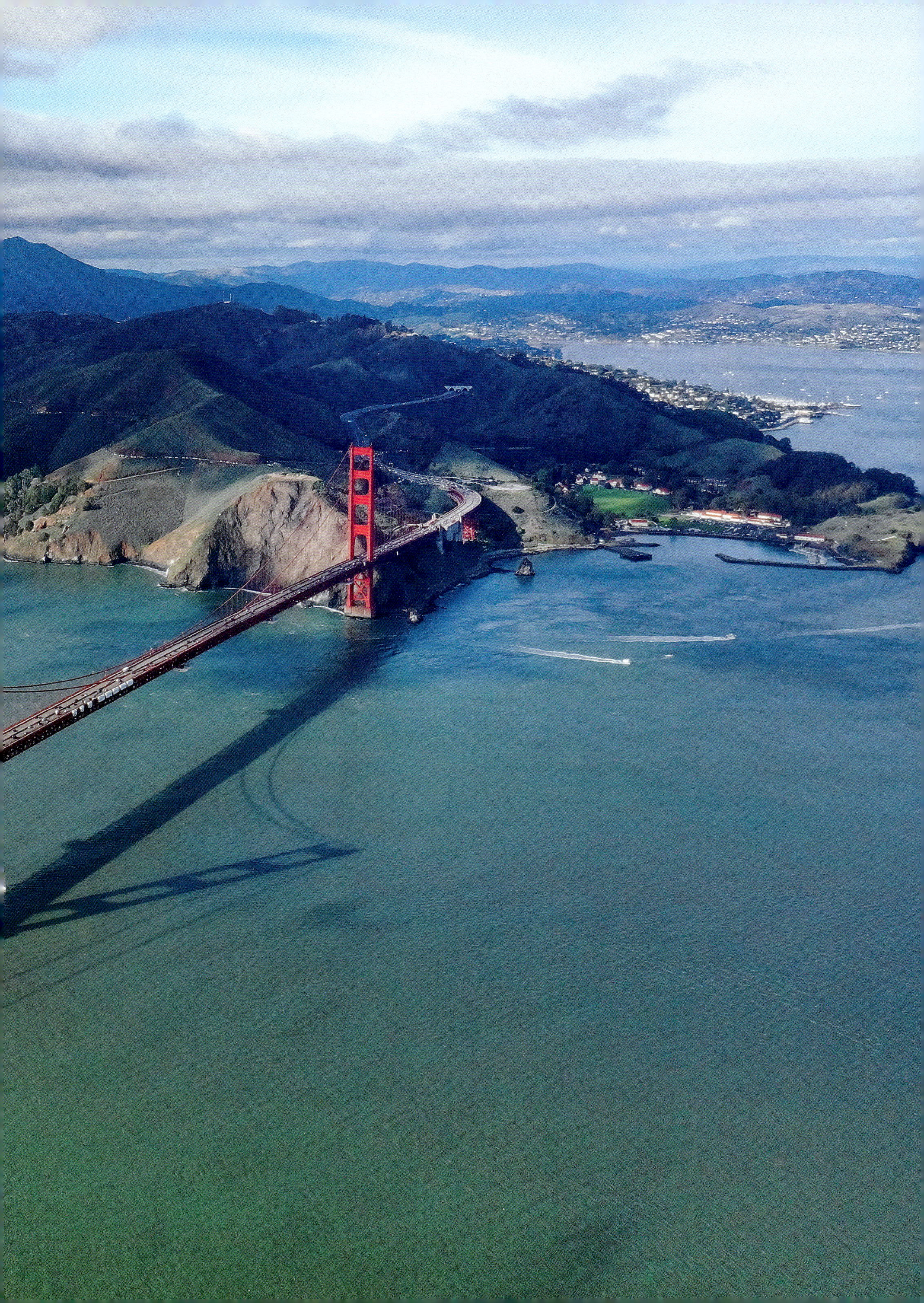

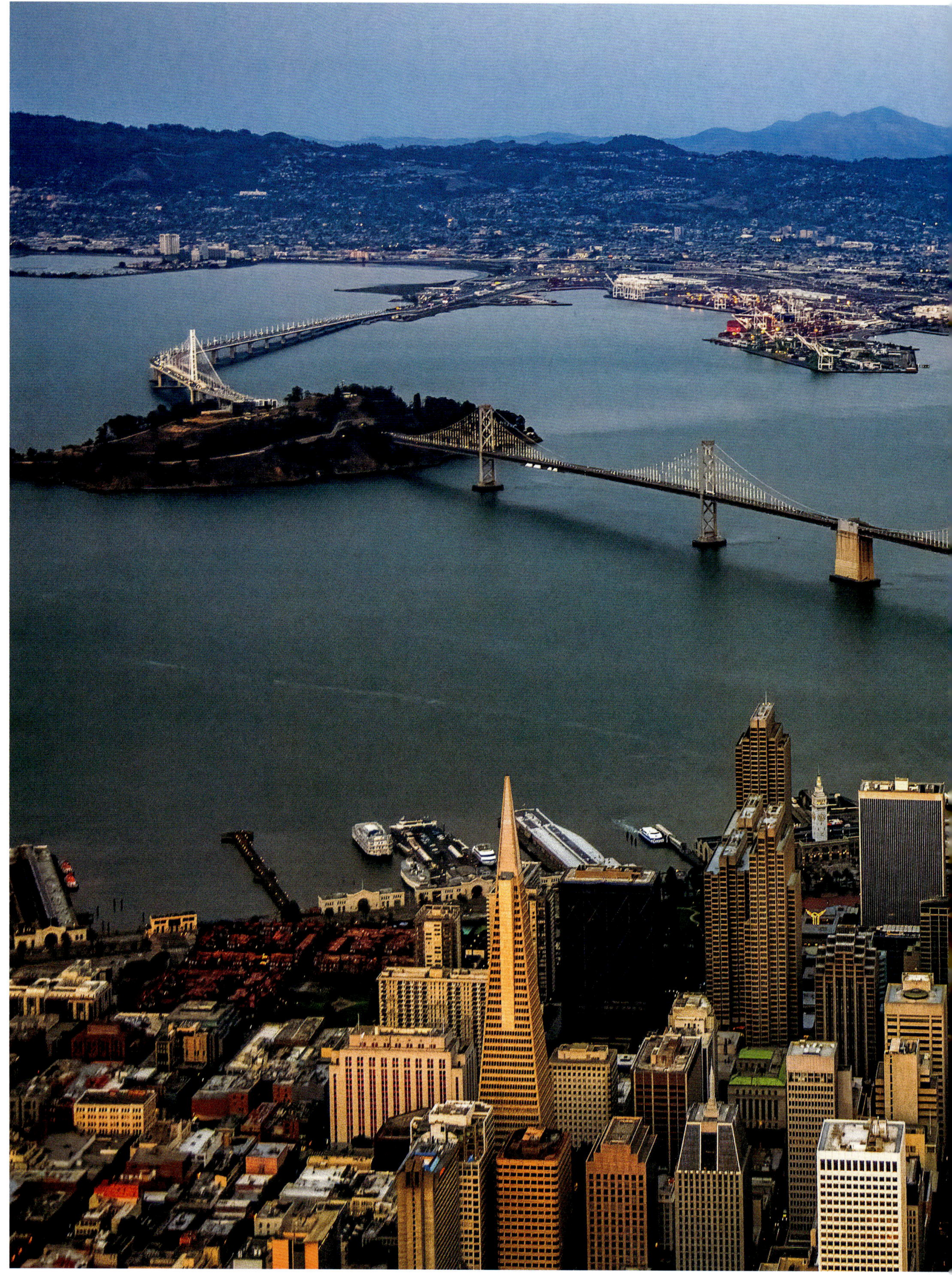

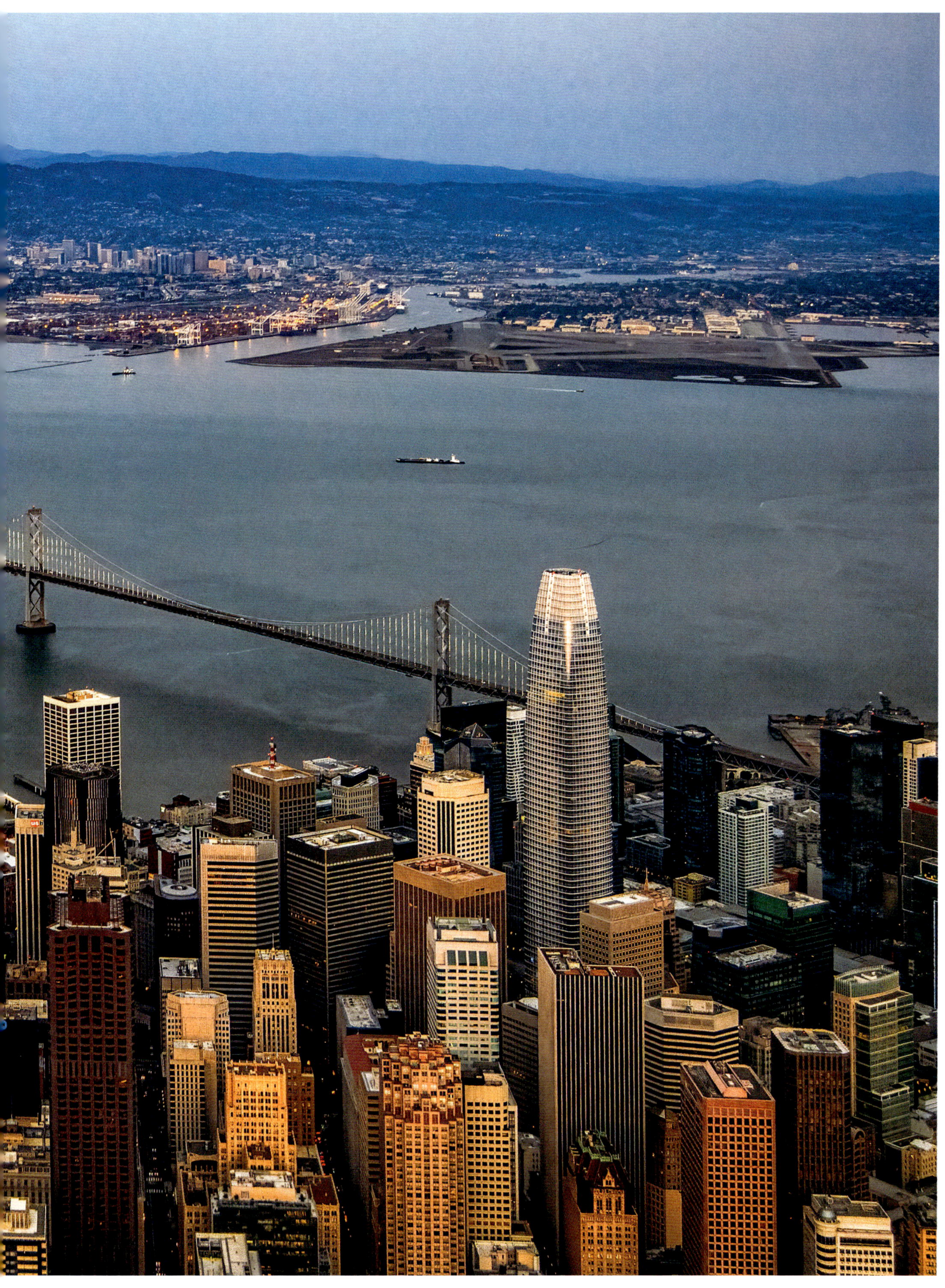

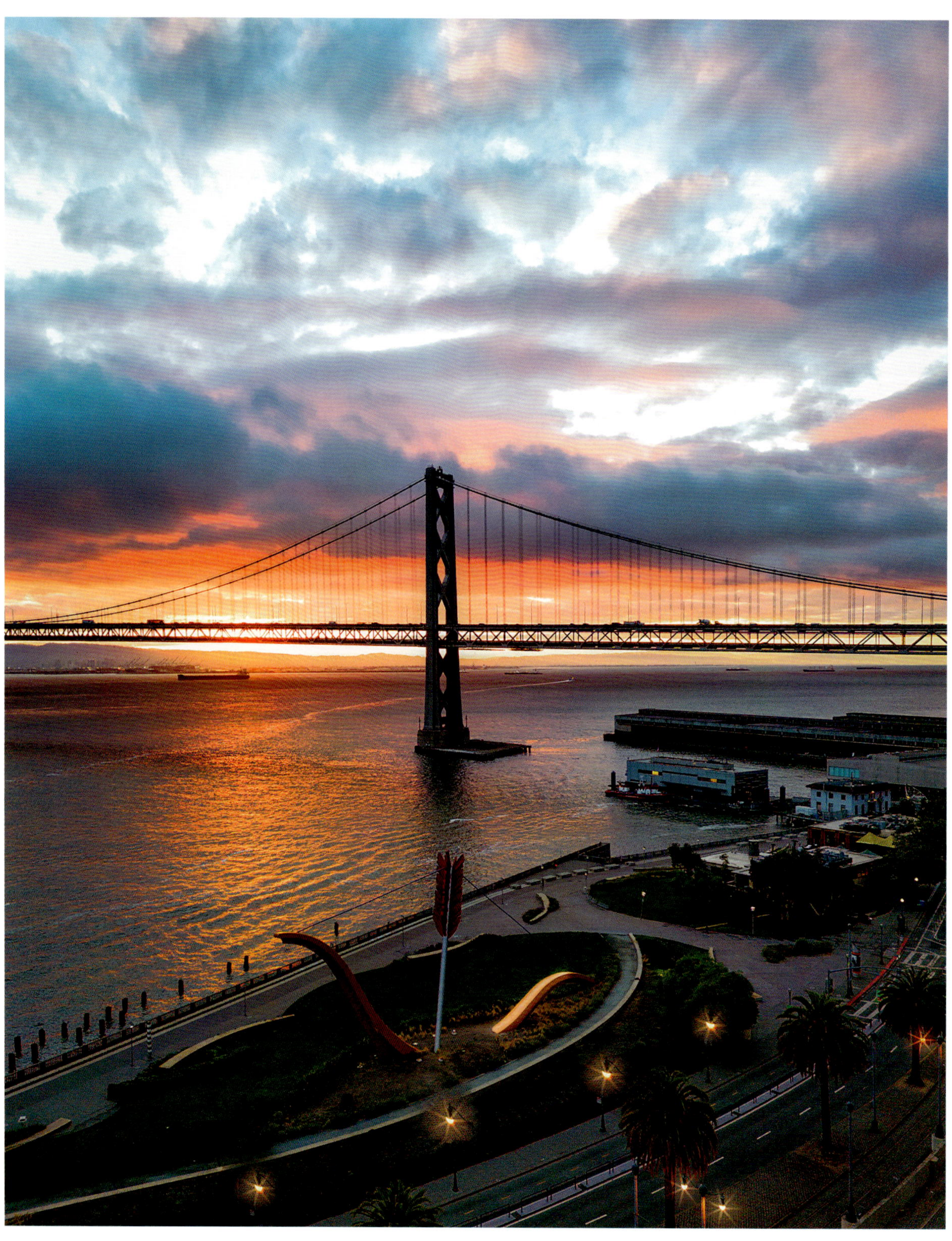

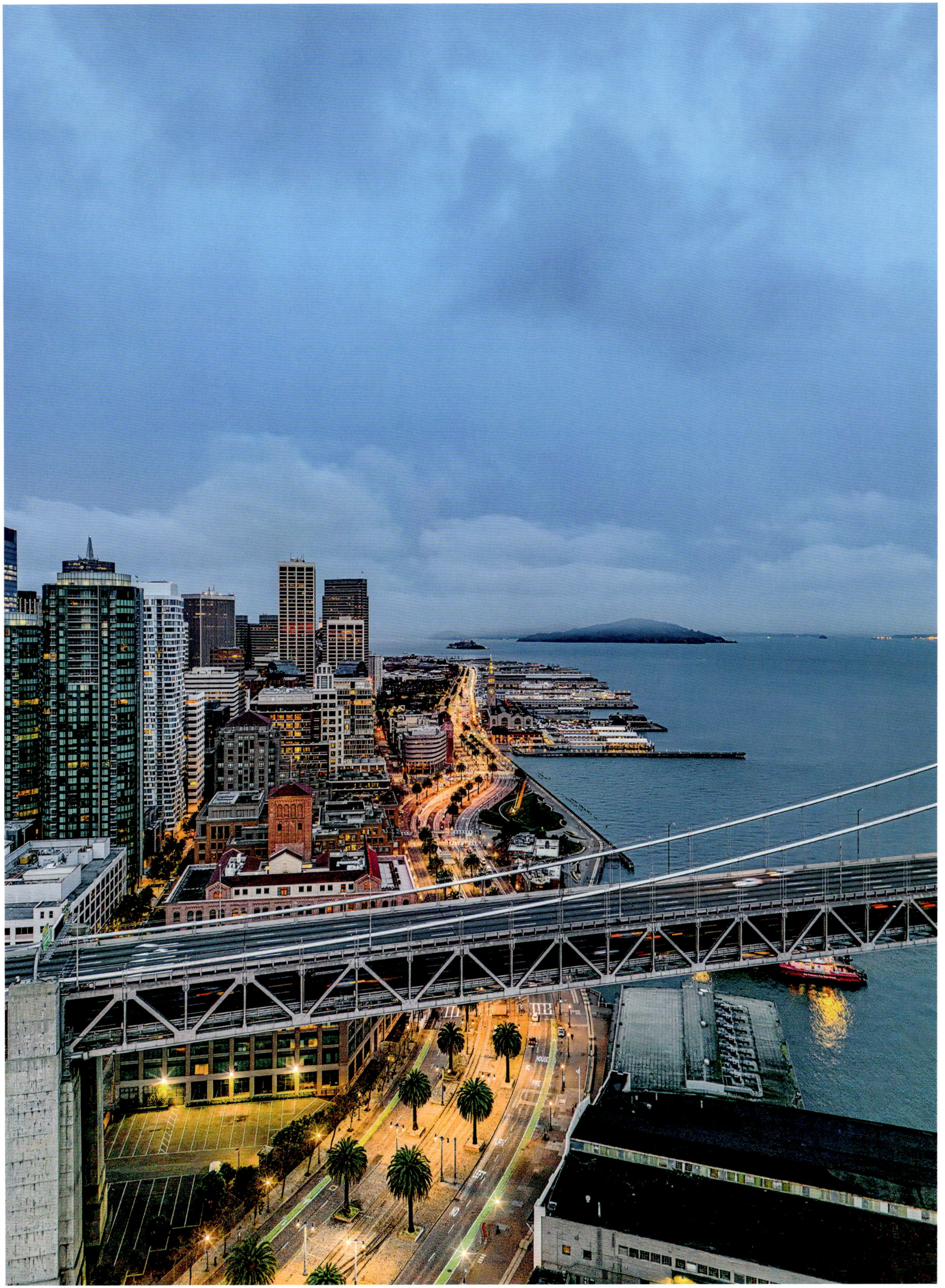

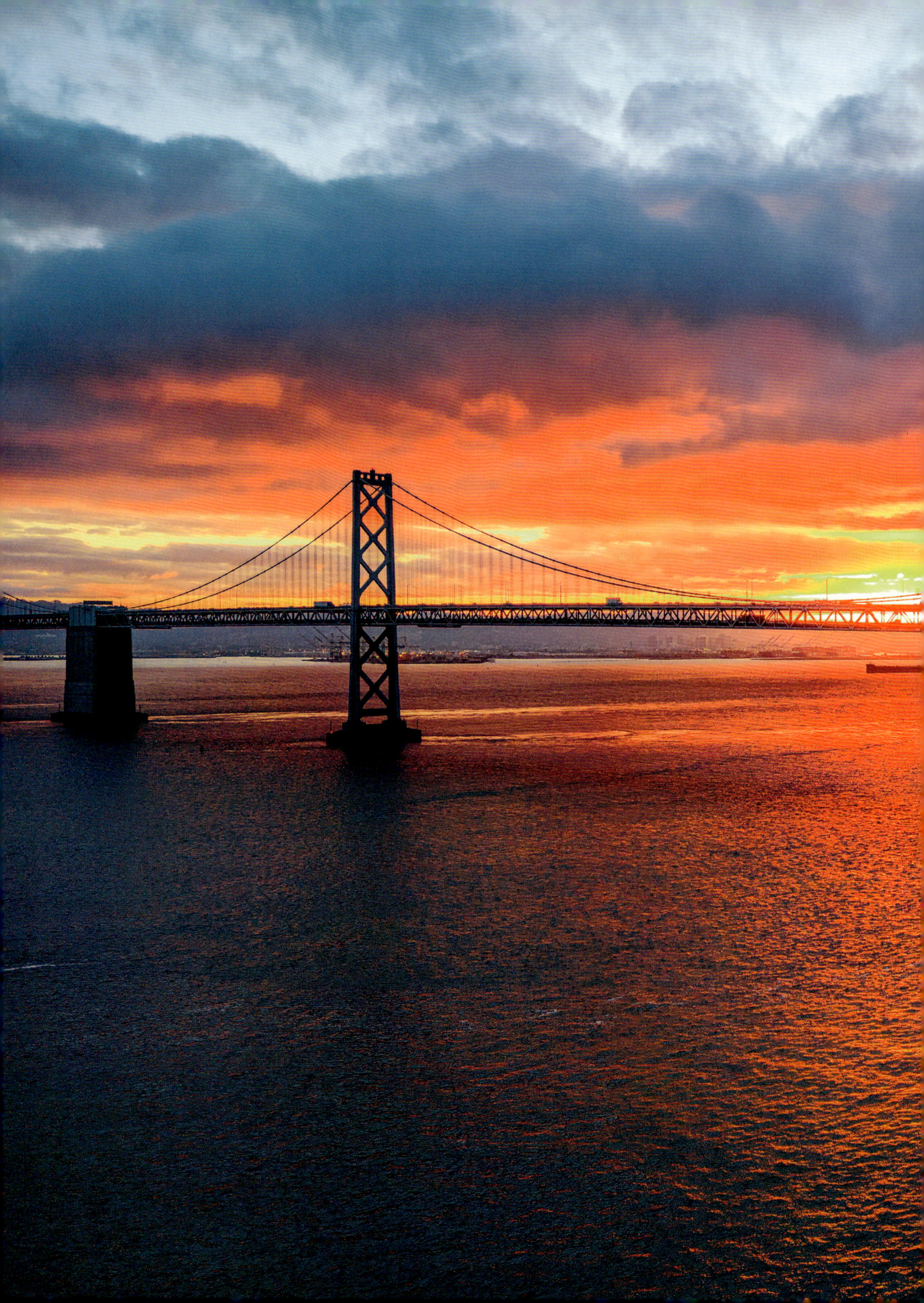

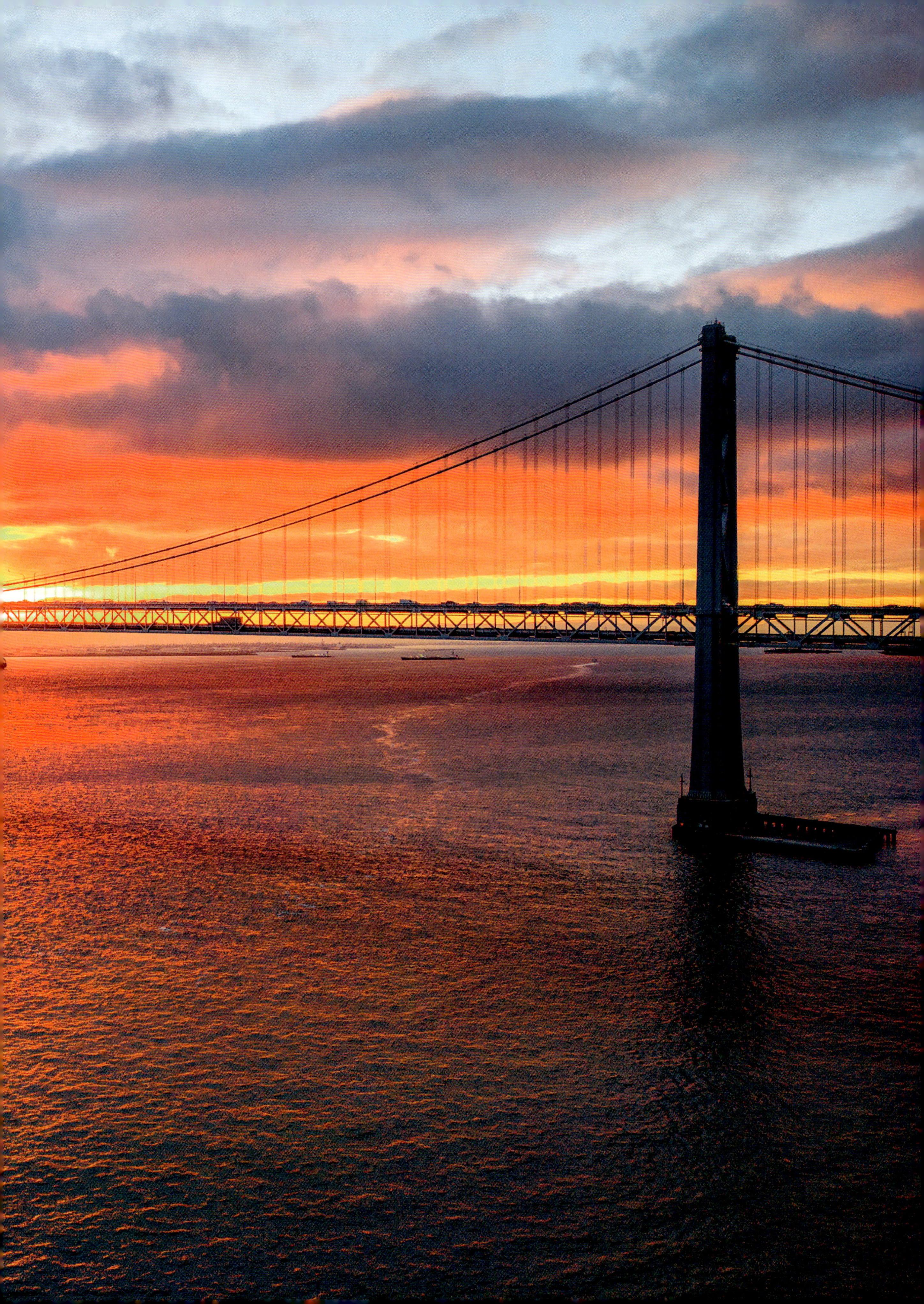

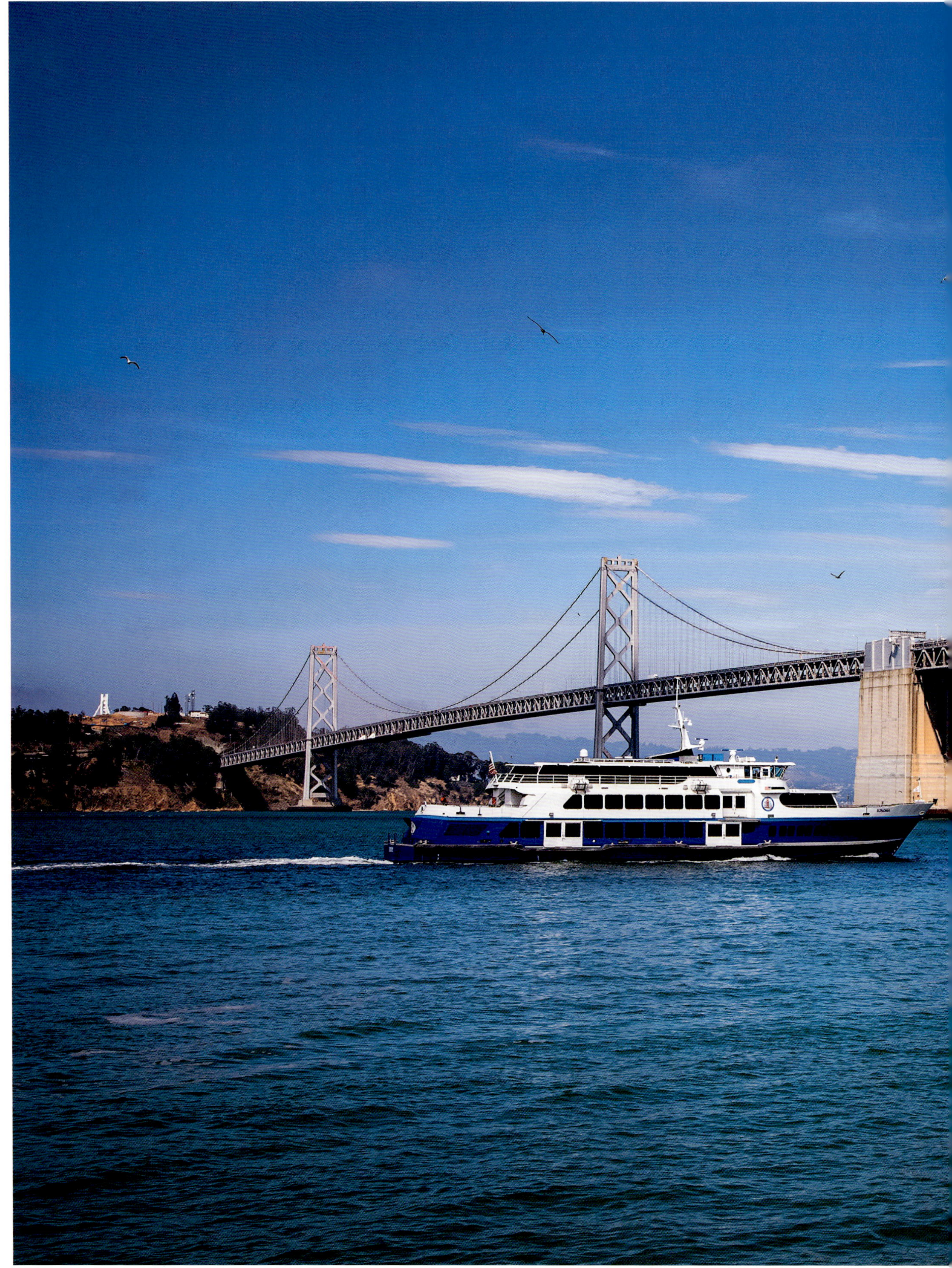

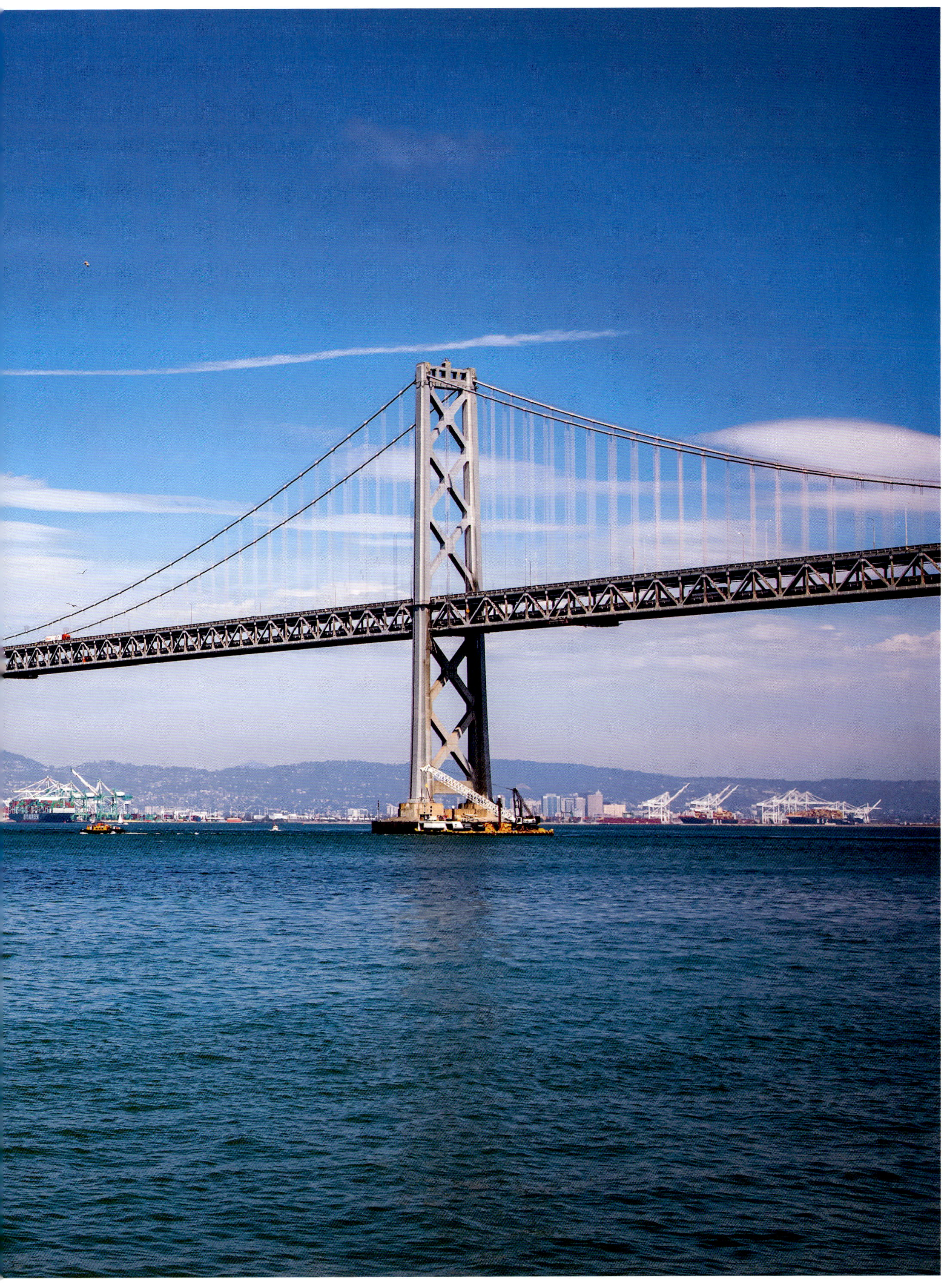

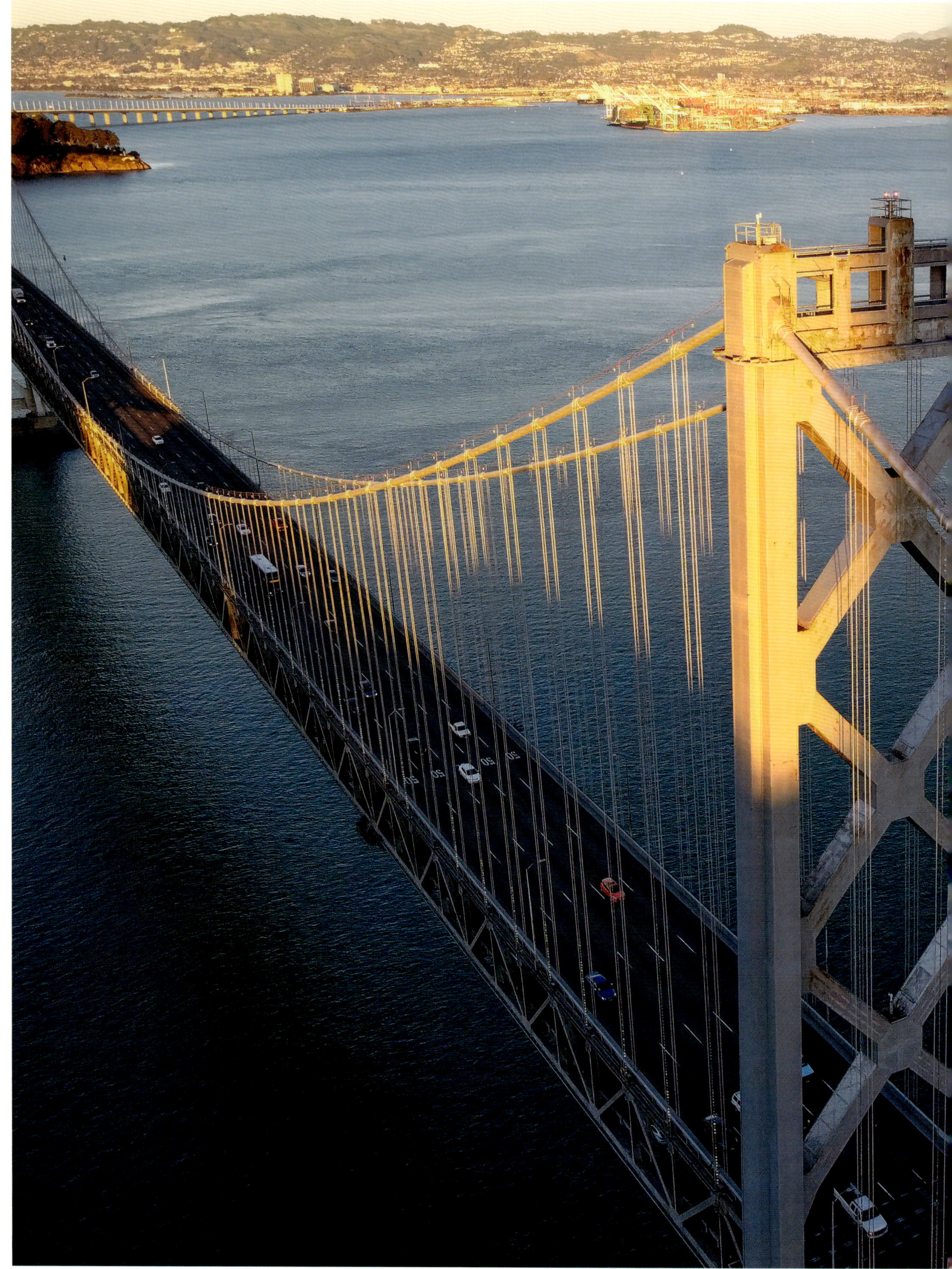

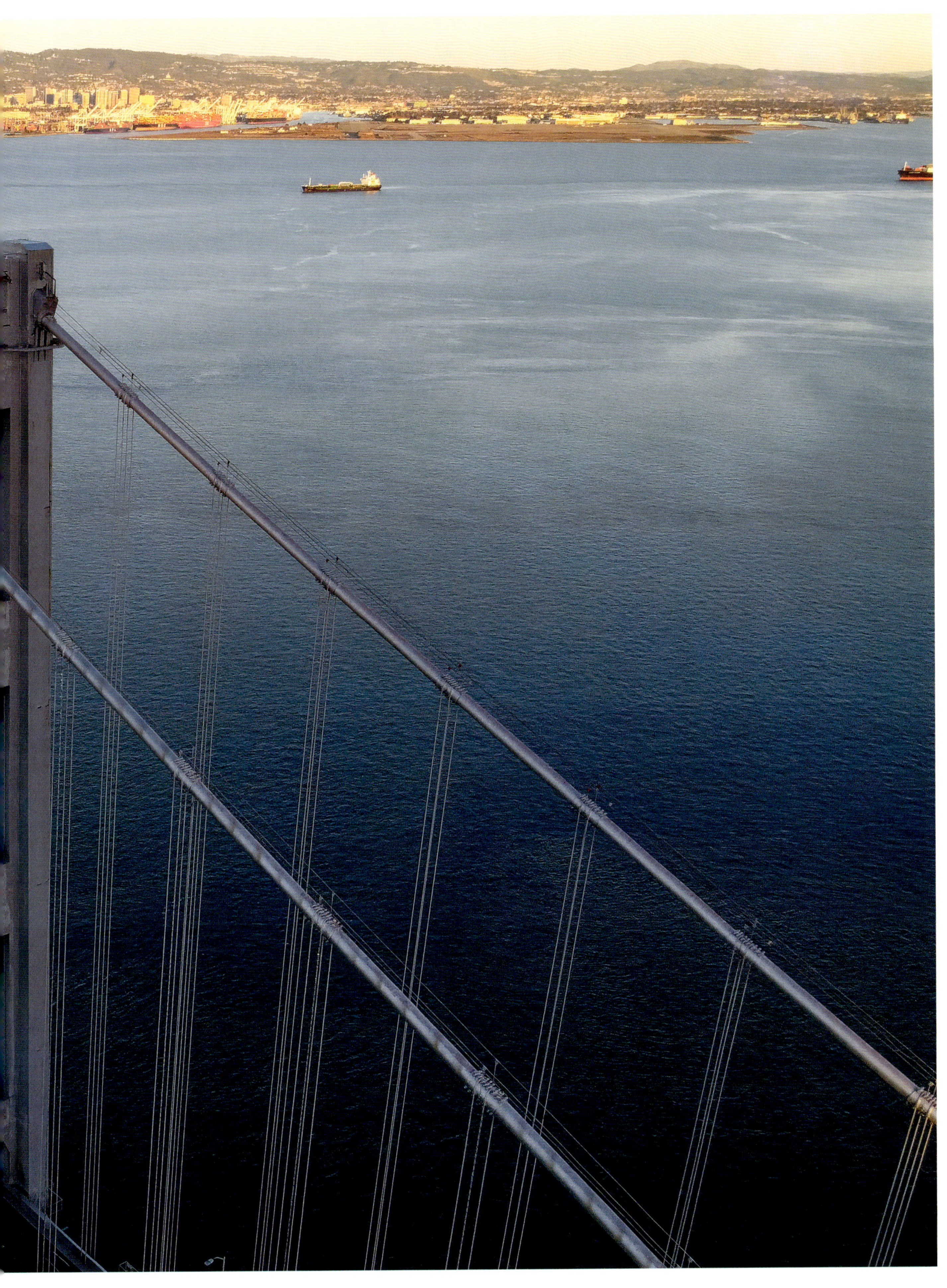

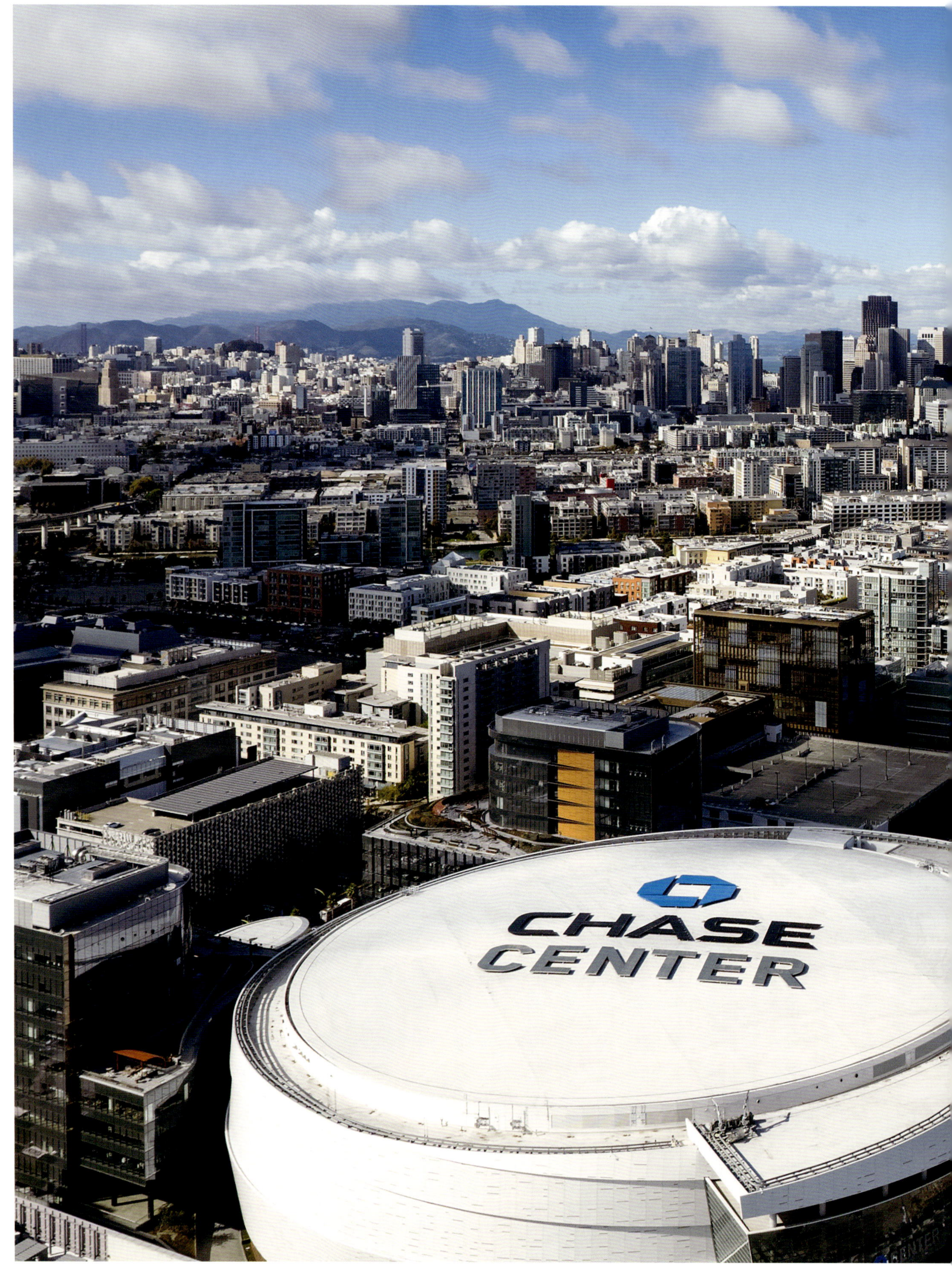
CHASE
CENTER

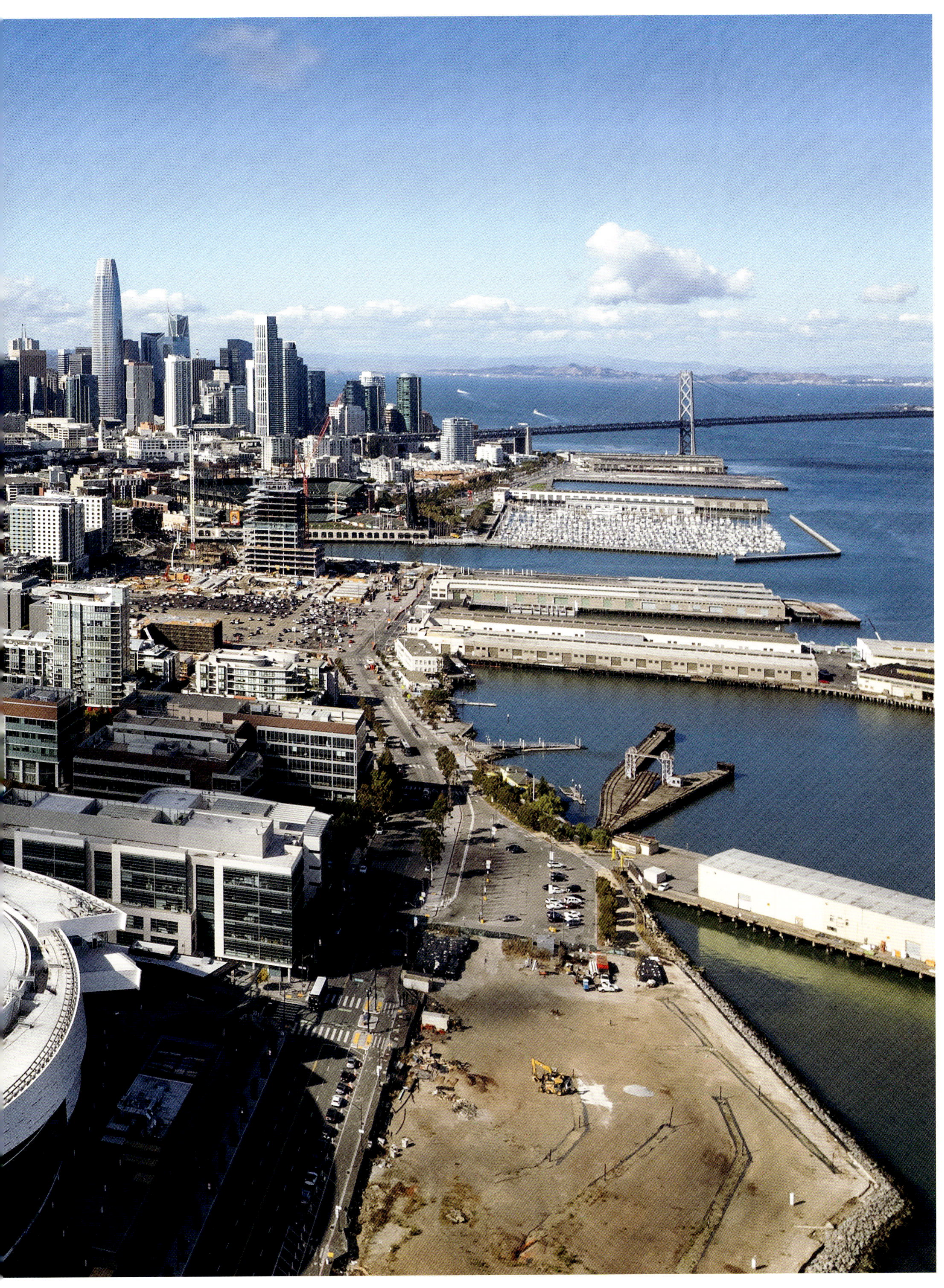

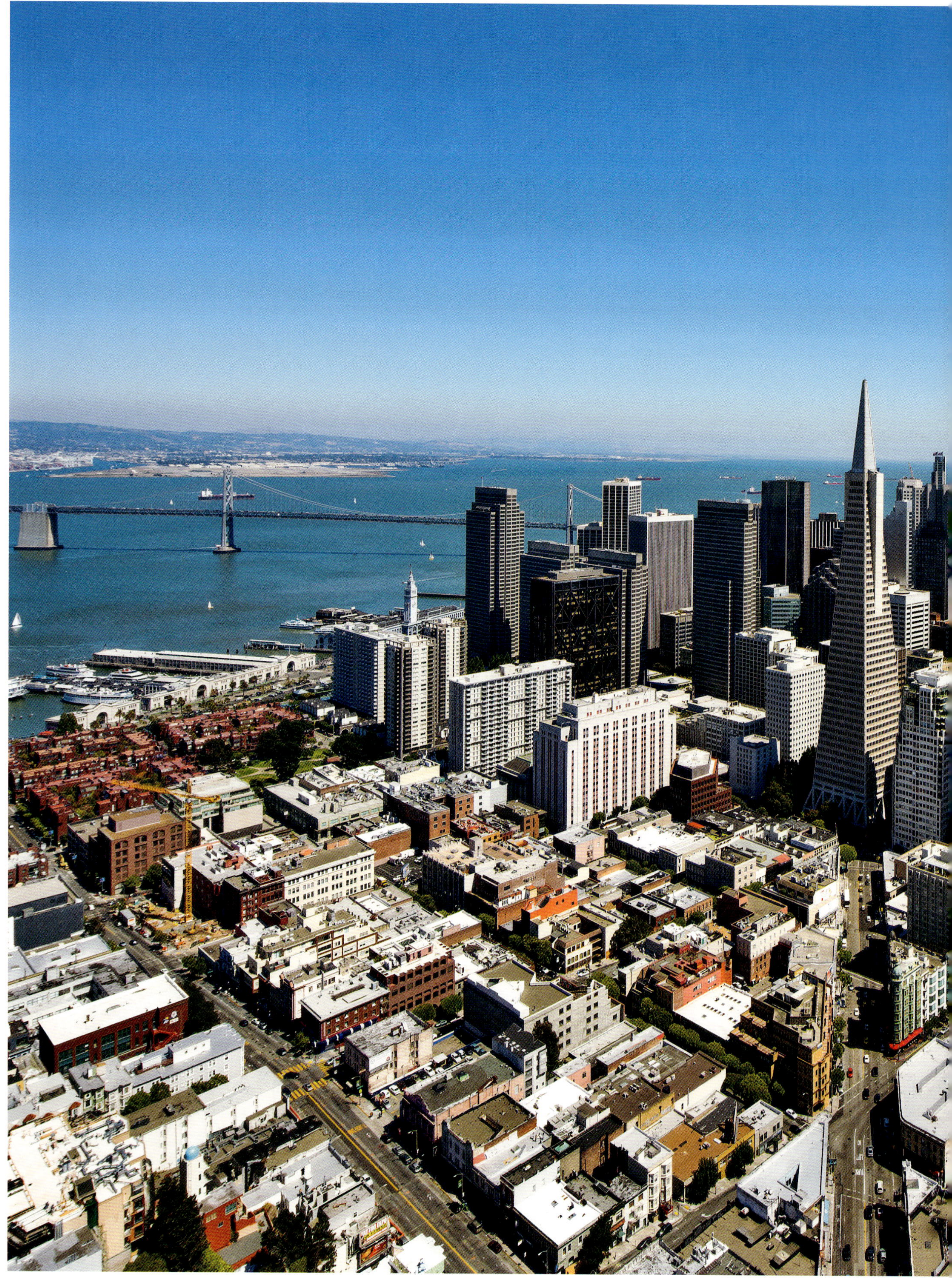

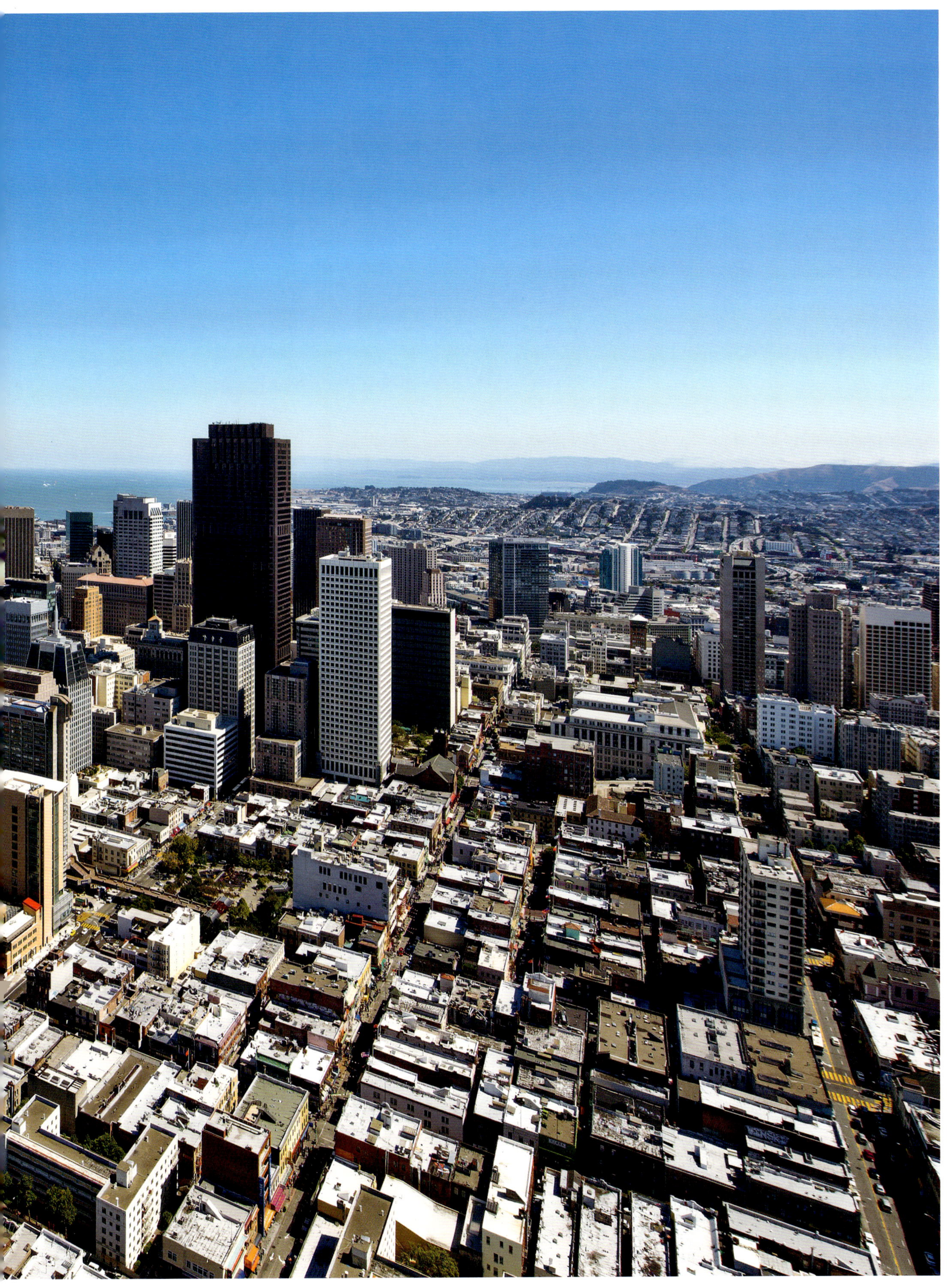

Fog ♦ In San Francisco, the fog is so enigmatic and well known that locals even have a name for it — Karl the Fog. Present throughout the year but particularly during the summer months, the fog is a product of San Francisco's unique geography with its nearby mountains and the gap at the Golden Gate. The combination of cold ocean currents and warm air creates the perfect conditions for fog formation, and as the moist air meets the cooler temperatures, it condenses into a thick, rolling mist. ♦ This weather phenomenon creates unique microclimates within San Francisco. While on the north side of the city, the Golden Gate Bridge may be blanketed by fog, just a few miles south in the Mission, residents may be lounging in a park soaking in the sunshine. It's not uncommon to have temperature swings of 20°F between different parts of the city, and residents know to dress in layers for the inevitable changes in microclimates. While fog is often present in the mornings, as the day progresses, the fog can burn off, only to return again in the evening, creating a mystical appearance as city lights shine through the mist. ♦ The fog not only causes inconsistent weather conditions, it also alters the San Francisco skyline, giving it a surreal, dreamlike appearance. As the tops of buildings, bridges, and skyscrapers are obscured, they appear to emerge out of the clouds, creating an almost otherworldly effect. And as the fog can move quickly, the appearance of the San Francisco skyline can change in minutes, making for incredibly dynamic photographs of the city. One moment, the city may be shrouded in dense fog; the next, it may clear, offering sweeping views. San Francisco's fog is a quintessential part of living in the Bay Area.

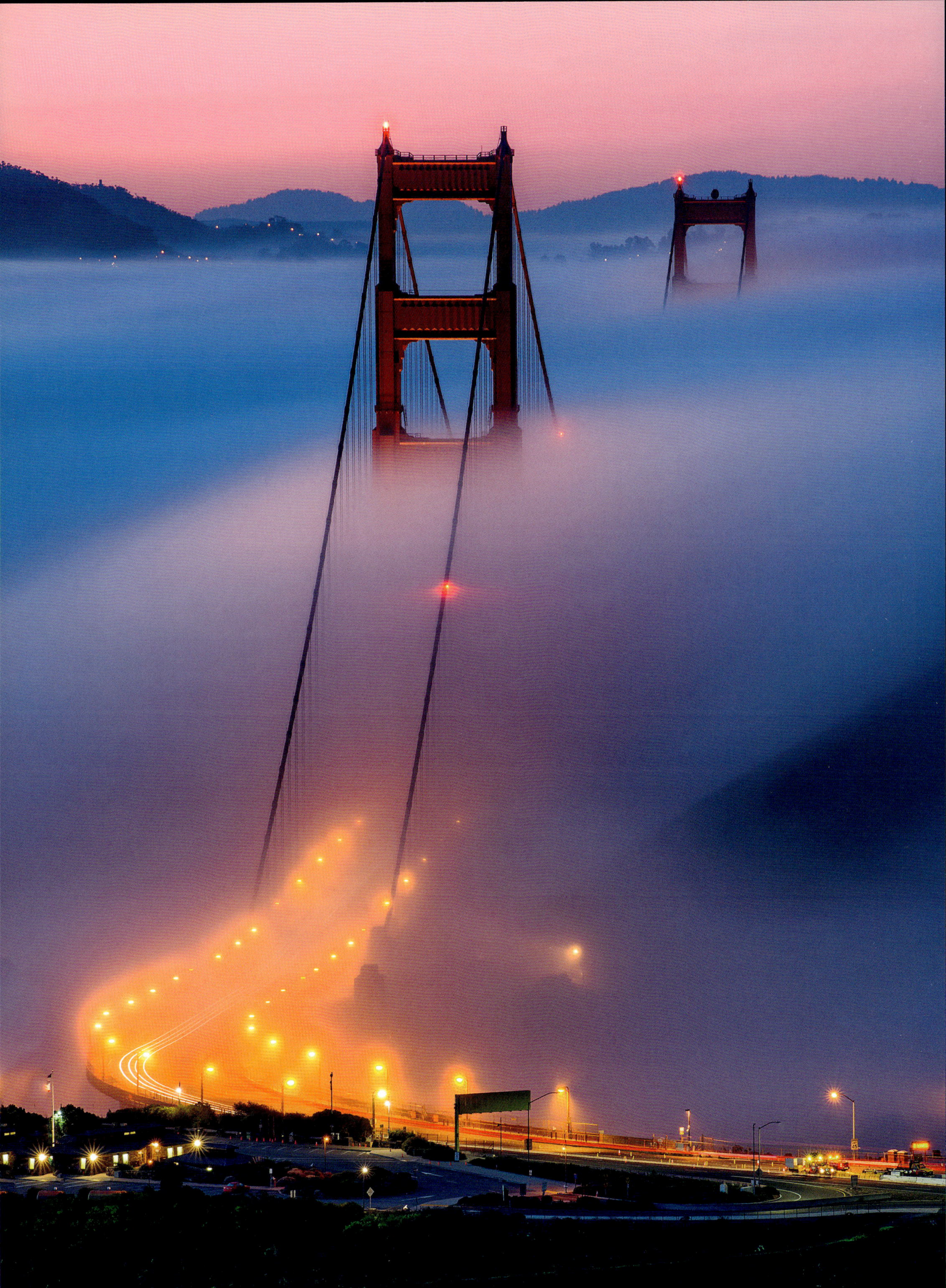

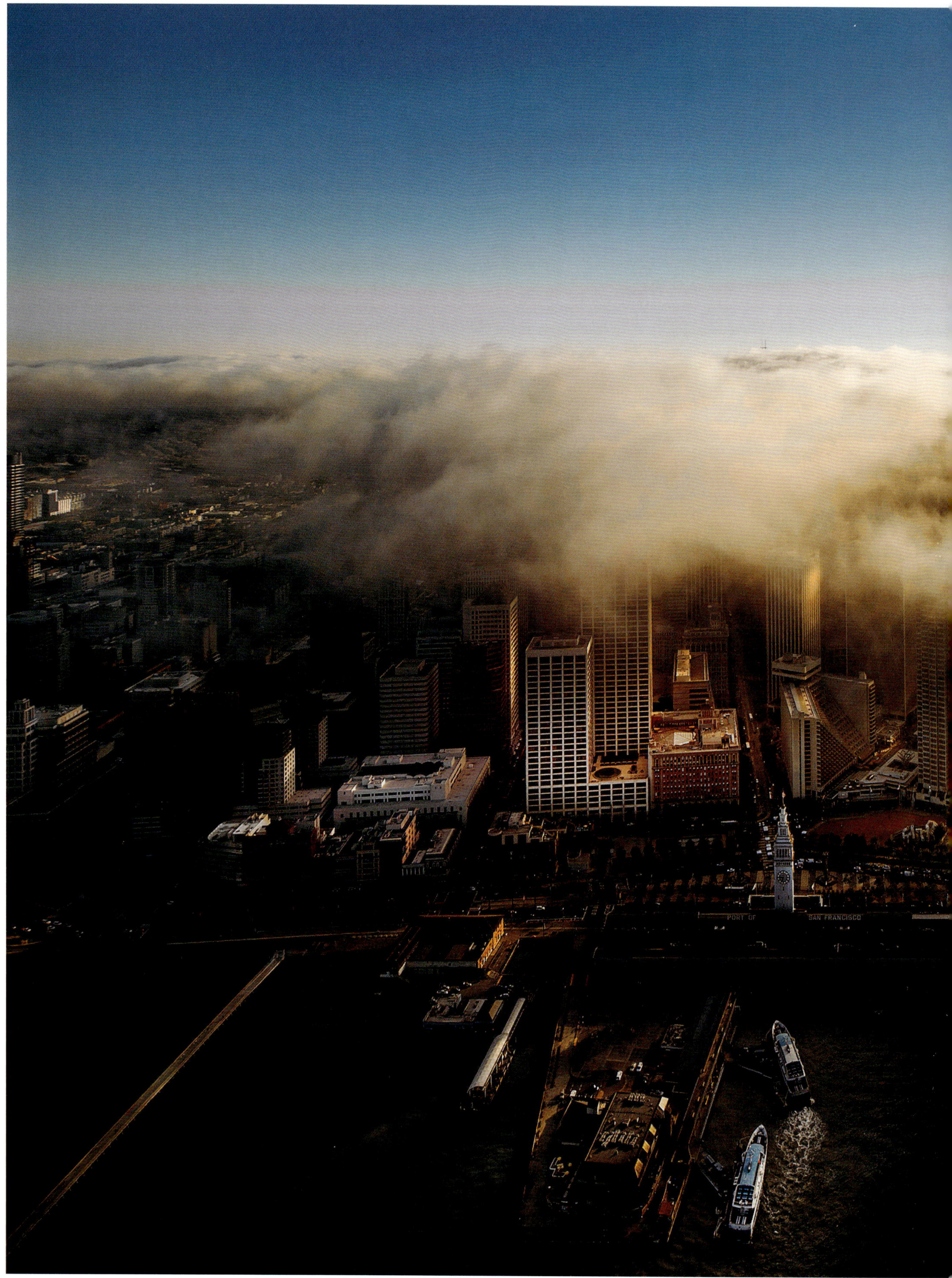
PORT OF SAN FRANCISCO

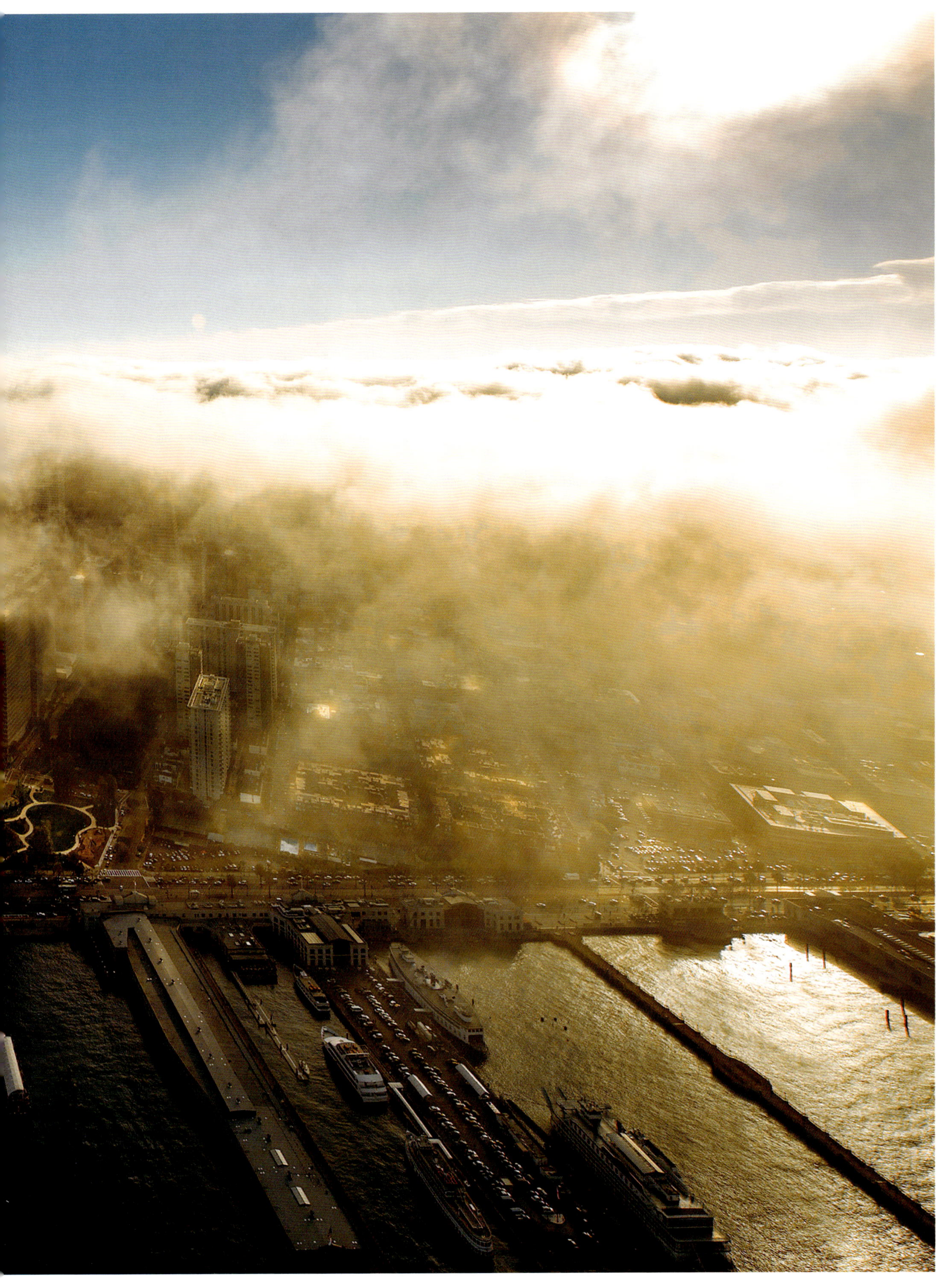

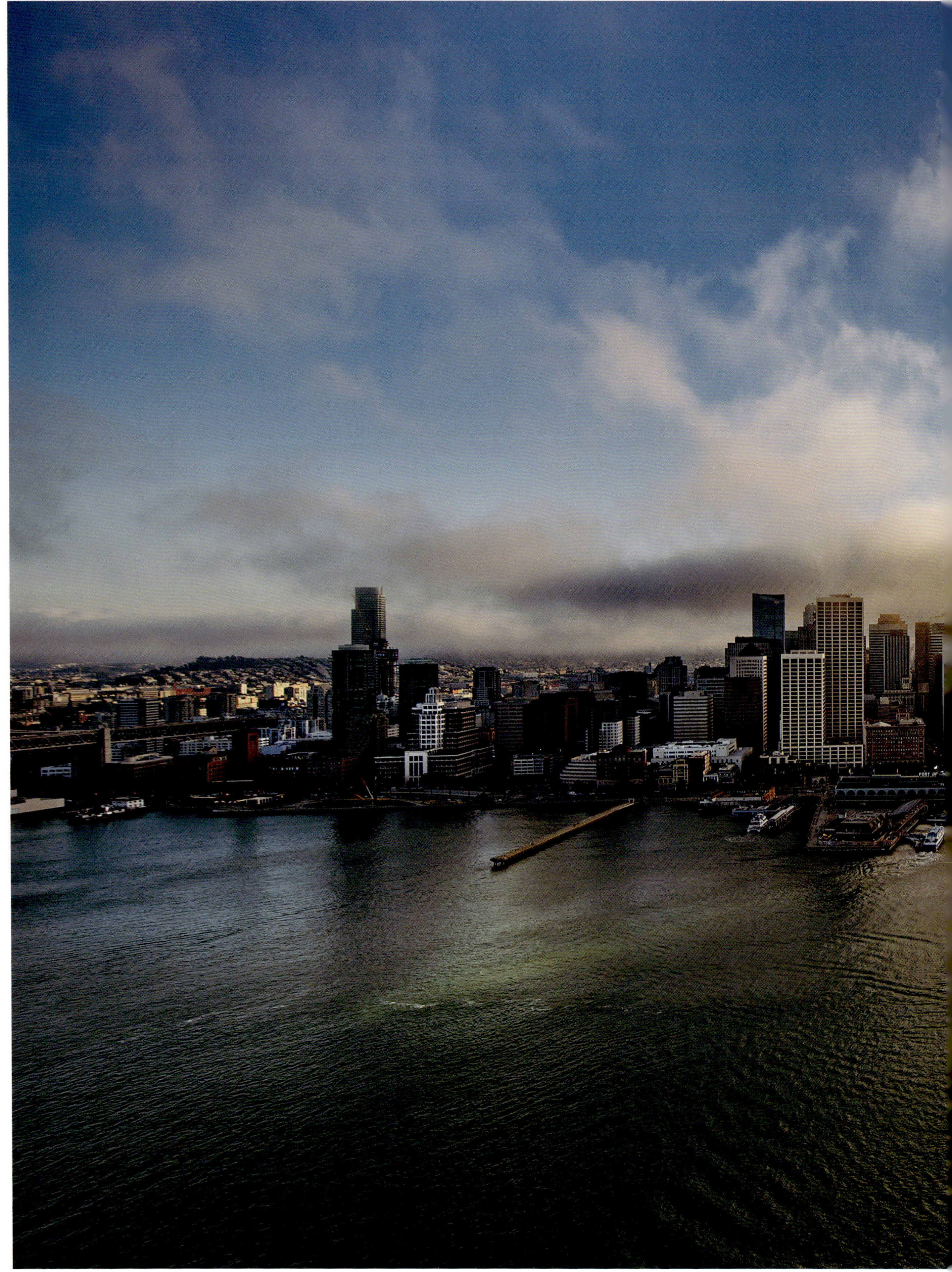

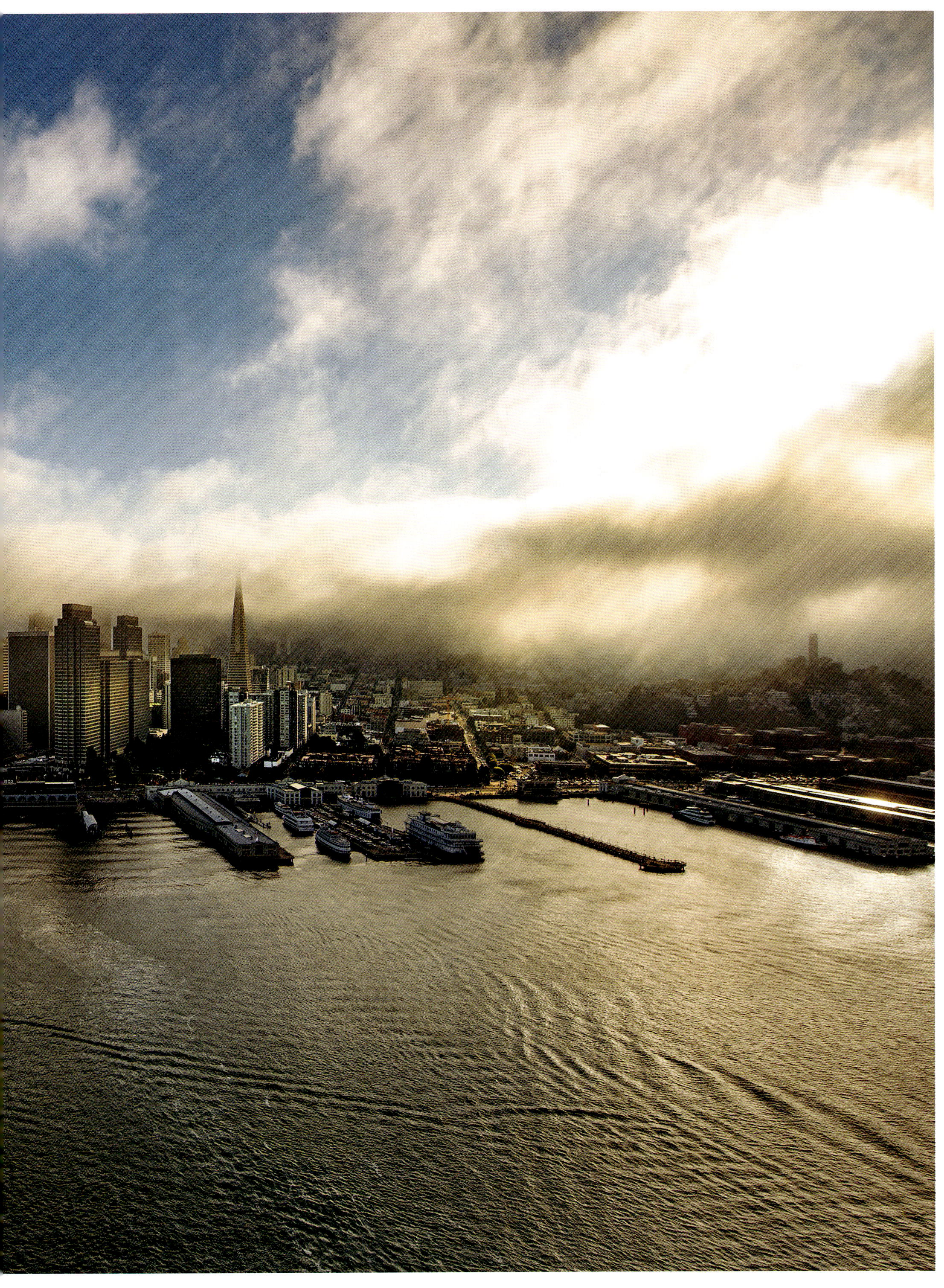

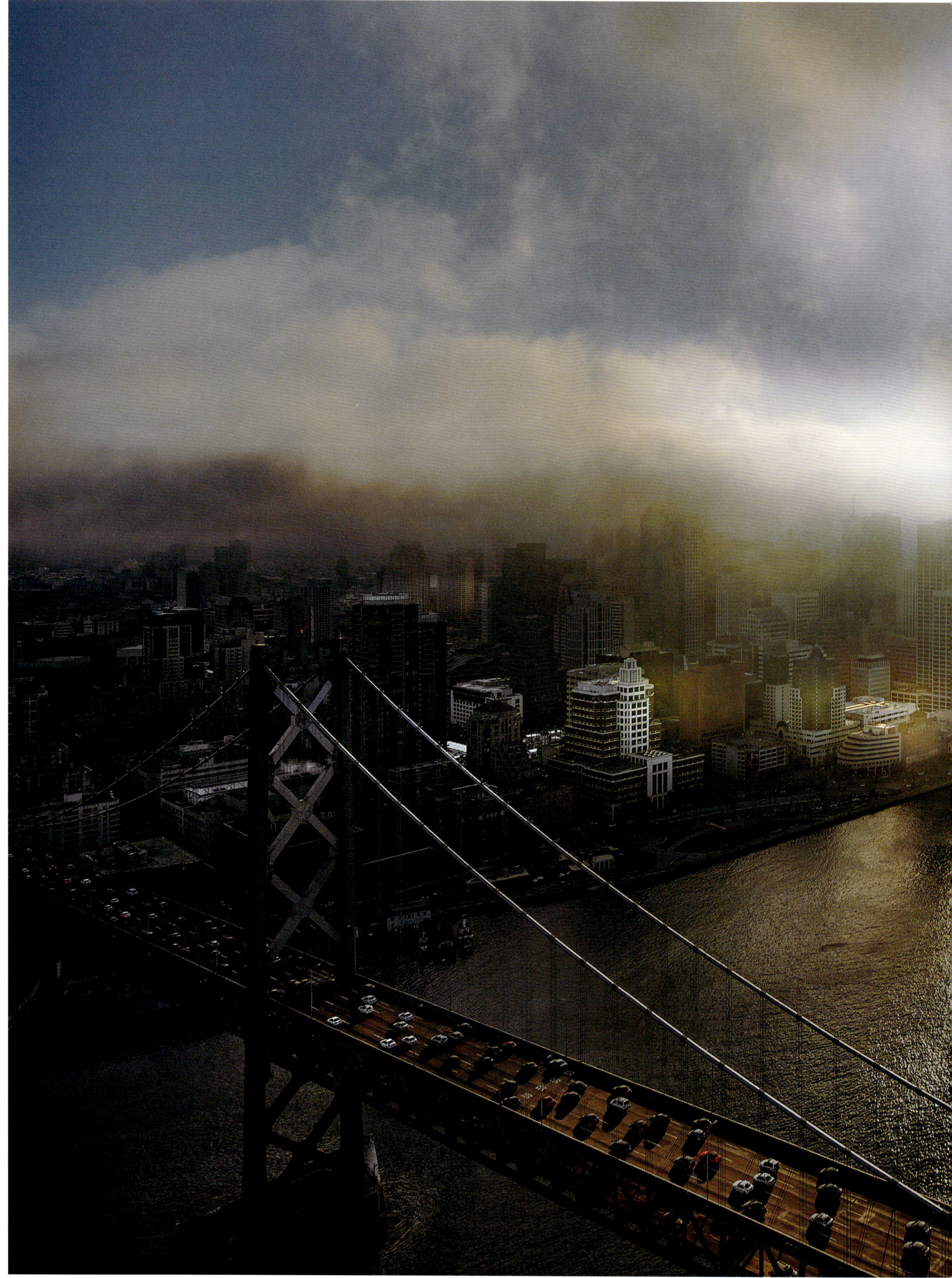

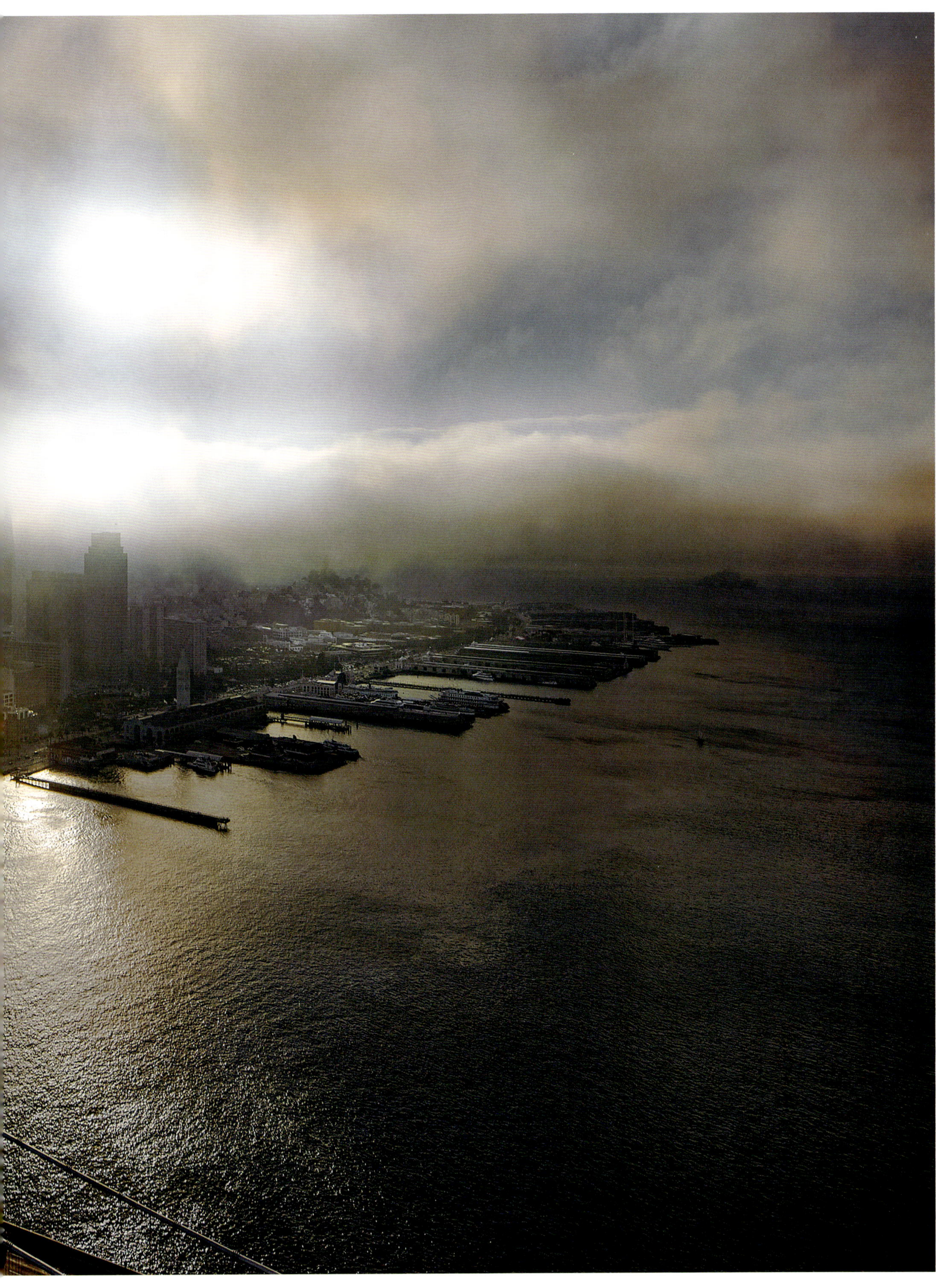

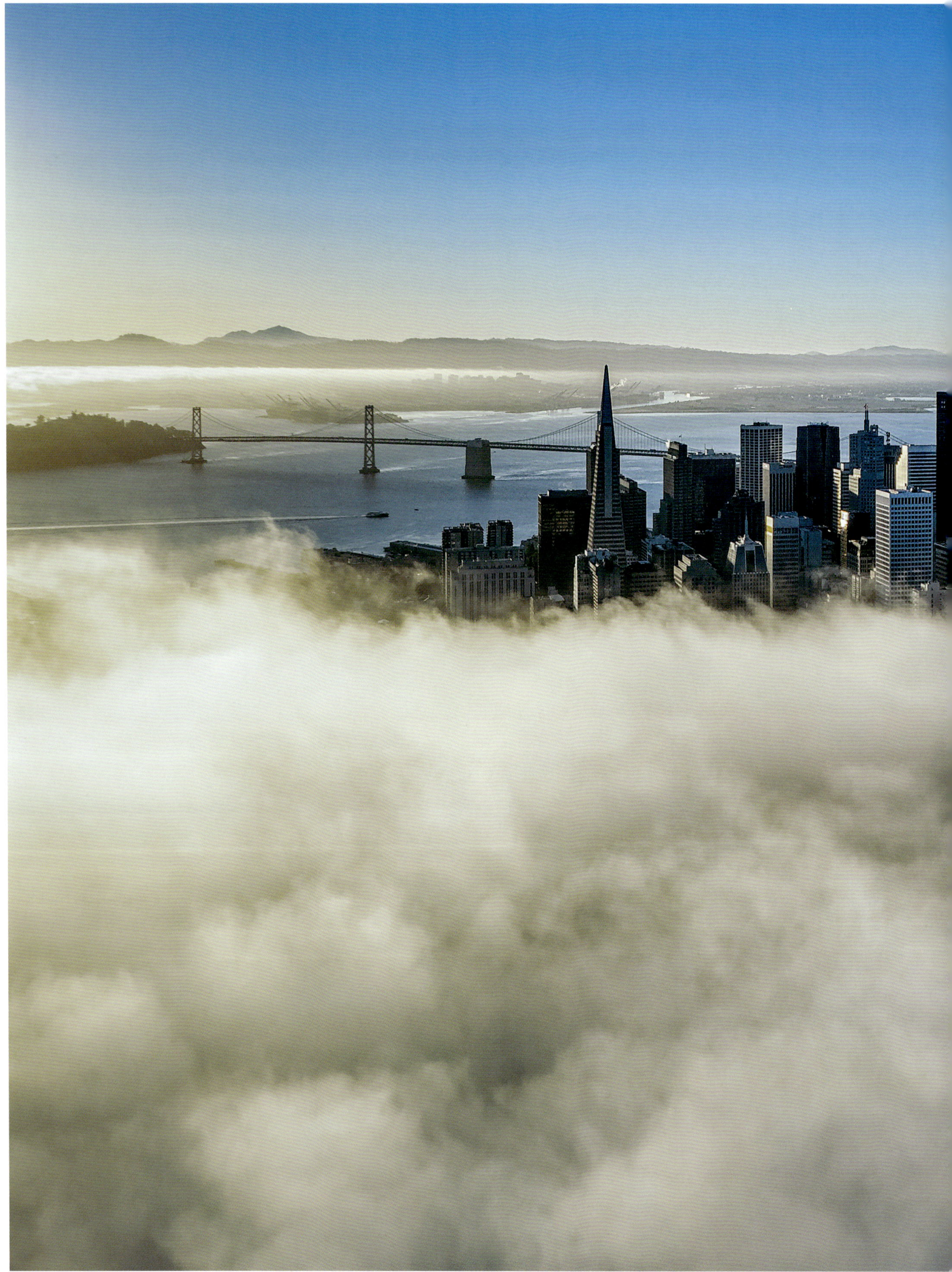

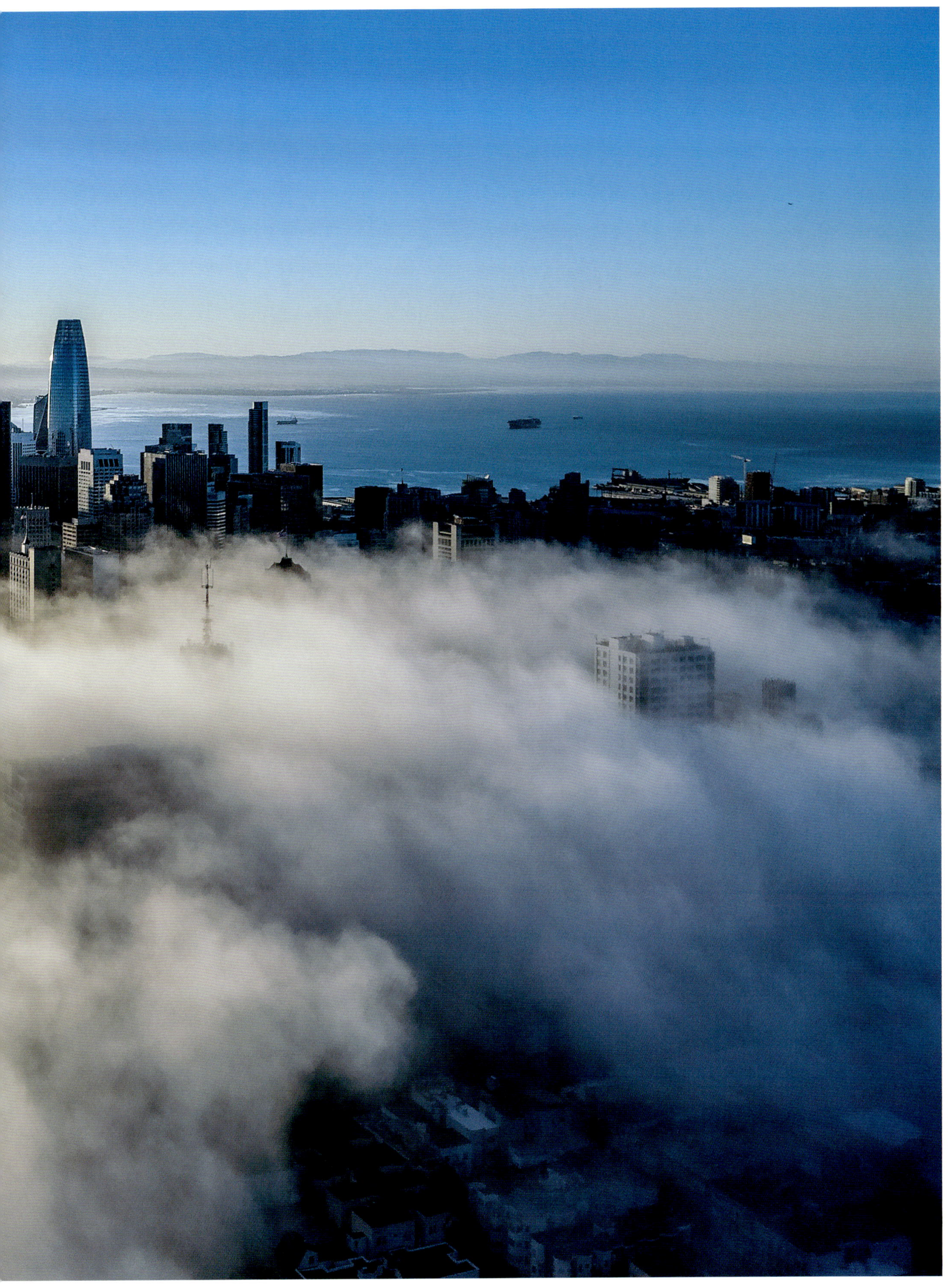

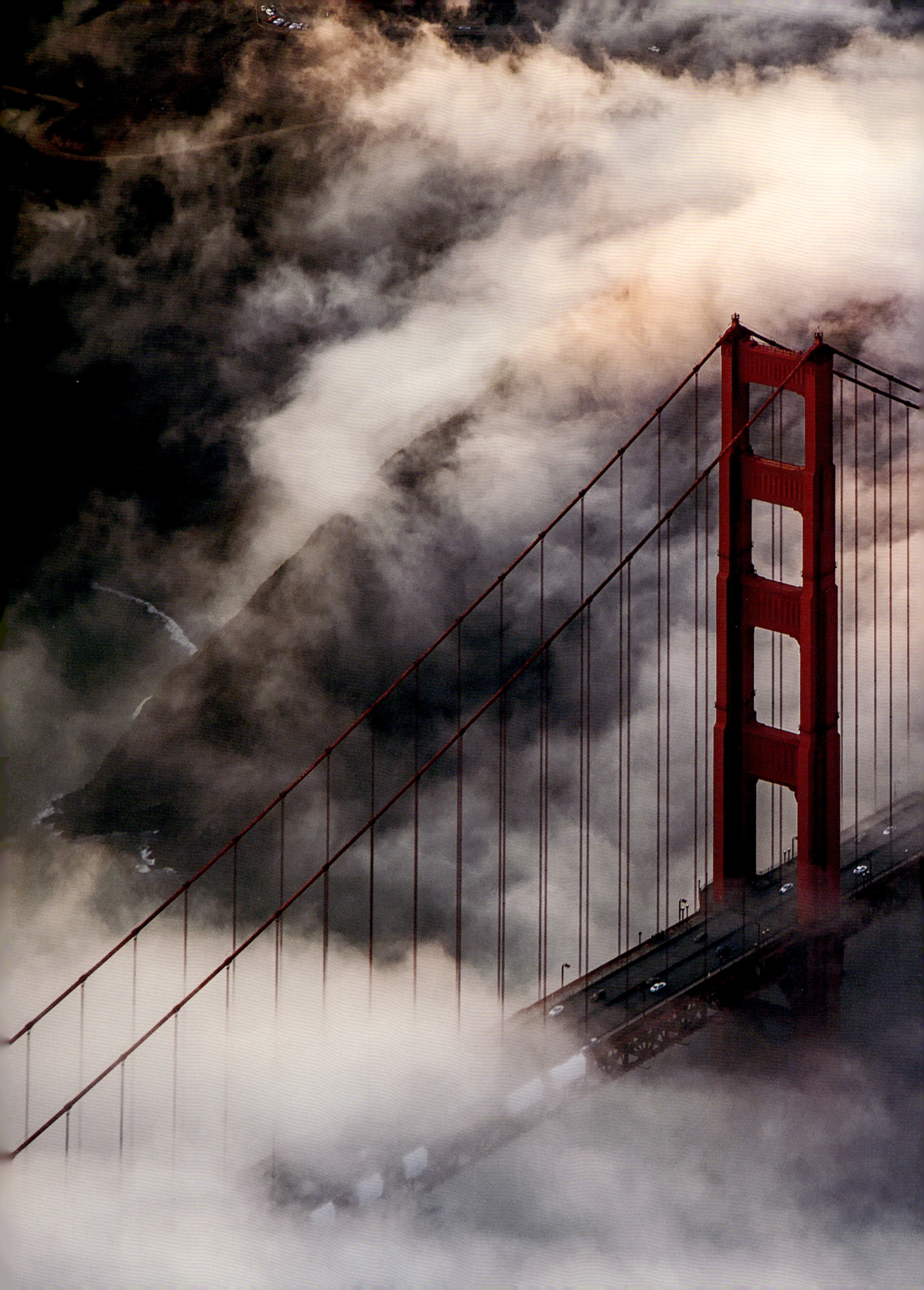

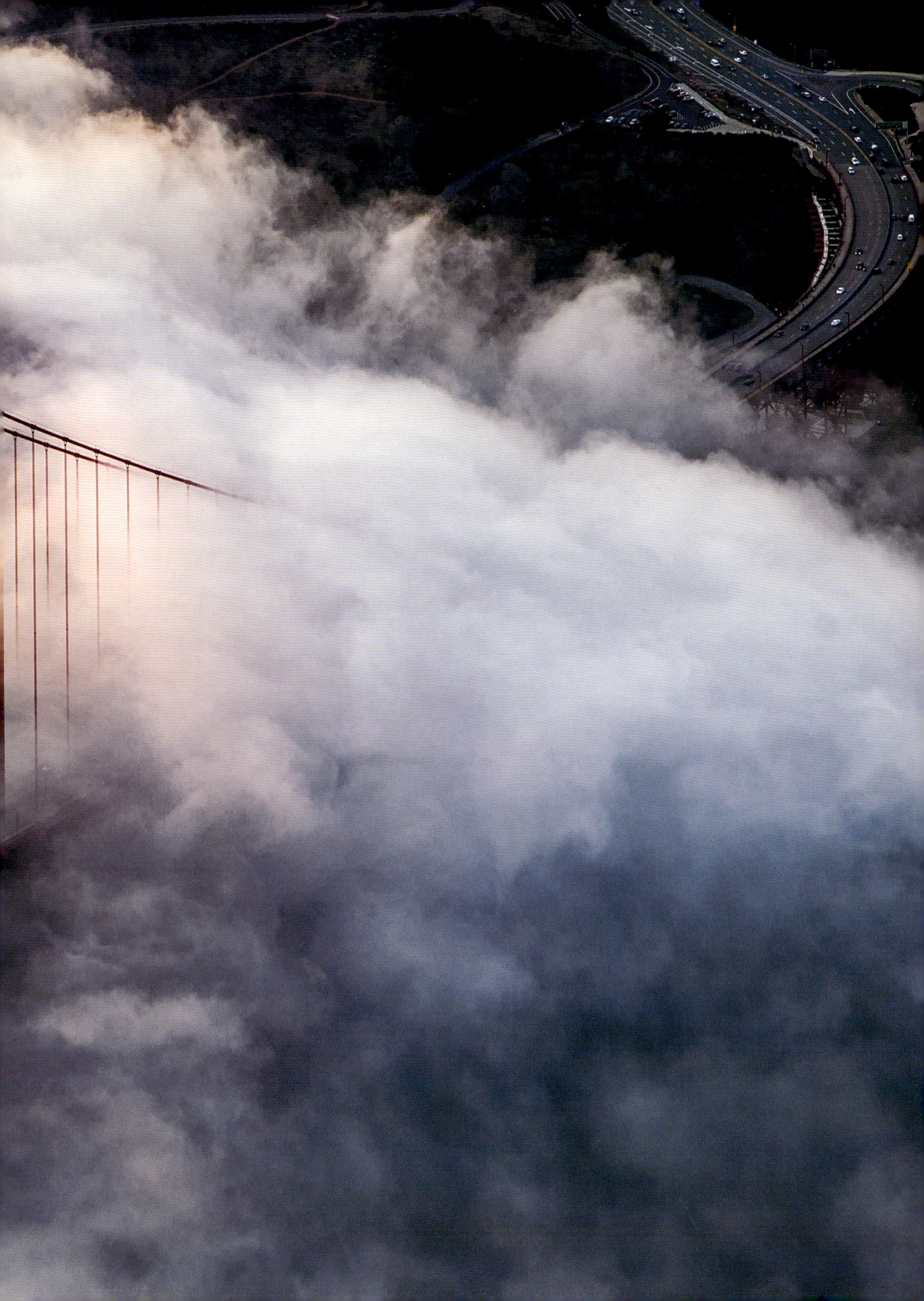

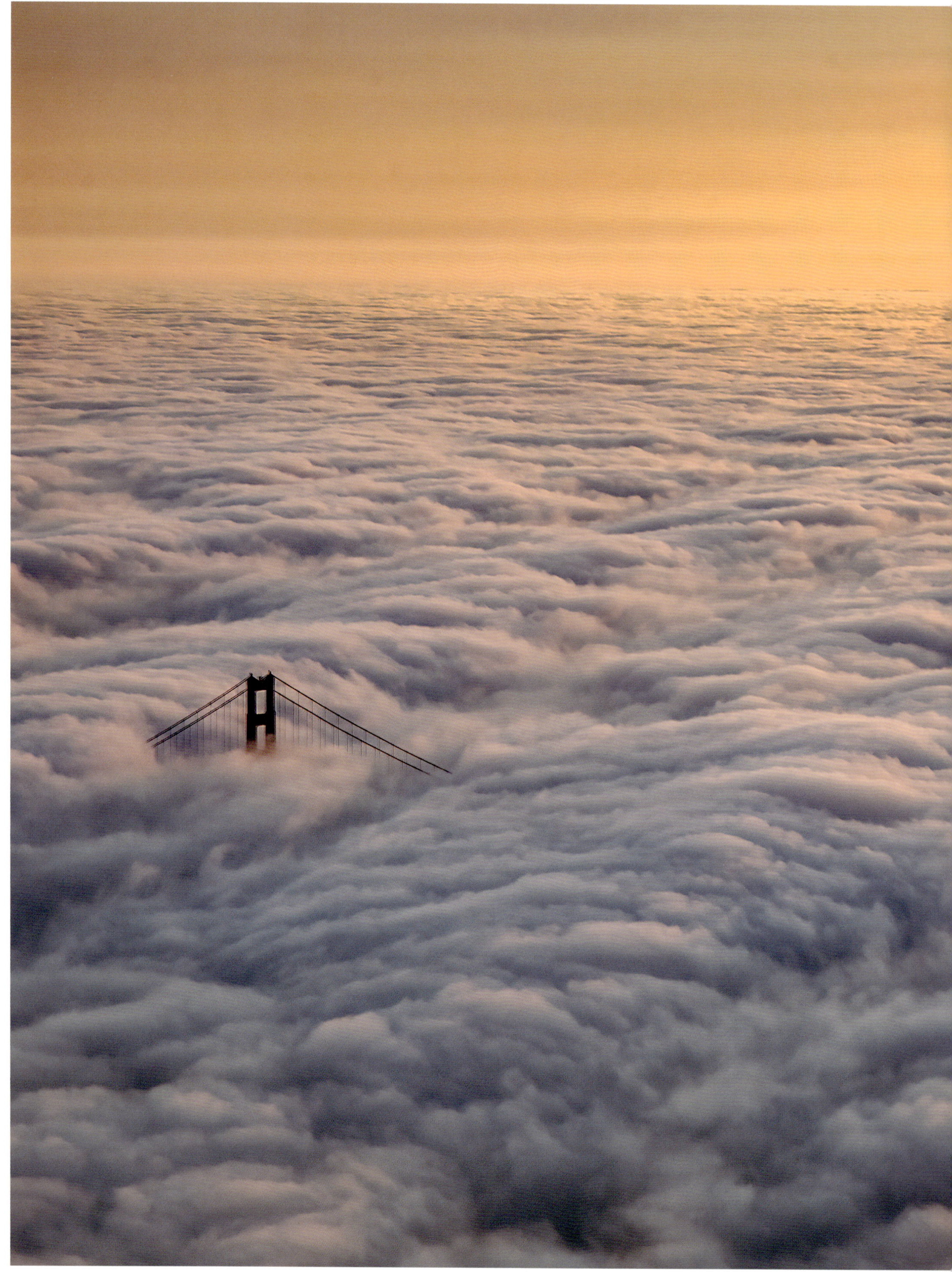

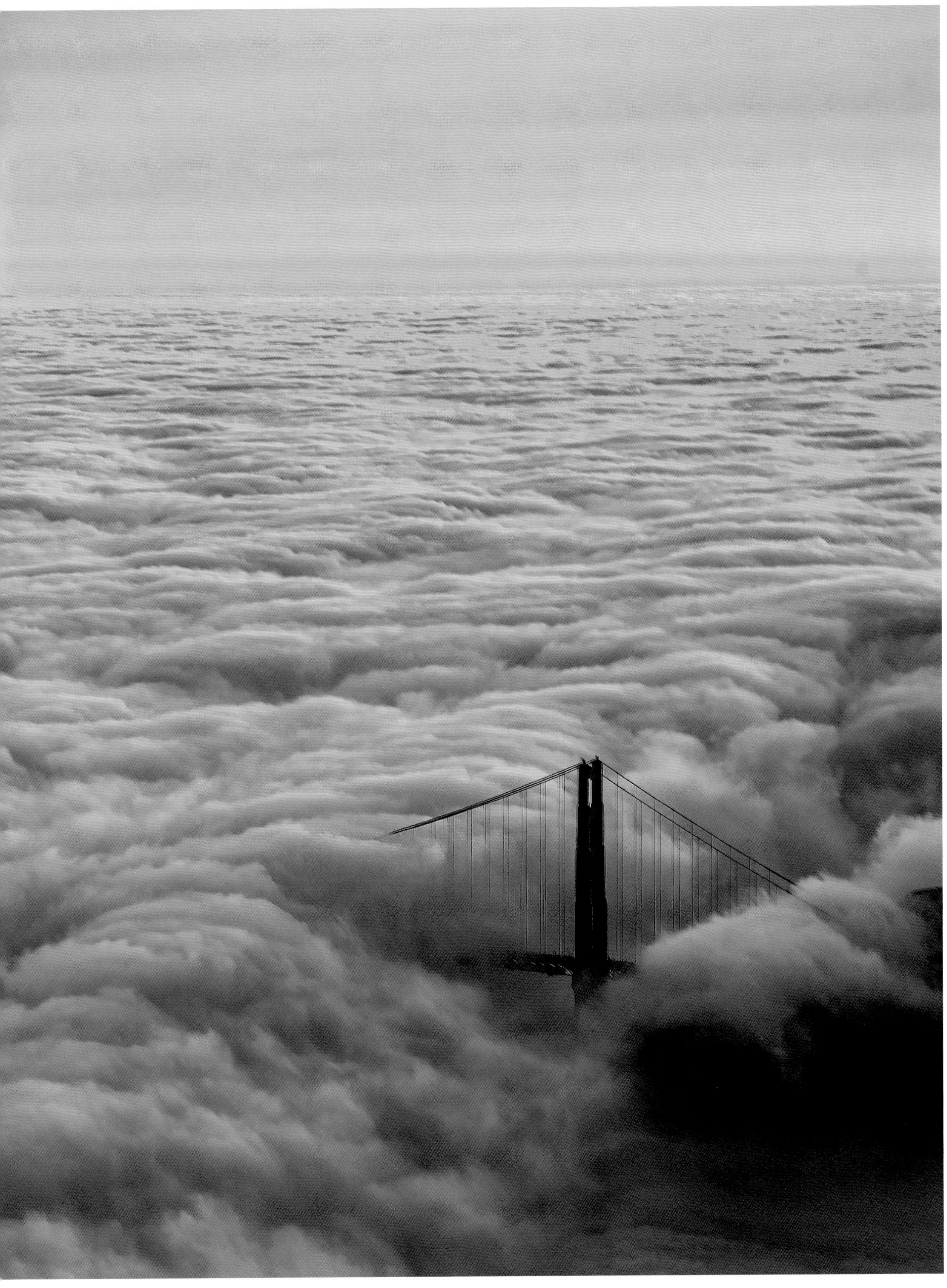

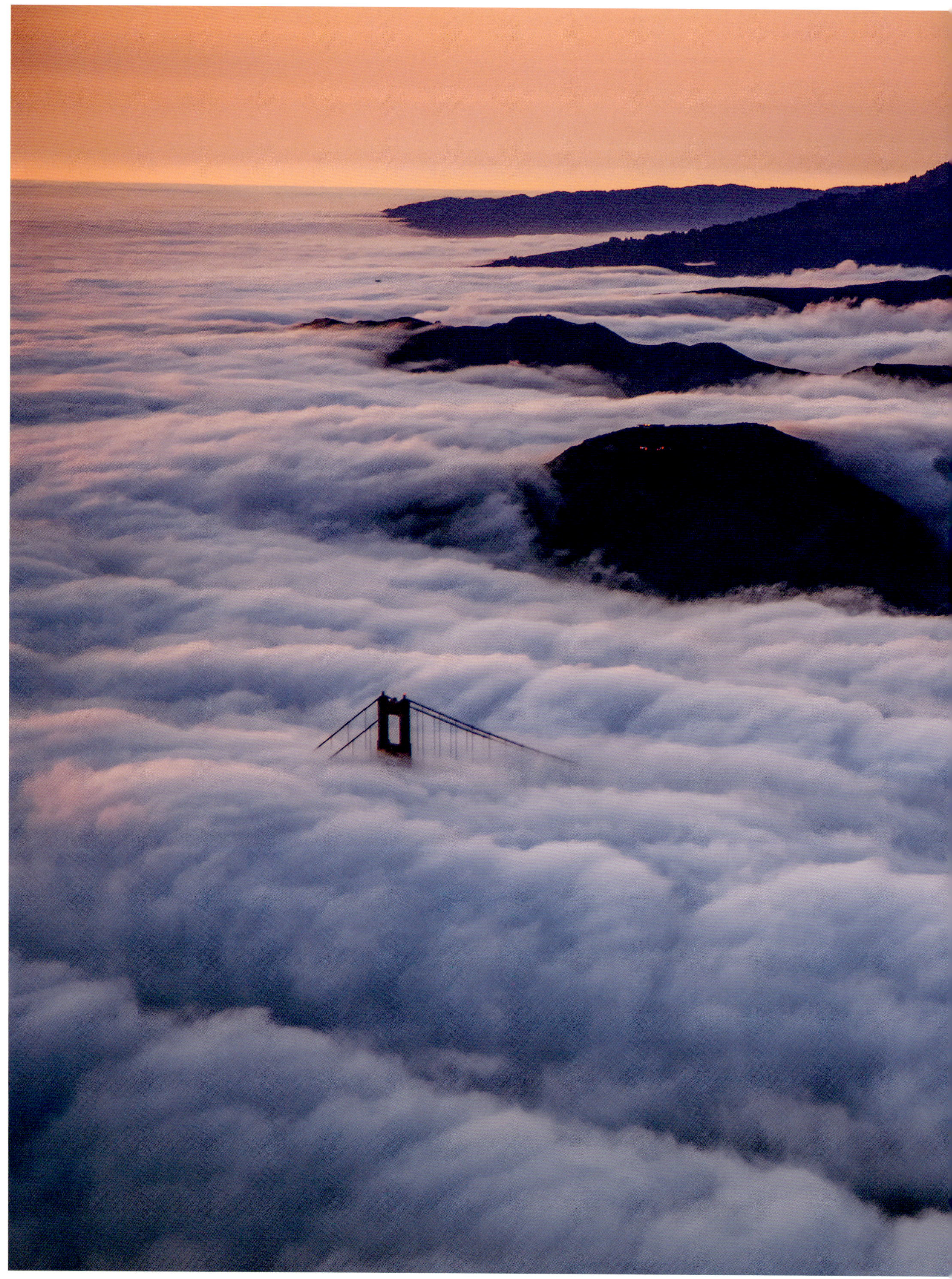

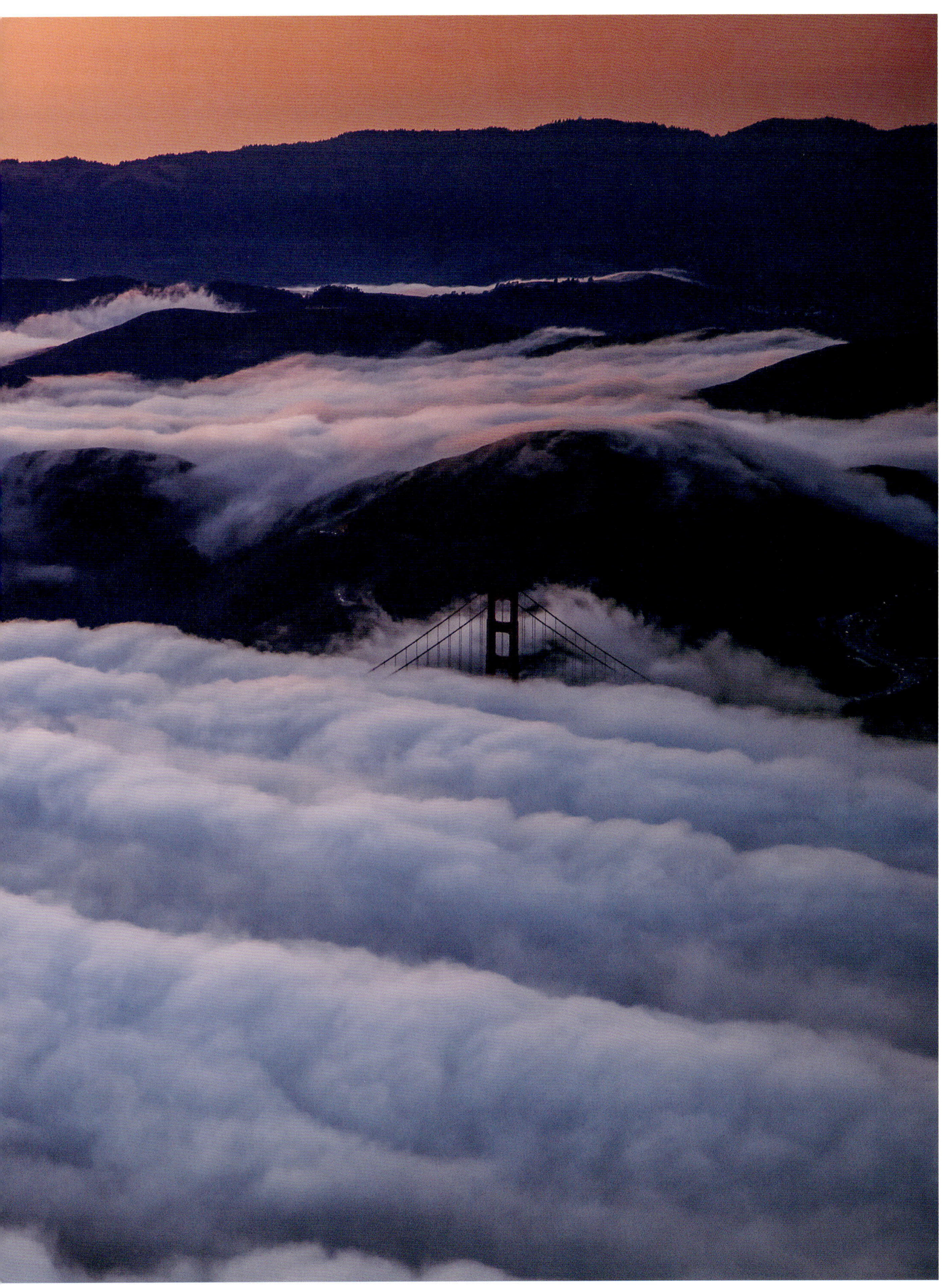

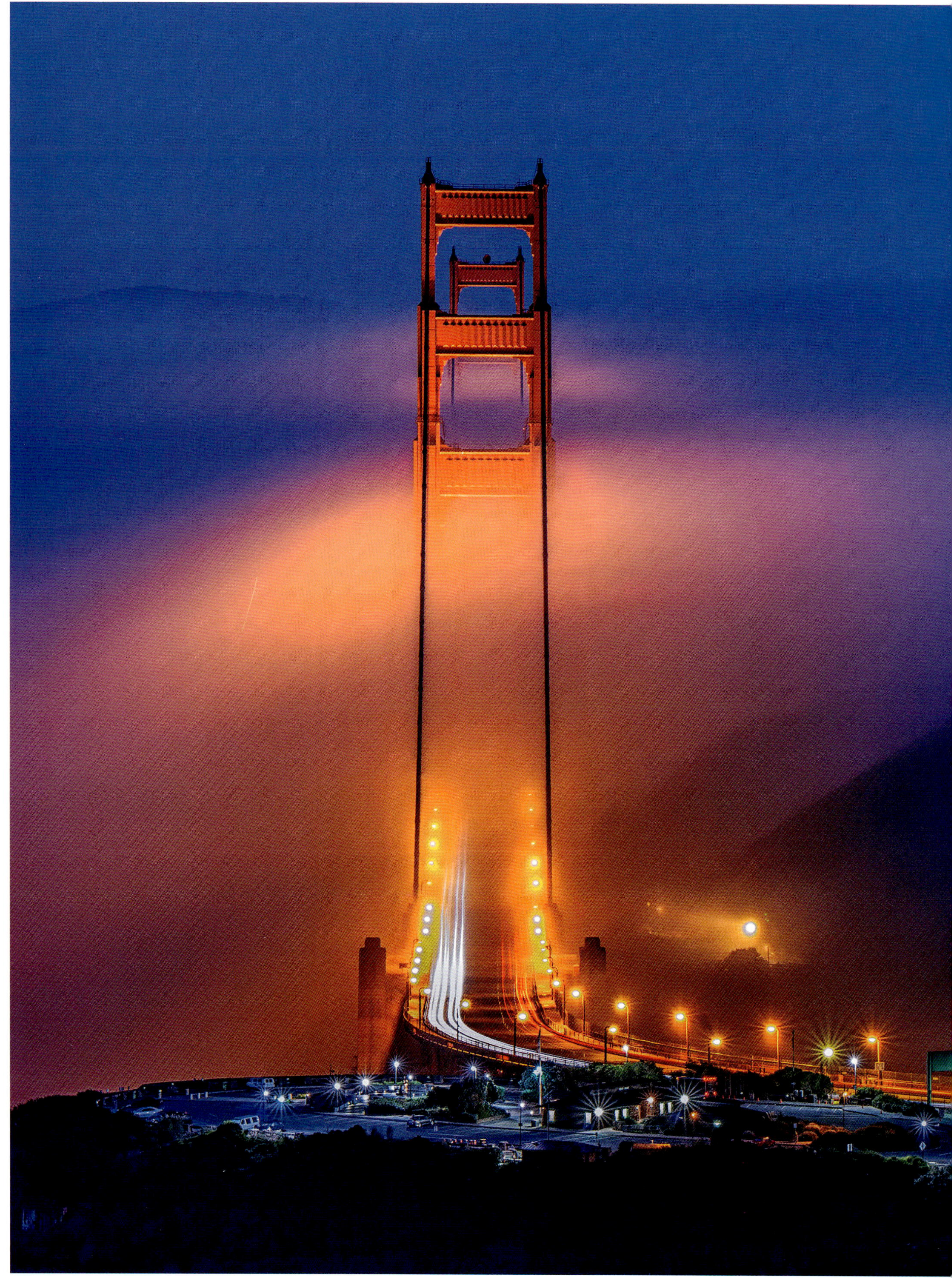

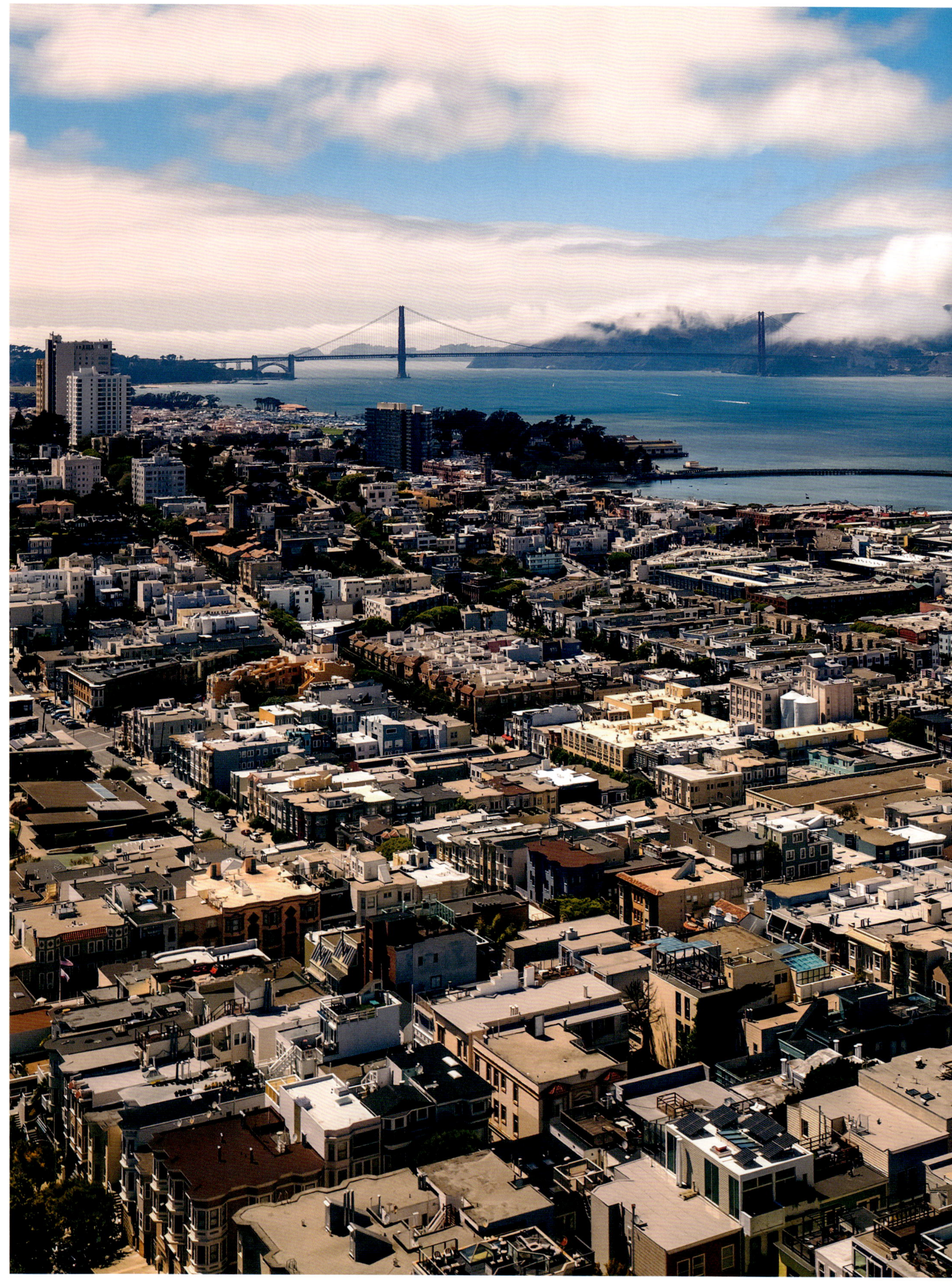

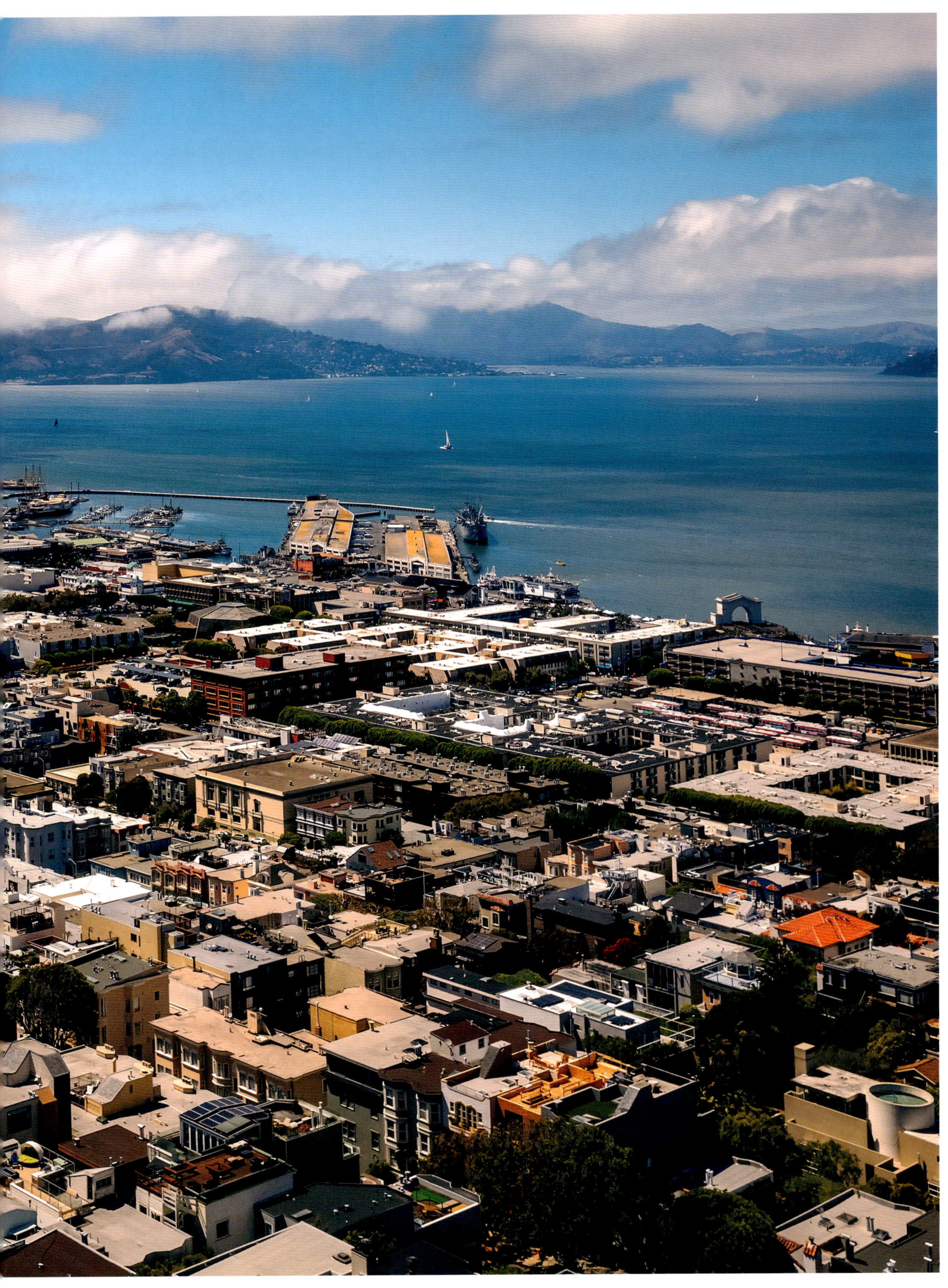

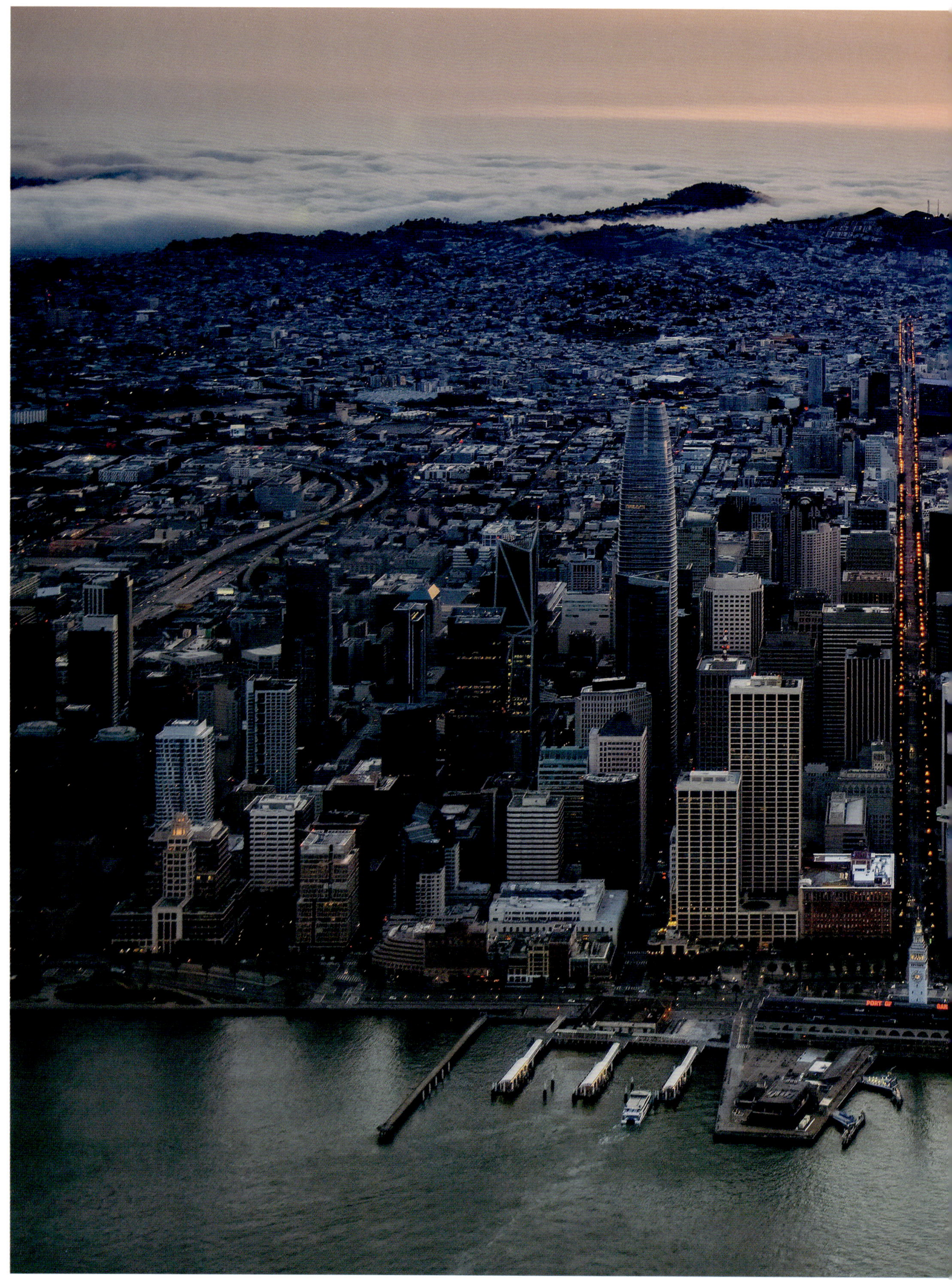

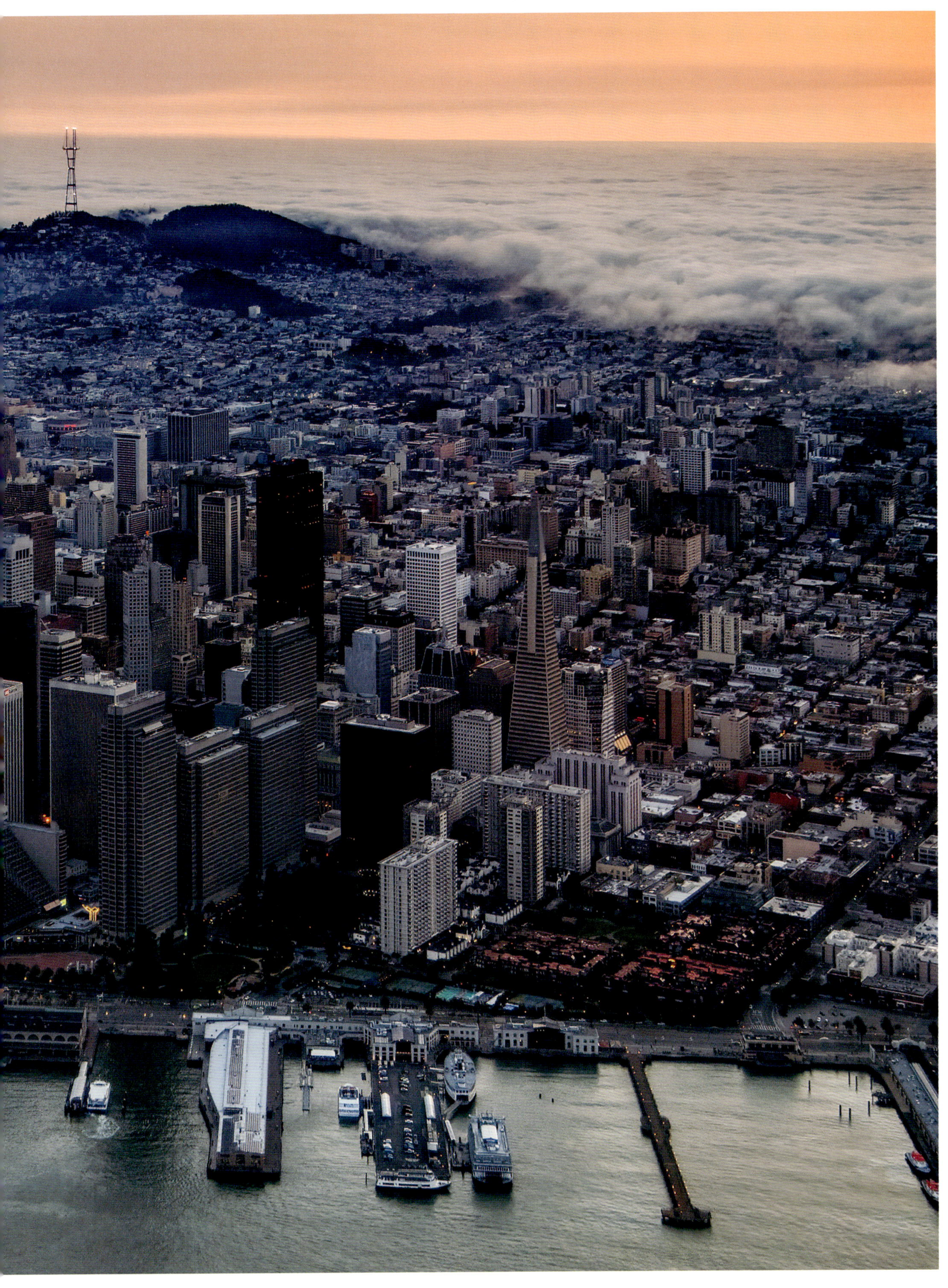

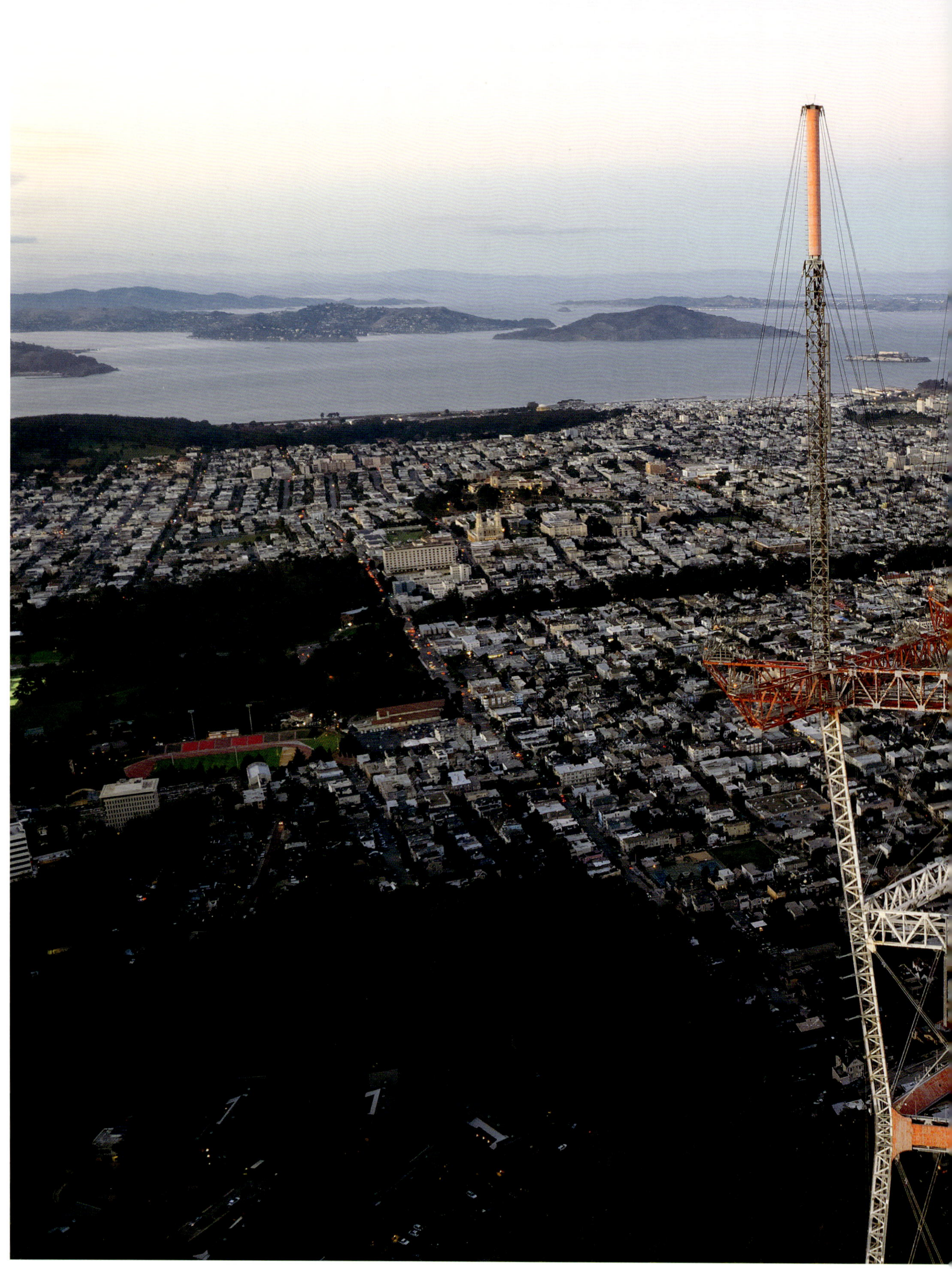

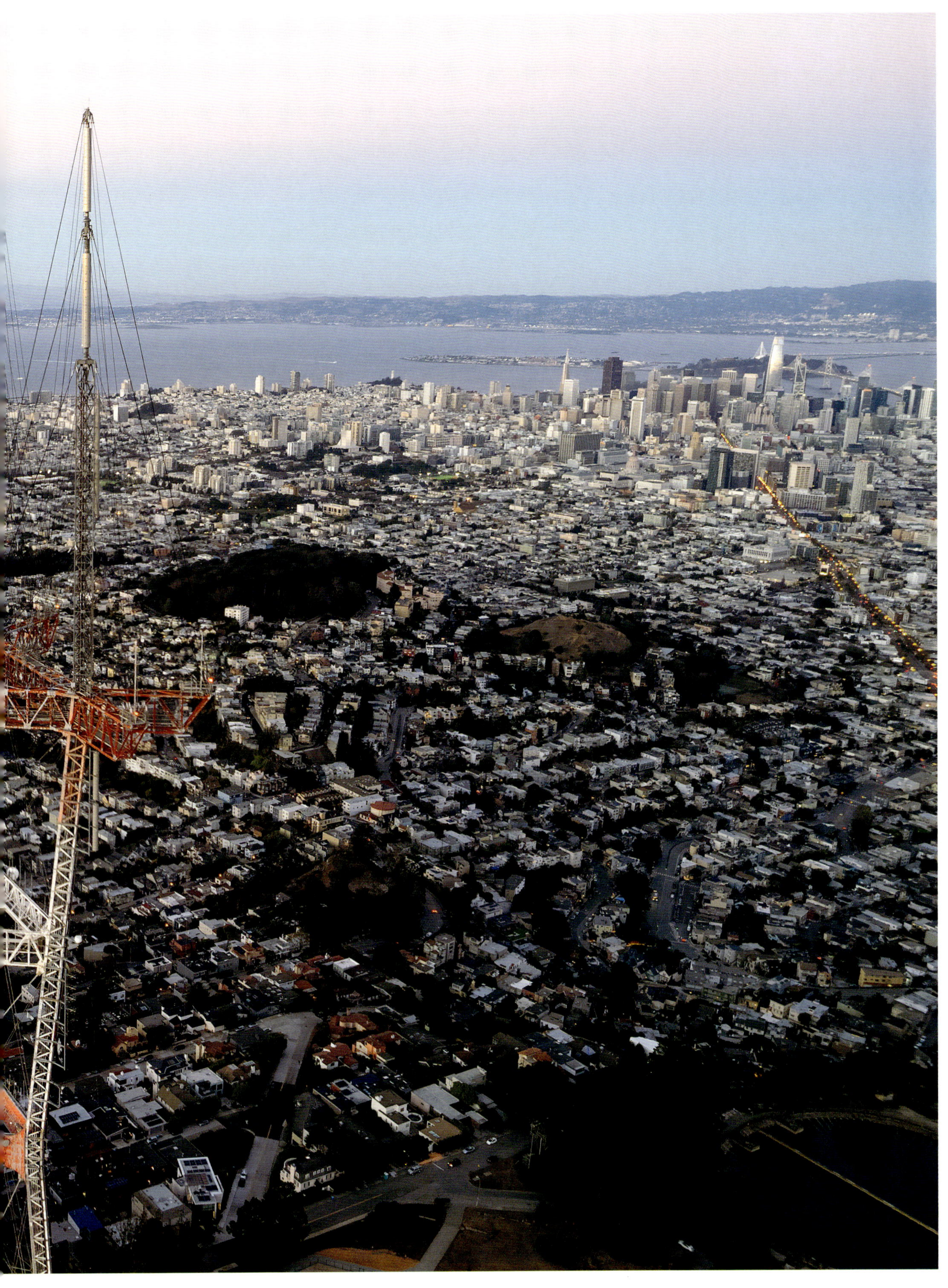

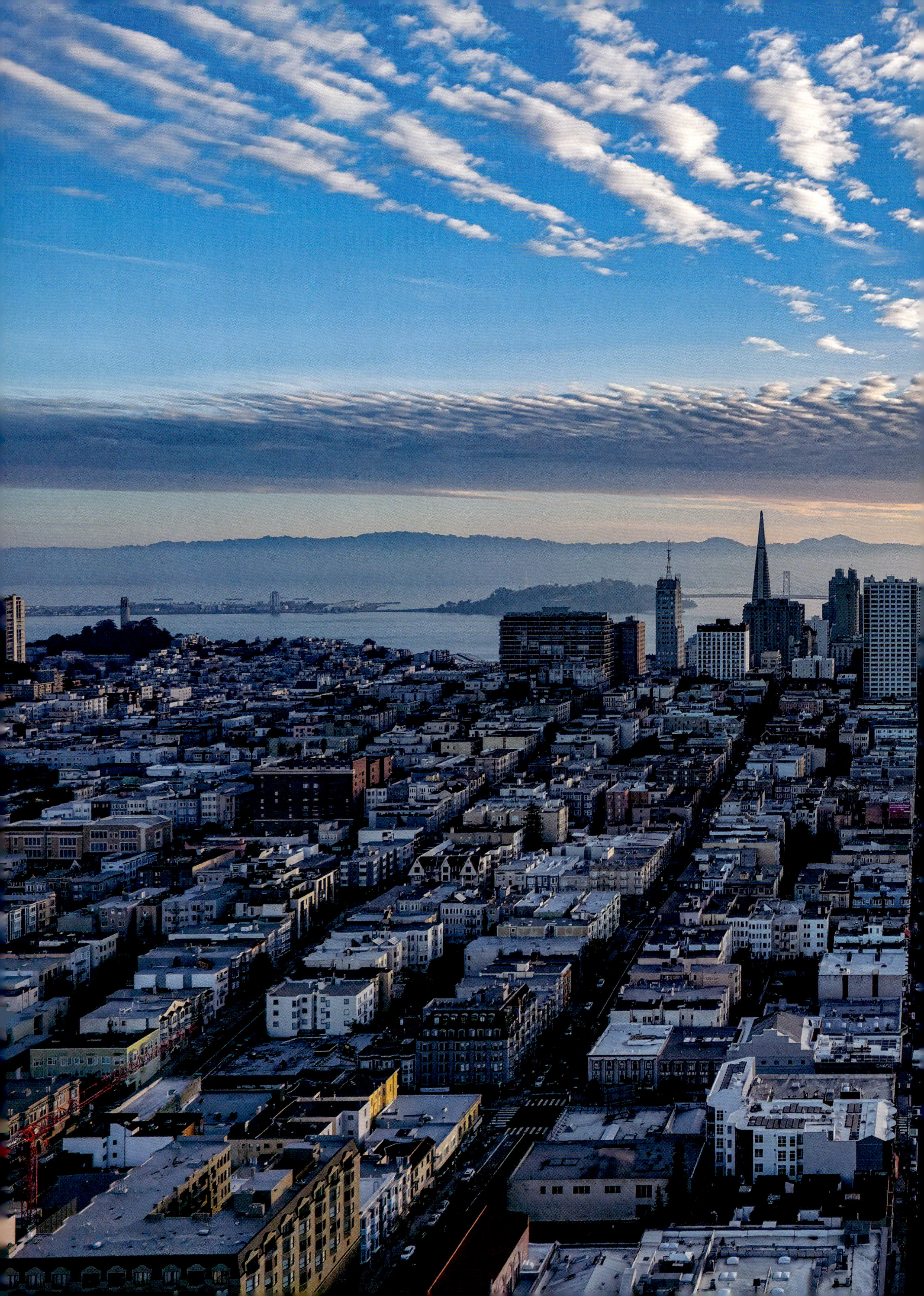

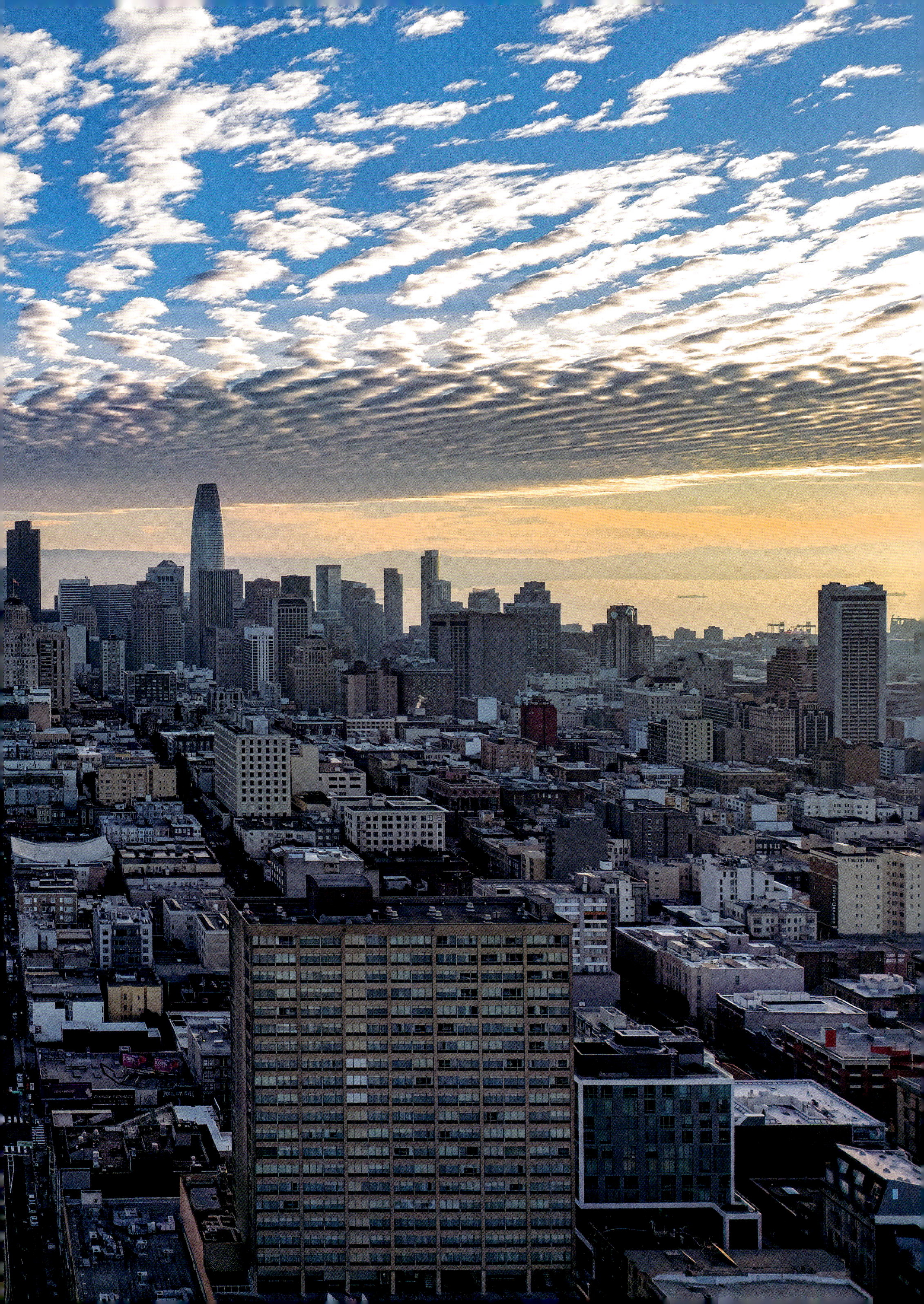

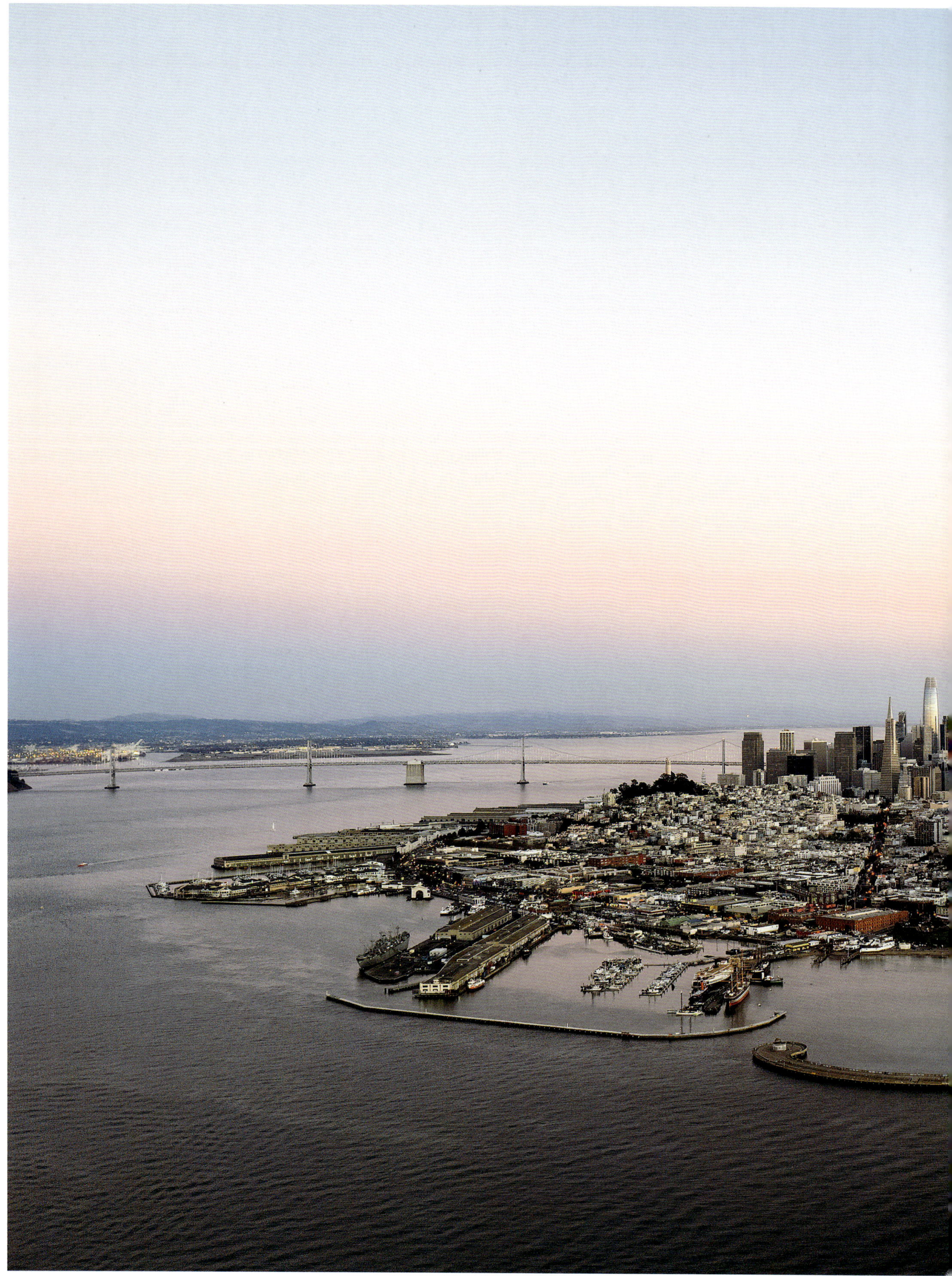

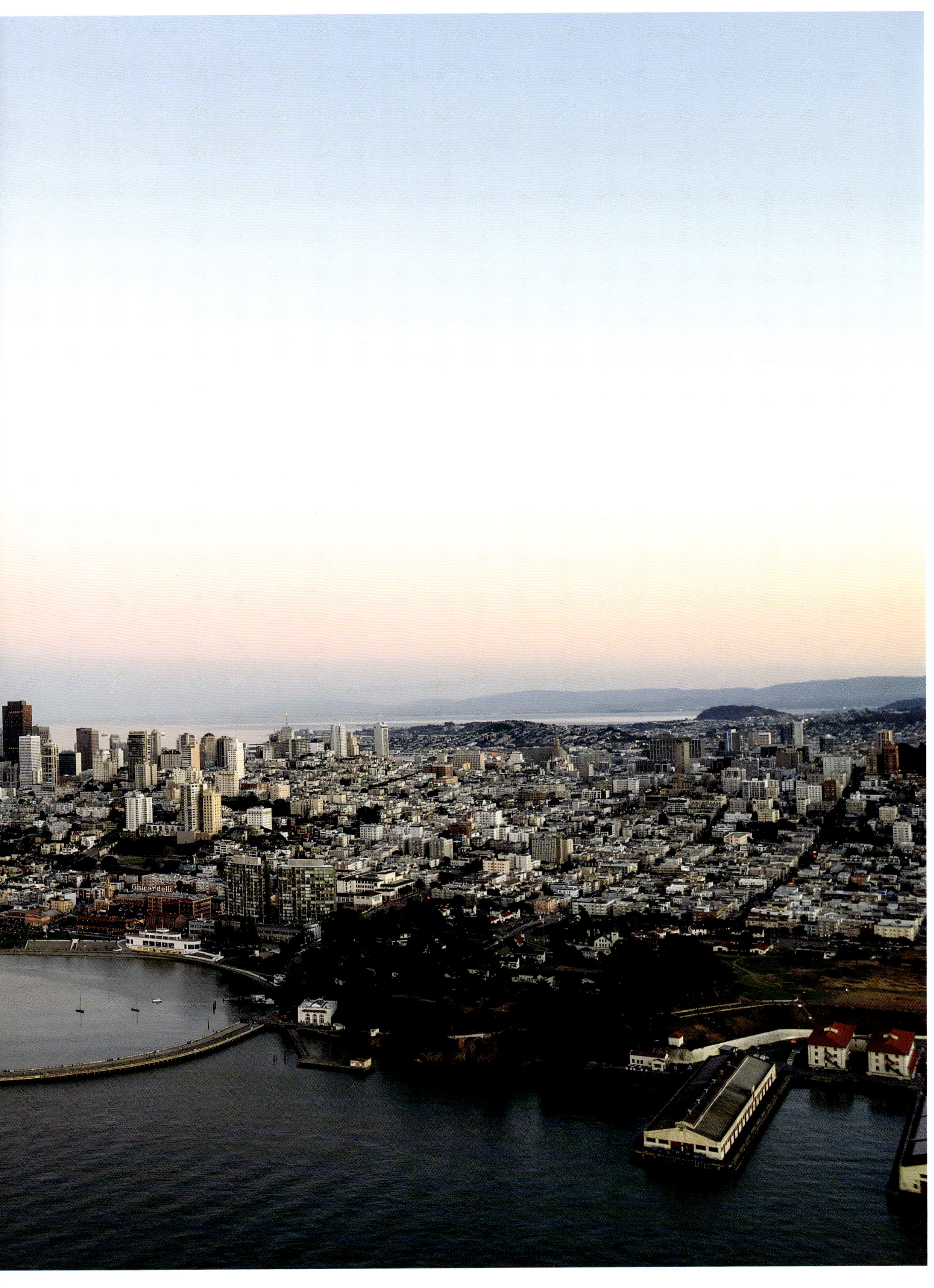

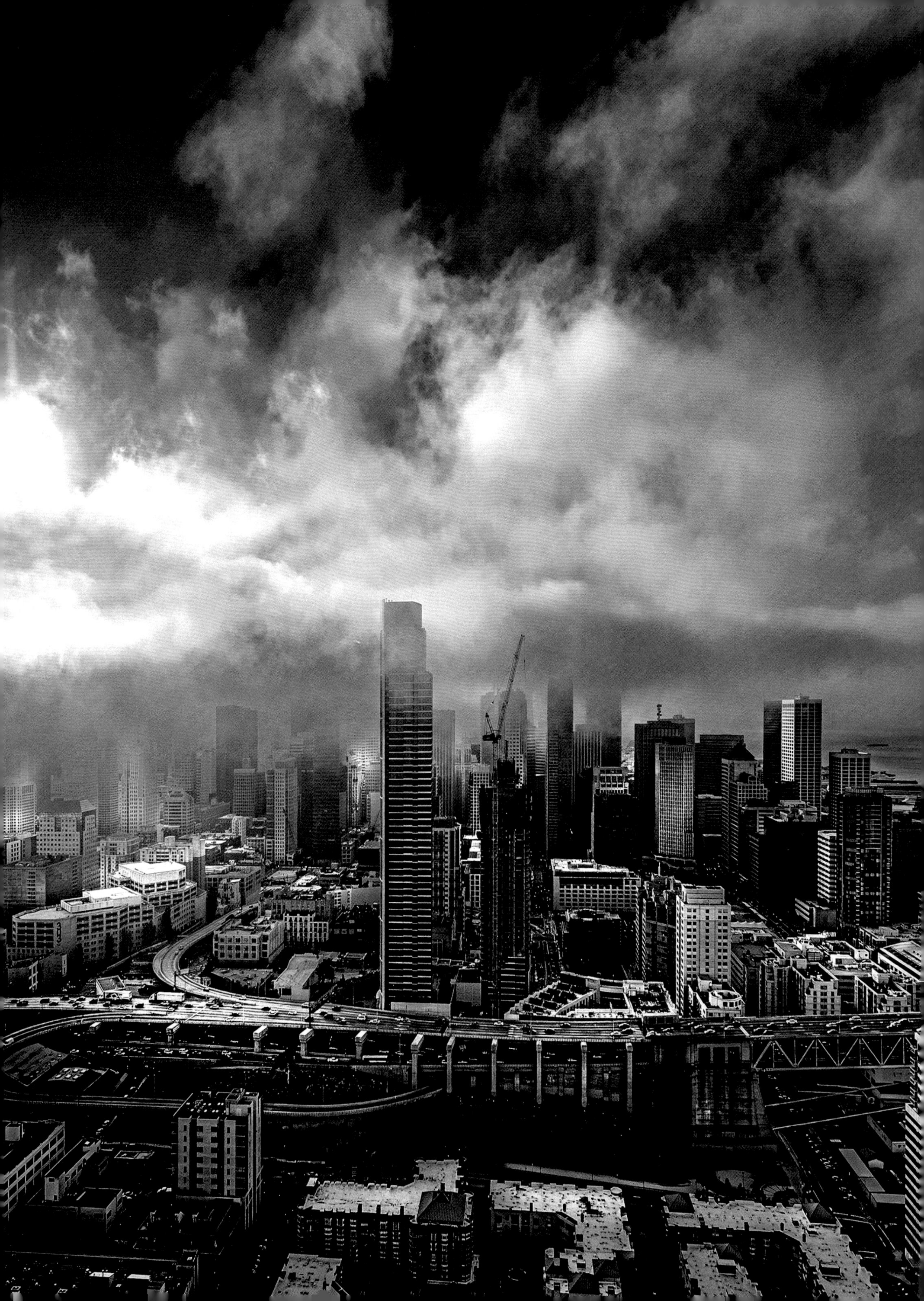

SAN FRANCISCO

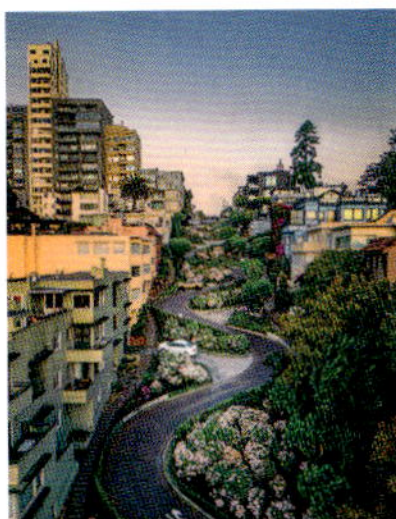

Front Cover
Diane Bentley Raymond
Above Lombard Street

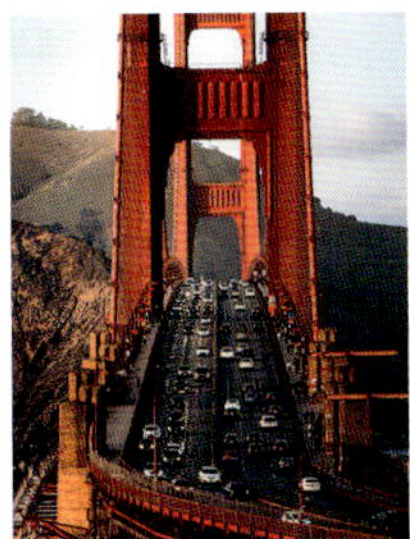

Back Cover
Kris Kuganathan
View of the Golden Gate Bridge

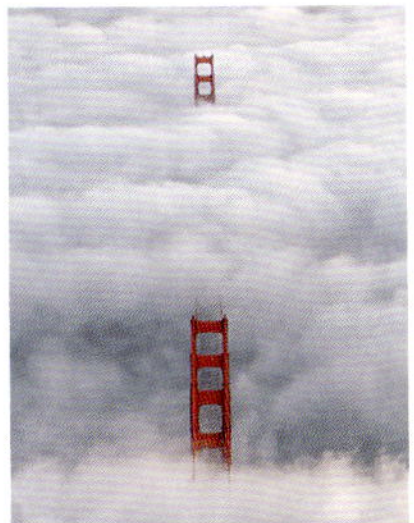

2 Jay Huang
Above the Golden
Gate Bridge

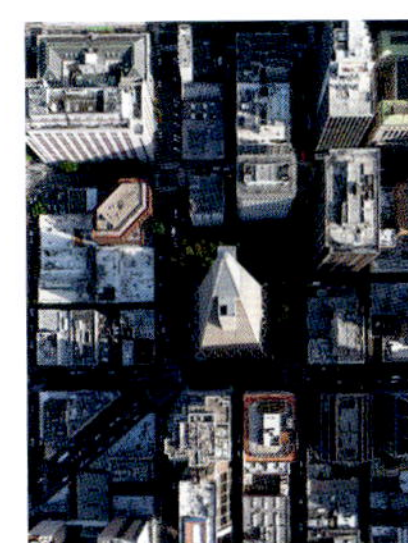

4 Jeffery Xin
Above the
Transamerica Pyramid

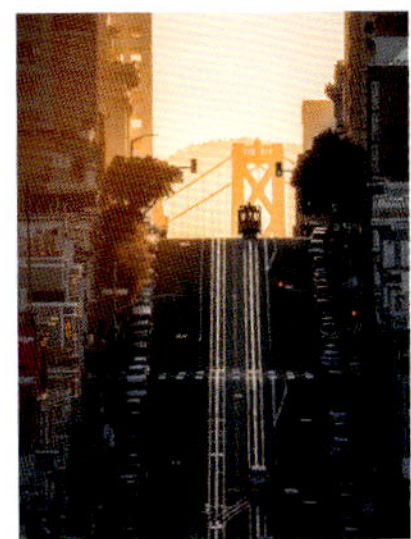

7 Kris Kuganathan
View of California Street
and the Bay Bridge

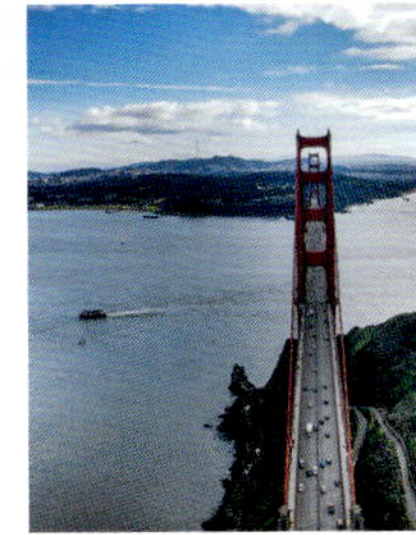

8 Lichao Liu
View of the Golden
Gate Bridge

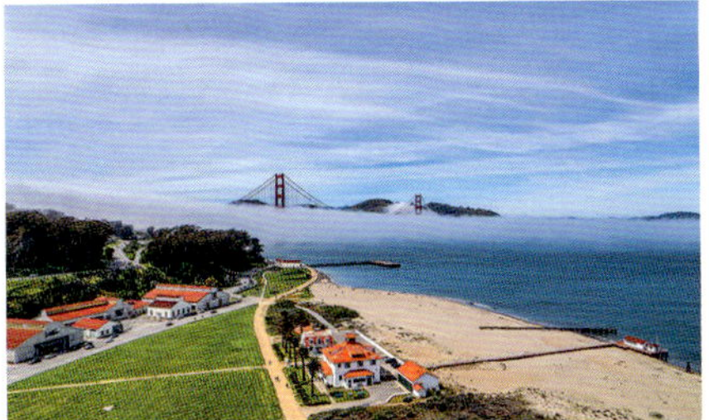

10-11 Diane Bentley Raymond
View of Crissy Field

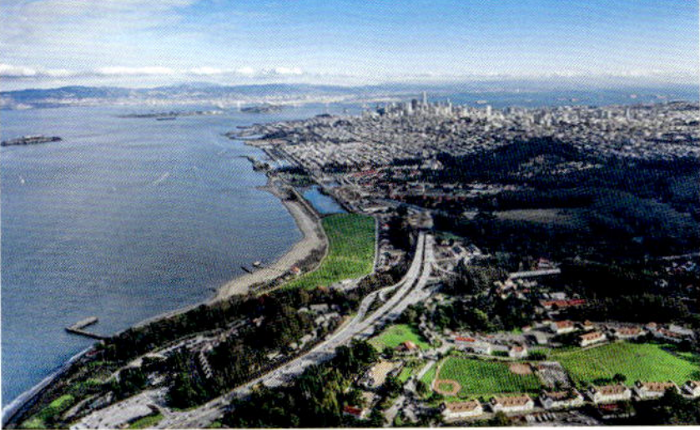

12-13 Lichao Liu
Above the Presidio

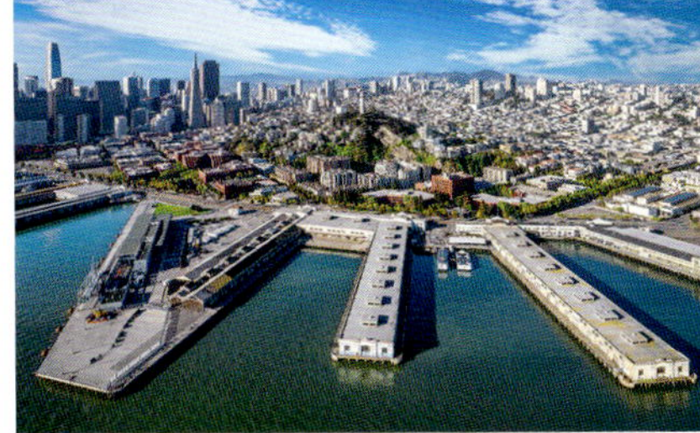

14-15 Diane Bentley Raymond
View of Pier 27, Pier 33, and Pier 35

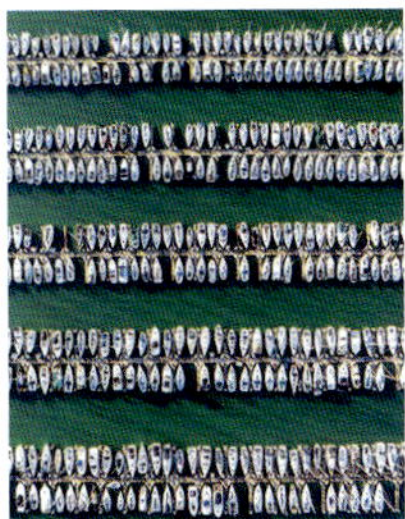

16 John Montoya
Above South Beach Harbor

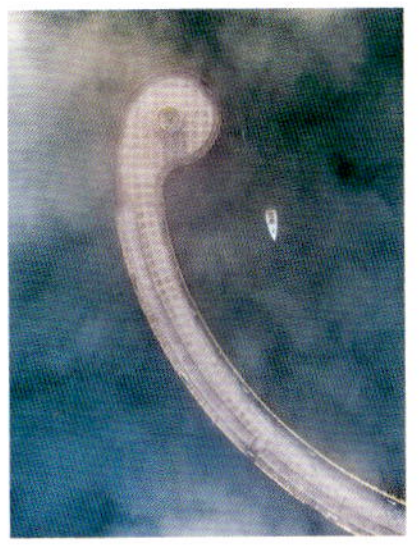

17 John Montoya
Above Aquatic Park Cove

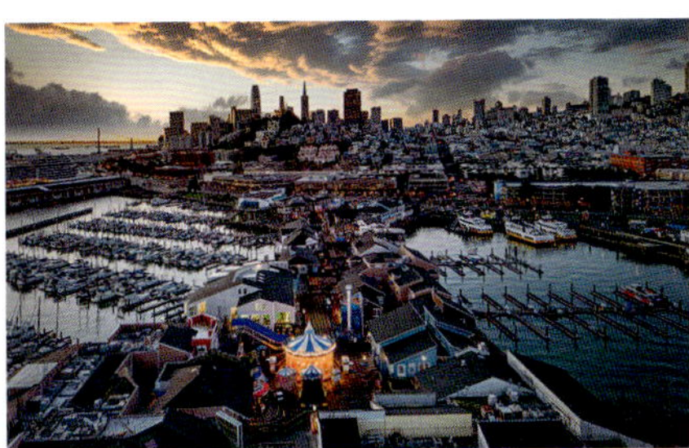

18-19 Diane Bentley Raymond
View of Fisherman's Wharf

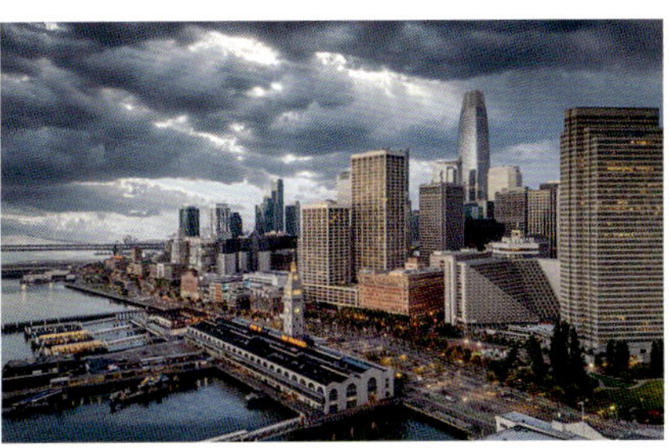

20-21 Diane Bentley Raymond
View of the Ferry Building and the Financial District

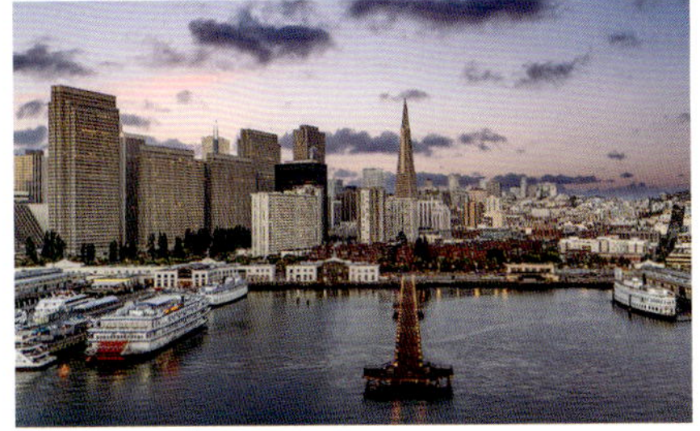

22-23 Diane Bentley Raymond
View of Pier 7 and the Financial District

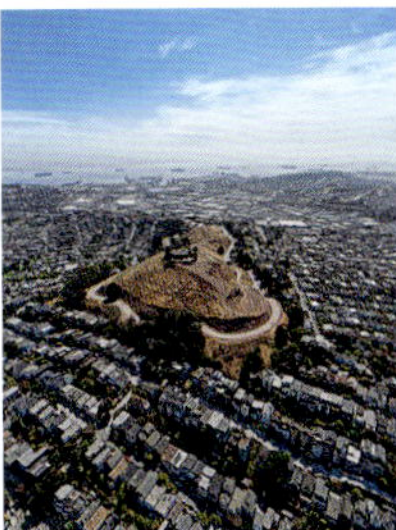

24 John Montoya
View of Bernal Heights Park

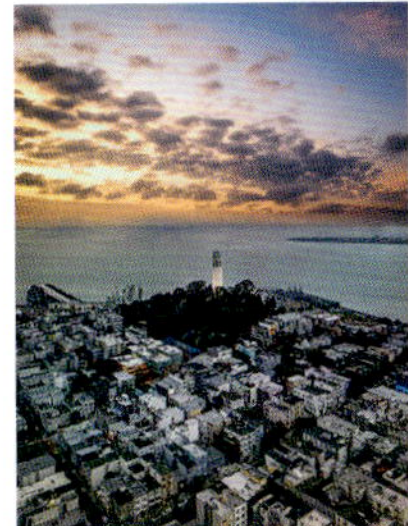

25 Diane Bentley Raymond
View of Coit Tower

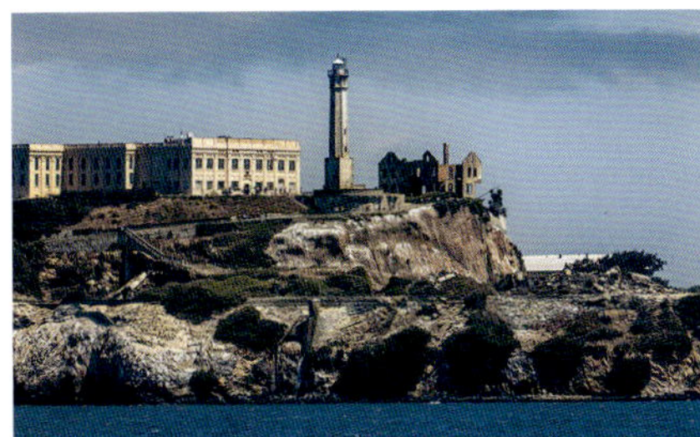

26-27 Jack Landau
View of Alcatraz Island

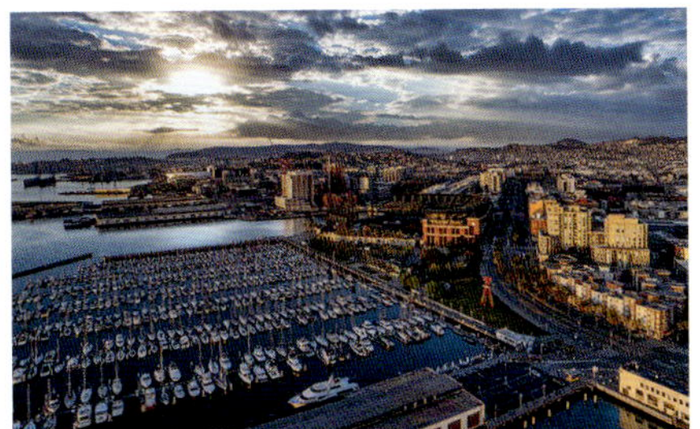

28-29 Diane Bentley Raymond
Above South Beach Harbor and Oracle Park

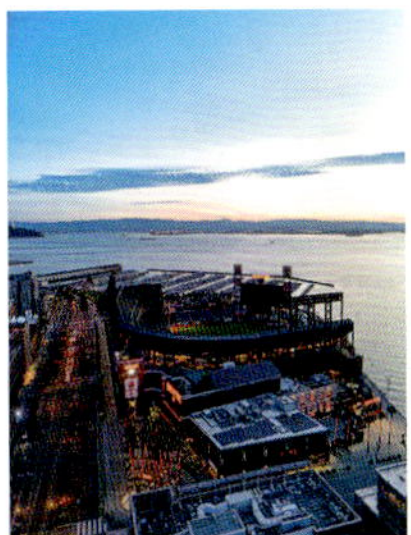

30 Diane Bentley Raymond
Above Oracle Park

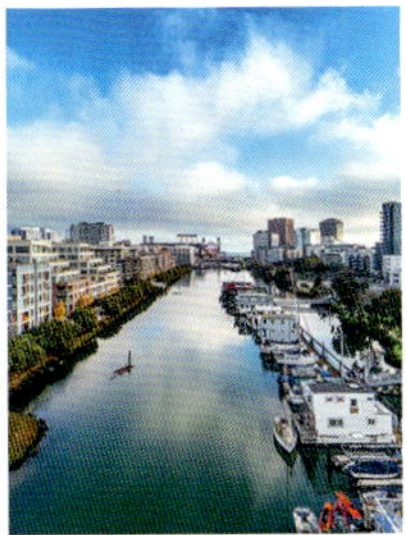

31 Diane Bentley Raymond
View of Mission Creek
Channel

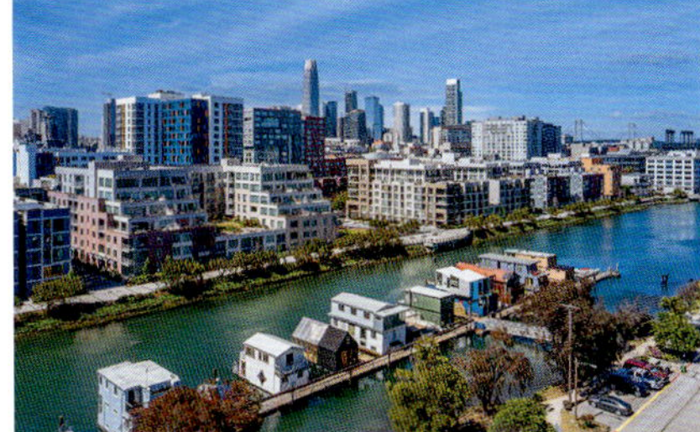

32-33 Diane Bentley Raymond
View of Mission Creek Channel

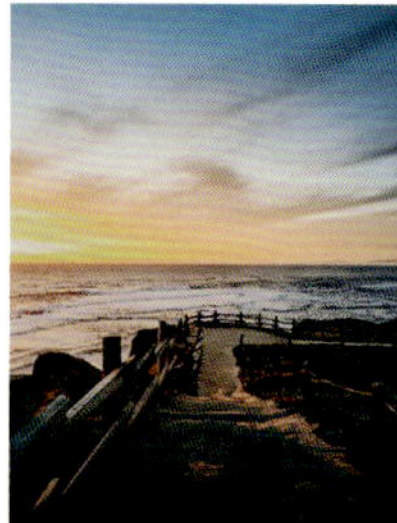

34 Cocu Liu
View from Lands End Trail

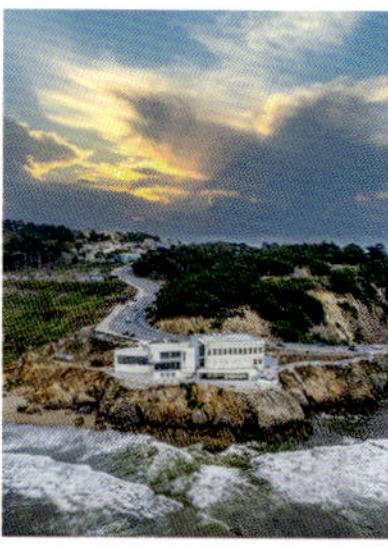

35 Diane Bentley Raymond
View of the Cliff House

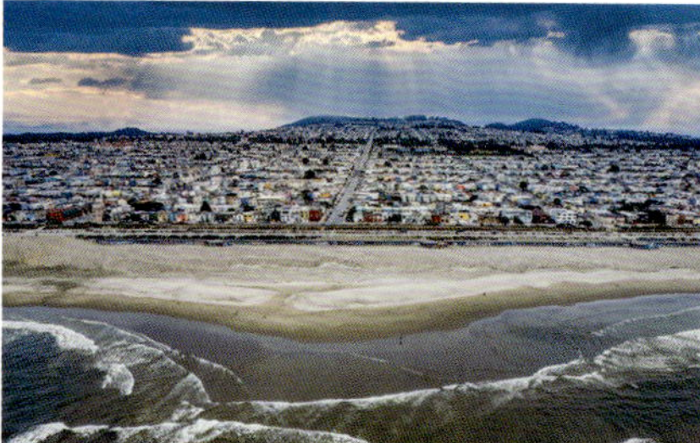

36-37 Diane Bentley Raymond
View of Ocean Beach and the Sunset District

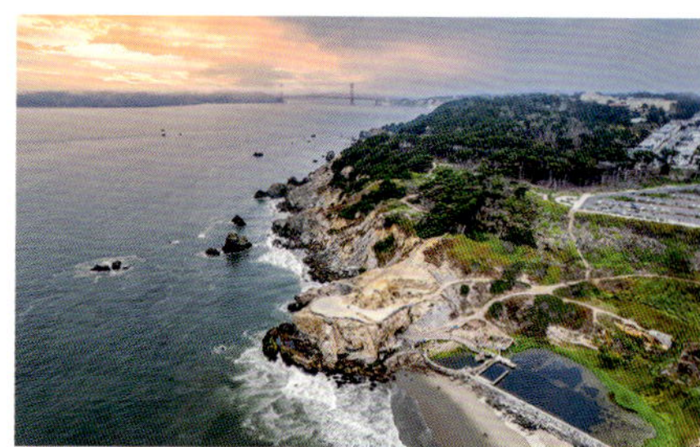

38-39 Diane Bentley Raymond
View of Point Lobos

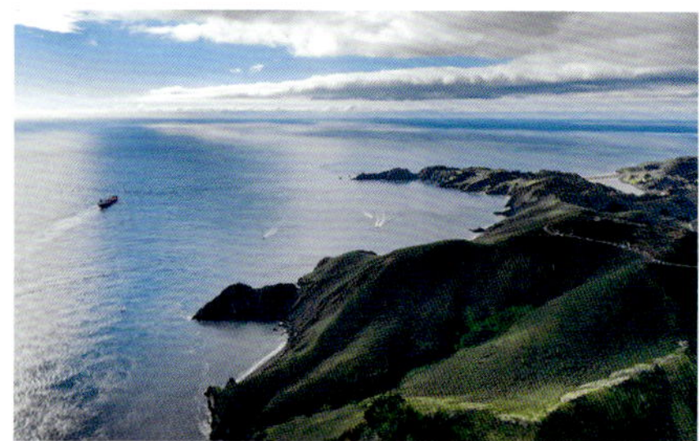

40-41 Lichao Liu
Above the Farallon Islands

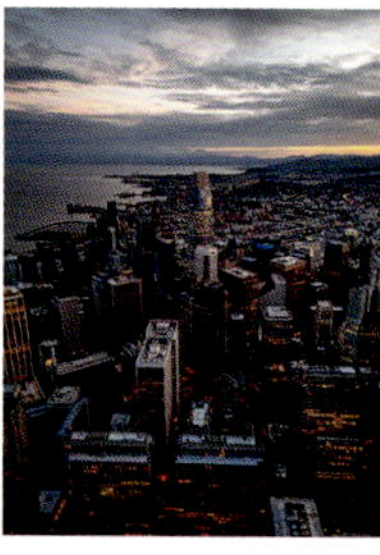

43 Kris Kuganathan
Above the Financial District

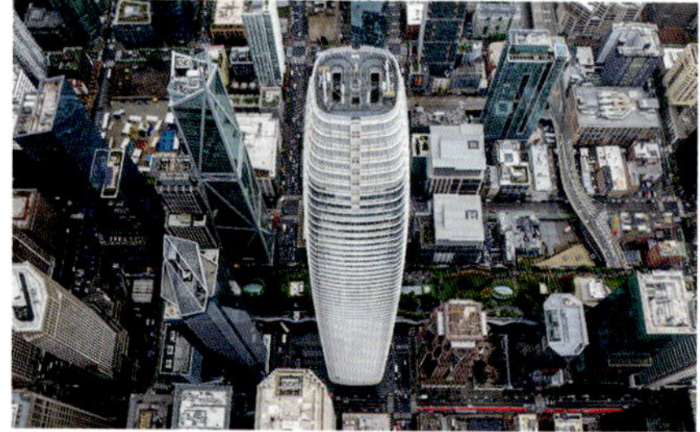

44-45 Jeffery Xin
View of Salesforce Tower

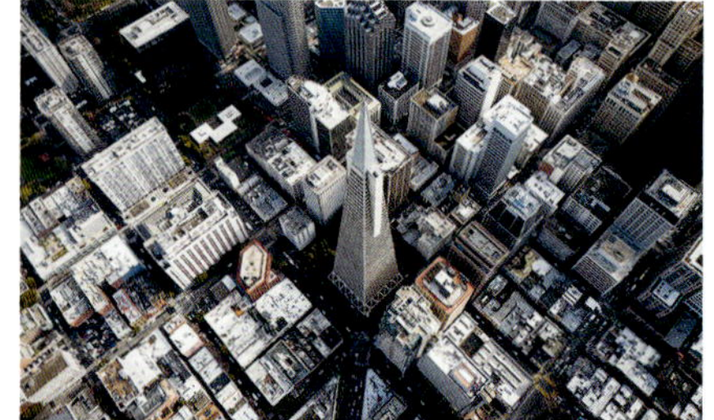

46-47 Jeffery Xin
Above the Transamerica Pyramid

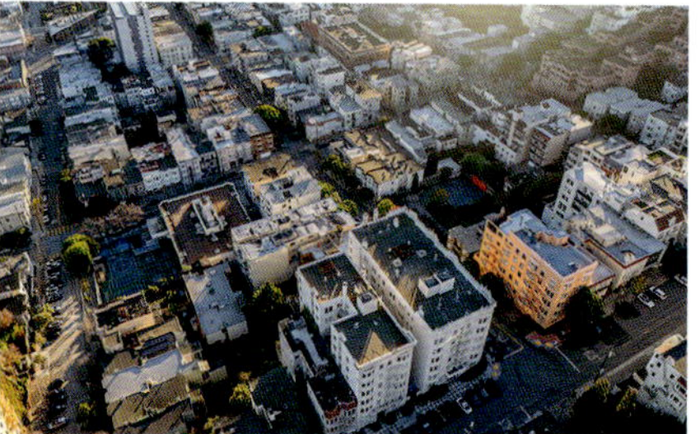

48 Jeffery Xin
Above Leavenworth Street and Greenwich Street

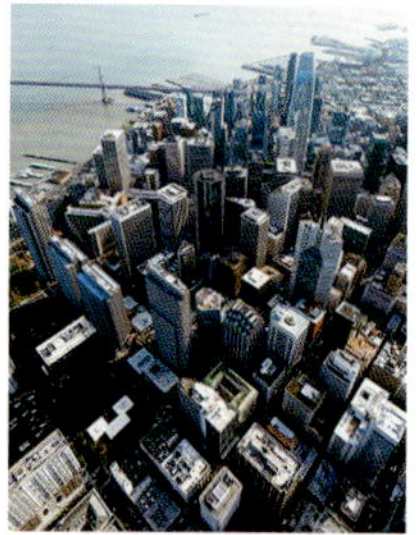

49 Jeffery Xin
Above the Financial District

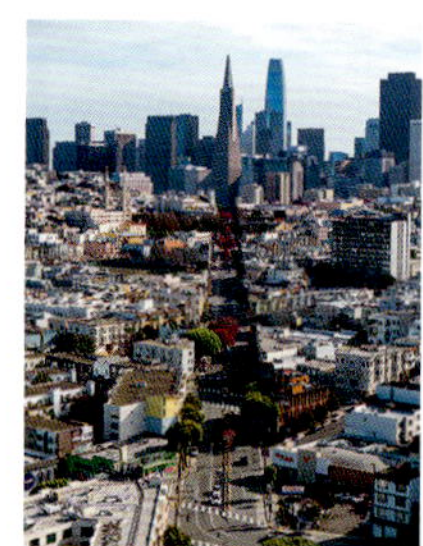

50 Jeffery Xin
Above Columbus Avenue

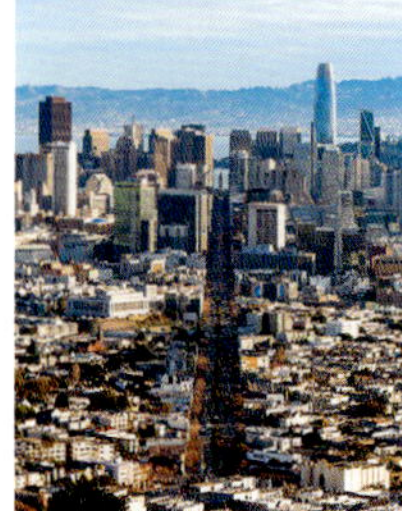

51 Jeffery Xin
Above Market Street

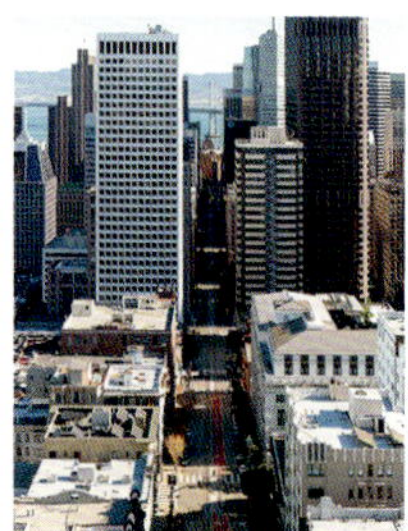

52 Jeffery Xin
Above California Street

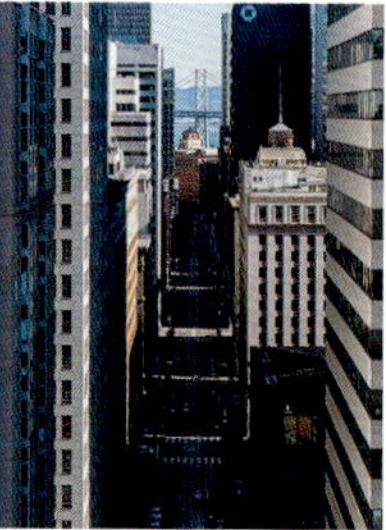

53 Jeffery Xin
Above California Street

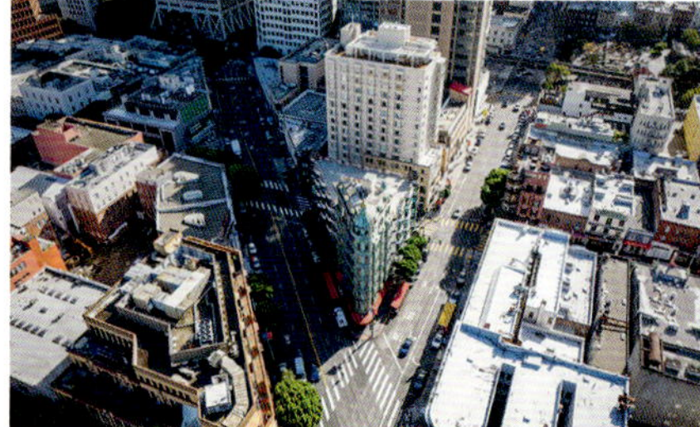

54-55 Jeffery Xin
Intersection of Columbus Avenue and Kearny Street

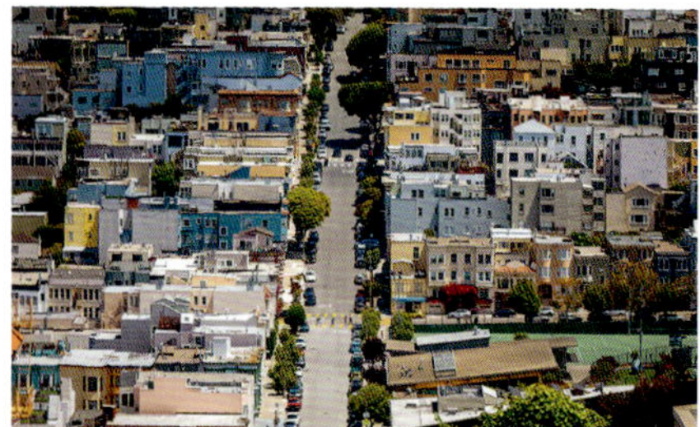

56-57 Jack Landau
View down Lombard Street

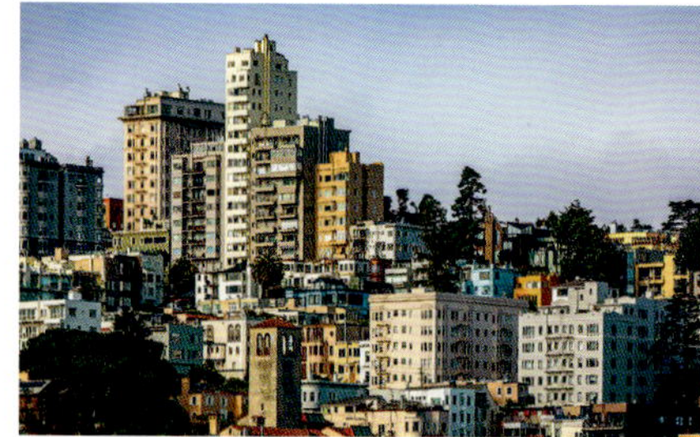

58-59 Jack Landau
View of Russian Hill

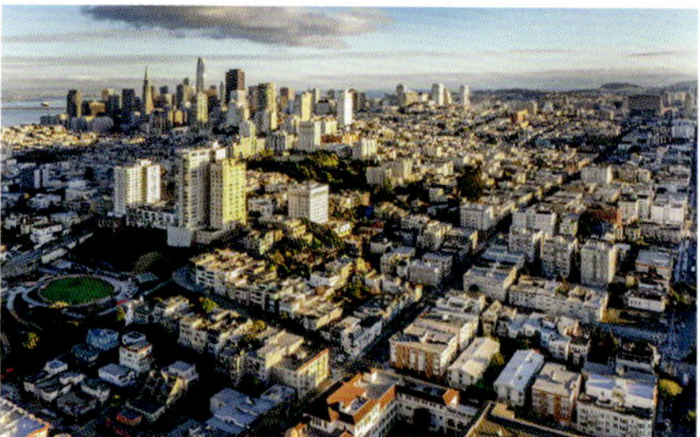

60-61 Lichao Liu
View across San Francisco

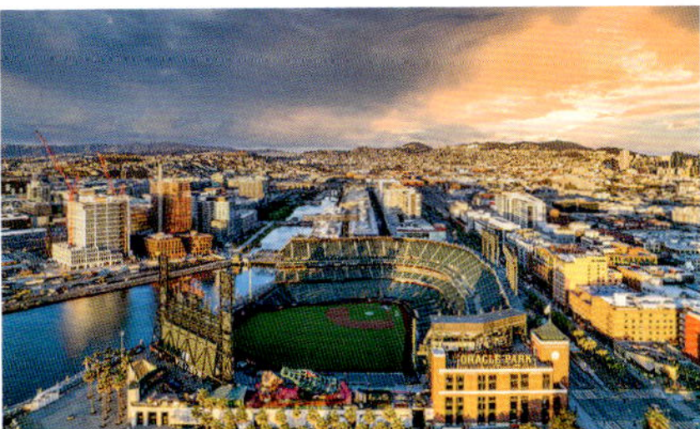

62-63 **Diane Bentley Raymond**
View of Oracle Park

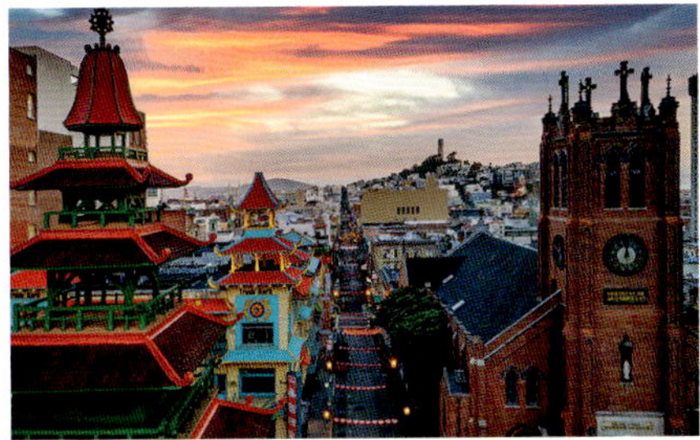

64-65 **Diane Bentley Raymond**
Above Grant Avenue

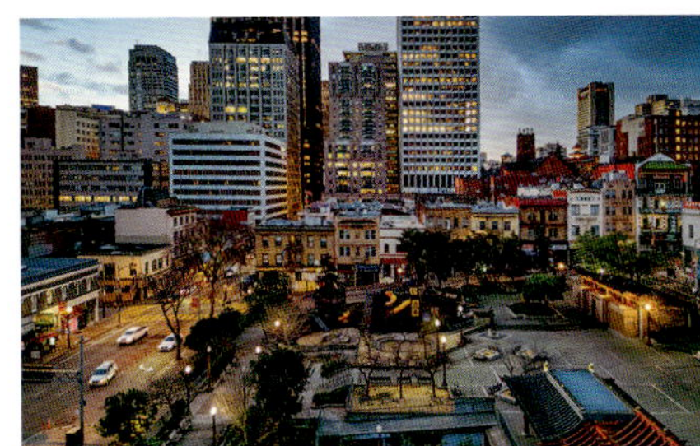

66-67 **Diane Bentley Raymond**
View of Portsmouth Square

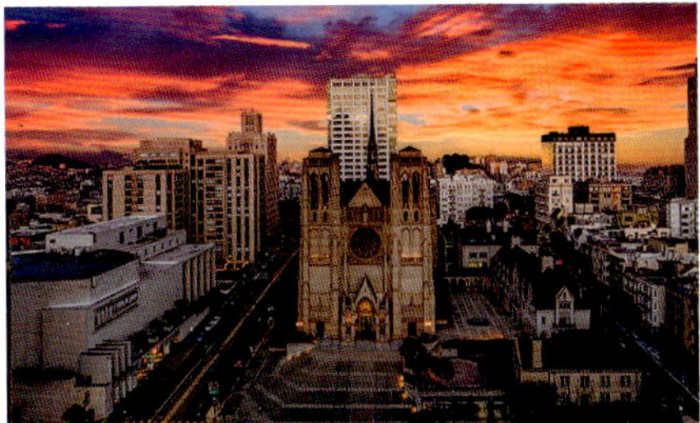

68-69 **Diane Bentley Raymond**
View of Grace Cathedral

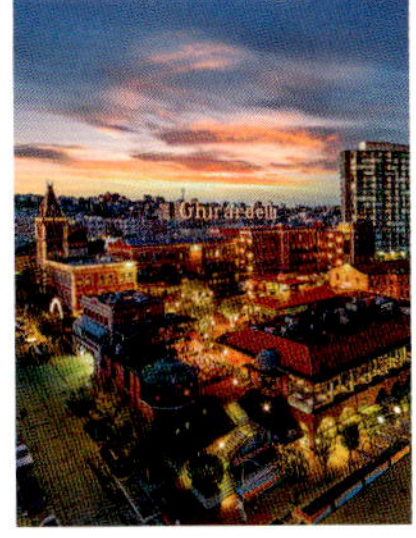

70 **Diane Bentley Raymond**
View of Ghirardelli Square

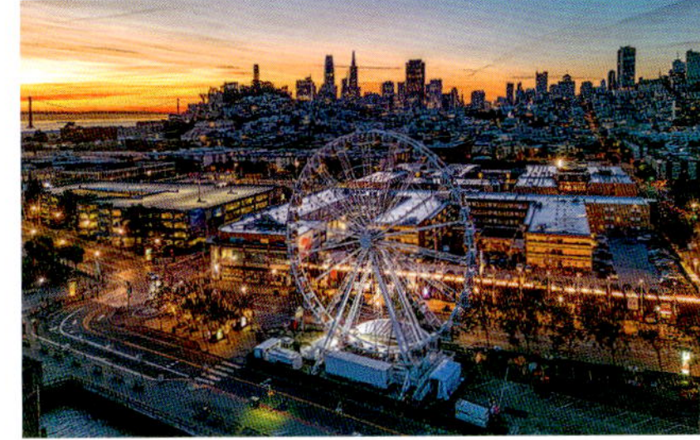

71 **Diane Bentley Raymond**
View of The Embarcadero

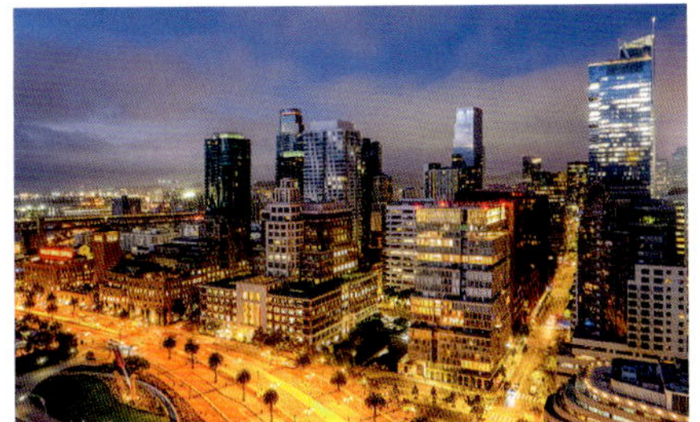

72-73 **Diane Bentley Raymond**
View of The Embarcadero

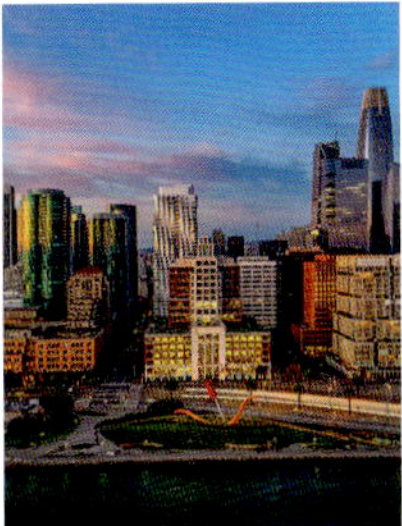

74 **Diane Bentley Raymond**
View of Rincon Park

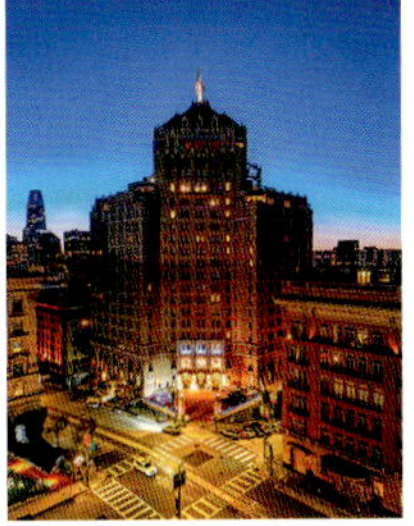

75 **Diane Bentley Raymond**
View of the InterContinental
Mark Hopkins San Francisco

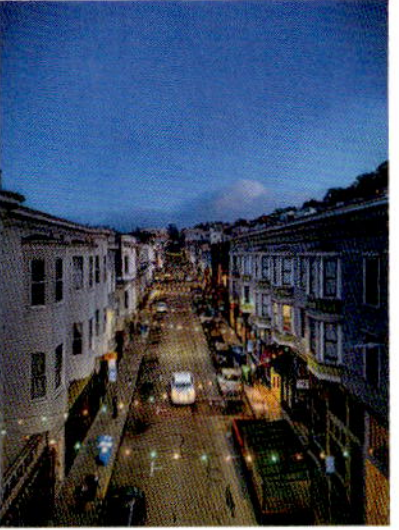

76 **Diane Bentley Raymond**
Above Grant Avenue

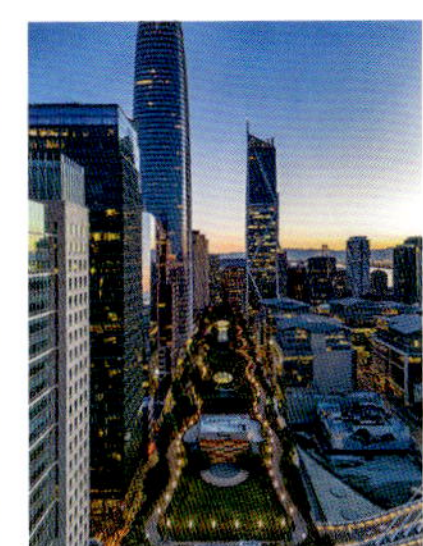

77 **Diane Bentley Raymond**
View of Salesforce Park

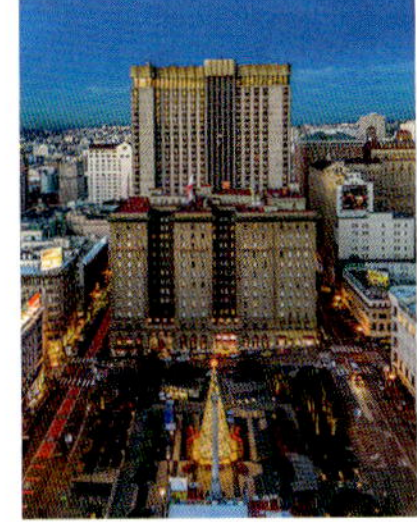

78 **Diane Bentley Raymond**
Above Union Square

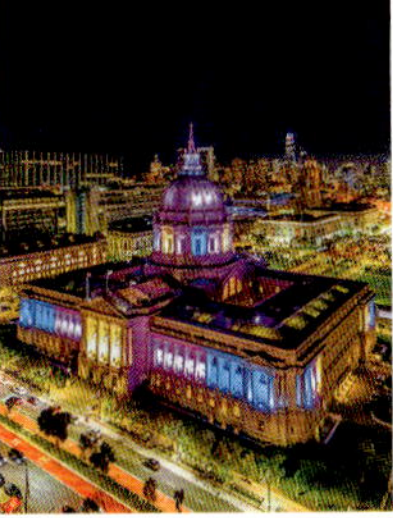

79 **Diane Bentley Raymond**
View of San Francisco
City Hall

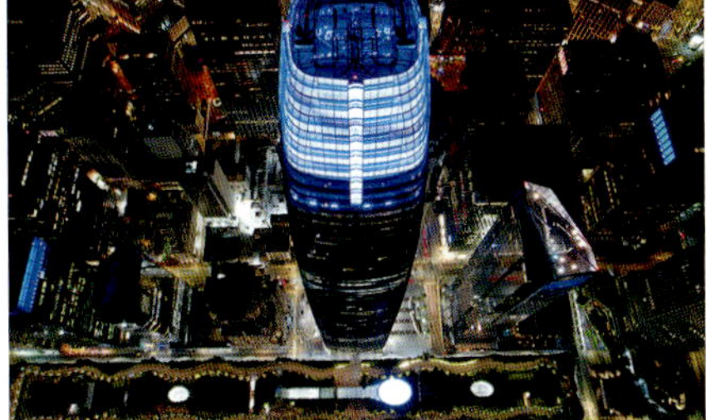

80-81 **John Montoya**
View of Salesforce Tower

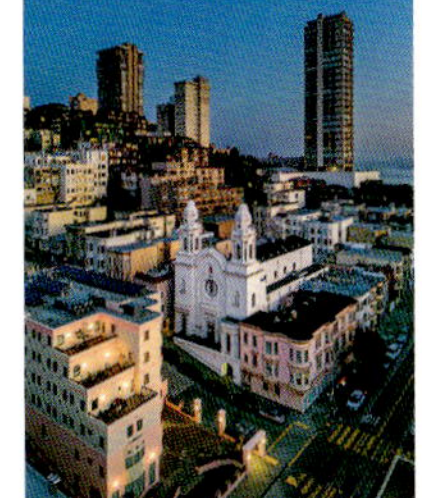

82 **Diane Bentley Raymond**
Intersection of Mason Street
and Broadway

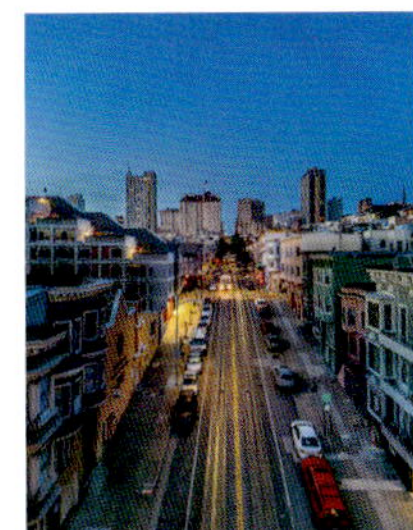

83 **Diane Bentley Raymond**
Above Mason Street

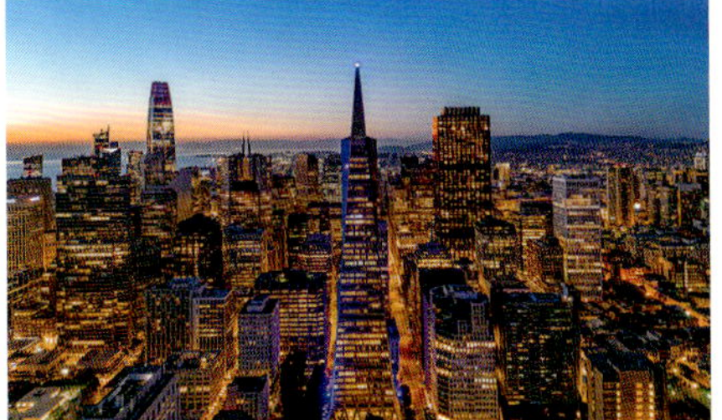

84-85 **Diane Bentley Raymond**
View of the Financial District

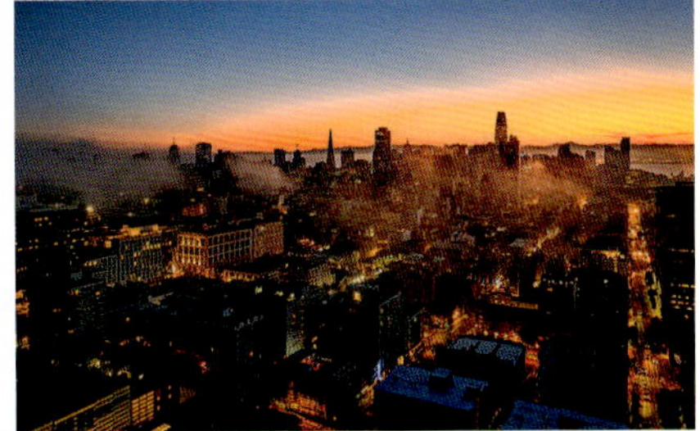

86-87 **Diane Bentley Raymond**
View of San Francisco skyline

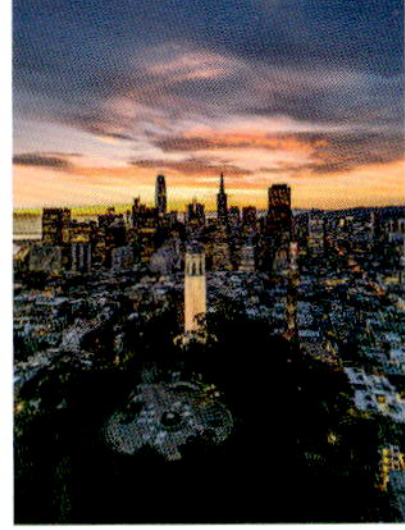

89 **Diane Bentley Raymond**
View of Coit Tower

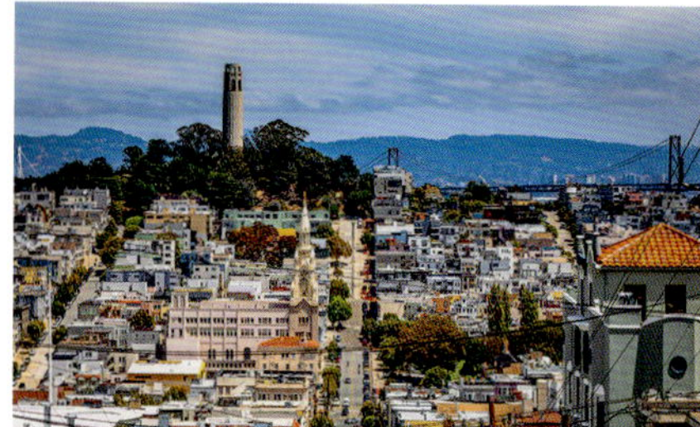

90-91 Jack Landau
View of Filbert Street and Coit Tower

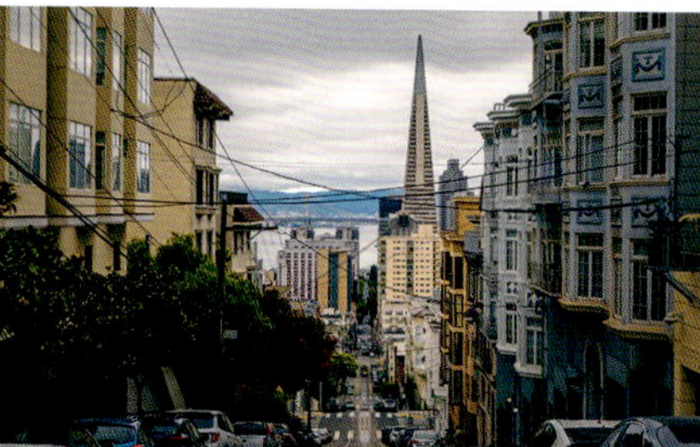

92-93 Jack Landau
View of Washington Street

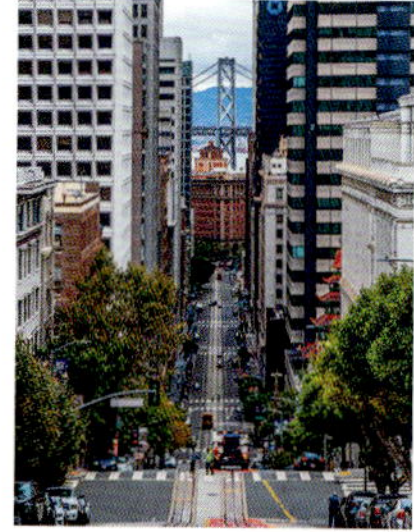

94 Jack Landau
View of California Street

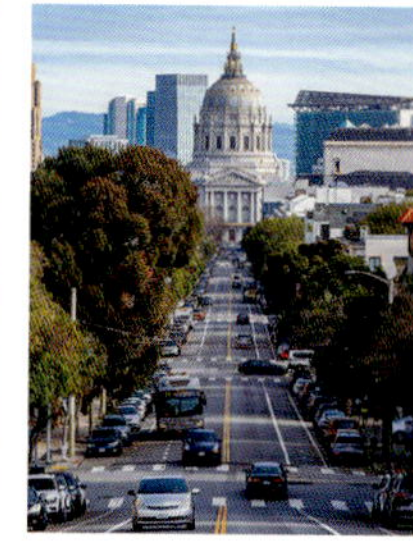

95 Jeffery Xin
View of San Francisco
City Hall

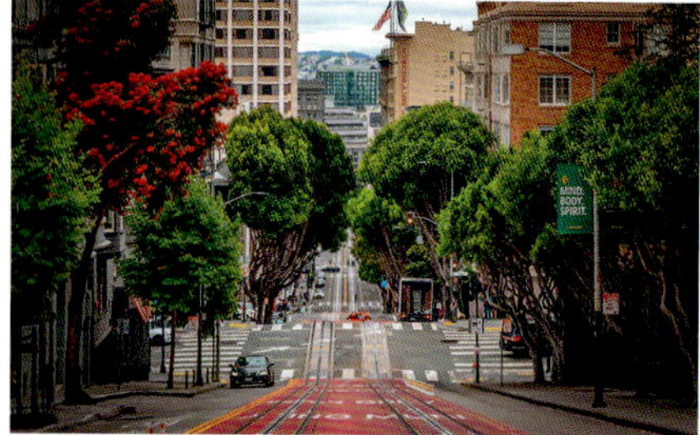

96-97 Jack Landau
View of Powell Street

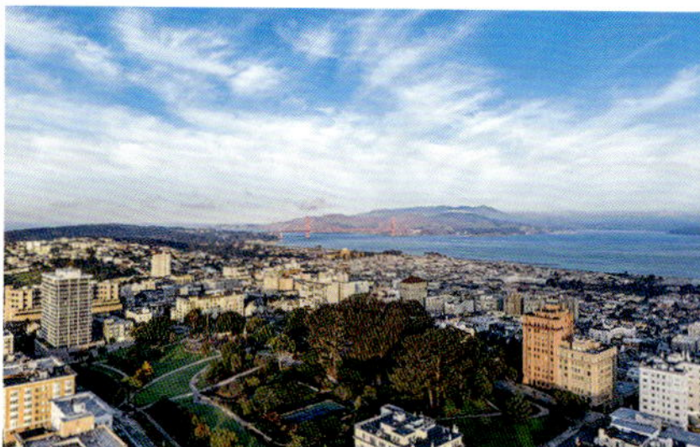

98-99 Diane Bentley Raymond
View of Lafayette Park

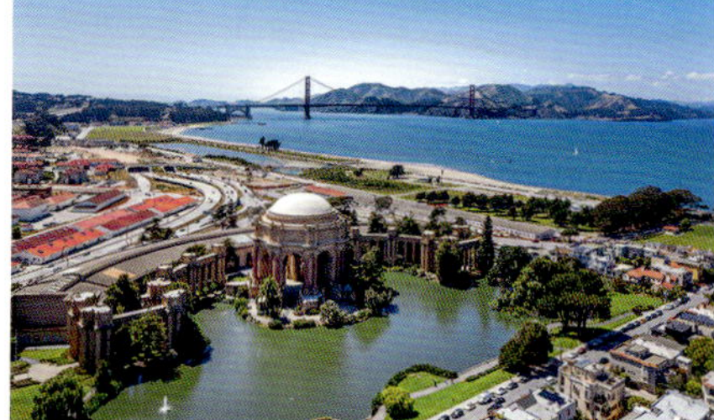

100-101 Diane Bentley Raymond
View of the Palace of Fine Arts

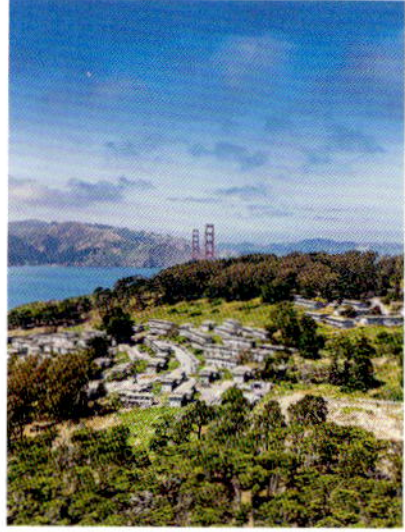

102 Diane Bentley Raymond
Above the Presidio

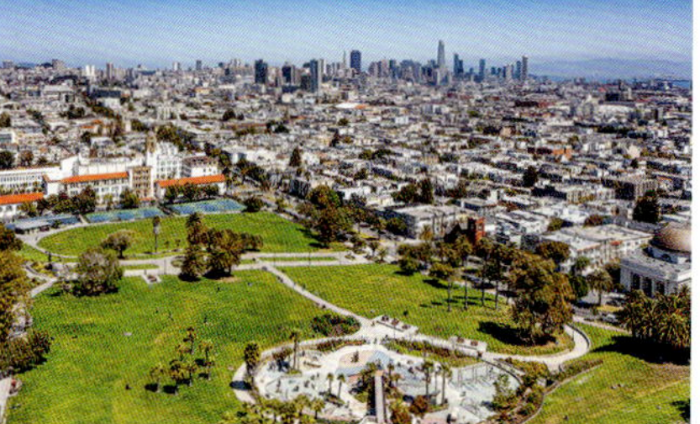

103 Diane Bentley Raymond
View of Dolores Park

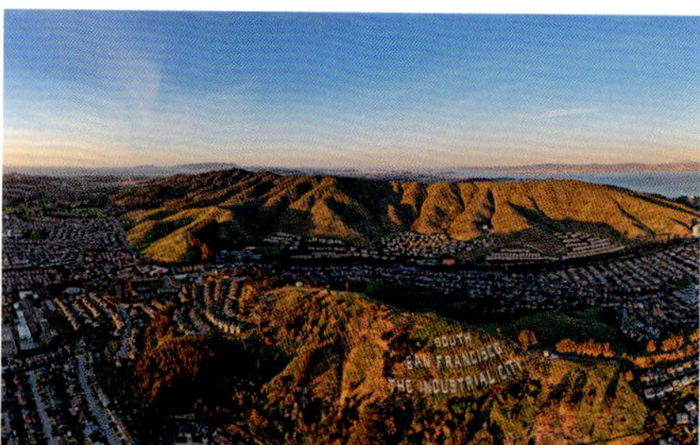

104-105 John Montoya
View of Sign Hill Park

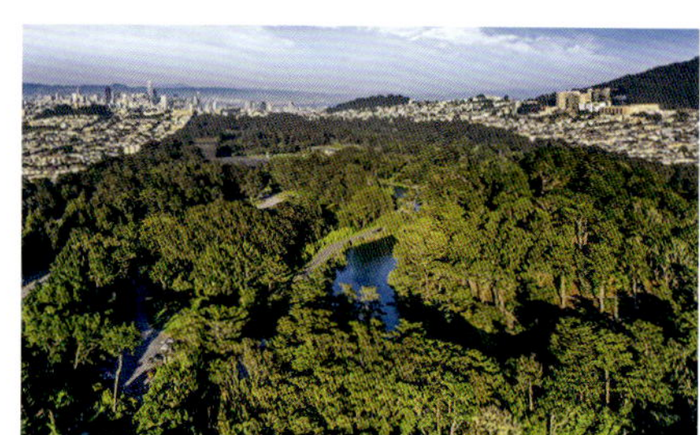

106-107 Diane Bentley Raymond
View of Stow Lake, Golden Gate Park

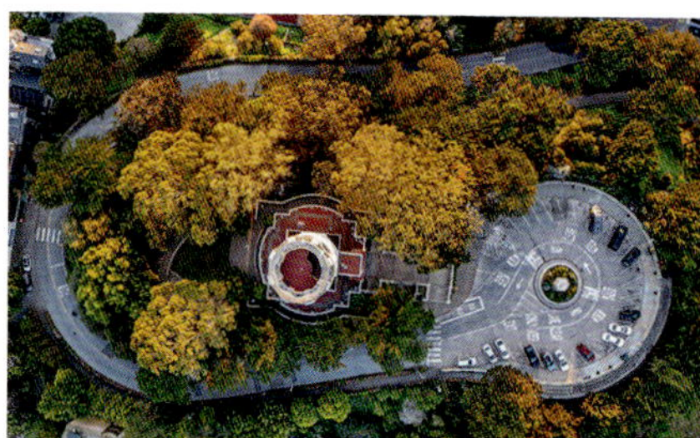

108-109 Diane Bentley Raymond
Above Coit Tower and Pioneer Park

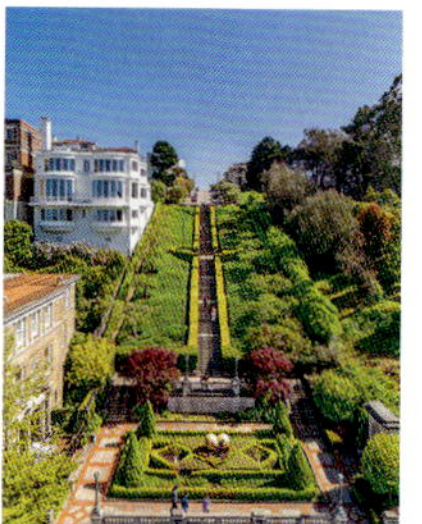

110 Diane Bentley Raymond
View of Lyon Street Steps

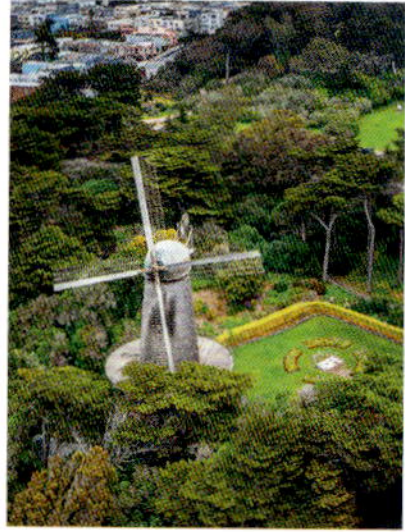

111 Diane Bentley Raymond
View of Dutch Windmill,
Golden Gate Park

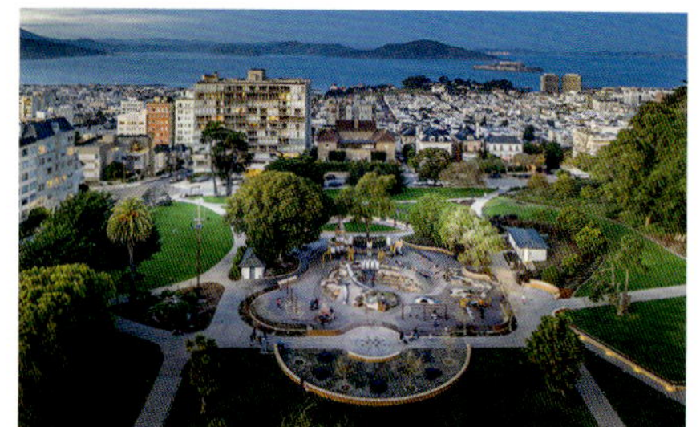

112-113 Diane Bentley Raymond
Above Lafayette Park

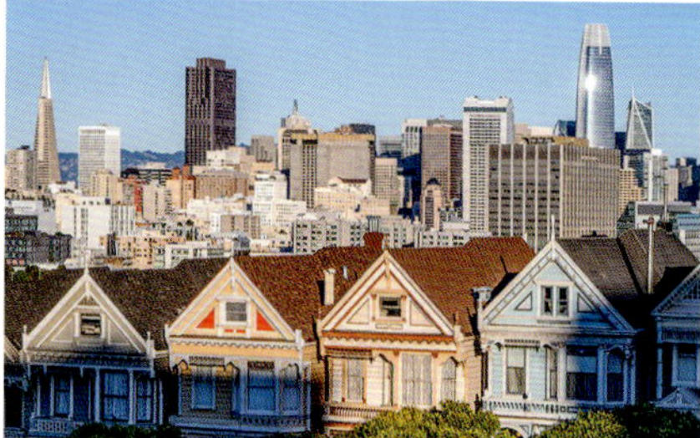

114-115 Jeffery Xin
View of the Painted Ladies of Alamo Square

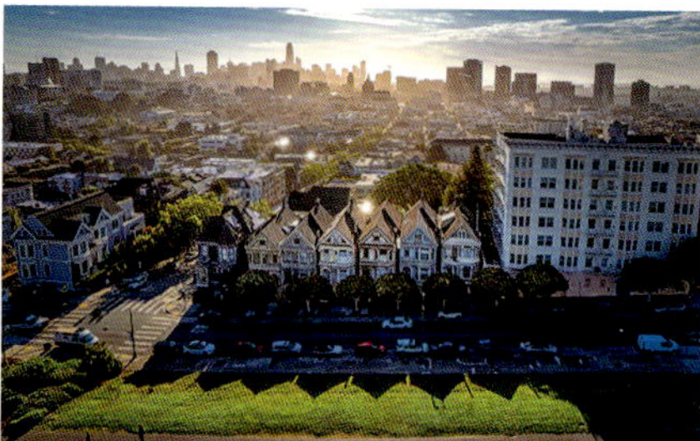

116-117 Diane Bentley Raymond
Above the Painted Ladies of Alamo Square and Steiner Street

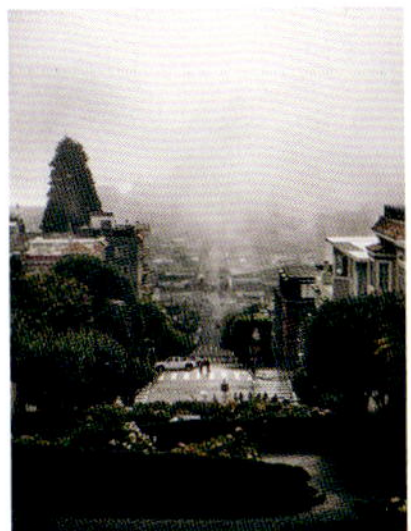

118 Cocu Liu
View of Lombard Street

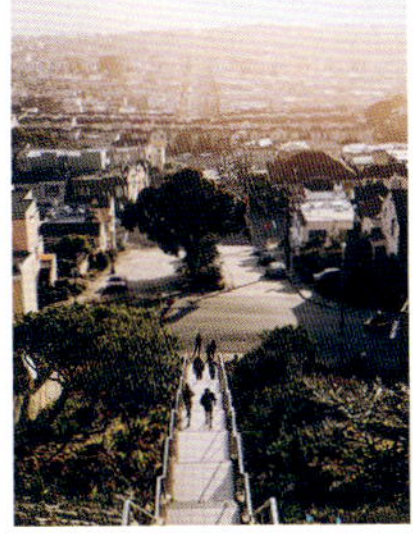

119 Cocu Liu
Above the Moraga Steps

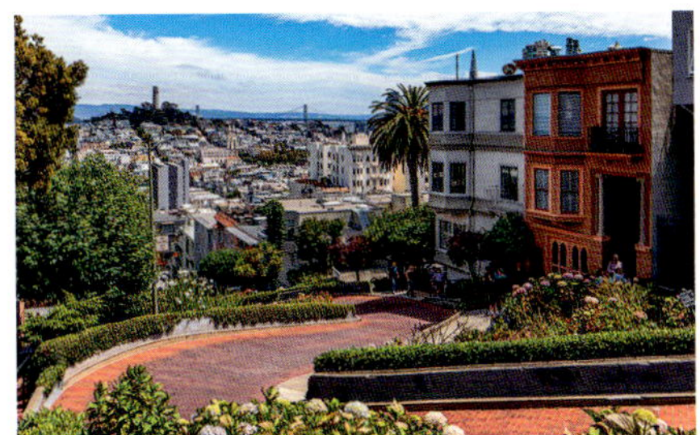

120-121 Jack Landau
View of Lombard Street

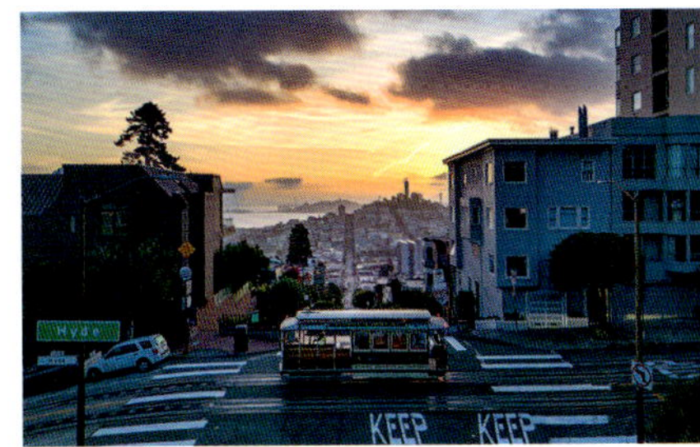

122-123 Diane Bentley Raymond
Intersection of Lombard Street and Hyde Street

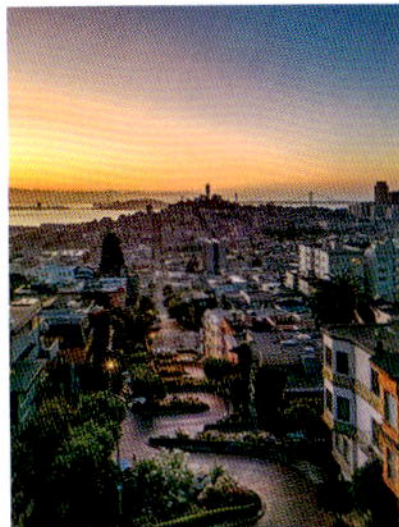

124 Diane Bentley Raymond
Above Lombard Street

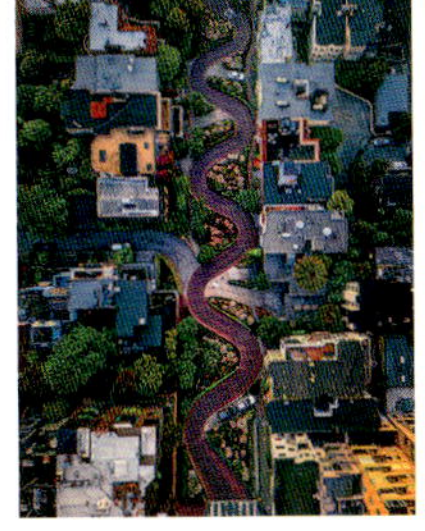

125 Diane Bentley Raymond
Above Lombard Street

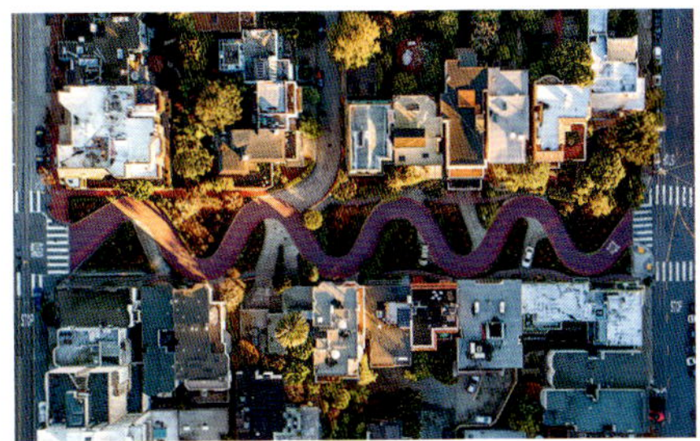

126-127 Jeffery Xin
Above Lombard Street

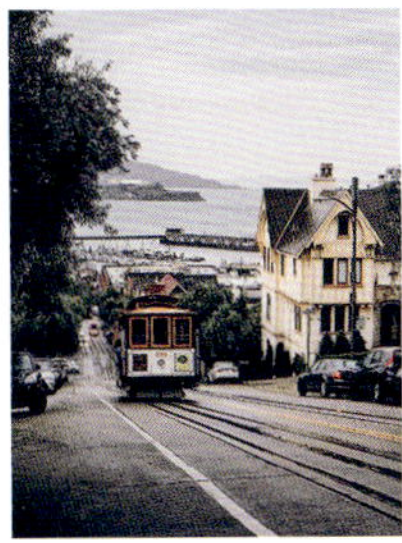

128 Cocu Liu
View of Hyde Street

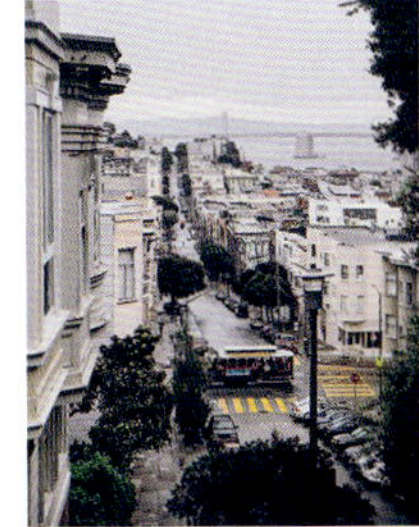

129 Cocu Liu
View of Jackson Street

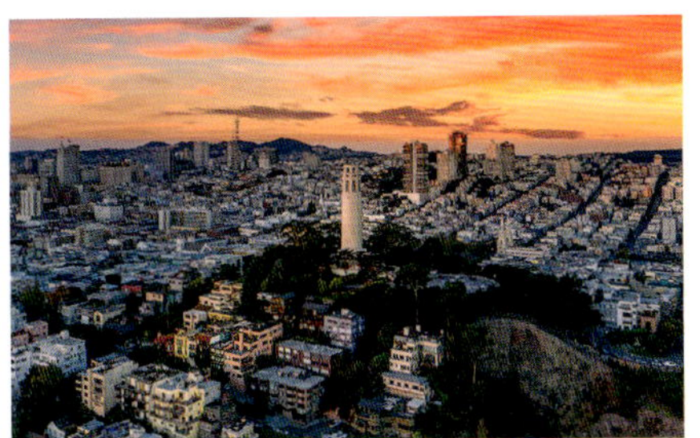

130-131 Diane Bentley Raymond
View of Coit Tower and Telegraph Hill

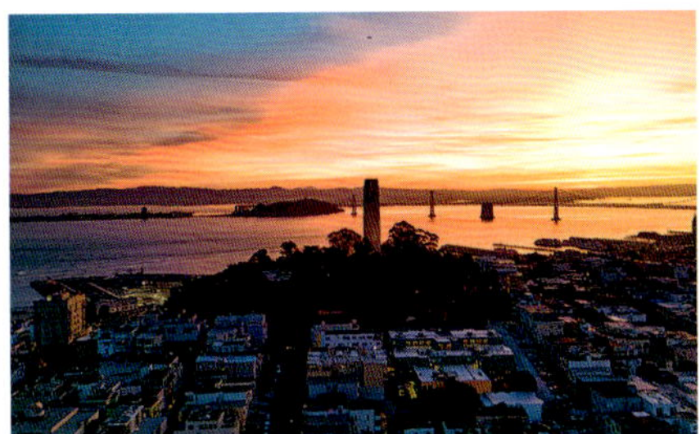

132-133 Diane Bentley Raymond
View of Coit Tower

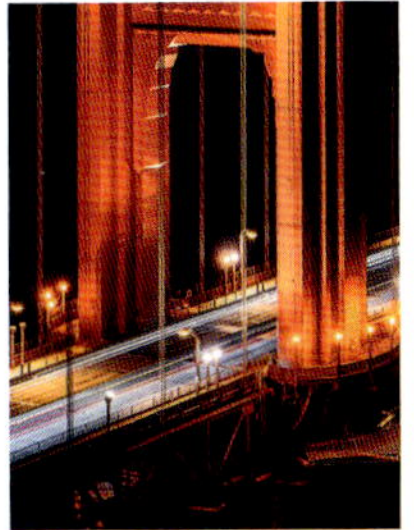

135 Kris Kuganathan
View of the Golden
Gate Bridge

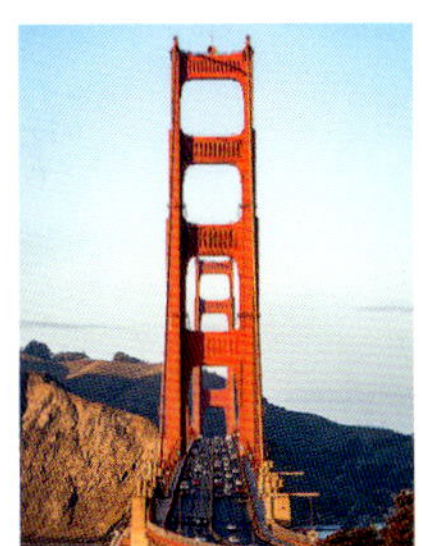

136 Jeffery Xin
View of the Golden
Gate Bridge

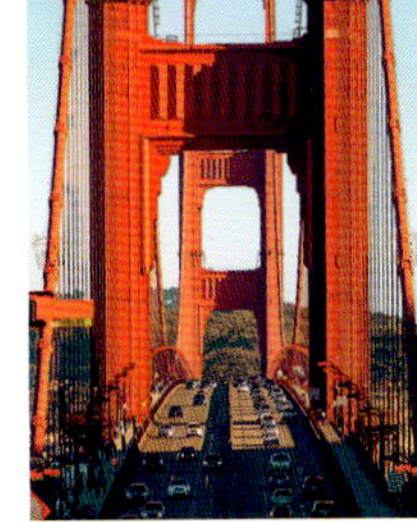

137 Jack Landau
View of the Golden
Gate Bridge

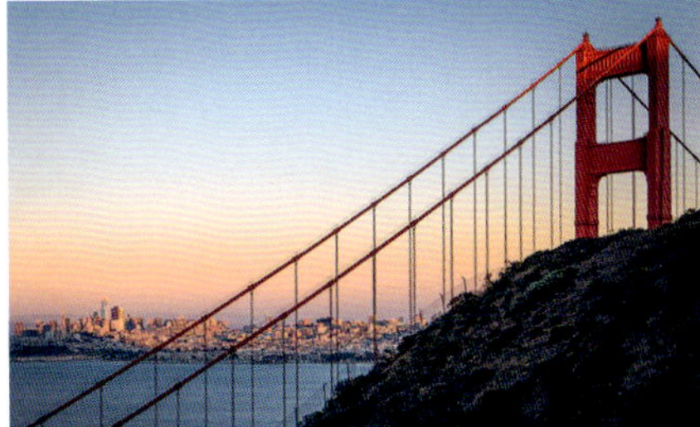

138-139 Jack Landau
View of the Golden Gate Bridge

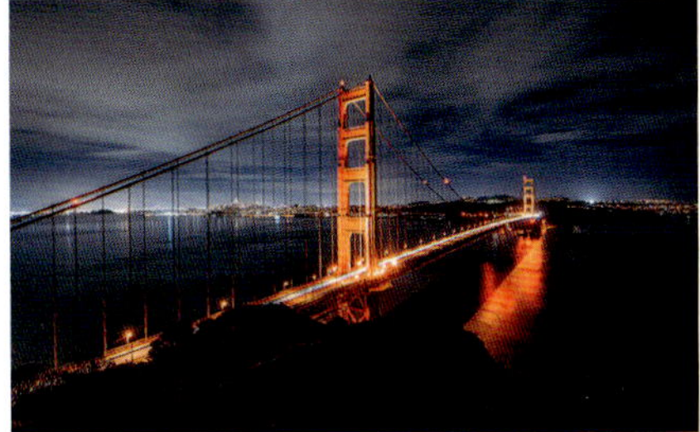

140-141 Kris Kuganathan
View of the Golden Gate Bridge

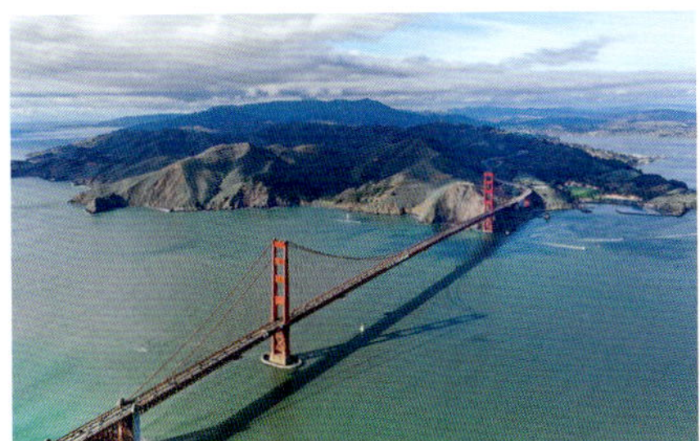

142-143 Lichao Liu
Above the Golden Gate Bridge

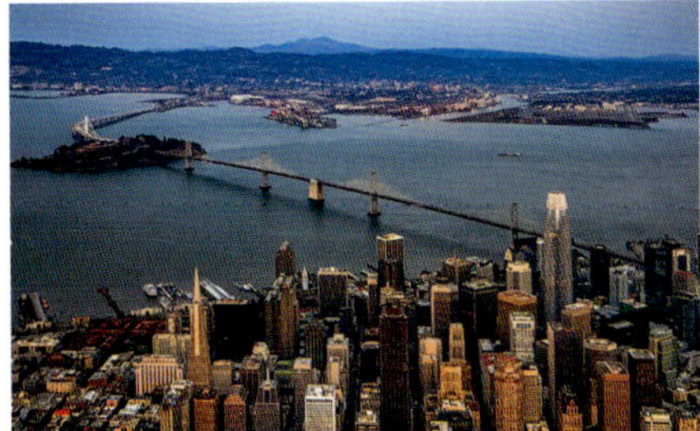

144-145 Jay Huang
View of the Bay Bridge

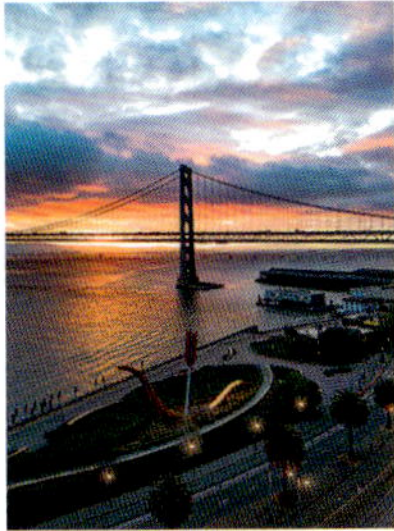

146 Diane Bentley Raymond
View of Rincon Park and
the Bay Bridge

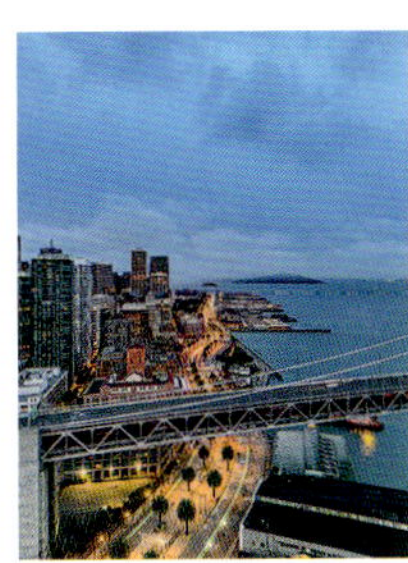

147 Diane Bentley Raymond
View of The Embarcadero

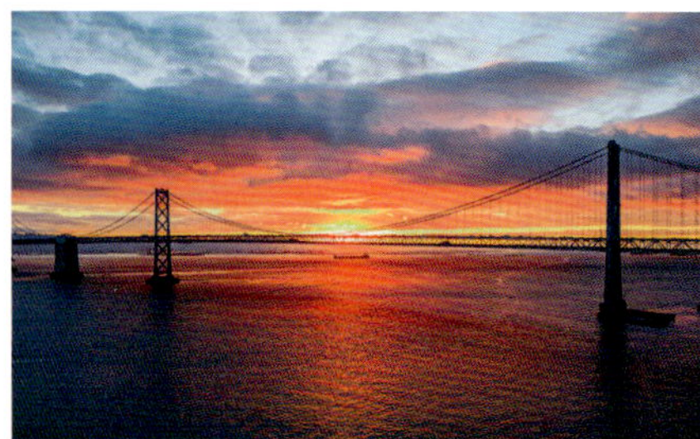

148-149 Diane Bentley Raymond
View of the Bay Bridge

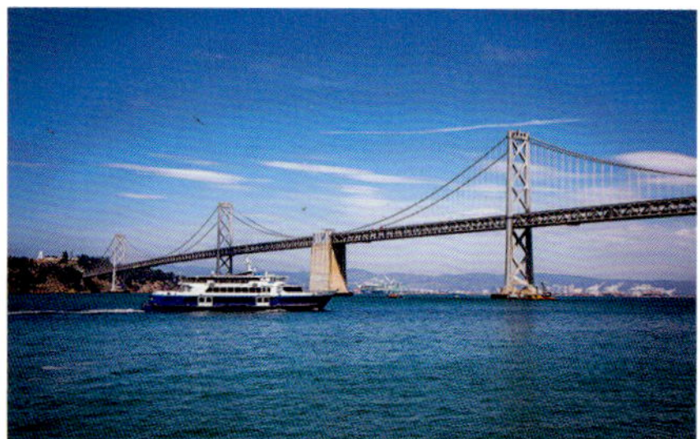

150-151 Jack Landau
View of the Bay Bridge

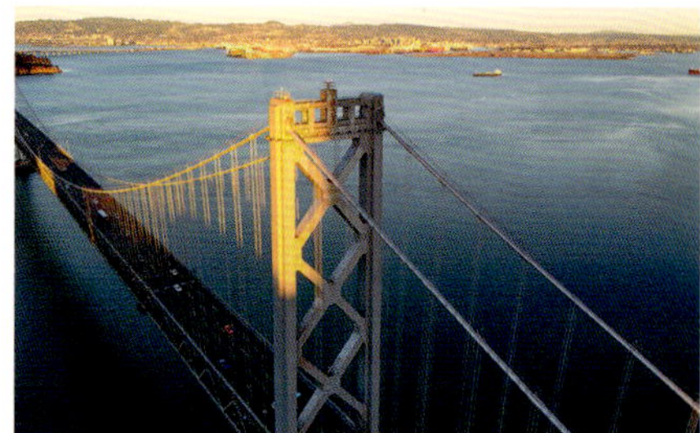

152-153 John Montoya
View of the Bay Bridge

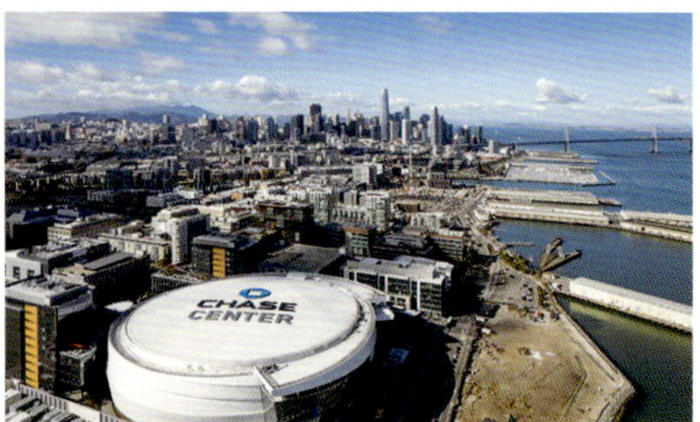

154-155 John Montoya
Above Chase Center and Mission Bay

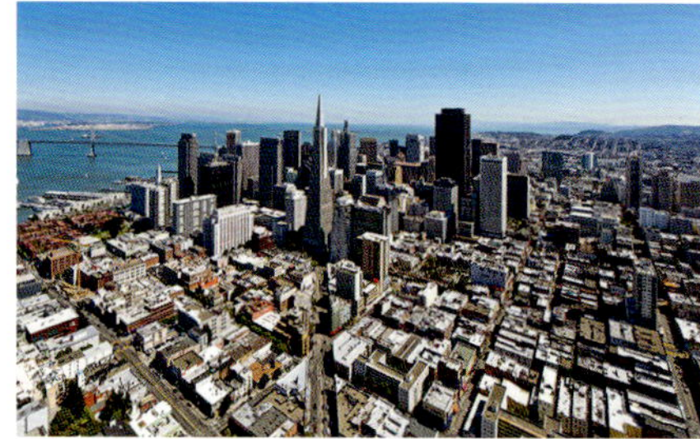

156-157 Howard Kingsnorth
Above the Financial District

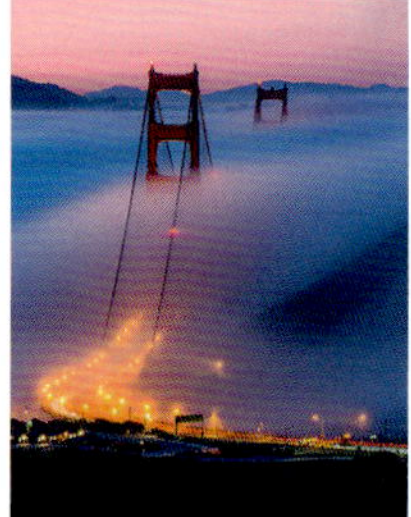

159 Jay Huang
View of the Golden
Gate Bridge

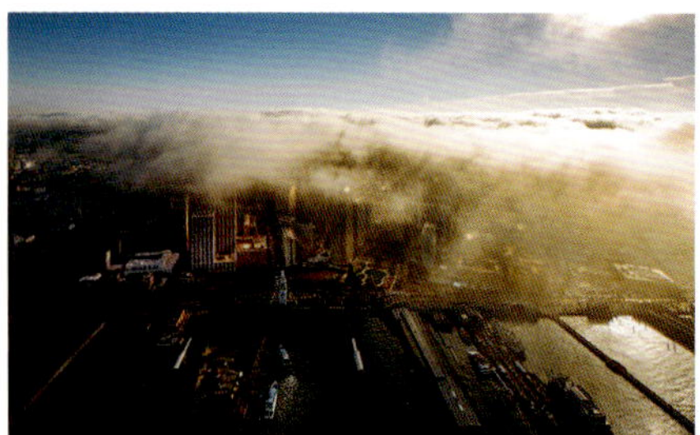

160-161 Howard Kingsnorth
Above the Ferry Building

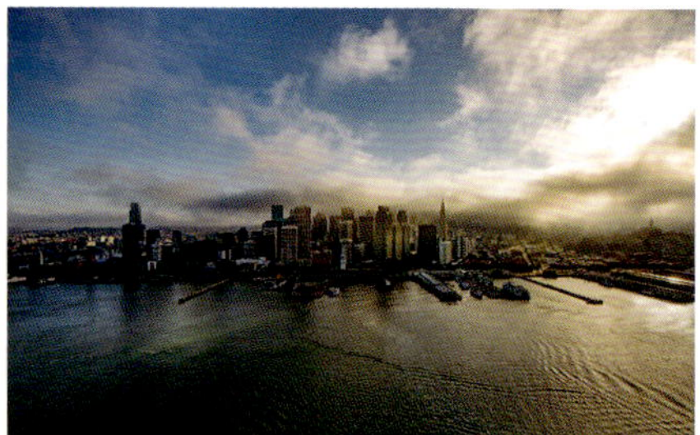

162-163 Howard Kingsnorth
View of the San Francisco skyline

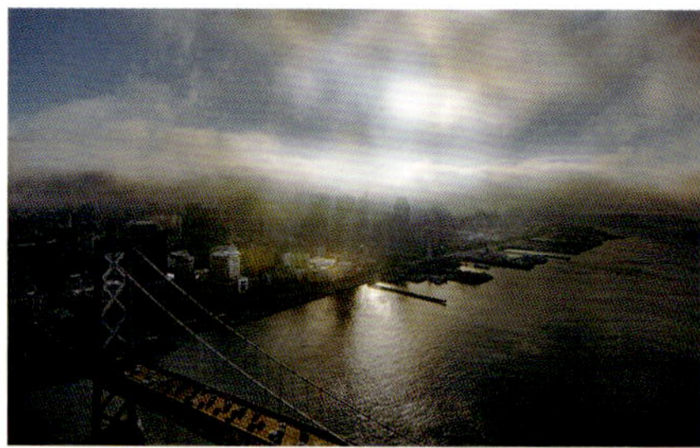

164-165 Howard Kingsnorth
View of the Bay Bridge and San Francisco Bay

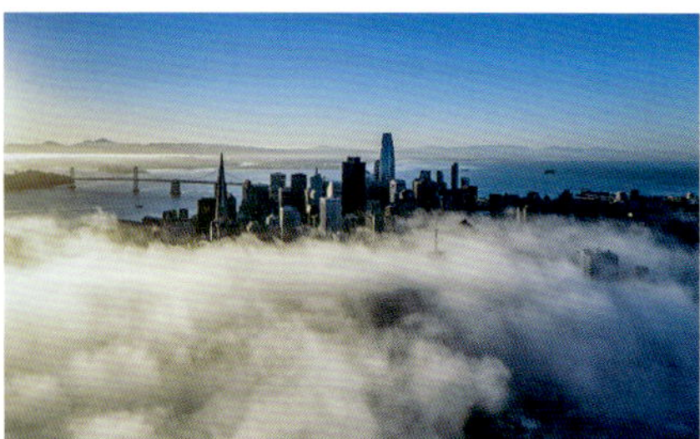

166-167 Diane Bentley Raymond
View of the San Francisco skyline

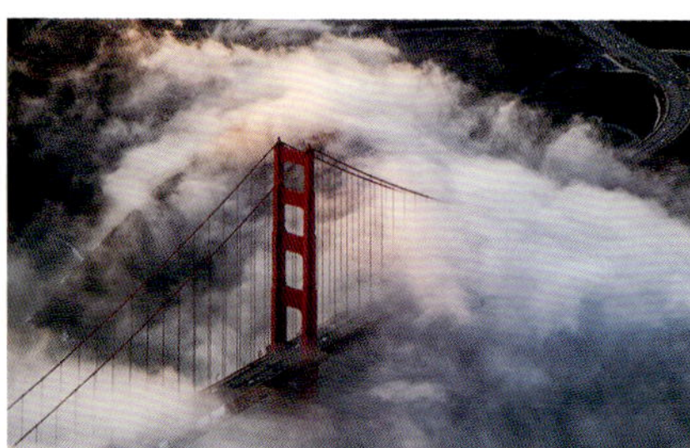

168-169 Jay Huang
Above the Golden Gate Bridge

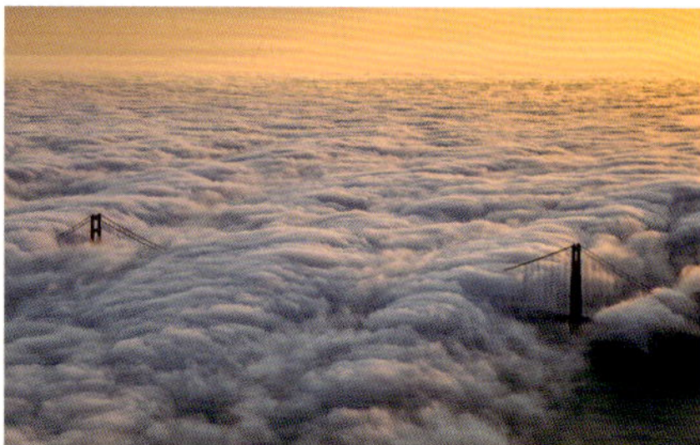

170-171 Jay Huang
Above the Golden Gate Bridge

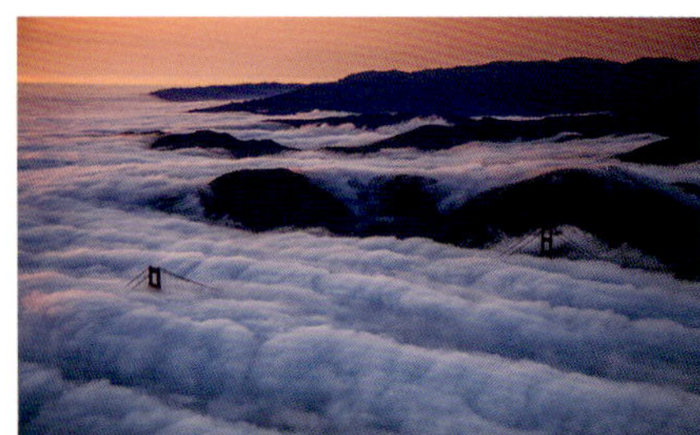

172-173 Jay Huang
Above the Golden Gate Bridge

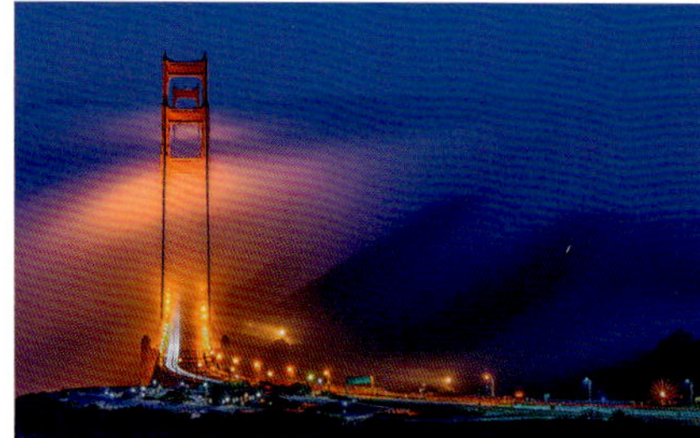

174-175 Jay Huang
View of the Golden Gate Bridge

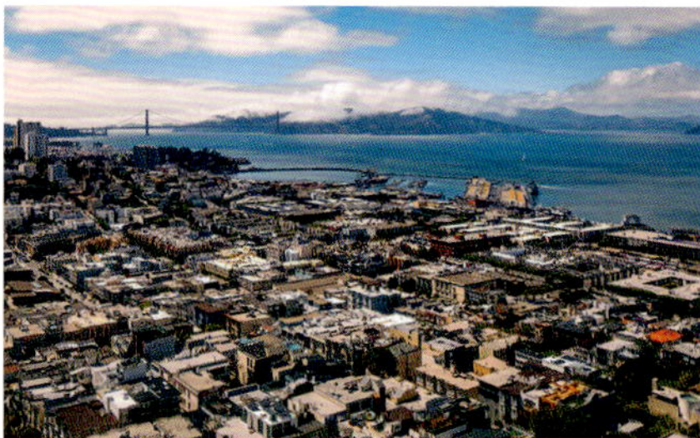

176-177 Jack Landau
View of the Golden Gate Bridge and Mt. Tamalpais

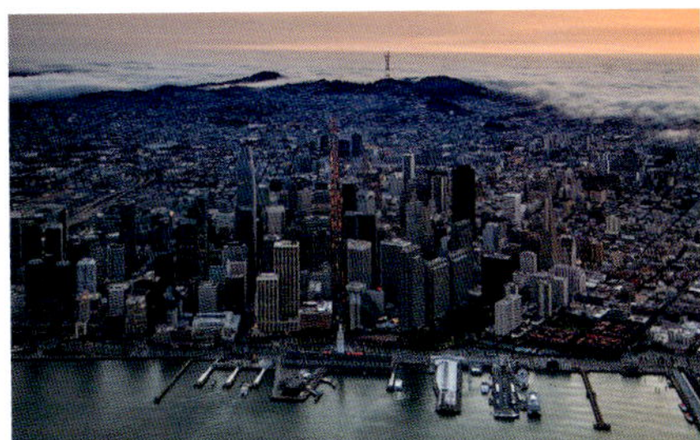

178-179 Jay Huang
View of the Ferry Building

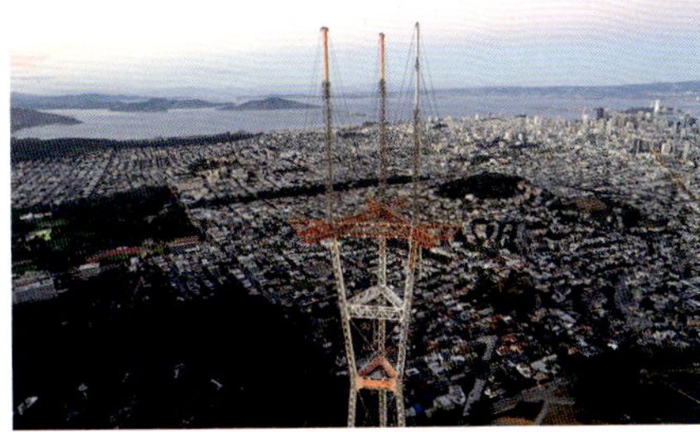

180-181 John Montoya
Above Sutro Tower

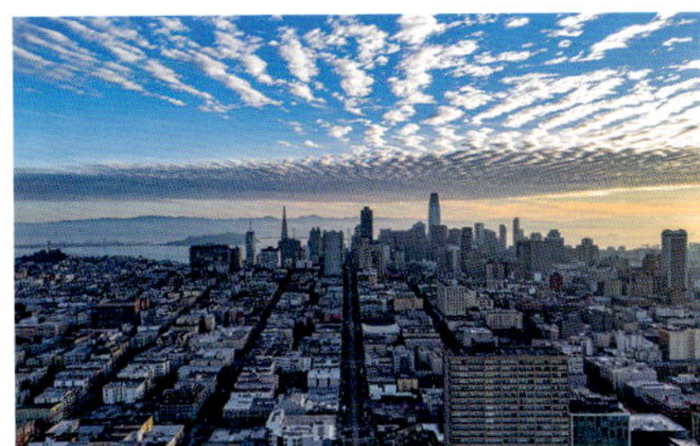

182-183 Diane Bentley Raymond
View of the San Francisco skyline

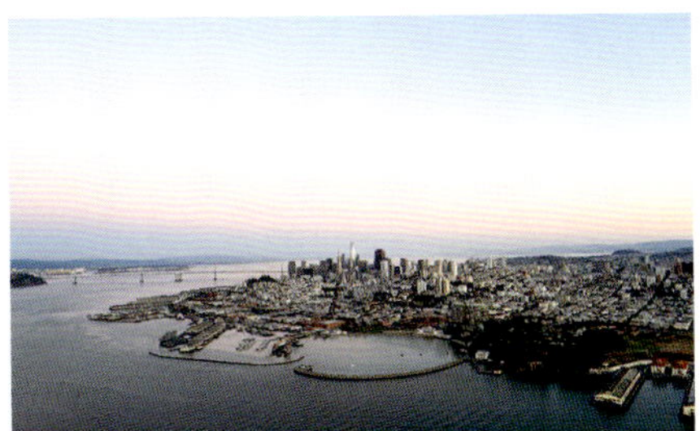

184-185 John Montoya
Above Aquatic Cove and Fisherman's Wharf

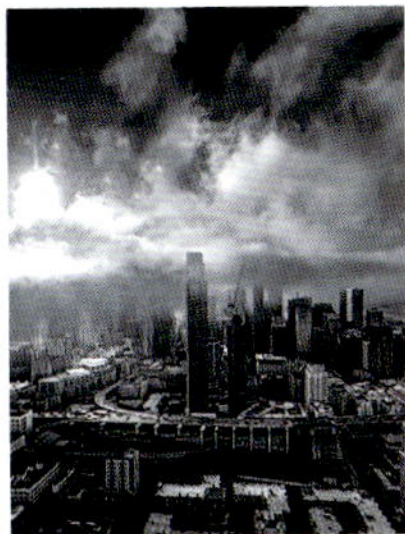

186 Howard Kingsnorth
Above SoMa

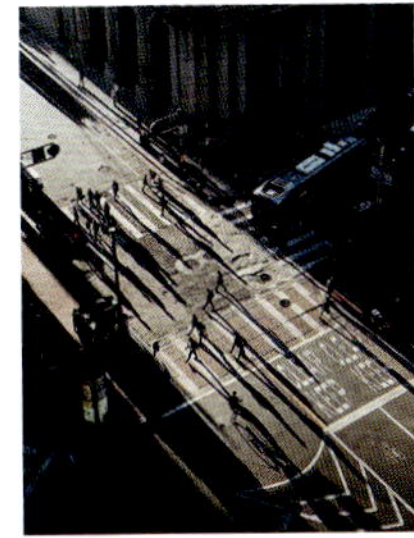

196 Cocu Liu
Intersection of Sansome
Street and Sutter Street

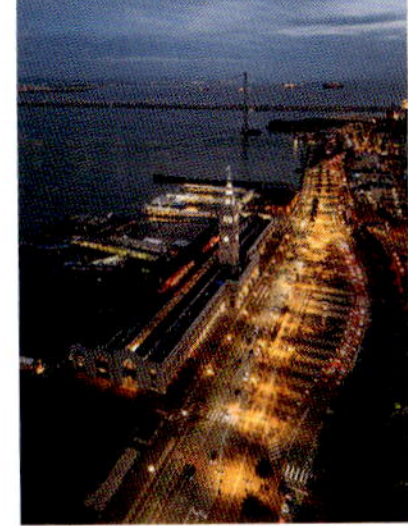

198 Kris Kuganathan
Above the Ferry Building

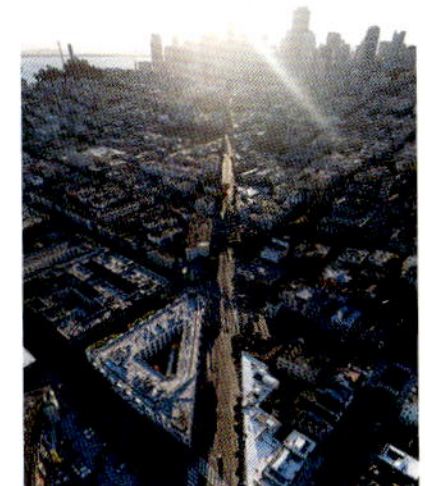

200 Jeffery Xin
Above Columbus Avenue
and Bay Street

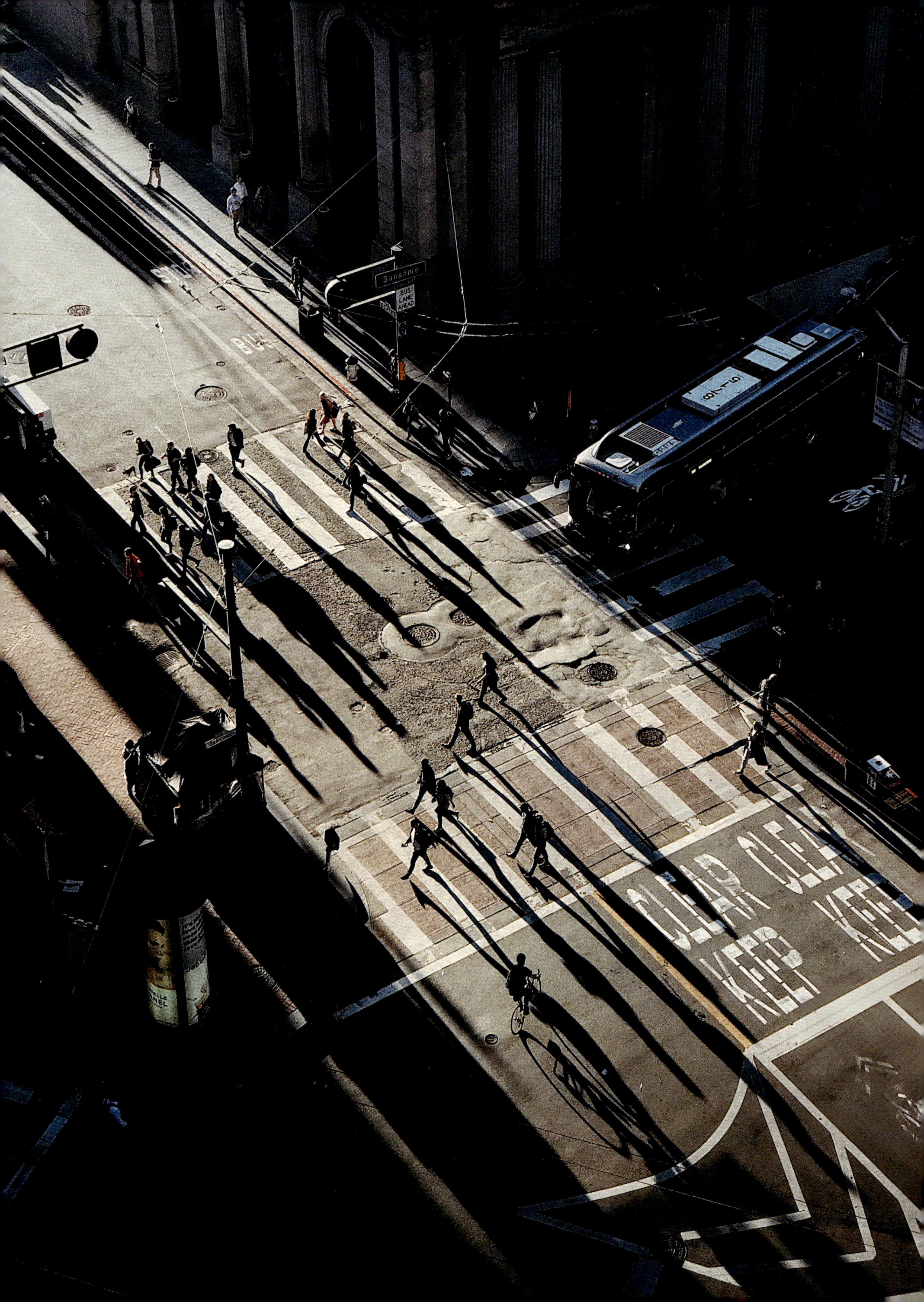

Sansome
BUS
LANE
AHEAD
CLEAR
KEEP
KEEP

PHOTOGRAPHERS

+ COCU LIU
Award-winning mobile photographer and product designer based in San Francisco.
@cocu_liu

+ DIANE BENTLEY RAYMOND
Aerial, architectural and travel photographer who loves seeing the world from different angles and calls San Francisco home.
@dianebentleyraymond

+ HOWARD KINGSNORTH
London based, worldly wise photographer with an adventurous eye for the darkly beautiful.
@howardkingsnorth

+ JACK LANDAU
Toronto-based journalist and photographer with a passion for uncovering the architecture and places that define cities around the world.
@jacklandauphotography

+ JAY HUANG
San Francisco-based amateur photographer specializing in landscape and cityscape.
@jaykhuangphotography

+ JEFFERY XIN
Interior designer and filmmaker with a passion for architectural and geometric elements, raised in Beijing and living in New York City.
@jeffery_bxin

+ JOHN MONTOYA
Drone photographer and food enthusiast from San Francisco California with a passion for community building and cooking.
@JohnMontoyaSF

+ KRIS KUGANATHAN
Southern California-based photographer specializing in cityscape, landscape, and aerial photography.
@kriskuganathan

+ LICHAO LIU
Architect who views photography as a form of frozen art that turns any fleeting moment into a tangible and lasting memory.
@jennylichao

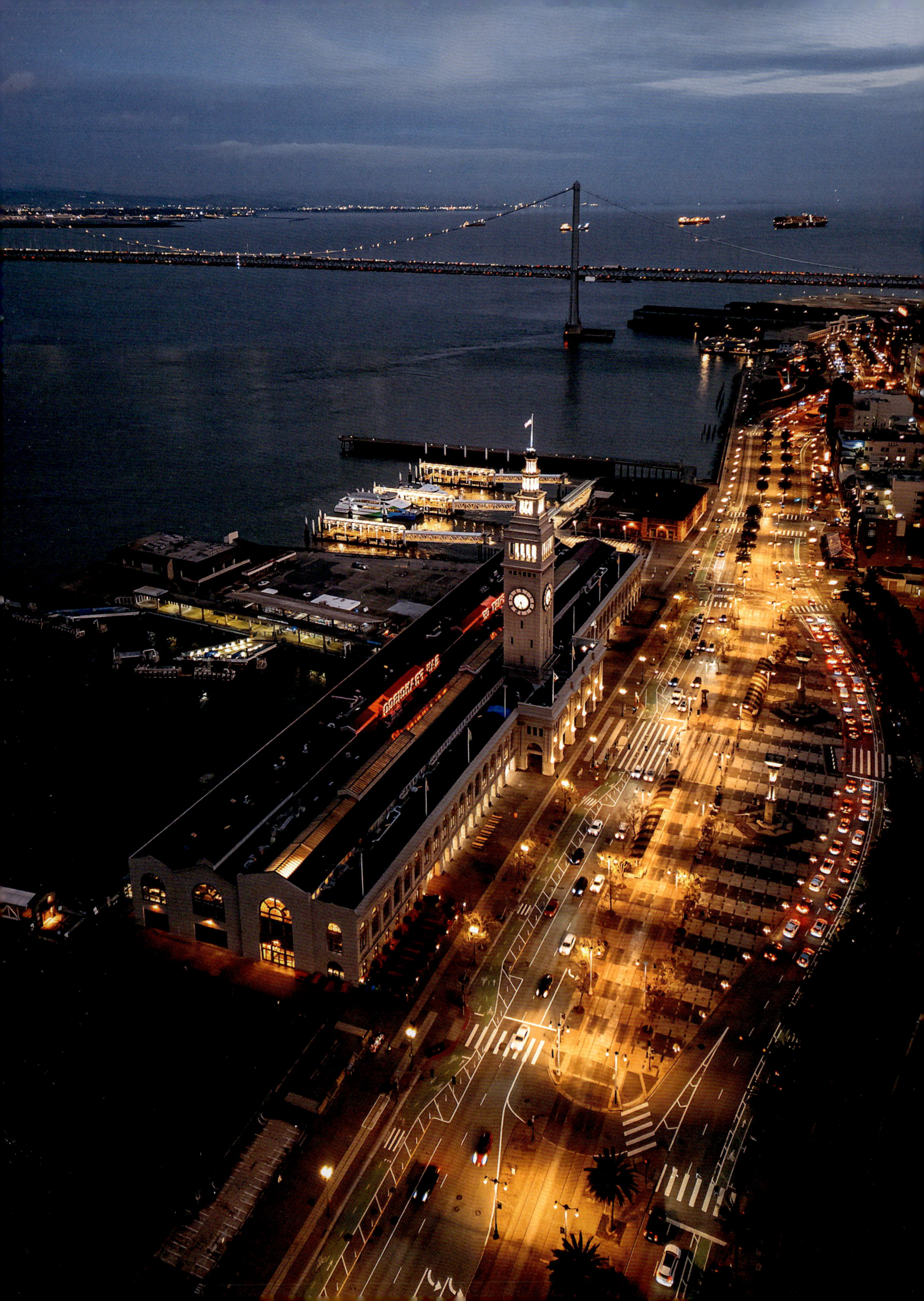

ACKNOWLEDGEMENTS

SPECIAL THANKS

+ We would like to thank all of the photographers who have generously donated their time and allowed us to use their images to create *Above & Across San Francisco.*

Additionally, we thank the following individuals who worked tirelessly through the production of *Above & Across San Francisco.*

+ STACY WILLIAMS

+ JACK VAN BOOM

+ KATE LANDERS

+ KENDRA HUSPASKA

LCCN: 2024946696
ISBN: 978-1-951963-32-3

Printed and bound in China
First printing, 2025

The photographs from *Above & Across San Francisco* are available for purchase. For inquiries, email the gallery at info@trope.com

ABOUT THE EDITORS

+ SAM LANDERS

Sam Landers is the Publisher and Editor at Trope Publishing Co. and has edited *Chicago*, *London*, *Hong Kong*, *Tokyo*, *Paris*, and *Los Angeles*, all titles in Trope's City Edition series, as well as *Above & Across Chicago*. Prior to launching Trope, Sam spent over two decades working in digital marketing. An avid photographer, Sam enjoys traveling, always taking his camera and notebook.

+ MICHELLE FITZGERALD

Michelle Fitzgerald is a veteran of the book publishing industry and the Associate Publisher at Trope Publishing Co. A fierce advocate for books, she served as editor on *Above & Across Chicago* and *Above & Across Atlanta*, as well as *New York*, *Paris*, and *Los Angeles*, all titles in Trope's City Edition series.

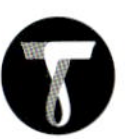

+ INFORMATION:
For additional information on our books and prints, visit WWW.TROPE.COM

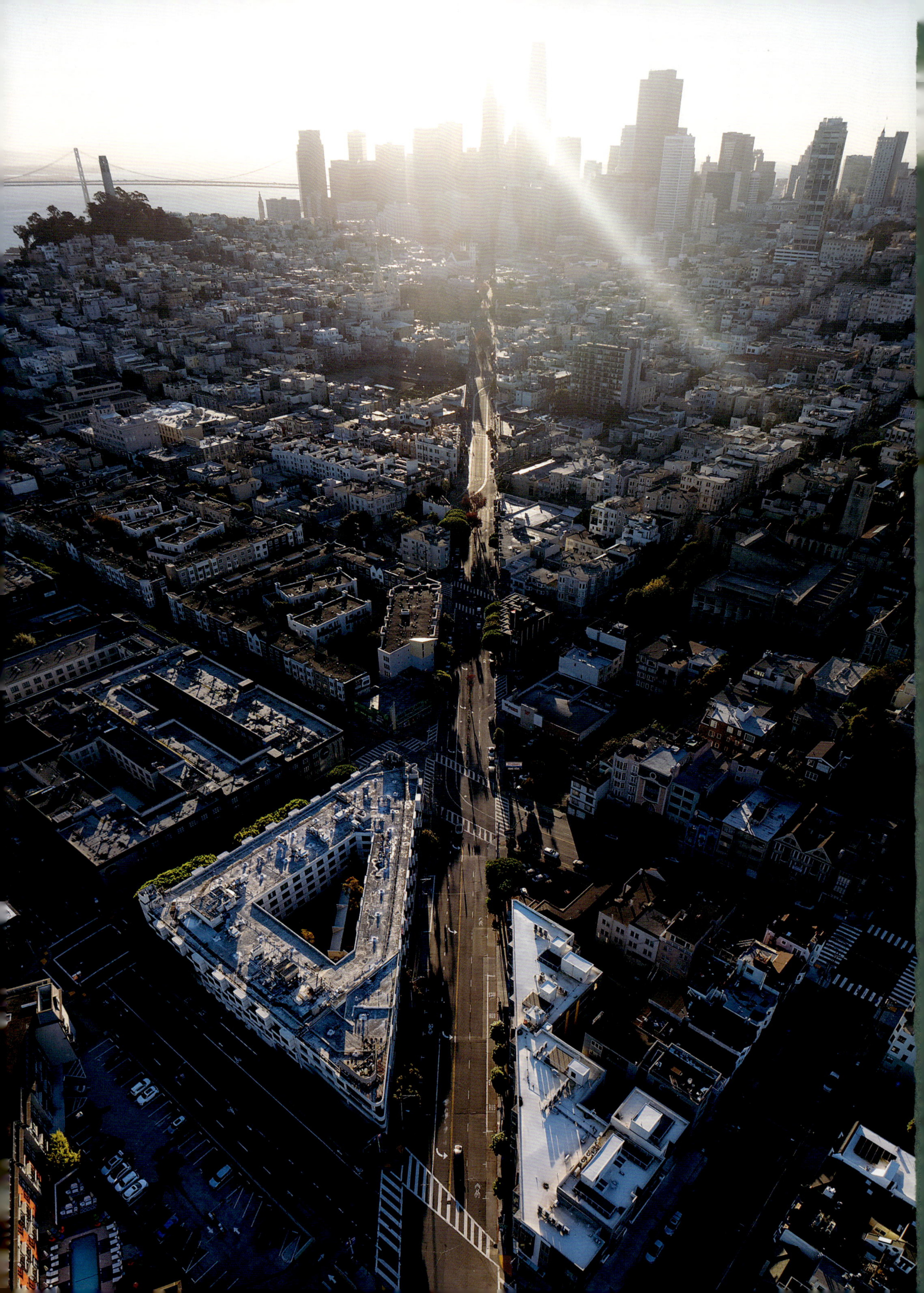